REMARKS

BY BILL NYE.

(EDGAR W. NYE.)

Ah Sin was his name;
And I shall not deny,
In regard to the same,
What the name might imply:
But his smile it was pensive and childlike,
As I frequent remarked to Bill Nye.
—BRET HARTE.

WITH OVER ONE HUNDRED AND FIFTY ILLUSTRATIONS,
BY J. H. SMITH.

PUBLISHED BY

F. T. NEELY.

CHICAGO. NEW YORK.

DIRECTIONS.

THIS book is not designed specially for any one class of people. It is for all. It is a universal repository of thought. Some of my best thoughts are contained in this book. Whenever I would think a thought that I thought had better remain unthought, I would omit it from this book. For that reason the book is not so large as I had intended. When a man coldly and dispassionately goes at it to eradicate from his work all that may not come up to his standard of merit, he can make a large volume shrink till it is no thicker than the bank book of an outspoken clergyman.

This is the fourth book that I have published in response to the clamorous appeals of the public. Whenever the public got to clamoring too loudly for a new book from me and it got so noisy that I could not ignore it any more, I would issue another volume. The first was a red book, succeeded by a dark blue volume, after which I published a green book, all of which were kindly received by the American people, and, under the present yielding system of international copyright, greedily snapped up by some of the tottering dynasties.

But I had long hoped to publish a larger, better and, if possible, a redder book than the first; one that would contain my better thoughts, thoughts that I had thought when I was feeling well; thoughts that I had emitted while my thinker was rearing up on its hind feet, if I may be allowed that term; thoughts that sprang forth with a wild whoop and demanded recognition.

This book is the result of that hope and that wish. It is my greatest and best book. It is the one that will live for weeks after other books have passed away. Even to those who cannot read, it will come like a benison when there is no benison in the house. To the ignorant, the pictures will be pleasing. The wise will revel in its wisdom, and the housekeeper will find that with it she may easily emphasize a statement or kill a cockroach.

The range of subjects treated in this book is wonderful, even to me. It is a library of universal knowledge, and the facts contained in it are different from any other facts now in use. I have carefully guarded, all the way through, against using hackneyed and moth-eaten facts. As a result, I am able to come before the people with a set of new and attractive statements, so fresh and so crisp that an unkind word would wither them in a moment.

I believe there is nothing more to add, except that I most heartily endorse the book. It has been carefully read over by the proof-reader and myself, so we do not ask the public to do anything that we were not willing to do ourselves.

☞ I cannot be responsible for the board of orphans whose parents read this book and leave their children in destitute circumstances.

BILL NYE.

CONTENTS.

WE WERE NOT ON TERMS OF INTIMACY.

My School Days.

LOOKING over my own school days, there are so many things that I would rather not tell, that it will take very little time and space for me to use in telling what I am willing that the carping public should know about my early history.

I began my educational career in a log school house. Finding that other great men had done that way, I began early to look around me for a log school house where I could begin in a small way to soak my system full of hard words and information.

For a time I learned very rapidly. Learning came to me with very little effort at first. I would read my lesson over once or twice and then take my place in the class. It never bothered me to recite my lesson and so I stood at the head of the class. I could stick my big toe through a knot-hole in the floor and work out the most difficult problem. This became at last a habit with me. With my knot-hole I was safe, without it I would hesitate.

A large red-headed boy, with feet like a summer squash and eyes like those of a dead codfish, was my rival. He soon discovered that I was very dependent on that knot-hole, and so one night he stole into the school house and plugged up the knot-hole, so that I could not work my toe into it and thus refresh my memory.

Then the large red-headed boy, who had not formed the knot-hole habit, went to the head of the class and remained there.

After I grew larger, my parents sent me to a military school. That is where I got the fine military learning and stately carriage that I still wear.

My room was on the second floor, and it was very difficult for me to leave it at night, because the turnkey locked us up at 9 o'clock every evening. Still, I used to get out once in a while and wander around in the starlight. I do not know yet why I did it, but I presume it was a kind of somnambulism. I would go to bed thinking so intently of my lessons that I would get up and wander away, sometimes for miles, in the solemn night.

One night I awoke and found myself in a watermelon patch. I was never so ashamed in my life. It is a very serious thing to be awakened so rudely out of a sound sleep, by a bull dog, to find yourself in the watermelon vineyard of a man with whom you are not acquainted. I was not on terms of social intimacy with this man or his dog. They did not belong to our set. We had never been thrown together before.

After that I was called the great somnambulist and men who had watermelon conservatories shunned me. But it cured me of my somnambulism. I have never tried to somnambule any more since that time.

There are other little incidents of my schooldays that come trooping up in my memory at this moment, but they were not startling in their nature. Mine is but the history of one who struggled on year after year, trying to do better, but most always failing to connect. The boys of Boston would do well to study carefully my record and then—do differently

Recollections of Noah Webster.

MR. WEBSTER, no doubt, had the best command of language of any American author prior to our day. Those who have read his ponderous but rather disconnected romance known as "Webster's Unabridged Dictionary, or How One Word Led on to Another," will agree with me that he was smart. Noah never lacked for a word by which to express himself. He was a brainy man and a good speller.

It would ill become me at this late day to criticise Mr. Webster's great work—a work that is now in almost every library, school-room and counting house in the land. It is a great book. I do believe that had Mr. Webster lived he would have been equally fair in his criticism of my books.

I hate to compare my own works with those of Mr. Webster, because it may seem egotistical in me to point out the good points in my literary labors; but I have often heard it said, and so do not state it solely upon my own responsibility, that Mr. Webster's book does not retain the interest of the reader all the way through.

He has tried to introduce too many characters, and so we cannot follow them all the way through. It is a good book to pick up and while away an idle hour with, perhaps, but no one would cling to it at night till the fire went out, chained to the thrilling plot and the glowing career of its hero.

Therein consists the great difference between Mr. Webster and myself. A friend of mine at Sing Sing once wrote me that from the moment he got hold of my book, he never left his room till he finished it. He seemed chained to the spot, he said, and if you can't believe a convict, who is entirely out of politics, who in the name of George Washington can you believe?

Mr. Webster was most assuredly a brilliant writer, and I have discovered in his later editions 118,000 words, no two of which are alike. This shows great fluency and versatility, it is true, but we need something else. The reader waits in vain to be thrilled by the author's wonderful word painting. There is not a thrill in the whole tome. I had heard so much of Mr. Webster that when I read his book I confess I was disappointed. It is cold, methodical and dispassionate in the extreme.

As I said, however, it is a good book to pick up for the purpose of whiling away an idle moment, and no one should start out on a long journey without Mr. Webster's tale in his pocket. It has broken the monotony of many a tedious trip for me.

Mr. Webster's "Speller" was a work of less pretentions, perhaps, and yet it had an immense sale. Eight years ago this book had reached a sale of 40,000,000, and yet it had the same grave defect. It was disconnected, cold, prosy and dull. I read it for years, and at last became a close student of Mr. Webster's style, yet I never found but one thing in this book, for which there seems to have been such a perfect stampede, that was even ordinarily interesting, and that was a little gem. It was so thrilling in its details, and so diametrically different from Mr. Webster's style, that I have often wondered who he got to write it for him. It related to the discovery of a boy by an elderly gentleman, in the crotch of an ancestral apple tree, and the feeling of bitterness and animosity that sprung up at the time between the boy and the elderly gentleman.

Though I have been a close student of Mr. Webster for years, I am free to say, and I do not wish to do an injustice to a great man in doing so, that his ideas of literature and my own are entirely dissimilar. Possibly his book has had a little larger sale than mine, but that makes no difference. When I write a book it must engage the interest of the reader, and show some plot to it. It must not be jerky in its style and scattering in its statements.

I know it is a great temptation to write a book that will sell, but we should have a higher object than that.

I do not wish to do an injustice to a man who has done so much for the world, and one who could spell the longest word without hesitation, but I speak of these things just as I would expect people to criticise my work. If we aspire to monkey with the literati of our day we must expect to be criticised. That's the way I look at it.

P. S.—I might also state that Noah Webster was a member of the Legislature of Massachusetts at one time, and though I ought not to throw it up to him at this date, I think it is nothing more than right that the public should know the truth.

To Her Majesty.

TO QUEEN VICTORIA, Regina Dei Gracia and acting mother-in-law, on the side:

DEAR MADAME.—Your most gracious majesty will no doubt be surprised to hear from me after my long silence. One reason that I have not written for some time is that I had hoped to see you ere this, and not because I had grown cold. I desire to congratulate you at this time upon your great success as a mother-in-law, and your very exemplary career socially. As a queen you have given universal satisfaction, and your family have married well.

ADVERTISING THE ENTERPRISE.

But I desired more especially to write you in relation to another matter. We are struggling here in America to establish an authors' international copyright arrangement, whereby the authors of all civilized nations may be protected in their rights to the profits of their literary labor, and the movement so far has met with generous encouragement. As an author we desire your aid and endorsement. Could you assist us? We are giving this season a series of authors' readings in New York to aid in prosecuting the work, and we would like to know whether we could not depend upon you to take a part in these readings, rendering selections from your late work.

I assure your most gracious majesty that you would meet some of our best literary people while here, and no pains would be spared to make your visit a pleasant one, aside from the reading itself. We would advertise your appearance extensively and get out a first-class audience on the occasion of your debut here.

An effort would be made to provide passes for yourself, and reduced rates, I think, could be secured for yourself and suite at the hotels. Of course you could do as you thought best about bringing suite, however. Some of us travel with our suites and some do not. I generally leave my suite at home, myself.

QUEEN VIC. READING.

You would not need to make any special change as to costume for the occasion. We try to make it informal, so far as possible, and though some of us wear full dress we do not make that obligatory on those who take a part in the exercises. If you decide to wear your every-day reigning clothes it will not excite comment on the part of our literati. We do not judge an author or authoress by his or her clothes.

You will readily see that this will afford you an opportunity to appear before some of the best people of New York, and at the same time you will aid in a deserving enterprise.

It will also promote the sale of your book.

Perhaps you have all the royalty you want aside from what you may receive from the sale of your works, but every author feels a pardonable pride in getting his books into every household.

I would assure your most gracious majesty that your reception here as an authoress will in no way suffer because you are an unnaturalized foreigner. Any alien who feels a fraternal interest in the international advancement of thought and the universal encouragement of the good, the true and the beautiful in literature, will be welcome on these shores.

This is a broad land, and we aim to be a broad and cosmopolitan people. Literature and free, willing genius are not hemmed in by State or national lines. They sprout up and blossom under tropical skies no less than beneath the frigid aurora borealis of the frozen North. We hail true merit just as heartily and uproariously on a throne as we would anywhere else. In fact, it is more deserving, if possible, for one who has never tried it little knows how difficult it is to sit on a hard throne all day and write well. We are to recognize struggling genius wherever it may crop out. It is no small matter for an almost unknown monarch to reign all day and then write an article for the press or a chapter for a serial story, only, perhaps, to have it returned by the publishers. All these things are drawbacks to a literary life, that we here in America know little of.

THE ACCOMPANIMENT.

I hope your most gracious majesty will decide to come, and that you will pardon this long letter. It will do you good to get out this way for a few weeks, and I earnestly hope that you will decide to lock up the house and come prepared to make quite a visit. We have some real good authors here now in America, and we are not ashamed to show them to any one. They are not only smart, but they are well behaved and know how to appear in company. We generally read selections from our own works, and can have a brass band to play between the selections, if thought best. For myself, I prefer to have a full brass band accompany me while I read. The audience also approves of this plan.

We have been having some very hot weather here for the past week, but it is now cooler. Farmers are getting in their crops in good shape, but wheat is still low in price, and cranberries are souring on the vines. All of our canned red raspberries worked last week, and we had to can them over again. Mr. Riel, who went into the rebellion business in Canada last winter, will be hanged in September if it don't rain. It will be his first appearance on the gallows, and quite a number of our leading American criminals are going over to see his dèbut.

Hoping to hear from you by return mail or prepaid cablegram, I beg leave to remain your most gracious and indulgent majesty's humble and obedient servant.

BILL NYE.

Habits of a Literary Man.

THE editor of an Eastern health magazine, having asked for information relative to the habits, hours of work, and style and frequency of feed adopted by literary men, and several parties having responded who were no more essentially saturated with literature than I am, I now take my pen in hand to reveal the true inwardness of my literary life, so that boys, who may yearn to follow in my footsteps and wear a laurel wreath the year round in place of a hat, may know what the personal habits of a literary party are.

I rise from bed the first thing in the morning, leaving my couch not because I am dissatisfied with it, but because I cannot carry it with me during the day

I then seat myself on the edge of the bed and devote a few moments to thought. Literary men who have never set aside a few moments on rising for thought will do well to try it.

I then insert myself into a pair of middle-aged pantaloons. It is needless to say that girls who may have a literary tendency will find little to interest them here.

Other clothing is added to the above from time to time. I then bathe myself. Still this is not absolutely essential to a literary life. Others who do not do so have been equally successful.

Some literary people bathe before dressing.

I then go down stairs and out to the barn, where I feed the horse. Some literary men feel above taking care of a horse, because there is really nothing in common between the care of a horse and literature, but simplicity is my watchword. T. Jefferson would have to rise early in the day to eclipse me in simplicity. I wish I had as many dollars as I have got simplicity.

I then go in to breakfast. This meal consists almost wholly of food. I am passionately fond of food, and I may truly say, with my hand on my heart, that I owe much of my great success in life to this inward craving, this constant yearning for something better.

During this meal I frequently converse with my family I do not feel above my family; at least, if I do, I try to conceal it as much as possible. Buckwheat pancakes in a heated state, with maple syrup on the upper side, are extremely conducive to literature. Nothing jerks the mental faculties around with greater rapidity than buckwheat pancakes.

After breakfast the time is put in to good advantage looking forward to the time when dinner will be ready. From 8 to 10 A. M., however, I frequently retire to my private library hot-bed in the hay mow, and write 1,200 words in my forthcoming book, the price of which will be $2.50 in cloth and $4 with Russia back.

I then play Copenhagen with some little girls 21 years of age, who live near by, and of whom I am passionately fond.

After that I dig some worms, with a view to angling. I then angle. After this I return home, waiting until dusk, however, as I do not like to attract attention. Nothing is more distasteful to a truly good man of wonderful literary acquirements, and yet with singular modesty, than the coarse and rude scrutiny of the vulger herd.

In winter I do not angle. I read the "Pirate Prince" or the "Missourian's Mash," or some other work, not so much for the plot as the style, that I may get my mind into correct channels of thought. I then play "old sledge" in a rambling sort of manner. I sometimes spend an evening at home, in order to excite remark and draw attention to my wonderful eccentricity.

I do not use alcohol in any form, if I know it, though sometimes I am basely deceived by those who know of my peculiar prejudice, and who do it, too, because they enjoy watching my odd and amusing antics at the time.

Alcohol should be avoided entirely by literary workers, especially young women. There can be no more pitiable sight to the tender hearted, than a young woman of marked ability writing an obituary poem while under the influence of liquor.

I knew a young man who was a good writer. His penmanship was very good, indeed. He once wrote an article for the press while under the influence of liquor. He sent it to the editor, who returned it at once with a cold and cruel letter, every line of which was a stab. The letter came at a time when he was full of remorse.

He tossed up a cent to see whether he should blow out his brains or go into the ready-made clothing business. The coin decided that he should die by his own hand, but his head ached so that he didn't feel like shooting into it. So he went into the ready-made clothing business, and now he pays taxes on $75,000, so he is probably worth $150,000. This, of course, salves over his wounded heart, but he often says to me that he might have been in the literary business to-day if he had let liquor alone.

A Father's Letter.

MY DEAR SON.—Your letter of last week reached us yesterday, and I enclose $13, which is all I have by me at the present time. I may sell the other shote next week and make up the balance of what you wanted. I will probably have to wear the old buffalo overcoat to meetings again this winter, but that don't matter so long as you are getting an education.

I hope you will get your education as cheap as you can, for it cramps your mother and me like Sam Hill to put up the money. Mind you, I don't complain. I knew education come high, but I didn't know the clothes cost so like sixty.

I want you to be so that you can go anywhere and spell the hardest word. I want you to be able to go among the Romans or the Medes and Persians and talk to any of them in their own native tongue.

I never had any advantages when I was a boy, but your mother and I decided that we would sock you full of knowledge, if your liver held out, regardless of expense. We calculate to do it, only we want you to go as slow on swallow-tail coats as possible till we can sell our hay.

Now, regarding that boat-paddling suit, and that baseball suit, and that bathing suit, and that roller-rinktum suit, and that lawn-tennis suit, mind, I don't care about the expense, because you say a young man can't really educate himself thoroughly without them, but I wish you'd send home what you get through with this fall, and I'll wear them through the winter under my other clothes. We have a good deal severer winters here than we used to, or else I'm failing in bodily health. Last winter I tried to go through without underclothes, the way I did when I was a boy, but a Manitoba wave came down our way and picked me out of a crowd with its eyes shet.

In your last letter you alluded to getting injured in a little "hazing scuffle with a pelican from the rural districts." I don't want any harm to come to you, my son, but if I went from the rural districts, and another young gosling from the rural districts undertook to haze me, I would meet him when the sun goes down, and I would swat him across the back of the neck with a fence board, and then I would meander across the pit of his stomach and put a blue forget-me-not under his eye.

Your father aint much on Grecian mythology and how to get the square root of a barrel of pork, but he wouldn't allow any educational institutions to

RETRIBUTIVE JUSTICE.

haze him with impunity Perhaps you remember once when you tried to haze your father a little, just to kill time, and how long it took you to recover. Anybody that goes at it right can have a good deal of fun with your father, but those who have sought to monkey with him, just to break up the monotony of life, have most always succeeded in finding what they sought.

I ain't much of a pensman, so you will have to excuse this letter. We are all quite well, except old Fan, who has a galded shoulder, and hope this will find you enjoying the same great blessing.

YOUR FATHER.

Archimedes.

ARCHIMEDES, whose given name has been accidentally torn off and swallowed up in oblivion, was born in Syracuse, 2,171 years ago last spring. He was a philosopher and mathematical expert. During his life he was never successfully stumped in figures. It ill befits me now, standing by his new-made grave, to say aught of him that is not of praise. We can only mourn his untimely death, and wonder which of our little band of great men will be the next to go.

Archimedes was the first to originate and use the word "Eureka." It has been successfully used very much lately, and as a result we have the Eureka baking powder, the Eureka suspender, the Eureka bed-bug buster, the Eureka shirt, and the Eureka stomach bitters. Little did Archimedes wot, when he invented this term, that it would come into such general use.

Its origin has been explained before, but it would not be out of place here for me to tell it as I call it to mind now, looking back over Archie's eventful life.

King Hiero had ordered an eighteen karat crown, size $7\frac{1}{8}$, and, after receiving it from the hands of the jeweler, suspected that it had been adulterated. He therefore applied to Archimedes to ascertain, if possible, whether such was the case or not. Archimedes had just got in on No. 3, two hours late, and covered with dust. He at once started for a hot and cold bath emporium on Sixteenth street, meantime wondering how the dickens he would settle that crown business.

He filled the bath-tub level full, and, piling up his raiment on the floor, jumped in. Displacing a large quantity of water, equal to his own bulk, he thereupon solved the question of specific gravity, and, forgetting his bill, forgetting his clothes, he sailed up Sixteenth street and all over Syracuse, clothed in shimmering sunlight and a plain gold ring, shouting "Eureka!" He ran head-first into a Syracuse policeman and howled "Eureka!" The policeman said: "You'll have to excuse me; I don't know him." He scattered the Syracuse Normal school on its way home, and tried to board a Fifteenth street bob-tail car, yelling "Eureka!" The car-driver told him that Eureka wasn't on the car, and referred Archimedes to a clothing store.

Everywhere he was greeted with surprise. He tried to pay his car-fare, but found that he had left his money in his other clothes.

Some thought it was the revised statute of Hercules; that he had become weary of standing on his pedestal during the hot weather, and had started out for fresh air. I give this as I remember it. The story is foundered on fact.

Archimedes once said. "Give me where I may stand, and I will move the world." I could write it in the original Greek, but, fearing that the nonpareil delirium tremens type might get short, I give it in the English language.

It may be tardy justice to a great mathematician and scientist, but I have a few resolutions of respect which I would be very glad to get printed on this solemn occasion, and mail copies of the paper to his relatives and friends:

"WHEREAS, It has pleased an All-wise Providence to remove from our midst Archimedes, who was ever at the front in all deserving labors and enterprises; and

"WHEREAS, We can but feebly express our great sorrow in the loss of Archimedes, whose front name has escaped our memory; therefore

"*Resolved*, That in his death we have lost a leading citizen of Syracuse, and one who never shook his friends—never weakened or gigged back on those he loved.

"*Resolved*, That copies of these resolutions will be spread on the moments of the meeting of the Common Council of Syracuse, and that they be published in the Syracuse papers eodtfpdq&cod, and that marked copies of said papers be mailed to the relatives of the deceased."

To the President-Elect.

DEAR SIR.—The painful duty of turning over to you the administration of these United States and the key to the front door of the White House has been assigned to me. You will find the key hanging inside the storm-door, and the cistern-pole up stairs in the haymow of the barn.

I have made a great many suggestions to the outgoing administration relative to the transfer of the Indian bureau from the department of the Interior to that of the sweet by-and-by The Indian, I may say, has been a great source of annoyance to me, several of their number having jumped one of my most valuable mining claims on White river. Still, I do not complain of that. This mine, however, I am convinced would be a good paying property if properly worked, and should you at any time wish to take the regular army and such other help as you may need and re-capture it from our red brothers, I would be glad to give you a controlling interest in it.

A DEARTH OF SOAP IN THE LAUNDRY AND BATH-ROOM.

You will find all papers in their appropriate pigeon-holes, and a small jar of cucumber pickles down cellar, which were left over and to which you will be perfectly welcome. The asperities and heart burnings that were the immediate result of a hot and unusually bitter campaign are now all buried. Take these pickles and use them as though they were your own. They are none too good for you. You deserve them. We may differ politically but that need not interfere with our warm personal friendship.

You will observe on taking possession of the administration, that the navy is a little bit weather-beaten and wormy. I would suggest that it be newly painted in the spring. If it had been my good fortune to receive a majority of the suffrages of the people for the office which you now hold, I should have painted the navy red. Still, that need not influence you in the course which you may see fit to adopt.

There are many affairs of great moment which I have not enumerated in this brief letter, because I felt some little delicacy and timidity about appearing to be at all dictatorial or officious about a matter wherein the public might charge me with interference.

I hope you will receive the foregoing in a friendly spirit, and whatever your convictions may be upon great questions of national interest, either foreign or domestic, that you will not undertake to blow out the gas on retiring, and that you will in other ways realize the fond anticipations which are now cherished in your behalf by a mighty people whose aggregated eye is now on to you.

BILL NYE.

P S.—You will be a little surprised, no doubt, to find no soap in the laundry or bath-rooms. It probably got into the campaign in some way and was absorbed.

B. N.

Anatomy.

THE word anatomy is derived from two Greek spatters and three poly-wogs, which, when translated, signify "up through" and "to cut," so that anatomy actually, when translated from the original wappy-jawed Greek, means to cut up through. That is no doubt the reason why the medical student proceeds to cut up through the entire course.

Anatomy is so called because its best results are obtained from the cutting or dissecting of organism. For that reason there is a growing demand in the neighborhood of the medical college for good second-hand organisms. Parties having well preserved organisms that they are not actually using, will do well to call at the side door of the medical college after 10 P M.

STUDYING ANATOMY.

The branch of the comparative anatomy which seeks to trace the unities of plan which are exhibited in diverse organisms, and which discovers, as far as may be, the principles which govern the growth and development of organized bodies, and which finds functional analogies and structural homologies, is denominated philosophical or transcendental anatomy (This statement, though strictly true, is not original with me.)

Careful study of the human organism after death, shows traces of functional analogies and structural homologies in people who were supposed to have been in perfect health all their lives.

Probably many of those we meet in the daily walks of life, many, too, who wear a smile and outwardly seem happy, have either one or both of these things. A man may live a false life and deceive his most intimate friends in the matter of anatomical analogies or homologies, but he cannot conceal it from the eagle eye of the medical student. The ambitious medical student makes a specialty of true inwardness.

The study of the structure of animals is called zootomy. The attempt to study the anatomical structure of the grizzly bear from the inside has not been crowned with success. When the anatomizer and the bear have been thrown together casually, it has generally been a struggle between the two organisms to see which would make a study of the structure of the other. Zootomy and moral suasion are not homogeneous, analogous, nor indigenous.

Vegetable anatomy is called phytonomy, sometimes. But it would not be safe to address a vigorous man by that epithet. We may call a vegetable that, however, and be safe.

Human anatomy is that branch of anatomy which enters into the description of the structure and geographical distribution of the elements of a human being. It also applies to the structure of the microbe that crawls out of jail every four years just long enough to whip his wife, vote and go back again.

Human anatomy is either general, specific, topographical or surgical. These terms do not imply the dissection and anatomy of generals, specialists, topographers and surgeons, as they might seem to imply, but really mean something else. I would explain here what they actually do mean if I had more room and knew enough to do it.

Anatomists divide their science, as well as their subjects, into fragments. Osteology treats of the skeleton, myology of the muscles, angiology of the blood vessels, splanchology the digestive organs or department of the interior, and so on.

People tell pretty tough stories of the young carvists who study anatomy on subjects taken from life. I would repeat a few of them here, but they are productive of insomnia, so I will not give them.

I visited a matinee of this kind once for a short time, but I have not been there since. When I have a holiday now, the idea of spending it in the dissecting-room of a large and flourishing medical college does not occur to me.

I never could be a successful surgeon, I fear. While I have no hesitation about mutilating the English, I have scruples about cutting up other nationalities. I should always fear, while pursuing my studies, that I might be called upon to dissect a friend, and I could not do that. I should like to do anything that would advance the cause of science, but I should not want to form the habit of dissecting people, lest some day I might be called upon to dissect a friend for whom I had a great attachment, or some creditor who had an attachment for me.

Mr. Sweeney's Cat.

ROBERT ORMSBY SWEENEY is a druggist of St. Paul, and though a recent chronological record reveals the fact that he is a direct descendant of a sure-enough king, and though there is mighty good purple, royal blood in his veins that dates back where kings used to have something to do to earn their salary, he goes right on with his regular business, selling drugs at the great sacrifice which druggists will make sometimes in order to place their goods within the reach of all.

As soon as I learned that Mr. Sweeney had barely escaped being a crowned head, I got acquainted with him and tried to cheer him up, and I told him that people wouldn't hold him in any way responsible, and that as it hadn't shown itself in his family for years he might perhaps finally wear it out.

He is a mighty pleasant man to meet, anyhow, and you can have just as much fun with him as you could with a man who didn't have any royal blood in his veins. You could be with him for days on a fishing trip and never notice it at all.

But I was going to speak more in particular about Mr. Sweeney's cat. Mr. Sweeney had a large cat, named Dr. Mary Walker, of which he was very fond. Dr. Mary Walker remained at the drug store all the time, and was known all over St. Paul as a quiet and reserved cat. If Dr. Mary Walker took in the town after office hours, nobody seemed to know anything about it. She would be around bright and cheerful the next morning and attend to her duties at the store just as though nothing whatever had happened.

One day last summer Mr. Sweeney left a large plate of fly-paper with water on it in the window, hoping to gather in a few quarts of flies in a deceased state. Dr. Mary Walker used to go to this window during the afternoon and look out on the busy street while she called up pleasant memories of her past life. That afternoon she thought she would call up some more memories, so she went over on the counter and from there jumped down on the window-sill, landing with all four feet in the plate of fly-paper.

At first she regarded it as a joke, and treated the matter very lightly, but later on she observed that the fly-paper stuck to her feet with great tenacity of purpose. Those who have never seen the look of surprise and deep sorrow that a cat wears when she finds herself glued to a whole sheet of fly-paper, cannot fully appreciate the way Dr. Mary Walker felt. She did not dash wildly through a $150 plate-glass window, as some cats would have done. She controlled herself and acted in the coolest manner, though you could have seen that mentally she suffered intensely. She sat down a moment to more fully outline a plan for the future. In doing so, she made a great mistake. The gesture

AT FIRST SHE REGARDED IT AS A JOKE.

resulted in gluing the fly-paper to her person in such a way that the edge turned up behind in the most abrupt manner, and caused her great inconvenience.

Some one at that time laughed in a coarse and heartless way, and I wish you could have seen the look of pain that Dr. Mary Walker gave him.

Then she went away. She did not go around the prescription case as the rest of us did, but strolled through the middle of it, and so on out through the glass door at the rear of the store. We did not see her go through the glass door, but we found pieces of fly-paper and fur on the ragged edges of a large aperture in the glass, and we kind of jumped at the conclusion that Dr. Mary Walker had taken that direction in retiring from the room.

Dr. Mary Walker never returned to St. Paul, and her exact whereabouts are not known, though every effort was made to find her. Fragments of fly-paper and brindle hair were found as far west as the Yellowstone National Park, and as far north as the British line, but the doctor herself was not found. My own theory is, that if she turned her bow to the west so as to catch the strong easterly gale on her quarter, with the sail she had set and her tail pointing directly toward the zenith, the chances for Dr. Mary Walker's immediate return are extremely slim.

The Heyday of Life.

THERE will always be a slight difference in the opinions of the young and the mature, relative to the general plan on which the solar system should be operated, no doubt. There are also points of disagreement in other matters, and it looks as though there always would be.

To the young the future has a more roseate hue. The roseate hue comes high, but we have to use it in this place. To the young there spreads out across the horizon a glorious range of possibilities. After the youth has endorsed for an intimate friend a few times, and purchased the paper at the bank himself later on, the horizon won't seem to horizon so tumultuously as it did aforetime. I remember at one time of purchasing such a piece of accommodation paper at a bank, and I still have it. I didn't need it any more than a cat needs eleven tails at one and the same time. Still the bank made it an object for me, and I secured it. Such things as these harshly knock the flush and bloom off the cheek of youth, and prompt us to turn the strawberry-box bottom side up before we purchase it.

Youth is gay and hopeful, age is covered with experience and scars where the skin has been knocked off and had to grow on again. To the young a dollar looks large and strong, but to the middle-aged and the old it is weak and inefficient.

When we are in the heyday and fizz of existence, we believe everything; but after awhile we murmur: "What's that you are givin' us," or words of like character. Age brings caution and a lot of shop-worn experience, purchased at the highest market price. Time brings vain regrets and wisdom teeth that can be left in a glass of water over night.

Still we should not repine. If people would repine less and try harder to get up an appetite by persweating in someone's vineyard at so much per diem, it would be better. The American people of late years seem to have a deeper and deadlier repugnance for mannish industry, and there seems to be a growing opinion that our crops are more abundant when saturated with foreign perspiration. European sweat, if I may be allowed to use such a low term, is very good in its place, but the native-born Duke of Dakota, or the Earl of York State should remember that the matter of perspiration and posterity should not be left solely to the foreigner.

There are too many Americans who toil not, neither do they spin. They would be willing to have an office foisted upon them, but they would rather blow their so-called brains out than to steer a pair of large steel-gray mules from day to day. They are too proud to hoe corn, for fear some great man will ride by and see the termination of their shirts extending out through the seats of their pantaloons, but they are not too proud to assign their shattered finances to a friend and their shattered remains to the morgue.

Pride is all right if it is the right kind, but the pride that prompts a man to kill his mother, because she at last refuses to black his boots any more, is an erroneous pride. The pride that induces a man to muss up the carpet with his brains because there is nothing left for him to do but to labor, is the kind that Lucifer had when he bolted the action of the convention and went over to the red-hot minority.

Youth is the spring-time of life. It is the time to acquire information, so that we may show it off in after years and paralyze people with what we know. The wise youth will "lay low" till he gets a whole lot of knowledge, and then in later days turn it loose in an abrupt manner. He will guard against telling what he knows, a little at a time. That is unwise. I once knew a youth who wore himself out telling people all he knew from day to day, so that when he became a bald-headed man he was utterly exhausted and didn't have anything left to tell anyone. Some of the things that we know should be saved for our own use. The man who sheds all his knowledge, and don't leave enough to keep house with, fools himself.

They Fell.

TWO delegates to the General Convocation of the Sons of Ice Water were sitting in the lobby of the Windsor, in the city of Denver, not long ago, strangers to each other and to everybody else. One came from Huerferno county, and the other was a delegate from the Ice Water Encampment of Correjos county.

From the beautiful billiard hall came the sharp rattle of ivory balls, and in the bar-room there was a glitter of electric light, cut glass, and French plate mirrors. Out of the door came the merry laughter of the giddy throng, flavored with fragrant Havana smoke and the delicate odor of lemon and mirth and pine apple and cognac.

The delegate from Correjos felt lonely, and he turned to the Ice Water representative from Huerferno:

"That was a bold and fearless speech you made this afternoon on the demon rum at the convocation."

"Think so?" said the sad Huerferno man.

"Yes, you entered into the description of rum's maniac till I could almost see the red-eyed centipedes and tropical hornets in the air. How could you describe the jimjams so graphically?"

"Well, you see, I'm a reformed drunkard. Only a little while ago I was in the gutter."

"So was I."

"How long ago?"

"Week ago day after to-morrow."

"Next Tuesday it'll be a week since I quit."

"Well, I swan!"

"Ain't it funny?"

"Tolerable."

* * * * * * * * *

"It's going to be a long, cold winter; don't you think so?"

"Yes, I dread it a good deal."

* * * * * * * * *

"It's a comfort, though, to know that you never will touch rum again."

"Yes, I am glad in my heart to-night that I am free from it. I shall never touch rum again."

When he said this he looked up at the other delegate, and they looked into each other's eyes earnestly, as though each would read the other's soul. Then the Huerferno man said:

"In fact, I never did care much for rum."

Then there was a long pause.

Finally the Correjos man ventured: "Do you have to use an antidote to cure the thirst?"

"Yes, I've had to rely on that a good deal at first. Probably this vain yearning that I now feel in the pit of the bosom will disappear after awhile."

"Have you got any antidote with you?"

"Yes, I've got some up in 232½. If you'll come up I'll give you a dose."

"There's no rum in it, is there?"

"No."

Then they went up the elevator. They did not get down to breakfast, but at dinner they stole in. The man from Huerferno dodged nervously through the archway leading to the dining-room as though he had doubts about getting through so small a space with his augmented head, and the man from Correjos looked like one who had wept his eyes almost blind over the woe that rum has wrought in our fair land.

When the waiter asked the delegate from Correjos for his desert order, the red-nosed Son of Ice Water said: "Bring me a cup of tea, some pudding without wine sauce, and a piece of mince pie. You may also bring me a cork-screw, if you please, to pull the brandy out of the mince pie with."

Then the two reformed drunkards looked at each other, and laughed a hoarse, bitter and joyous laugh.

At the afternoon session of the Sons of Ice Water, the Huerferno delegate couldn't get his regalia over his head.

Second Letter to the President.

TO THE PRESIDENT.—I write this letter not on my own account, but on behalf of a personal friend of mine who is known as a mugwump. He is a great worker for political reform, but he cannot spell very well, so he has asked me to write this letter. He knew that I had been thrown among great men all my life, and that, owing to my high social position and fine education, I would be peculiarly fitted to write you in a way that would not call forth disagreeable remarks, and so he has given me the points and I have arranged them for you.

WORKING FOR REFORM.

In the first place, my friend desires me to convey to you, Mr. President, in a delicate manner, and in such language as to avoid giving offense, that he is somewhat disappointed in your Cabinet. I hate to talk this way to a bran-new President, but my friend feels hurt and he desires that I should say to you that he regrets your short-sighted policy. He says that it seems to him there is very little in the course of the administration so far to encourage a man to shake off old party ties and try to make men better. He desires to say that after conversing with a large number of the purest men, men who have been in both political parties off and on for years and yet have never been corrupted by office, men who have left convention after convention in years past because those conventions were corrupt and endorsed other men than themselves for office, he finds that your appointment of Cabinet officers will only please two classes, viz: Democrats and Republicans.

Now, what do you care for an administration which will only gratify those two old parties? Are you going to snap your fingers in disdain at men who admit that they are superior to anybody else? Do you want history to chronicle the fact that President Cleveland accepted the aid of the pure and highly cultivated gentlemen who never did anything naughty or unpretty, and then appointed his Cabinet from men who had been known for years as rude, naughty Democrats?

My friend says that he feels sure you would not have done so if you had fully realized how he felt about it. He claims that in the first week of your administration you have basely truckled to the corrupt majority. You have shown yourself to be the friend of men who never claimed to be truly good.

If you persist in this course you will lose the respect and esteem of my friend and another man who is politically pure, and who has never smirched his escutcheon with an office. He has one of the cleanest and most vigorous escutcheons in that county. He never leaves it out over night during the summer, and in the winter he buries it in sawdust. Both of these men will go back to the Republican party in 1888 if you persist in the course you have thus far adopted. They would go back now if the Republican party insisted on it.

Mr. President, I hate to write to you in this tone of voice, because I know the pain it will give you. I once held an office myself, Mr. President, and it hurt my feelings very much to have a warm personal friend criticise my official acts.

The worst feature of the whole thing, Mr. President, is that it will encourage crime. If men who never committed any crime are allowed to earn their living by the precarious methods peculiar to manual labor, and if those who have abstained from office for years, by request of many citizens, are to be denied the endorsement of the administration, they will lose courage to go on and do right in the future. My friend desires to state vicariously, in the strongest terms, that both he and his wife feel the same way about it, and they will not promise to keep it quiet any longer. They feel like crippling the administration in every way they can if the present policy is to be pursued.

He says he dislikes to begin thus early to threaten a President who has barely taken off his overshoes and drawn his mileage, but he thinks it may prevent a recurrence of these unfortunate mistakes. He claims that you have totally misunderstood the principles of the mugwumps all the way through. You seem to regard the reform movement as one introduced for the purpose of universal benefit. This was not the case. While fully endorsing and supporting reform, he says that they did not go into it merely to kill time or simply for fun. He also says that when he became a reformer and supported you, he did not think there were so many prominent Democrats who would have claims upon you. He can only now deplore the great national poverty of offices and the boundless wealth of raw material in the Democratic party from which to supply even that meagre demand.

He wishes me to add, also, that you must have over-estimated the zeal of his party for civil service reform. He says that they did not yearn for civil service reform so much as many people seem to think.

I must now draw this letter to a close. We are all well with the exception of colds in the head, but nothing that need give you any uneasiness. Our large seal-brown hen last week, stimulated by a rising egg market, over-exerted herself, and on Saturday evening, as the twilight gathered, she yielded to a complication of pip and softening of the brain and expired in my arms. She certainly led a most exemplary life and the forked tongue of slander could find naught to utter against her.

Hoping that you are enjoying the same great blessing and that you will write as often as possible without waiting for me, I remain,

Very respectfully yours, BILL NYE.

[Dictated Letter.]

Milling in Pompeii.

WHILE visiting Naples, last fall, I took a great interest in the wonderful museum there, of objects that have been exhumed from the ruins of Pompeii. It is a remarkable collection, including, among other things, the cumbersome machinery of a large woolen factory, the receipts, contracts, statements of sales, etc., etc., of bankers, brokers, and usurers. I was told that the exhumist also ran into an Etruscan bucket-shop in one part of the city, but, owing to the long, dry spell, the buckets had fallen to pieces.

The object which engrossed my attention the most, however, was what seems to have been a circular issued prior to the great volcanic vomit of 79 A. D., and no doubt prior even to the Christian era. As the date is torn off, however, we are left to conjecture the time at which it was issued. I was permitted to make a copy of it, and with the aid of my hired man, I have translated it with great care.

OFFICE OF

LUCRETIUS & PROCALUS,

DEALERS IN

FLOUR, BRAN, SHORTS, MIDDLINGS, SCREENINGS, ETRUSCAN HEN FEED, AND OTHER CHOICE BRIC-A-BRAC.

Highest Cash Price Paid for Neapolitan Winter Wheat and Roman Corn. Why haul your Wheat through the sand to Herculaneum, when we pay the same price here?

OFFICE AND MILL, VIA VIII, NEAR THE STABIAN GATE, ONLY THIRTEEN BLOCKS FROM THE P. O., POMPEII.

DEAR SIR: This circular has been called out by another one issued last month by Messrs. Toecorneous & Chilblainicus, alleged millers and wheat buyers of Herculaneum, in which they claim to pay a quarter to a half-cent more per bushel than we do for wheat, and charge us with docking the farmers around Pompeii a pound per bushel more than necessary for cockle, wild buckwheat, and pigeon-grass seed. They make the broad statement that we have made all our money in that way, and claim that Mr. Lucretius, of our mill, has erected a fine house, which the farmers allude to as the "wild buckwheat villa."

We do not, as a general rule, pay any attention to this kind of stuff; but when two snide romans, who went to Herculaneum without a dollar and drank stale beer out of an old Etruscan tomato-can the first year they were there, assail our integrity, we feel justified in making a prompt and final reply. We desire to state to the Roman farmers that we do not test their wheat with the crooked brass tester that has made more money for Messrs. Toecorneous & Chilblainicus than their old mill has. We do not do that kind of business. Neither do we buy a man's wheat at a cash price and then work off four or five hundred pounds of XXXX Imperial hog feed on him in part payment. When we buy a man's wheat we pay him in money. We do not seek to fill him up with sour Carthagenian cracked wheat and orders on the store.

TWO OLD ROMANS.

We would also call attention to the improvements that we have just made in our mill. Last week we put a handle in the upper burr, and we have also engaged one of the best head millers in Pompeii to turn the crank day-times. Our old head miller will oversee the business at night, so that the mill will be in full blast night and day, except when the head miller has gone to his meals or stopped to spit on his hands.

The mill of our vile contemporaries at Herculaneum is an old one that was used around Naples one hundred years ago to smash rock for the Neapolitan road, and is entirely out of repair. It was also used in a brick-yard here near Pompeii; then an old junk man sold it to a tenderfoot from Jerusalem as an ice-cream freezer. He found that it would not work, and so used it to grind up potato bugs for blisters. Now it is grinding ostensible flour at Herculaneum.

We desire to state to the farmers about Pompeii and Herculaneum that we aim to please. We desire to make a grade of flour this summer that will not have to be run through the coffee mill before it can be used. We will also pay you the highest price for good wheat, and give you good weight. Our capacity is now greatly enlarged, both as to storage and grinding. We now turn out a sack of flour, complete and ready for use, every little while. We have an extra handle for the mill, so that in case of accident to the one now in use, we need not shut down but a few moments. We call attention to our XXXX Git-there brand of flour. It is the best flour in the market for making angels' food and other celestial groceries. We fully warrant it, and will agree that for every sack containing whole kernels of corn, corncobs, or other foreign substances, not thoroughly pulverized, we will refund the money already paid, and show the person through our mill.

ANCIENT ROMAN MILLER.

We would also like to call the attention of farmers and housewives around Pompeii to our celebrated Dough Squatter. It is purely automatic in its operation, requiring only two men to work it. With this machine two men will knead all the bread they can eat and do it easily, feeling thoroughly refreshed at night. They also avoid that dark maroon taste in the mouth so common in Pompeii on arising in the morning.

To those who do not feel able to buy one of these machines, we would say that we have made arrangements for the approaching season, so that those who wish may bring their dough to our mammoth squatter and get it treated at our place at the nominal price of two bits per squat. Strangers calling for their squat or unsquat dough, will have to be identified.

☞ Do not forget the place, Via VIII, near Stabian gate.

LUCRETIUS & PROCALUS,

Dealers in choice family flour, cut feed and oatmeal with or without clinkers in it. Try our lumpless bran for indigestion. ☜

Broncho Sam.

SPEAKING about cowboys, Sam Stewart, known from Montana to Old Mexico as Broncho Sam, was the chief. He was not a white man, an Indian, a greaser or a negro, but he had the nose of an Indian warrior, the curly hair of an African, and the courtesy and equestrian grace of a Spaniard. A wide reputation as a "broncho breaker" gave him his name. To master an untamed broncho and teach him to lead, to drive and to be safely ridden was Sam's mission during the warm weather when he was not riding the range. His special delight was to break the war-like heart of the vicious wild pony of the plains and make him the servant of man.

I've seen him mount a hostile "bucker," and, clinching his italic legs around the body of his adversary, ride him till the blood would burst from Sam's nostrils and spatter horse and rider like rain. Most everyone knows what the bucking of the barbarous Western horse means. The wild horse probably learned it from the antelope, for the latter does it the same way, *i. e.*, he jumps straight up into the air, at the same instant curving his back and coming down stiff-legged, with all four of his feet in a bunch. The concussion is considerable.

I tried it once myself. I partially rode a roan broncho one spring day, which will always be green in my memory The day, I mean, not the broncho.

It occupied my entire attention to safely ride the cunning little beast, and when he began to ride me I put in a minority report against it.

I have passed through an earthquake and an Indian outbreak, but I would rather ride an earthquake without saddle or bridle than to bestride a successful broncho eruption. I remember that I wore a large pair of Mexican spurs, but I forgot them until the saddle turned. Then I remembered them. Sitting down on them in an impulsive way brought them to my mind. Then the broncho steed sat down on me, and that gave the spurs an opportunity to make a more lasting impression on my mind.

To those who observed the charger with the double "cinch" across his back and the saddle in front of him like a big leather corset, sitting at the same time on my person, there must have been a tinge of amusement; but to me it was not so frolicsome.

There may be joy in a wild gallop across the boundless plains, in the crisp morning, on the back of a fleet broncho; but when you return with your ribs sticking through your vest, and find that your nimble steed has returned to town two hours ahead of you, there is a tinge of sadness about it all.

A BRONCO ERUPTION.

Broncho Sam, however, made a specialty of doing all the riding himself. He wouldn't enter into any compromise and allow the horse to ride him.

In a reckless moment he offered to bet ten dollars that he could mount and ride a wild Texas steer. The money was put up. That settled it. Sam never took water. This was true in a double sense. Well, he climbed the cross-bar of the corral-gate, and asked the other boys to turn out their best steer, Marquis of Queensbury rules.

As the steer passed out, Sam slid down and wrapped those parenthetical legs of his around that high-headed, broad-horned brute, and he rode him till the fleet-footed animal fell down on the buffalo grass, ran his hot red tongue out across the blue horizon, shook his tail convulsively, swelled up sadly and died.

It took Sam four days to walk back.

A ten-dollar bill looks as large to me as the star spangled banner, sometimes; but that is an avenue of wealth that had not occurred to me.

I'd rather ride a buzz-saw at two dollars a day and found.

How Evolution Evolves.

THE following paper was read by me in a clear, resonant tone of voice, before the Academy of Science and Pugilism at Erin Prairie, last month, and as I have been so continually and so earnestly importuned to print it that life was no longer desirable, I submit it to you for that purpose, hoping that you will print my name in large caps, with astonishers at the head of the article, and also in good display type at the close:

SOME FEATURES OF EVOLUTION.

No one could possibly, in a brief paper, do the subject of evolution full justice. It is a matter of great importance to our lost and undone race. It lies near to every human heart, and exercises a wonderful influence over our impulses and our ultimate success or failure. When we pause to consider the opaque and fathomless ignorance of the great masses of our fellow men on the subject of evolution, it is not surprising that crime is rather on the increase, and that thousands of our race are annually filling drunkards' graves, with no other visible means of support, while multitudes of enlightened human beings are at the same time obtaining a livelihood by meeting with felons' dooms.

These I would ask in all seriousness and in a tone of voice that would melt the stoniest heart: "Why in creation do you do it?" The time is rapidly approaching when there will be two or three felons for each doom. I am sure that within the next fifty years, and perhaps sooner even than that, instead of handing out these dooms to Tom, Dick and Harry as formerly, every applicant for a felon's doom will have to pass through a competitive examination, as he should do.

It will be the same with those who desire to fill drunkards' graves. The time is almost here when all positions of profit and trust will be carefully and judiciously handed out, and those who do not fit themselves for those positions will be left in the lurch, whatever that may be.

It is with this fact glaring me in the face that I have consented to appear before you to-day and lay bare the whole hypothesis, history, rise and fall, modifications, anatomy, physiology and geology of evolution. It is for this that I have poured over such works as Huxley, Herbert Spencer, Moses in the bulrushes, Anaxagoras, Lucretius and Hoyle. It is for the purpose of advancing the cause of common humanity and to jerk the rising generation out of barbarism into the dazzling effulgence of clashing intellects and fermenting brains that I have sought the works of Pythagoras, Democritus and Epluribus. Whenever I could find any book that bore upon the subject of evolution, and could borrow it, I have done so while others slept.

That is a matter which rarely enters into the minds of those who go easily and carelessly through life. Even the general superintendent of the Academy of Science and Pugilism here in Erin Prairie, the hotbed of a free and untrammeled, robust democracy, does not stop to think of the midnight and other kinds of oil that I have consumed in order to fill myself full of information and to soak my porous mind with thought. Even the O'Reilly College of this place, with its strong mental faculty, has not informed itself fully relative to the great effort necessary before a lecturer may speak clearly, accurately and exhaustingly of evolution.

And yet, here in this place, where education is rampant, and the idea is patted on the back, as I may say; here in Erin Prairie, where progress and some other sentiments are written on everything; here where I am addressing you to-night for $2 and feed for my horse, I met a little child with a bright and cheerful smile, who did not know that evolution consisted in a progress from the homogeneous to the heterogeneous.

So you see that you never know where ignorance lurks. The hydra-headed upas tree and bete noir of self-acting progress, is such ignorance as that, lurking in the very shadow of magnificent educational institutions and hard words of great cast. Nothing can be more disagreeable to the scientist than a bete noir. Nothing gives him greater satisfaction than to chase it up a tree or mash it between two shingles.

For this reason, as I said, it gives me great pleasure to address you on the subject of evolution, and to go into details in speaking of it. I could go on for hours as I have been doing, delighting you with the intricacies and peculiarities of evolution, but I must desist. It would please me to do so, and you would no doubt remain patiently and listen, but your business might suffer while you were away, and so I will close, but I hope that anyone now within the sound of my voice, and in whose breast a sudden hunger for more light on this great subject may have sprung up, will feel perfectly free to call on me and ask me about it or immerse himself in the numerous tomes that I have collected from friends, and which relate to this matter.

In closing I wish to say that I have made no statements in this paper relative to evolution which I am not prepared to prove; and, if anything, I have been over-conservative. For that reason I say now, that the person who doubts a single fact as I have given it to-night, bearing upon the great subject of evolution, will have to do so over my dumb remains.

And a man who will do that is no gentleman. I presume that many of these statements will be snapped up and sharply criticised by other theologians and many of our foremost thinkers, but they will do well to pause before they draw me into a controversy, for I have other facts in relation to evolution, and some personal reminiscences and family history, which I am prepared to introduce, if necessary, together with ideas that I have thought up myself. So I say to those who may hope to attract notice and obtain notoriety by drawing me into a controversy, beware. It will be to your interest to beware!

Hours With Great Men.

I PRESUME that I could write an entire library of personal reminiscences relative to the eminent people with whom I have been thrown during a busy life, but I hate to do it, because I always regarded such things as sacred from the vulgar eye, and I felt bound to respect the confidence of a prominent man just as much as I would that of one who was less before the people. I remember very well my first meeting with General W T. Sherman. I would not mention it here if it were not for the fact that the people seem so be yearning for personal reminiscences of great men, and that is perfectly right, too.

It was since the war that I met General Sherman, and it was on the line of the Union Pacific Railway, at one of those justly celebrated eating-houses, which I understand are now abandoned. The colored waiter had cut off a strip of the omelette with a pair of shears, the scorched oatmeal had been passed around, the little rubber door mats fried in butter and called pancakes had been dealt around the table, and the cashier at the end of the hall had just gone through the clothes of a party from Vermont, who claimed a rebate on the ground that the waiter had refused to bring him anything but his bill. There was no sound in the dining-room except the weak request of the coffee for more air and stimulents, or perhaps the cry of pain when the butter, while practicing with the dumb-bells, would hit a child on the head; then all would be still again.

General Sherman sat at one end of the table, throwing a life-preserver to a fly in the milk pitcher

We had never met before, though for years we had been plodding along life's rugged way—he in the war department, I in the postoffice department. Unknown to each other, we had been holding up opposite corners of the great national fabric, if you will allow me that expression.

I remember, as well as though it were but yesterday, how the conversation began. General Sherman looked sternly at me and said:

"I wish you would overpower that butter and send it up this way."

"All right," said I, "if you will please pass those molasses."

That was all that was said, but I shall never forget it, and probably he never will. The conversation was brief, but yet how full of food for thought! How true, how earnest, how natural! Nothing stilted or false about it. It was the natural expression of two minds that were too great to be verbose or to monkey with social, conversational flapdoodle.

AN ENCOUNTER WITH THE BUTTER.

I remember, once, a great while ago, I was asked by a friend to go with him in the evening to the house of an acquaintance, where they were going to have a kind of musicale, at which there was to be some noted pianist, who had kindly consented to play a few strains. I did not get the name of the professional, but I went, and when the first piece was announced I saw that the light was very uncertain, so I kindly volunteered to get a lamp from another room. I held that big lamp, weighing about twenty-nine pounds, for half an hour, while the pianist would tinky tinky up on the right hand, or bang, boomy to bang down on the bass, while he snorted and slugged that old concert grand piano and almost knocked its teeth down its throat, or gently dawdled with the keys like a pale moonbeam shimmering through the bleached rafters of a deceased horse, until at last there was a wild jangle, such as the accomplished musician gives to an instrument to show the audience that he has disabled the piano, and will take a slight intermission while it is sent to the junk shop.

With a sigh of relief I carefully put down the twenty-nine pound lamp, and my friend told me that I had been standing there like liberty enlightening the world, and holding that heavy lamp for Blind Tom.

* * * * * * * * *

I had never seen him before, and I slipped out of the room before he had a chance to see me.

Concerning Coroners.

I AM glad to notice that in the East there is a growing disfavor in the public mind for selecting a practicing physician for the office of coroner. This matter should have attracted attention years ago. Now it gratifies me to notice a finer feeling on the part of the people, and an awakening of those sensibilities which go to make life more highly prized and far more enjoyable.

I had the misfortune at one time to be under the medical charge of a coroner who had graduated from a Chicago morgue and practiced medicine along with his inquest business with the most fiendish delight. I do not know which he enjoyed best, holding the inquest or practicing on his patient and getting the victim ready for the quest.

One day he wrote out a prescription and left it for me to have filled. I was surprised to find that he had made a mistake and left a rough draft of the verdict in my own case and a list of jurors which he had made in memorandum, so as to be ready for the worst. I was alarmed, for I did not know that I was in so dangerous a condition. He had the advantage of me, for he knew just what he was giving me, and how long human life could be sustained under his treatment. I did not.

That is why I say that the profession of medicine should not be allowed to conflict with the solemn duties of the coroner. They are constantly clashing and infringing upon each other's territory. This coroner had a kind of tread-softly-bow-the-head way of getting around the room that made my flesh creep. He had a way, too, when I was asleep, of glancing hurriedly through the pockets of my pantaloons as they hung over a chair, probably to see what evidence he could find that might aid the jury in arriving at a verdict. Once I woke up and found him examing a draft that he had found in my pocket. I asked him what he was doing with my funds, and he said that he thought he detected a draft in the room and he had just found out where it came from.

After that I hoped that death would come to my relief as speedily as possible. I felt that death would be a happy release from the cold touch of the amateur coroner and pro tem physician. I could look forward with pleasure, and even joy, to the moment when my physician would come for the last time in his professional capacity and go to work on me officially Then the county would be obliged to pay him, and the undertaker could take charge of the fragments left by the inquest.

The duties of the physician are with the living, those of the coroner with the dead. No effort, therefore, should be made to unite them. It is in violation of all the finer feelings of humanity When the physician decides that his tendencies point mostly toward immortality and the names of his patients are nearly all found on the moss-covered stones of the cemetery, he may abandon the profession with safety and take hold of politics. Then, should his tastes lead him to the inquest, let him gravitate toward the office of coroner; but the two should not be united.

No man ought to follow his fellow down the mysterious river that defines the boundary between the known and the unknown, and charge him professionally till his soul has fled, and then charge a per diem to the county for prying into his internal economy and holding an inquest over the debris of mortality. I therefore hail this movement with joy and wish to encourage it in every way It points toward a degree of enlightenment which will be in strong contrast with the darker and more ignorant epochs of time, when the practice of medicine was united with the profession of the barber, the well-digger, the farrier, the veterinarian or the coroner.

Why, this physician plenipotentiary and coroner extraordinary that I have referred to, didn't know when he got a call whether to take his morphine syringe or his venire for a jury. He very frequently went to see a patient with a lung tester under one arm and the revised statutes under the other. People never knew when they saw him going to a neighbor's house, whether the case had yielded to the coroner's treatment or not. No one ever knew just when over-taxed nature would yield to the statutes in such case made and provided. When the jury was impanelled, however, we always knew that the medical treatment had been successfully fatal.

Once he charged the county with an inquest he felt sure of, but in the night the patient got delirious, eluded his nurse, the physician and coroner, and fled to the foot-hills, where he was taken care of and finally recovered.

The experiences of some of the patients who escaped from this man read more like fiction than fact. One man revived during the inquest, knocked the foreman of the jury through the window, kicked the coroner in the stomach, fed him a bottle of violet ink, and, with a shriek of laughter, fled. He is now traveling under an assumed name with a mammoth circus, feeding his bald head to the African lion twice a day at $9 a week and found.

Down East Rum.

RUM has always been a curse to the State of Maine. The steady fight that Maine has made, for a century past, against decent rum, has been worthy of a better cause.

Who hath woe? who hath sorrow and some more things of that kind? He that monkeyeth with Maine rum; he that goeth to seek emigrant rum.

In passing through Maine the tourist is struck with the ever-varying styles of mystery connected with the consumption of rum.

In Denver your friend says. "Will you come with me and shed a tear?" or "Come and eat a clove with me."

In Salt Lake City a man once said to me: "William, which would you rather do, take a dose of Gentile damnation down here on the corner, or go over across the street and pizen yourself with some real old Mormon Valley tan, made last week from ground feed and prussic acid?" I told him that I had just been to dinner, and the doctor had forbidden my drinking any more, and that I had promised several people on their death beds never to touch liquor, and besides, I had just taken a large drink, so he would have to excuse me.

But in Maine none of these common styles of invitation prevail. It is all shrouded in mystery. You give the sign of distress to any member in good standing, pound three times on the outer gate, give two hard kicks and one soft one on the inner door, give the password, "Rutherford B. Hayes," turn to the left, through a dark passage, turn the thumbscrew of a mysterious gas fixture 90 deg. to the right, holding the goblet of the encampment under the gas fixture, then reverse the thumbscrew, shut your eyes, insult your digester, leave twenty-five cents near the gas fixture, and hunt up the nearest cemetery, so that you will not have to be carried very far.

If a man really wants to drink himself into a drunkard's grave, he can certainly save time by going to Maine. Those desiring the most prompt and vigorous style of jim-jams at cut rates will do well to examine Maine goods before going elsewhere. Let a man spend a week in Boston, where the Maine liquor law, I understand, is not in force, and then, with no warning whatever, be taken into the heart of Maine; let him land there a stranger and a partial orphan, with no knowledge of the underground methods of securing a drink, and to him the world seems very gloomy, very sad, and extremely arid.

At the Bangor depot a woman came up to me and addressed me. She was rather past middle age, a perfect lady in her manners, but a little full.

I said: "Madam, I guess you will have to excuse me. You have the advantage. I can't just speak your name at this moment. It has been now thirty years since I left Maine, a child two years old. So people have changed. You've no idea how people have grown out of my knowledge. I don't see but you look just as young as you did when I went away, but I'm a poor hand to remember names, so I can't just call you to mind."

She was perfectly ladylike in her manner, but a little bit drunk. It is singular how drunken people will come hundreds of miles to converse with me. I have often been alluded to as the "drunkard's friend." Men have been known to get intoxicated and come a long distance to talk with me on some subject, and then they would lean up against me and converse by the hour. A drunken man never seems to get tired of talking with me. As long as I am willing to hold such a man up and listen to him, he will stand and tell me about himself with the utmost confidence, and, no matter who goes by, he does not seem to be ashamed to have people see him talking with me.

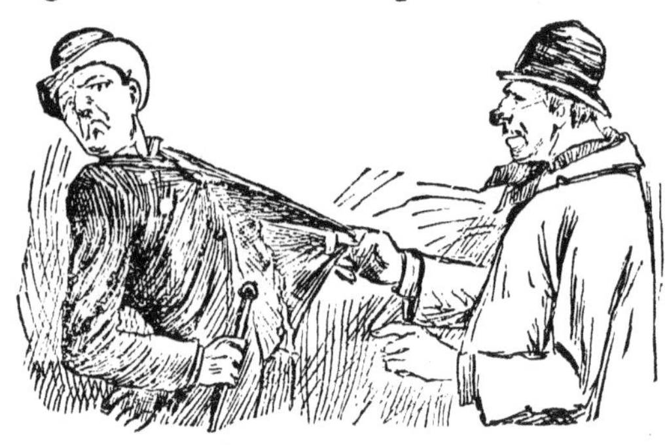
THAT BUTTONHOLE.

I once had a friend who was very much liked by every one, so he drifted into politics. For seven years he tried to live on free whiskey and popular approval, but it wrecked him at last. Finally he formed the habit of meeting me every day and explaining it to me, and giving me free exhibitions of a breath that he had acquired at great expense. After he got so feeble that he could not walk any more, this breath of his used to pull him out of bed and drag him all over town. It don't seem hardly possible, but it is so. I can show you the town yet.

He used to take me by the buttonhole when he conversed with me. This is a diagram of the buttonhole.

If I had a son I would warn him against trying to subsist solely on popular approval and free whiskey It may do for a man engaged solely in sedentary pursuits, but it is not sufficient in cases of great muscular exhaustion. Free whiskey and popular approval on an empty stomach are highly injurious.

Railway Etiquette.

MANY people have traveled all their lives and yet do not know how to behave themselves when on the road. For the benefit and guidance of such, these few crisp, plain, horse-sense rules of etiquette have been framed.

In traveling by rail on foot, turn to the right on discovering an approaching train. If you wish the train to turn out, give two loud toots and get in between the rails, so that you will not muss up the right of way Many a nice, new right of way has been ruined by getting a pedestrian tourist spattered all over its first mortgage.

On retiring at night on board the train, do not leave your teeth in the ice-water tank. If every one should do so, it would occasion great confusion in case of wreck. It would also cause much annoyance and delay during the resurrection. Experienced tourists tie a string to their teeth and retain them during the night.

If you have been reared in extreme poverty, and your mother supported you until you grew up and married, so that your wife could support you, you will probably sit in four seats at the same time, with your feet extended into the aisles so that you can wipe them off on other people, while you snore with your mouth open clear to your shoulder blades.

If you are prone to drop to sleep and breathe with a low death rattle, like the exhaust of a bath tub, it would be a good plan to tie up your head in a feather bed and then insert the whole thing in the linen closet; or, if you cannot secure that, you might stick it out of the window and get it knocked off against a tunnel. The stockholders of the road might get mad about it, but you could do it in such a way that they wouldn't know whose head it was.

Ladies and gentlemen should guard against traveling by rail while in a beastly state of intoxication.

the dining car, while eating, do not comb your moustache with your fork. By all means do not comb your moustache with the fork of another. It is better to refrain altogether from combing the moustache with a fork while traveling, for the motion of the train might jab the fork into your eye and irritate it.

If your desert is very hot and you do not discover it until you have burned the rafters out of the roof of your mouth, do not utter a wild yell of agony and spill your coffee all over a total stranger, but control yourself, hoping to know more next time.

In the morning is a good time to find out how many people have succeeded in getting on the passenger train, who ought to be in the stock car.

Generally, you will find one male and one female. The male goes into the wash room, bathes his worthless carcass from daylight until breakfast time, walking on the feet of any man who tries to wash his face during that time. He wipes himself on nine different towels, because when he gets home he knows he will have to wipe his face on an old door mat. People who have been reared on hay all their lives, generally want to fill themselves full of pie and colic when they travel.

The female of this same mammal, goes into the ladies' department and remains there until starvation drives her out. Then the real ladies have about thirteen seconds apiece in which to dress.

If you never rode in a varnished car before, and never expect to again, you will probably roam up and down the car, meandering over the feet of the porter while he is making up the berths. This is a good way to let people see just how little sense you had left after your brain began to soften.

In traveling, do not take along a lot of old clothes that you know you will never wear.

B. Franklin, Deceased.

BENJAMIN FRANKLIN, formerly of Boston, came very near being an only child. If seventeen children had not come to bless the home of Benjamin's parents, they would have been childless. Think of getting up in the morning and picking out your shoes and stockings from among seventeen pairs of them. Imagine yourself a child, gentle reader, in a family where you would be called upon, every morning, to select your own cud of spruce gum from a collection of seventeen similar cuds stuck on a window sill. And yet B. Franklin never murmured or repined. He desired to go to sea, and to avoid this he was apprenticed to his brother James, who was a printer. It is said that Franklin at once took hold of the great Archimedean lever, and jerked it early and late in the interests of freedom. It is claimed that Franklin at this time invented the deadly weapon known as the printer's towel. He found that a common crash towel could be saturated with glue, molasses, antimony, concentrated lye, and roller composition, and that after a few years of time and perspiration it would harden so that the "Constant Reader" or "Veritas" could be stabbed with it and die soon.

A DEADLY ONSLAUGHT.

Many believe that Franklin's other scientific experiments were productive of more lasting benefit to mankind than this, but I do not agree with them.

This paper was called the *New England Courant.* It was edited jointly by James and Benjamin Franklin, and was started to supply a long-felt want. Benjamin edited a part of the time and James a part of the time. The idea of having two editors was not for the purpose of giving volume to the editorial page, but it was necessary for one to run the paper while the other was in jail. In those days you couldn't sass the king, and then, when the king came in the office the next day and stopped his paper, and took out his ad., you couldn't put it off on "our informant" and go right along with the paper. You had to go to jail, while your subscribers wondered why their paper did not come, and the paste soured in the tin dippers in the sanctum, and the circus passed by on the other side.

STOPPING HIS PAPER.

How many of us to-day, fellow journalists, would be willing to stay in jail while the lawn festival and the kangaroo came and went? Who, of all our company, would go to a prison cell for the cause of freedom while a double-column ad. of sixteen aggregated circuses, and eleven congresses of ferocious beasts, fierce and fragrant from their native lair, went by us?

At the age of 17, Ben got disgusted with his brother, and went to Philadelphia and New York, where he got a chance to "sub" for a few weeks, and then got a regular "sit." Franklin was a good printer, and finally got to be a foreman. He made an excellent foreman, sitting by the hour in the composing room and spitting on the stone, while he cussed the make-up and press work of the other papers. Then he would go into the editorial rooms and scare the editors to death with a wild shriek for more copy. He knew just how to conduct himself as a foreman, so that strangers would think he owned the paper.

In 1730, at the age of 24, Franklin married and established the *Pennsylvania Gazette.* He was then regarded as a great man, and most everyone took his paper. Franklin grew to be a great journalist, and spelled hard words with great fluency He never tried to be a humorist in any of his newspaper work, and everybody respected him.

Along about 1746 he began to study the construction and habits of lightning, and inserted a local in his paper, in which he said that he would be obliged to any of his readers who might notice any new or odd specimens of lightning, if they would send them into the *Gazette* office by express for examination. Every time there was a thunder storm, Franklin would tell the foreman to edit the paper, and, armed with a string and an old fruit jar, he would go out on the hills and get enough lightning for a mess.

"HOW'S TRADE?"

In 1753 Franklin was made postmaster-general of the colonies. He made a good postmaster-general, and people say there were less mistakes in distributing their mail than there has ever been since. If a man mailed a letter in those days, old Ben Franklin saw that it went where it was addressed.

Franklin frequently went over to England in those days, partly on business, and partly to shock the king. He used to delight in going to the castle with his breeches tucked in his boots, figuratively speaking, and attract a good deal of attention. It looked odd to the English, of course, to see him come into the royal presence, and, leaving his wet umbrella up against the throne, ask the king: "How's trade?" Franklin never put on any frills, but he was not afraid of a crowned head. He used to say, frequently, that to him a king was no more than a seven spot.

He did his best to prevent the Revolutionary war, but he couldn't do it,

Patrick Henry had said that the war was inevitable, and given it permission to come, and it came. He also went to Paris and got acquainted with a few crowned heads there. They thought a good deal of him in Paris, and offered him a corner lot if he would build there and start a paper. They also promised him the county printing, but he said no, he would have to go back to America, or his wife might get uneasy about him.

Franklin wrote "Poor Richard's Almanac" in 1732–57, and it was republished in England. Benjamin Franklin had but one son, and his name was William. William was an illegitimate son, and, though he lived to be quite an old man, he never got over it entirely, but continued to be but an illegitimate son all his life. Everybody urged him to do differently, but he steadily refused to do so.

Life Insurance as a Health Restorer.

LIFE Insurance is a great thing. I would not be without it. My health is greatly improved since I got my new policy Formerly I used to have a seal-brown taste in my mouth when I arose in the morning, but that has entirely disappeared. I am more hopeful and happy, and my hair if getting thicker on top. I would not try to keep house without life insurance. Last September I was caught in one of the most destructive cyclones that ever visited a Republican form of government. A great deal of property was destroyed and many lives were lost, but I was spared. People who had no insurance were mowed down on every hand, but aside from a broken leg I was entirely unharmed.

PROTECTED BY LIFE INSURANCE.

I look upon life insurance as a great comfort, not only to the beneficiary, but to the insured, who very rarely lives to realize anything pecuniarily from his venture. Twice I have almost raised my wife to affluence and cast a gloom over the community in which I lived, but something happened to the physician for a few days so that he could not attend to me, and I recovered. For nearly two years I was under the doctor's care. He had his finger on my pulse or in my pocket all the time. He was a young western physician, who attended me on Tuesdays and Fridays. The rest of the week he devoted his medical skill to horses that were mentally broken down. He said he attended me largely for my society. I felt flattered to know that he enjoyed my society after he had been thrown among horses all the week that had much greater advantages than I.

My wife at first objected seriously to an insurance on my life, and said she would never, never touch a dollar of the money if I were to die, but after I had been sick nearly two years, and my disposition had suffered a good deal, she said that I need not delay the obsequies on that account. But the life insurance slipped through my fingers somehow, and I recovered.

In these days of dynamite and roller rinks, and the gory meat-ax of a new administration, we ought to make some provision for the future.

The Opium Habit.

I Have always had a horror of opiates of all kinds. They are so seductive and so still in their operations. They steal through the blood like a wolf on the trail, and they seize upon the heart at last with their white fangs till it is still forever.

Up the Laramie there is a cluster of ranches at the base of the Medicine Bow, near the north end of Sheep Mountain, and in sight of the glittering, eternal frost of the snowy range. These ranches are the homes of the young men from Massachusetts, Pennsylvania and Ohio, and now there are several "younger sons" of Old England, with herds of horses, steers and sheep, worth millions of dollars. These young men are not of the kind of whom the metropolitan ass writes as saying "youbetcherlife," and calling everybody "pardner." They are many of them college graduates, who can brand a wild Maverick or furnish the easy gestures for a Strauss waltz.

They wear human clothes, talk in the United States language, and have a bank account. This spring they may be wearing chaparajos and swinging a quirt through the thin air, and in July they may be at Long Branch, or coloring a meerschaum pipe among the Alps.

Well, a young man whom we will call Curtis lived at one of these ranches years ago, and, though a quiet, mind-your-own-business fellow, who had absolutely no enemies among his companions, he had the misfortune to incur the wrath of a tramp sheep-herder, who waylaid Curtis one afternoon and shot him dead as he sat in his buggy. Curtis wasn't armed. He didn't dream of trouble till he drove home from town, and, as he passed through the gates of a corral, saw the-hairy face of the herder, and at the same moment the flash of a Winchester rifle. That was all.

A rancher came into town and telegraphed to Curtis' father, and then a half dozen citizens went out to help capture the herder, who had fled to the sage brush of the foot-hills.

They didn't get back till toward daybreak, but they brought the herder with them. I saw him in the gray of the morning, lying in a coarse gray blanket, on the floor of the engine house. He was dead.

I asked, as a reporter, how he came to his death, and they told me—opium! I said, did I understand you to say "ropium?" They said no, it was opium. The murderer had taken poison when he found that escape was impossible.

I was present at the inquest, so that I could report the case. There was very little testimony, but all the evidence seemed to point to the fact that life was extinct, and a verdict of death by his own hand was rendered.

It was the first opium work I had ever seen, and it aroused my curiosity. Death by opium, it seems, leaves a dark purple ring around the neck. I did not know this before. People who die by opium also tie their hands together before they die. This is one of the eccentricities of opium poisoning that I have never seen laid down in the books. I bequeath it to medical science. Whenever I run up against a new scientific discovery, I just hand it right over to the public without cost.

Ever since the above incident, I have been very apprehensive about people who seem to be likely to form the opium habit. It is one of the most deadly of narcotics, especially in a new country. High up in the pure mountain atmosphere, this man could not secure enough air to prolong life, and he expired. In a land where clear, crisp air and delightful scenery are abundant, he turned his back upon them both and passed away. Is it not sad to contemplate?

More Paternal Correspondence.

MY DEAR SON.—I tried to write to you last week, but didn't get around to it, owing to circumstances. I went away on a little business tower for a few days on the cars, and then when I got home the sociable broke loose in our onct happy home.

While on my commercial tower down the Omehaw railroad buying a new well-diggin' machine of which I had heard a good deal pro and con, I had the pleasure of riding on one of them sleeping-cars that we read so much about.

I am going on 50 years old, and that's the first time I ever slumbered at the rate of forty-five miles per hour, including stops.

I got acquainted with the porter, and he blacked my boots in the night unbeknownst to me, while I was engaged in slumber. He must have thought that I was your father, and that we rolled in luxury at home all the time, and that it was a common thing for us to have our boots blacked by menials. When I left the car this porter brushed my clothes till the hot flashes ran up my spinal column, and I told him that he had treated me square, and I rung his hand when he held it out toards me, and I told him that at any time he wanted a good, cool drink of buttermilk, to just heller through our telephone. We had the sociable at our house last week, and when I got home your mother set me right to work borryin' chairs and dishes. She had solicited some cakes and other things. I don't know whether you are on the skedjule by which these sociables are run or not. The idea is a novel one to me.

The sisters in our set, onct in so often, turn their houses wrong side out for the purpose of raising four dollars to apply on the church debt. When I was a boy we worshiped with less frills than they do now. Now it seems that the debt is a part of the worship.

Well, we had a good time and used up 150 cookies in a short time. Part of these cookies was devoured and the balance was trod into our all-wool carpet. Several of the young people got to playing Copenhagen in the setting-room and stepped on the old cat in such a way as to disfigure him for life. They also had a disturbance in the front room and knocked off some of the plastering. So your mother is feeling slim and I am not very chipper myself. I hope that you are working hard at your books so that you will be an ornament to society. Society is needing some ornaments very much. I sincerely hope

ROUGH ON THE OLD CAT.

that you will not begin to monkey with rum. I should hate to have you meet with a felon's doom or fill a drunkard's grave. If anybody has got to fill a drunkard's grave, let him do it himself. What has the drunkard ever done for you, that you should fill his grave for him?

I expect you to do right, as near as possible. You will not do exactly right all the time, but try to strike a good average. I do not expect you to let your studies encroach too much on your polo, but try to unite the two so that you will not break down under the strain. I should feel sad and mortified to have you come home a physical wreck. I think one physical wreck in a family is enough, and I am rapidly getting where I can do the entire physical wreck business for our neighborhood.

I see by your picture that you have got one of them pleated coats with a belt around it, and short pants. They make you look as you did when I used to spank you in years gone by, and I feel the same old desire to do it now that I did then. Old and feeble as I am, it seems to me as though I could spank a boy that wears knickerbocker pants buttoned onto a Garabaldy waist and a pleated jacket. If it wasn't for them cute little camel's hair whiskers of yours I would not believe that you had grown to be a large, expensive boy, grown up with thoughts. Some of the thoughts you express in your letters are far beyond your years. Do you think them yourself, or is there some boy in the school that thinks all the thoughts for the rest?

Some of your letters are so deep that your mother and I can hardly grapple with them. One of them, especially, was so full of foreign stuff that you had got out of a bill of fare, that we will have to wait till you come home before we can take it in. I can talk a little Chippewa, but that is all the foreign language I am familiar with. When I was young we had to get our foreign languages the best we could, so I studied Chippewa without a master. A Chippewa chief took me into his camp and kept me there for some time while I acquired his language. He became so much attached to me that I had great difficulty in coming away. I wish you would write in the United States dialect as much as possible, and not try to paralize your parents with imported expressions that come too high for poor people.

Remember that you are the only boy we've got, and we are only going through the motions of living here for your sake. For us the day is wearing out, and it is now way long into the shank of the evening. All we ask of you is to improve on the old people. You can see where I fooled myself, and you can do better. Read and write, and sifer, and polo, and get nolledge, and try not to be ashamed of your uncultivated parents.

When you get that checkered little sawed-off coat on, and that pair of knee panties, and that poker-dot necktie, and the sassy little boys holler "rats" when you pass by, and your heart is bowed down, remember that, no matter how foolish you may look, your parents will never sour on you. YOUR FATHER.

Twombley's Tale.

MY name is Twombley, G. O. P Twombley is my full name and I have had a checkered career. I thought it would be best to have my career checked right through, so I did so.

My home is in the Wasatch Mountains. Far up, where I can see the long, green, winding valley of the Jordan, like a glorious panorama below me, I dwell. I keep a large herd of Angora goats. That is my business. The Angora goat is a beautiful animal—in a picture. But out of a picture he has a style of perspiration that invites adverse criticism.

Still, it is an independent life, and one that has its advantages, too.

When I first came to Utah, I saw one day, in Salt Lake City, a young girl arrive. She was in the heyday of life, but she couldn't talk our language. Her face was oval; rather longer than it was wide, I noticed, and, though she was still young, there were traces of care and other foreign substances plainly written there.

She was an emigrant, about seventeen years of age, and, though she had been in Salt Lake City an hour and a half, she was still unmarried.

She was about the medium height, with blue eyes, that somehow, as you examined them carefully in the full, ruddy light of a glorious September afternoon, seemed to resemble each other. Both of them were that way.

I know not what gave me the courage, but I stepped to her side, and in a low voice told her of my love and asked her to be mine.

She looked askance at me. Nobody ever did that to me before and lived to tell the tale. But her sex made me overlook it. Had she been any other sex that I can think of, I would have resented it. But I would not strike a woman, especially when I had not been married to her and had no right to do so.

I turned on my heel and I went away I most always turn on my heel when I go away. If I did not turn on my own heel when I went away, whose heel would a lonely man like me turn upon?

Years rolled by. I did nothing to prevent it. Still that face came to me in my lonely hut far up in the mountains. That look still rankled in my memory. Before that my memory had been all right. Nothing had ever rankled in it very much. Let the careless reader who never had his memory rankle in hot weather, pass this by. This story is not for him.

After our first conversation we did not meet again for three years, and then by the merest accident. I had been out for a whole afternoon, hunting an elderly goat that had grown childish and irresponsible. He had wandered away, and for several days I had been unable to find him. So I sought for him till darkness found me several miles from my cabin. I realized at once that I must hurry back, or lose my way and spend the night in the mountains. The darkness became more rapidly obvious. My way became more and more uncertain.

Finally I fell down an old prospect shaft. I then resolved to remain where I was until I could decide what was best to be done. If I had known that the prospect shaft was there, I would have gone another way. There was another way that I could have gone, but it did not occur to me until too late.

I hated to spend the next few weeks in the shaft, for I had not locked up my cabin when I left it, and I feared that someone might get in while I was absent and play on the piano. I had also set a batch of bread and two hens that morning, and all of these would be in sad knead of me before I could get my business into such shape that I could return.

I could not tell accurately how long I had been in the shaft, for I had no matches by which to see my watch. I also had no watch.

All at once, someone fell down the shaft. I knew that it was a woman, because she did not swear when she landed at the bottom. Still, this could be accounted for in another way. She was unconscious when I picked her up.

I did not know what to do. I was perfectly beside myself, and so was she. I had read in novels that when a woman became unconscious people generally chafed her hands, but I did not know whether I ought to chafe the hands of a person to whom I had never been introduced.

I could have administered alcoholic stimulants to her but I had neglected to provide myself with them when I fell down the shaft. This should be a warning to people who habitually go around the country without alcoholic stimulants.

Finally she breathed a long sigh and murmured, "where am I?" I told her that I did not know, but wherever it might be, we were safe, and that whatever she might say to me, I would promise her, should go no farther.

Then there was a long pause.

To encourage further conversation I asked her if she did not think we had been having a rather backward spring. She said we had, but she prophesied a long, open fall.

Then there was another pause, after which I offered her a seat on an old red empty powder can. Still, she seemed shy and reserved. I would make a remark to which she would reply briefly, and then there would be a pause of a little over an hour. Still it seemed longer.

Suddenly the idea of marriage presented itself to my mind. If we never got out of the shaft, of course an engagement need not be announced. No one had ever plighted his or her troth at the bottom of a prospect shaft before. It was certainly unique, to say the least. I suggested it to her.

She demurred to this on the ground that our acquaintance had been so brief, and that we had never been thrown together before. I told her that this would be no objection, and that my parents were so far away that I did not think they would make any trouble about it.

She said that she did not mind her parents so much as she did the violent temper of her husband.

I asked her if her husband had ever indulged in polygamy. She replied that he had, frequently. He had several previous wives. I convinced her that in the eyes of the law, and under the Edmunds bill, she was not bound to him. Still she feared the consequences of his wrath.

Then I suggested a desperate plan. We would elope!

I was now thirty-seven years old, and yet had never eloped. Neither had she. So, when the first streaks of rosy dawn crept across the soft, autumnal sky and touched the rich and royal coloring on the rugged sides of the grim old mountains, we got out of the shaft and eloped.

On Cyclones.

I DESIRE to state that my position as United States Cyclonist for this Judicial District is now vacant. I resigned on the 9th day of September, A. D. 1884.

I have not the necessary personal magnetism to look a cyclone in the eye and make it quail. I am stern and even haughty in my intercourse with men, but when a Manitoba simoon takes me by the brow of my pantaloons and throws me across Township 28, Range 18, West of the 5th Principal Meridian, I lose my mental reserve and become anxious and even taciturn. For thirty years I had yearned to see a grown up cyclone, of the ring-tail-puller variety, mop up the green earth with huge forest trees and make the landscape look tired. On the 9th day of September, A. D. 1884, my morbid curiosity was gratified.

As the people came out into the forest with lanterns and pulled me out of the crotch of a basswood tree with a "tackle and fall," I remember I told them I didn't yearn for any more atmospheric phenomena. The old desire for a hurricane that would blow a cow through a penitentiary was satiated. I remember when the doctor pried the bones of my leg together, in order to kind of draw my attention away from the limb, he asked me how I liked the fall style of Zephyr in that locality

I said it was all right, what there was of it. I said this in a tone of bitter irony.

Cyclones are of two kinds, viz: the dark maroon cyclone; and the iron gray cyclone with pale green mane and tail. It was the latter kind I frolicked with on the above-named date.

My brother and I were riding along in the grand old forest, and I had just been singing a few bars from the opera of "Whoop 'em Up, Lizzie Jane," when I noticed that the wind was beginning to sough through the trees. Soon after that, I noticed that I was soughing through the trees also, and I am really no slouch of a sougher, either, when I get started.

The horse was hanging by the breeching from the bough of a large butternut tree, waiting for some one to come and pick him.

I did not see my brother at first, but after a while he disengaged himself from a rail fence and came where I was hanging, wrong end up, with my personal effects spilling out of my pockets. I told him that as soon as the wind kind of softened down, I wished he would go and pick the horse. He did so, and at midnight a party of friends carried me into town on a stretcher. It was quite an ovation. To think of a torchlight procession coming way out there into the woods at midnight, and carrying me into town on their shoulders in triumph! And yet I was once only a poor boy!

WAITING TO BE PICKED.

It shows what may be accomplished by anyone if he will persevere and insist on living a different life.

The cyclone is a natural phenomenon, enjoying the most robust health. It may be a pleasure for a man with great will power and an iron constitution to study more carefully into the habits of the cyclone, but as far as I am concerned, individually, I could worry along some way if we didn't have a phenomenon in the house from one year's end to another.

As I sit here, with my leg in a silicate of soda corset, and watch the merry throng promenading down the street, or mingling in the giddy torchlight procession, I cannot repress a feeling toward a cyclone that almost amounts to disgust.

The Arabian Language.

THE Arabian language belongs to what is called the Semitic or Shemitic family of languages, and, when written, presents the appearance of a general riot among the tadpoles and wrigglers of the United States.

The Arabian letter "jeem" or "jim," which corresponds with our J, resembles some of the spectacular wonders seen by the delirium tremens expert. I do not know whether that is the reason the letter is called jeem or jim, or not.

The letter "sheen" or "shin," which is some like our "sh" in its effect, is a very pretty letter, and enough of them would make very attractive trimming for pantalets or other clothing. The entire Arabic alphabet, I think, would work up first-rate into trimming for aprons, skirts, and so forth.

Still it is not so rich in variety as the Chinese language. A Chinaman who desires to publish a paper in order to fill a long felt want, must have a small fortune in order to buy himself an alphabet. In this country we get a press, and then, if we have any money left, we lay it out in type; but in China the editor buys himself an alphabet and then regards the press as a mere annex. If you go to a Chinese type maker and ask him to show you his goods, he will ask you whether you want a two or a three story alphabet.

The Chinese compositor spends most of his time riding up and down the elevator, seeking for letters and dusting them off with a feather duster. In large and wealthy offices the compositor sits at his case with the copy before him, and has five or six boys running from one floor to another, bringing him the letters of this wild and peculiar alphabet.

Sometimes they have to stop in the middle of a long editorial and send down to Hong Kong and have a letter cast specially for that editorial.

Chinese compositors soon die from heart disease, because they have to run up stairs and down so much in order to get the different letters needed.

One large publisher tried to have his case arranged in a high building without floors, so that the compositor could reach each type by means of a long pole, but one day there was a slight earthquake shock that spilled the entire alphabet out of the case, all over the floor, and although that was ninety-seven years ago last April, there are still two bushels of pi on the floor of that office. The paper employs rat printers, and as they have been engaged in assorting and distributing this mass of pi, it is called rat pi in China, and the term is quite popular.

When the editor underscores a word, the Chinese compositor charges $9 extra for italicizing it. This is nothing more than fair, for he may have to go all over the empire, and climb twenty-seven flights of stairs to find the necessary italics. So it is much more economical in China to use body type mostly in setting up a paper, and the old journalist will avoid caps and italics, unless he is very wealthy.

Arabian literature is very rich, and more especially so in verse. How the Arabian poets succeeded so well in writing their verse in their own language, I can hardly understand. I find it very difficult to write poetry which will be greedily snapped up and paid for, even when written in the English language but if I had to paw around for an hour to get a button-hook for the end of the fourth line, so that it would rhyme with the button-hook in the second line of the same verse, I believe it would drive me mad.

The Arabian writer is very successful in a tale of fiction. He loves to take a tale and re-write it for the press by carefully expunging the facts. It is in lyric and romantic writing that he seems to excel.

The Arabian Nights is the most popular work that has survived the harsh touch of time. Its age is not fully known, and as the author has been dead several hundred years, I feel safe in saying that a number of the incidents contained in this book are grossly inaccurate.

It has been translated several times with more or less success by various writers, and some of the statements contained in the book are well worthy of the advanced civilization, and wild word painting incident to a heated presidential campaign.

Verona.

WE arrived in Verona day before yesterday. Most every one has heard of the Two Gentlemen of Verona. This is the place they came from. They have never returned. Verona is not noted for its gentlemen now. Perhaps that is the reason I was regarded as such a curiosity when I came here.

Verona is a good deal older town than Chicago, but the two cities have points of resemblance after all. When the southern simoon from the stock yards is wafted across the vinegar orchards of Chicago, and a load of Mormon emigrants get out at the Rock Island depot and begin to move around and squirm and emit the fragrance of crushed Limburger cheese, it reminds one of Verona.

THE ODORS OF VERONA.

The sky is similar, too. At night, when it is raining hard, the sky of Chicago and Verona is not dissimilar. Chicago is the largest place, however, and my sympathies are with her. Verona has about 68,000 people now, aside from myself. This census includes foreigners and Indians not taxed.

Verona has an ancient skating rink, known in history as the amphitheatre. It is 404½ feet by 516 in size, and the wall is still 100 feet high in places. The people of Verona wanted me to lecture there, but I refrained. I was afraid that some late comers might elbow their way in and leave one end of the amphitheatre open and then there would be a draft. I will speak more fully on the subject of amphitheatres in another letter. There isn't room in this one.

Verona is noted for the Capitular library, as it is called. This is said to be the largest collection of rejected manuscripts in the world. I stood in with the librarian and he gave me an opportunity to examine this wonderful store of literary work. I found a Virgil that was certainly over 1,600 years old. I also found a well preserved copy of "Beautiful Snow." I read it. It was very touching indeed. Experts said it was 1,700 years old, which is no doubt correct. I am no judge of the age of MSS. Some can look at the teeth of a literary production and tell within two weeks how old it is, but I can't. You can also fool me on the age of wine. My rule used to be to observe how old I felt the next day and to fix that as the age of the wine, but this rule I find is not infallible. One time I found myself feeling the next day as though I might be 138 years old, but on investigation we found that the wine was extremely new, having been made at a drug store in Cheyenne that same day

THE NEXT MORNING.

Looking these venerable MSS. over, I noticed that the custom of writing with a violet pencil on both sides of the large foolscap sheet, and then folding it in sixteen directions and carrying it around in the pocket for two or three centuries, is not a late American invention, as I had been led to suppose. They did it in Italy fifteen centuries ago. I was permitted also to examine the celebrated institutes of Gains. Gains was a poor penman, and I am convinced from a close examination of his work that he was in the habit of carrying his manuscript around in his pocket with his smoking tobacco. The guide said that was impossible, for smoking tobacco was not introduced into Italy until a comparatively late day. That's all right, however. You can't fool me much on the odor of smoking tobacco.

The churches of Verona are numerous, and although they seem to me a little different from our own in many ways, they resemble ours in others. One thing that pleased me about the churches of Verona was the total absence of the church fair and festival as conducted in America. Salvation seems to be handed out in Verona without ice cream and cake, and the odor of sancity and stewed oysters do not go inevitably hand in hand. I have already been in the place more than two days and I have not yet been invited to help lift the old church debt on the cathedral. Perhaps they think I am not wealthy, however. In fact there is nothing about my dress or manner that would betray my wealth. I have been in Europe now six weeks and have kept my secret well. Even my most intimate traveling companions do not know that I am the Laramie City postmaster in disguise.

The cathedral is a most imposing and massive pile. I quote this from the guide book. This beautiful structure contains a baptismal font cut out of one solid block of stone and made for immersion, with an inside diameter of ten feet. A man nine feet high could be baptized there without injury. The Venetians have a great respect for water. They believe it ought not to be used for anything else but to wash away sins, and even then they are very economical about it.

There is a nice picture here by Titian. It looks as though it had been left in the smoke house 900 years and overlooked. Titian painted a great deal. You find his works here ever and anon. He must have had all he could do in Italy in an early day, when the country was new. I like his pictures first rate, but I haven't found one yet that I could secure at anything like a bed rock price.

A Great Upheaval.

I HAVE just received the following letter, which I take the liberty of publishing, in order that good may come out of it, and that the public generally may be on the watch

WILLIAM NYE, ESQ.—*Dear Sir:* There has been a great religious upheaval here, and great anxiety on the part of our entire congregation, and I write to you, hoping that you may have some suggestions to offer that we could use at this time beneficially.

All the bitter and irreverent remarks of Bob Ingersoll have fallen harmlessly upon the minds of our people. The flippant sneers and wicked sarcasms of the modern infidel, wise in his own conceit, have alike passed over our heads without damage or disaster. These times that have tried men's souls have only rooted us more firmly in the faith, and united us more closely as brothers and sisters.

We do not care whether the earth was made in two billion years or two minutes, so long as it was made and we are satisfied with it. We do not care whether Jonah swallowed the whale or the whale swallowed Jonah. None of these things worry us in the least. We do not pin our faith on such little matters as those, but we try to so live that when we pass on beyond the flood we may have a record to which we may point with pride.

But last Sabbath our entire congregation was visibly moved. People who had grown gray in this church got right up during the service and went out, and did not come in again. Brothers who had heard all kinds of infidelity and scorned to be moved by it, got up, and kicked the pews, and slammed the doors, and created a young riot.

For many years we have sailed along in the most peaceful faith, and through joy or sorrow we came to the church together to worship. We have laughed and wept as one family for a quarter of a century, and an humble dignity and Christian style of etiquette have pervaded our incomings and our outgoings.

That is the reason why a clear case of disorderly conduct in our church has attracted attention and newspaper comment. That is the reason why we want in some public way to have the church set right before we suffer from unjust criticism and worldly scorn.

It has been reported that one of the brothers, who is sixty years of age, and a model Christian, and a good provider, rose during the first prayer, and, waving his plug hat in the air, gave a wild and blood-curdling whoop, jumped over the back of his pew, and lit out. While this is in a measure true, it is not accurate. He did do some wild and startling jumping, but he did not jump over the pew He tried to, but failed. He was too old.

It has also been stated that another brother, who has done more to build up the church and society here than any other one man of his size, threw his hymn book across the church, and, with a loud wail that sounded like the word "Gosh!" hissed through clenched teeth, got out through the window and went away This is overdrawn, though there is an element of truth in it, and I do not try to deny it.

There were other similar strong evidences of feeling throughout the congregation, none of which had ever been noticed before in this place. Our clergyman was amazed and horrified. He tried to ignore the action of the brethren, but when a sister who has grown old in our church, and been such a model and example of rectitude that all the girls in the county were perfectly discouraged about trying to be anywhere near equal to her; when she rose with a wild snort, got up on the pew with her feet, and swung her parasol in a way that indicated that she would not go home till morning, he paused and briefly wound up the services.

Of course there were other little eccentricities on the part of the congregation, but these were the ones that people have talked about the most, and have done us the most damage abroad.

Now, my desire is that through the medium of the press you will state that this great trouble which has come upon us, by reason of which the ungodly have spoken lightly of us, was not the result of a general tendency to dissent from the statements made by our pastor, and therefore an exhibition of our disapproval of his doctrines, but that the janitor had started a light fire in the furnace, and that had revived a large nest of common, streaked, hot-nosed wasps in the warm air pipe, and when they came up through the register and united in the services, there was more or less of an ovation.

Sometimes Christianity gets sluggish and comatose, but not under the above circumstances. A man may slumber on softly with his bosom gently rising and falling, and his breath coming and going through one corner of his mouth like the death rattle of a bath-tub, while the pastor opens out a new box of theological thunders and fills the air full of the sullen roar of sulphurous waves, licking the shores of eternity and swallowing up the great multitudes of the eternally lost; but when one little wasp, with a red-hot revelation, goes gently up the leg of that same man's pantaloons, leaving large, hot tracks whenever he stopped and sat down to think it over, you will see a sudden awakening and a revival that will attract attention.

I wish that you would take this letter, Mr. Nye, and write something from it in your own way, for publication, showing how we happened to have more zeal than usual in the church last Sabbath, and that it was not directly the result of the sermon which was preached on that day.

Yours, with great respect,

WILLIAM LEMONS.

The Weeping Woman.

I HAVE not written much for publication lately, because I did not feel well. I was fatigued. I took a ride on the cars last week and it shook me up a good deal.

The train was crowded somewhat, and so I sat in a seat with a woman who got aboard at Minkin's Siding. I noticed as we pulled out of Minkin's Siding, that this woman raised the window so that she could bid adieu to a man in a dyed moustache. I do not know whether he was her dolce far niente, or her grandson by her second husband. I know that if he had been a relative of mine, however, I would have cheerfully concealed the fact.

She waved a little 2x6 handkerchief out of the window, said "good-bye," allowed a fresh zephyr from Cape Sabine to come in and play a xylophone interlude on my spinal column, and then burst into a paroxysm of damp, hot tears.

SHE SOBBED SEVERAL MORE TIMES.

I had to go into another car for a moment, and when I returned a pugilist from Chicago had my seat. When I travel I am uniformly courteous, especially to pugilists. A pugilist who has started out as an obscure boy with no money, no friends, and no one to practice on, except his wife or his mother, with no capital aside from his bare hands; a man who has had to fight his way through life, as it were, and yet who has come out of obscurity and attracted the attention of the authorities, and won the good will of those with whom he came in contact, will always find me cordial and pacific. So I allowed this self-made man with the broad, high, intellectual shoulder blades, to sit in my seat with his feet on my new and expensive traveling bag, while I sat with the tear-bedewed memento from Minkin's Siding.

She sobbed several more times, then hove a sigh that rattled the windows in the car, and sat up. I asked her if I might sit by her side for a few miles and share her great sorrow. She looked at me askance. I did not resent it. She allowed me to take the seat, and I looked at a paper for a few moments so that she could look me over through the corners of her eyes. I also scrutinized her lineaments some.

She was dressed up considerably, and, when a woman dresses up to ride in a railway train, she advertises the fact that her intellect is beginning to totter on its throne. People who have more than one suit of clothes should not pick out the fine raiment for traveling purposes. This person was not handsomely dressed, but she had the kind of clothes that look as though they had tried to present the appearance of affluence and had failed to do so.

This leads me to say, in all seriousness, that there is nothing so sad as the sight of a man or woman who would scorn to tell a wrong story, but who will persist in wearing bogus clothes and bogus jewelry that wouldn't fool anybody.

My seat-mate wore a cloak that had started out to bamboozle the American people with the idea that it was worth $100, but it wouldn't mislead anyone who might be nearer than half a mile. I also discovered that it had an air about it that would indicate that she wore it while she cooked the pancakes and fried the doughnuts. It hardly seems possible that she would do this, but the garment, I say, had that air about it.

She seemed to want to converse after awhile, and she began on the subject of literature, picking up a volume that had been left in her seat by the train boy, entitled: "Shadowed to Skowhegan and Back; or, The Child Fiend, price $2," we drifted on pleasantly into the broad domain of letters.

Incidentally I asked her what authors she read mostly.

"O, I don't remember the authors so much as I do the books," said she; "I am a great reader. If I should tell you how much I have read, you wouldn't believe it."

I said I certainly would. I had frequently been called upon to believe things that would make the ordinary rooster quail.

If she discovered the true inwardness of this Anglo-American "Jewdesprit," she refrained from saying anything about it.

"I read a good deal," she continued, "and it keeps me all strung up. I weep, O so easily." Just then she lightly laid her hand on my arm, and I could see that the tears were rising to her eyes. I felt like asking her if she had ever tried running herself through a clothes wringer every morning? I did feel that someone ought to chirk her up, so I asked her if she remembered the advice of the editor who received a letter from a young lady troubled the same way She stated that she couldn't explain it, but every little while, without any apparent cause, she would shed tears, and the editor asked her why she didn't lock up the shed.

We conversed for a long time about literature, but every little while she would get me into deep water by quoting some author or work that I had never read. I never realized what a hopeless ignoramus I was till I heard about the scores of books that had made her shed the scalding, and yet that I had never, never read. When she looked at me with that far-away expression in her eyes, and with her hand resting lightly on my arm in such a way as to give the gorgeous two karat Rhinestone from Pittsburg full play, and told me how such works as "The New Made Grave; or The Twin Murderers" had cost her many and many a copious tear, I told her I was glad of it. If it be a blessed boon for the student of such books to weep at home and work up their honest perspiration into scalding tears, far be it from me to grudge that poor boon.

I hope that all who may read these lines, and who may feel that the pores of their skin are getting torpid and sluggish, owing to an inherited antipathy toward physical exertion, and who feel that they would rather work up their perspiration into woe and shed it in the shape of common red-eyed weep, will keep themselves to this poor boon. People have different ways of enjoying themselves, and I hope no one will hesitate about accepting this or any other poor boon that I do not happen to be using at the time.

The Crops.

I HAVE just been through Iowa, Minnesota and Wisconsin, on a tour of inspection. I rode for over ten days in these States in a sleeping-car. examining crops, so that I could write an intelligent report.

Grain in Northern Wisconsin suffered severely in the latter part of the season from rust, chintz bug, Hessian fly and trichina. In the St. Croix valley wheat will not average a half crop. I do not know why farmers should insist upon leaving their grain out nights in July, when they know from the experience of former years that it will surely rust.

In Southern Wisconsin too much rain has almost destroyed many crops, and cattle have been unable to get enough to eat, unless they were fed, for several weeks. This is a sad outlook for the farmer at this season.

In the northern part of the State many fields of grain were not worth cutting, while others barely yielded the seed, and even that of a very inferior quality

The ruta-baga is looking unusually well this fall, but we cannot subsist entirely upon the ruta-baga. It is juicy and rich if eaten in large quantities, but it is too bulky to be popular with the aristocracy

Cabbages in most places are looking well, though in some quarters I notice an epidemic of worms. To successfully raise the cabbage, it will be necessary at all times to be well supplied with vermifuge that can be readily administered at any hour of the day or night.

The crook-neck squash in the Northwest is a great success this season. And what can be more beautiful, as it calmly lies in its bower of green vines in the crisp and golden haze of autumn, than the cute little crook-neck squash, with yellow, warty skin, all cuddled up together in the cool morning, like the discarded wife of an old Mormon elder—his first attempt in the matrimonial line, so to speak, ere he had gained wisdom by experience.

The full-dress, low-neck-and-short-sleeve summer squash will be worn as usual this fall, with trimmings of salt and pepper in front and revers of butter down the back.

N. B.—It will not be used much as an outside wrap, but will be worn mostly inside.

Hop-poles in some parts of Wisconsin are entirely killed. I suppose that continued dry weather in the early summer did it.

Hop-lice, however, are looking well. Many of our best hop-breeders thought that when the hop-pole began to wither and die, the hop-louse could not survive the intense dry heat; but hop-lice have never looked better in this State than they do this fall.

I can remember very well when Wisconsin had to send to Ohio for hop-lice. Now she could almost supply Ohio and still have enough to fill her own coffers.

ENJOYING HIMSELF AT THE DANCE.

I do not know that hop-lice are kept in coffers, and I may be wrong in speaking thus freely of these two subjects, never having seen either a hop-louse or a coffer, but I feel that the public must certainly and naturally expect me to say something on these subjects. Fruit in the Northwest this season is not a great success. Aside from the cranberry and choke-cherry, the fruit yield in the northern district is light. The early dwarf crab, with or without worms, as desired—but mostly with—is unusually poor this fall. They make good cider. This cider when put into a brandy flask that has not been drained too dry, and allowed to stand until Christmas, puts a great deal of expression into a country dance. I have tried it once myself, so that I could write it up for your valuable paper.

People who were present at that dance, and who saw me frolic around there like a thing of life, say that it was well worth the price of admission. Stone fence always flies right to the weakest spot. So it goes right to my head and makes me eccentric,

The violin virtuoso who "fiddled," "called off" and acted as justice of the peace that evening, said that I threw aside all reserve and entered with great zest into the dance, and seemed to enjoy it much better than those who danced in the same set with me. Since that, the very sight of a common crab apple makes my head reel. I learned afterward that this cider had frozen, so that the alleged cider which we drank that night was the clear, old-fashioned brandy, which of course would not freeze.

We should strive, however, to lead such lives that we will never be ashamed to look a cider barrel square in the bung.

Literary Freaks.

PEOPLE who write for a livelihood get some queer propositions from those who have crude ideas about the operation of the literary machine. There is a prevailing idea among those who have never dabbled in literature very much, that the divine afflatus works a good deal like a corn sheller. This is erroneous.

To put a bushel of words into the hopper and have them come out a poem or a sermon, is a more complicated process than it would seem to the casual observer.

I can hardly be called literary, though I admit that my tastes lie in that direction, and yet I have had some singular experiences in that line. For instance, last year I received flattering overtures from three young men who wanted me to write speeches for them to deliver on the Fourth of July They could do it themselves, but hadn't the time. If I would write the speeches they would be willing to revise them. They seemed to think it would be a good idea to write the speeches a little longer than necessary and then the poorer parts of the effort could be cut out. Various prices were set on these efforts, from a dollar to "the kindest regards." People who have squeezed through one of our adult winters in this latitude, subsisting on kind regards, will please communicate with the writer, stating how they like it.

One gentleman, who was in the confectionery business, wanted a lot of "humorous notices wrote for to put into conversation candy." It was a big temptation to write something that would be in every lady's mouth, but I refrained. Writing gum drop epitaphs may properly belong to the domain of literature, but I doubt it. Surely I do not want to be haughty and above my business, but it seems to me that this is irrelevant.

Another man wanted me to write a "piece for his boy to speak," and if I would do so, I could come to his house some Saturday night and stay over Sunday. He said that the boy was "a perfect little case to carry on and folks didn't know whether he would develop into a condemb fool or a youmerist." So he wanted a piece of one of them tomfoolery kind for the little cuss to speak the last day of school.

A coal dealer who had risen to affluence by selling coal to the poor by apothecaries' weight, wrote to ask me for a design to be used as a family crest and a motto to emblazon on his arms. I told him I had run out of crests, but that "weight for the wagon, we'll all take a ride," would be a good motto; or he might use the following: "The fuel and his money are soon parted." He might emblazon this on his arms, or tattoo it on any other part of his system where he thought it would be becoming to his complexion. I never heard from him again, and I do not know whether he was offended or not.

HIS MOTTO.

Two young men in Massachusetts wrote me a letter in which they said they "had a good thing on mother." They wanted it written up in a facetious vein. They said that their father had been on the coast a few weeks before, engaged in the eeling industry. Being a good man, but partially full, he had mingled himself in the flowing tide and got drowned. Finally, after several days' search, the neighbors came in sadly and told the old lady that they had found all that was mortal of James, and there were two eels in the remains. They asked for further instructions as to deceased. The old lady swabbed out her weeping eyes, braced herself against the sink and told the men to "bring in the eels and set him again."

The boys thought that if this could be properly written up, "it would be a mighty good joke on mother." I was greatly shocked when I received this letter. It seemed to me heartless for young men to speak lightly of their widowed mother's great woe. I wrote them how I felt about it, and rebuked them severely for treating their mother's grief so lightly. Also for trying to impose upon me with an old chestnut.

A Father's Advice to his Son.

MY DEAR HENRY.—Your pensive favor of the 20th inst., asking for more means with which to persecute your studies, and also a young man from Ohio, is at hand and carefully noted.

I would not be ashamed to have you show the foregoing sentence to your teacher, if it could be worked, in a quiet way, so as not to look egotistic on my part. I think myself that it is pretty fair for a man that never had any advantages.

But, Henry, why will you insist on fighting the young man from Ohio? It is not only rude and wrong, but you invariably get licked. There's where the enormity of the thing comes in.

It was this young man from Ohio, named Williams, that you hazed last year, or at least that's what I gether from a letter sent me by your warden. He maintains that you started in to mix Mr. Williams up with the campus in some way, and that in some way Mr. Williams resented it and got his fangs tangled up in the bridge of your nose.

You never wrote this to me or to your mother, but I know how busy you are with your studies, and I hope you won't ever neglect your books just to write to us.

Your warden, or whoever he is, said that Mr. Williams also hung a hand-painted marine view over your eye and put an extra eyelid on one of your ears.

I wish that, if you get time, you would write us about it, because, if there's anything I can do for you in the arnica line, I would be pleased to do so.

The president also says that in the scuffle you and Mr Williams swapped belts as follows, to-wit: That Williams snatchod off the belt of your little Norfolk jacket, and then gave you one in the eye.

From this I gether that the old prez, as you faseshusly call him, is an youmorist. He is not a very good penman, however; though, so far, his words have all been spelled correct.

I would hate to see you permanently injured, Henry, but I hope that when you try to tramp on the toes of a good boy simply because you are a seanyour and he is a fresh, as you frequently state, that he will arise and rip your little pleated jacket up the back and make your spinal colyum look like a corderoy bridge in the spring tra la. (This is from a Japan show I was to last week.)

Why should a seanyour in a colledge tromp onto the young chaps that come in there to learn? Have you forgot how I fatted up the old cow and beefed her so that you could go and monkey with youclid and algebray? Have you forgot how the other boys pulled you through a mill pond and made you tobogin down hill in a salt barrel with brads in it? Do you remember how your mother went down there to nuss you for two weeks and I stayed to home, and done my own work and the housework too and cooked my own vittles for the whole two weeks?

And now, Henry, you call yourself a seanyour, and therefore, because you are simply older in crime, you want to muss up Mr. Williams's features so that his mother will have to come over and nuss him. I am glad that your little pleated coat is ripped up the back, Henry, under the circumstances, and I am also glad that you are wearing the belt—over your off eye. If there's anything I can do to add to the hilarity of the occasion, please let me know and I will tend to it.

The lop-horned heifer is a parent once more, and I am trying in my poor, weak way to learn her wayward offspring how to drink out of a patent pail without pushing your old father over into the hay-mow. He is a cute little quadruped, with a wild desire to have fun at my expense. He loves to swaller a part of my coat-tail Sunday morning, when I am dressed up, and then return it to me in a moist condition. He seems to know that when I address the sabbath school the children will see the joke and enjoy it.

Your mother is about the same, trying in her meek way to adjust herself to a new set of teeth that are a size too large for her. She has one large bunion in the roof of her mouth already, but is still resolved to hold out faithful, and hopes these few lines will find you enjoying the same great blessing.

You will find inclosed a dark-blue money-order for four eighty-five. It is money that I had set aside to pay my taxes, but there is no novelty about paying taxes. I've done that before, so it don't thrill me as it used to.

Give my congratulations to Mr. Williams. He has got the elements of greatness to a wonderful degree. If I happened to be participating in that colledge of yours, I would gently but firmly decline to be tromped onto.

So good-bye for this time. YOUR FATHER.

Eccentricity in Lunch.

OVER at Kasota Junction, the other day, I found a living curiosity. He was a man of about medium height, perhaps 45 years of age, of a quiet disposition, and not noticeable or peculiar in his general manner. He runs the railroad eating-house at that point, and the one odd characteristic which he has, makes him well known all through three or four States. I could not illustrate his eccentricity any better than by relating a circumstance that occurred to me at the Junction last week. I had just eaten breakfast there and paid for it. I stepped up to the cigar case and asked this man if he had "a rattling good cigar."

THE ANTIQUE LUNCH.

Without knowing it I had struck the very point upon which this man seems to be a crank, if you will allow me that expression, though it doesn't fit very well in this place. He looked at me in a sad and subdued manner and said, "No, sir; I haven't a rattling good cigar in the house. I have some cigars there that I bought for Havana fillers, but they are mostly filled with pieces of Colorado Maduro overalls. There's a box over yonder that I bought for good, straight ten cent cigars, but they are only a chaos of hay and Flora, Fino and Damfino, all socked into a Wisconsin wrapper. Over in the other end of the case is a brand of cigars that were to knock the tar out of all other kinds of weeds, according to the urbane rustler who sold them to me, and then drew on me before I could light one of them. Well, instead of being a fine Colorado Claro with a high-priced wrapper, they are common Mexicano stinkaros in a Mother Hubbard wrapper. The commercial tourist who sold me those cigars and then drew on me at sight was a good deal better on the draw than his cigars are. If you will notice, you will see that each cigar has a spinal column to it, and this outer debris is wrapped around it. One man bought a cigar out of that box last week. I told him, though, just as I am telling you, that they were no good, and if he bought one he would regret it. But he took one and went out on the veranda to smoke it. Then he stepped on a melon rind and fell with great force on his side. When we picked him up he gasped once or twice and expired. We opened his vest hurriedly and found that, in falling, this bouquet de Gluefactoro cigar, with the spinal column, had been driven through his breast bone and had penetrated his heart. The wrapper of the cigar never so much as cracked."

"But doesn't it impair your trade to run on in this wild, reckless way about your cigars?"

"It may at first, but not after awhile. I always tell people what my cigars are made of, and then they can't blame me; so, after awhile they get to believe what I say about them. I often wonder that no cigar man ever tried this way before. I do just the same way about my lunch counter. If a man steps up and wants a fresh ham sandwich I give it to him if I've got it, and if I haven't it I tell him so. If you turn my sandwiches over, you will find the date of its publication on every one. If they are not fresh, and I have no fresh ones, I tell the cutomer that they are not so blamed fresh as the young man with the gauze moustache, but that I can remember very well when they were fresh, and if his artificial teeth fit him pretty well he can try one.

"It's just the same with boiled eggs. I have a rubber dating stamp, and as soon as the eggs are turned over to me by the hen for inspection, I date them. Then they are boiled and another date in red is stamped on them. If one of my clerks should date an egg ahead, I would fire him too quick.

"On this account, people who know me will skip a meal at Missouri Junction, in order to come here and eat things that are not clouded with mystery. I do not keep any poor stuff when I can help it, but if I do, I don't conceal the horrible fact.

"Of course a new cook will sometimes smuggle a late date onto a mediæval egg and sell it, but he has to change his name and flee.

"I suppose that if every eating-house should date everything, and be square with the public, it would be an old story and wouldn't pay; but as it is, no one trying to compete with me, I do well out of it, and people come here out of curiosity a good deal.

"The reason I try to do right and win the public esteem is that the general public never did me any harm and the majority of people who travel are a kind that I may meet in a future state. I should hate to have a thousand traveling men holding nuggets of rancid ham sandwiches under my nose through all eternity, and know that I had lied about it. It's an honest fact, if I knew I'd got to stand up and apologize for my hand-made, all-around, seamless pies, and quarantine cigars, Heaven would be no object."

Insomnia in Domestic Animals.

IF there be one thing above another that I revel in, it is science. I have devoted much of my life to scientific research, and though it hasn't made much stir in the scientific world so far, I am positive that when I am gone the scientists of our day will miss me, and the red-nosed theorist will come and shed the scalding tear over my humble tomb.

My attention was first attracted to insomnia as the foe of the domestic animal, by the strange appearance of a favorite dog named Lucretia Borgia. I did not name this animal Lucretia Borgia. He was named when I purchased him. In his eccentric and abnormal thirst for blood he favored Lucretia, but in sex he did not. I got him partly because he loved children. The owner said Lucretia Borgia was an ardent lover of children, and I found that he was. He seemed to love them best in the spring of the year, when they were tender. He would have eaten up a favorite child of mine, if the youngster hadn't left a rubber ball in his pocket which clogged the glottis of Lucretia till I could get there and disengage what was left of the child.

Lucretia soon after this began to be restless. He would come to my casement and lift up his voice, and howl into the bosom of the silent night. At first I thought that he had found some one in distress, or wanted to get me out of doors and save my life. I went out several nights in a weird costume that I had made up of garments belonging to different members of my family. I dressed carefully in the dark and stole out to kill the assassin referred to by Lucretia, but he was not there. Then the faithful animal would run up to me and with almost human, pleading eyes, bark and run away toward a distant alley I immediately decided that some one was suffering there. I had read in books about dogs that led their masters away to the suffering and saved people's lives; so, when Lucretia came to me with his great, honest eyes and took little mementoes out of the calf of my leg, and then galloped off seven or eight blocks, I followed him in the chill air of night and my Mosaic clothes. I wandered away to where the dog stopped behind a livery stable, and there, lying in a shuddering heap on the frosty ground, lay the still, white features of a soup bone that had outlived its usefulness.

On the way back, I met a physician who had been up town to swear in an American citizen who would vote twenty-one years later, if he lived. The physician stopped me and was going to take me to the home of the friendless, when he discovered who I was.

EXCITING PUBLIC CURIOSITY.

You wrap a tall man, with a William H. Seward nose, in a flannel robe, cut plain, and then put a plug hat and a sealskin sacque and Arctic overshoes on him, and put him out in the street, under the gaslight, with his trim, purple ankles just revealing themselves as he madly gallops after a hydrophobia infested dog, and it is not, after all, surprising that people's curiosity should be a little bit excited.

After I had introduced myself to the physician and asked him for a cigar, explaining that I could not find any in the clothes I had on, I asked him about

Lucretia Borgia. I told the doctor how Lucretia seemed restless nights and nervous and irritable days, and how he seemed to be almost a mental wreck, and asked him what the trouble was.

He said it was undoubtedly "insomnia." He said that it was a bad case of it, too. I told him I thought so myself. I said I didn't mind the insomnia that Lucretia had so much as I did my own. I was getting more insomnia on my hands than I could use.

He gave me something to administer to Lucretia. He said I must put it in a link of sausage and leave the sausage where it would appear that I didn't want the dog to get it, and then Lucretia would eat it greedily.

I did so. It worked well so far as the administration of the remedy was concerned, but it was fatal to my little, high strung, yearnful dog. It must have contained something of a deleterious character, for the next morning a coarse man took Lucretia Borgia by the tail and laid him where the violets blow. Malignant insomnia is fast becoming the great foe to the modern American dog.

Along Lake Superior.

I HAVE just returned from a brief visit to Duluth. After strolling along the Bay of Naples and watching old Vesuvius vomit red-hot mud, vapor and other campaign documents, Duluth is quite a change. The ice in the bay at Duluth was thirty-eight inches in depth when I left there the last week in March, and we rode across it with the utmost impunity By the time these lines fall beneath the eye of the genial, courteous and urbane reader, the new railroad bridge across the bay, over a mile and a half long, will have been completed, so that you may ride from Chicago to Duluth over the Northwestern and Omaha railroads with great comfort. I would be glad to digress here and tell about the beauty of the summer scenery along the Omaha road, and the shy and beautiful troutlet, and the dark and silent Chippewa squawlet and her little bleached out pappooselet, were it not for the unkind and cruel thrusts that I would invoke from the scenery cynic who believes that a newspaper man's opinions may be largely warped with a pass.

Duluth has been joked a good deal, but she stands it first-rate and takes it good naturedly She claims 16,000 people, some of whom I met at the opera house there. If the rest of the 16,000 are as pleasant as those I conversed with that evening, Duluth must be a pleasant place to live in. Duluth has a very pleasant and beautiful opera house that seats 1,000 people. A few more could have elbowed their way into tho opora house the evening that I spoke there, but they preferred to suffer on at home.

Lake Superior is one of the largest aggregations of fresh wetness in the world, if not the largest. When I stop to think that some day all this cold, cold water will have to be absorbed by mankind, it gives me a cramp in the geographical center.

Around the west end of Lake Superior there is a string of towns which stretches along the shore for miles under one name or another, all waiting for the boom to strike and make the northern Chicago. You cannot visit Duluth or Superior without feeling that at any moment the tide of trade will rise and designate the point where the future metropolis of the northern lakes is to be. I firmly believe that this summer will decide it, and my guess is that what is now known as West Superior is to get the benefit. For many years destiny has been hovering over the west end of this mighty lake, and now the favored point is going to be designated. Duluth has past prosperity and expensive improvements in her favor, and in fact the whole locality is going to be benefited, but if I had a block in West Superior with a roller rink on it, I would wear my best clothes every day and claim to be a millionaire in disguise. Ex-President R. B. Hayes has a large brick block in Duluth, but he does not occupy it. Those who go to Duluth hoping to meet Mr. Hayes will be bitterly disappointed.

The streams that run into Lake Superior are alive with trout, and next summer I propose to go up there and roast until I have so thoroughly saturated my system with trout that the trout bones will stick out through my clothes in every direction and people will regard me as a beautiful toothpick holder.

Still there will be a few left for those who think of going up there. All I will need will be barely enough to feed Albert Victor and myself from day to day People who have never seen a crowned head with a peeled nose on it are cordially invited to come over and see us during office hours. Albert is not at all haughty, and I intend to throw aside my usual reserve this summer also—for the time. P Wales' son and I will be far from the cares that crowd so thick and fast on greatness. People who come to our cedar bark wigwam to show us their mosquito bites, will be received as cordially as though no great social chasm yawned between us.

Many will meet us in the depths of the forest and go away thinking that we are just common plugs of whom the world wots not; but there is where they will fool themselves.

Then, when the season is over, we will come back into the great maelstrom of life, he to wait for his grandmother's overshoes and I to thrill waiting millions from the rostrum with my "Tale of the Broncho Cow." And so it goes with us all. Adown life's rugged pathway some must toil on from daylight to dark to earn their meagre pittance as kings, while others are born to wear a swallow-tail coat every evening and wring tears of genuine anguish from their audiences.

They tell some rather wide stories about people who have gone up there total physical wrecks and returned strong and well. One man said that he knew a young college student, who was all run down and weak, go up there on the Brule and eat trout and fight mosquitoes a few months, and when he returned to his Boston home he was so stout and well and tanned up that his parents did not know him. There was a man in our car who weighed 300 pounds. He seemed to be boiling out through his clothes everywhere. He was the happiest looking man I ever saw. All he seemed to do in this life was to sit all day and whistle and laugh and trot his stomach, first on one knee and then on the other.

He said that he went up into the pine forests of the Great Lake region a broken-down hypochondriac and confirmed consumptive. He had been measured for a funeral sermon three times, he said, and had never used either of them. He knew a clergyman named Brayley who went up into that region with Bright's justly celebrated disease. He was so emaciated that he couldn't carry a watch. The ticking of the watch rattled his bones so that it made him nervous, and at night they had to pack him in cotton so that he wouldn't break a leg when he turned over. He got to sleeping out nights on a bed of balsam and spruce boughs and eating venison and trout.

When he came down in the spring, he passed through a car of lumbermen and one of them put a warm, wet quid of tobacco in his plug hat for a joke. There were a hundred of these lumbermen when the preacher began, and when the train got into Eau Claire there were only three of them well enough to go around to the office and draw their pay

This is just as the story was given to me and I repeat it to show how bracing the climate near Superior is. Remember, if you please, that I do not want the story to be repeated as coming from me, for I have nothing left now but my reputation for veracity, and that has had a very hard winter of it.

I Tried Milling.

I THINK I was about 18 years of age when I decided that I would be a miller, with flour on my clothes and a salary of $200 per month. This was not the first thing I had decided to be, and afterward changed my mind about.

I engaged to learn my profession of a man called Sam Newton, I believe; at least I will call him that for the sake of argument. My business was to weigh wheat, deduct as much as possible on account of cockle, pigeon grass and wild buckwheat, and to chisel the honest farmer out of all he would stand. This was the programme with Mr. Newton; but I am happy to say that it met with its reward, and the sheriff afterward operated the mill.

On stormy days I did the book-keeping, with a scoop shovel behind my ear, in a pile of middlings on the fifth floor. Gradually I drifted into doing a good deal of this kind of brain work. I would chop the ice out of the turbine wheel at 5 o'clock A. M., and then frolic up six flights of stairs and shovel shorts till 9 o'clock P. M.

By shoveling bran and other vegetables 16 hours a day, a general knowledge of the milling business may be readily obtained. I used to scoop middlings till I could see stars, and then I would look out at the landscape and ponder.

I got so that I piled up more ponder, after a while, than I did middlings.

One day the proprietor came up stairs and discovered me in a brown study, whereupon he cursed me in a subdued Presbyterian way, abbreviated my salary from $26 per month to $18 and reduced me to the ranks.

Afterward I got together enough desultory information so that I could superintend the feed stone. The feed stone is used to grind hen feed and other luxuries. One day I noticed an odor that reminded me of a hot overshoe trying to smother a glue factory at the close of a tropical day. I spoke to the chief floor walker of the mill about it, and he said "dod gammit" or something that sounded like that, in a course and brutal manner. He then kicked my person in a rude and hurried tone of voice, and told me that the feed stone was burning up.

He was a very fierce man, with a violent and ungovernable temper, and, finding that I was only increasing his brutal fury, I afterward resigned my position. I talked it over with the proprietor, and both agreed that it would be best. He agreed to it before I did, and rather hurried up my determination to go.

I rather hated to go so soon, but he made it an object for me to go, and I went. I started in with the idea that I would begin at the bottom of the ladder, as it were, and gradually climb to the bran bin by my own exertions, hoping by honesty, industry, and carrying two bushels of wheat up nine flights of stairs, to become a wealthy man, with corn meal in my hair and cracked wheat in my coat pocket, but I did not seem to accomplish it.

Instead of having ink on my fingers and a chastened look of woe on my clear-cut Grecian features, I might have poured No. 1 hard wheat and buckwheat flour out of my long taper ears every night, if I had stuck to the profession. Still, as I say, it was for another man's best good that I resigned. The head miller had no control over himself and the proprietor had rather set his heart on my resignation, so it was better that way.

HE MADE IT AN OBJECT FOR ME TO GO.

Still I like to roll around in the bran pile, and monkey in the cracked wheat. I love also to go out in the kitchen and put corn meal down the back of the cook's neck while my wife is working a purple silk Kensington dog, with navy blue mane and tail, on a gothic lambrequin.

I can never cease to hanker for the rumble and grumble of the busy mill, and the solemn murmur of the millstones and the machinery are music to me. More so than the solemn murmur of the proprietor used to be when he came in at an inopportune moment, and in that impromptu and extemporaneous manner of his, and found me admiring the wild and beautiful scenery. He may have been a good miller, but he had no love for the beautiful. Perhaps that is why he was always so cold and cruel toward me. My slender, willowy grace and mellow, bird-like voice never seemed to melt his stony heart.

Our Forefathers.

SEATTLE, W. T., December 12.—I am up here on the Sound in two senses. I rode down to-day from Tacoma on the Sound, and to-night I shall lecture at Frye's Opera House.

Seattle is a good town. The name lacks poetic warmth, but some day the man who has invested in Seattle real estate will have reason to pat himself on the back and say "ha ha," or words to that effect. The city is situated on the side of a large hill and commands a very fine view of that world's most calm and beautiful collection of water, Puget Sound.

I cannot speak too highly of any sheet of water on which I can ride all day with no compunction of digestion. He who has tossed for days upon the briny deep, will understand this and appreciate it; even if he never tossed upon the angry deep, if it happened to be all he had, he will be glad to know that the Sound is a good piece of water to ride on. The gentle reader who has crossed the raging main and borrowed high-priced meals of the steamship company for days and days, will agree with me that when we can find a smooth piece of water to ride on we should lose no time in crossing it.

In Washington Territory the women vote. That is no novelty to me, of course, for I lived in Wyoming for seven years where women vote, and I held office all the time. And still they say that female voters are poor judges of men, and that any pleasing $2 adonis who comes along and asks for their suffrages will get them.

Not much! ! !

Woman is a keen and correct judge of mental and moral worth. Without stopping to give logical reasons for her course, perhaps, she still chooses with unerring judgment at the polls.

Anyone who doubts this statement, will do well to go to the old poll books in Wyoming and examine my overwhelming majorities—with a powerful magnifier.

I have just received from Boston a warm invitation to be present in that city on Forefathers' day, to take part in the ceremonies and join in the festivities of that occasion.

Forefathers, I thank you! Though this reply will not reach you for a long time, perhaps, I desire to express to you my deep appreciation of your kindness, and, though I can hardly be regarded as a forefather myself, I assure you that I sympathize with you.

Nothing would give me greater pleasure than to be with you on this day of your general jubilee and to-talk over old times with you.

One who has never experienced the thrill of genuine joy that wakens a man to a glad realization of the fact that he is a forefather, cannot understand its full significance. You alone know how it is yourself, you can speak from experience.

In fancy's dim corridors I see you stand, away back in the early dawn of our national day, with the tallow candle drooping and dying in its socket, as you waited for the physician to come and announce to you that you were a forefather.

Forefathers, you have done well. Others have sought to outdo you and wrest the laurels from your brow, but they did not succeed. As forefathers you have never been successfully scooped.

I hope that you will keep up your justly celebrated organization. If a forefather allows his dues to get in arrears, go to him kindly and ask him like a brother to put up. If he refuses to do so, fire him. There is no reason why a man should presume upon his long standing as a forefather to become insolent to other forefathers who are far his seniors. As a rule, I notice it is the young amateur forefather who has only been so a few days, in fact, who is arrogant and disobedient.

I have often wished that we could observe Forefathers' day more generally in the West. Why we should allow the Eastern cities to outdo us in this matter, while we hold over them in other ways, I cannot understand. Our church sociables and homicides in the West will compare favorably with those of the effeter cities of the Atlantic slope. Our educational institutions and embezzlers are making rapid strides, especially our embezzlers. We are cultivating a certain air of refinement and haughty reserve which enables us at times to fool the best judges. Many of our Western people have been to the Atlantic seaboard and remained all summer without falling into the hands of the bunko artist. A cow gentleman friend of mine who bathed his plump limbs in the Atlantic last summer during the day, and mixed himself up in the mazy dance at night, told me on his return that he had enjoyed the summer immensely, but that he had returned financially depressed.

"Ah," said I, with an air of superiority which I often assume while talking to men who know more than I do, "you fell into the hands of the cultivated confidence man?"

"No, William," he said sadly, "worse than that. I stopped at a seaside hotel. Had I gone to New York City and hunted up the gentlemanly bunko man and the Wall street dealer in lamb's pelts, as my better judgment prompted, I might have returned with funds. Now I am almost insolvent. I begin life again with great sorrow, and the same old Texas steer with which I went into the cattle industry five years ago."

But why should we, here in the West, take readily to all other institutions common to the cultured East and ignore the forefather industry? I now make this public announcement, and will stick to it, viz: I will be one of ten full-blooded American citizens to establish a branch forefather's lodge in the West, with a separate fund set aside for the benefit of forefathers who are no longer young. Forefathers are just as apt to become old and helpless as anyone else. Young men who contemplate becoming forefathers should remember this.

In Acknowledgment.

TO THE METROPOLITAN GUIDE PUBLISHING CO., New York.

GENTLEMEN.—I received the copy of your justly celebrated "Guide to rapid Affluence, or How to Acquire Wealth Without Mental Exertion," price twenty-five cents. It is a great boon.

I have now had this book sixteen weeks, and, as I am wealthy enough, I return it. It is not much worn, and if you will allow me fifteen cents for it, I would be very grateful. It is not the intrinsic value of the fifteen cents that I care for so much, but I would like it as a curiosity

The book is wonderfully graphic and thorough in all its details, and I was especially pleased with its careful and useful recipe for ointments. One style of ointment spoken of and recommended by your valuable book, is worthy of a place in history. I made some of it according to your formula. I tried it on a friend of mine. He wore it when he went away, and he has not as yet returned. I heard, incidentally, that it adhered to him. People who have examined it say that it retains its position on his person similar to a birth-mark.

Your cement does not have the same peculiarity It does everything but adhere. Among other specialties it effects a singular odor. It has a fragrance that ought to be utilized in some way Men have harnessed the lightning, and it seems to me that the day is not far distant when a man will be raised up who can control this latent power. Do you not think that possibly you have made a mistake and got your ointment and cement formula mixed? Your cement certainly smells like a corrupt administration in a warm room.

Your revelations in the liquor manufacture, and how to make any mixed drink with one hand tied, is well worth the price of the book. The chapter on bar etiquette is also excellent. Very few men know how to properly enter a bar-room and what to do after they arrive. How to get into a bar-room without attracting attention, and how to get out without police interference, are points upon which our American drunkards are lamentably ignorant. How to properly address a bar tender, is also a page that no student of good breeding could well omit.

I was greatly surprised to read how simple the manufacture of drinks under your formula is. You construct a cocktail without liquor and then rob intemperance of its sting. You also make all kinds of liquor without the use of alcohol, that demon under whose iron heel thousands of our sons and brothers go down to death and delirium annually Thus you are doing a good work.

You also unite aloes, tobacco and Rough on Rats, and, by a happy combination, construct a style of beer that is non-intoxicating.

No one could, by any possible means, become intoxicated on your justly celebrated beer. He would not have time. Before he could get inebriated he would be in the New Jerusalem.

Those who drink your beer will not fill drunkards' graves. They will close their career and march out of this life with perforated stomachs and a look of intense anguish.

Your method of making cider without apples is also frugal and ingenious. Thousands of innocent apple worms annually lose their lives in the manufac-

HOW TO WIN AFFECTION.

ture of cider. They are also, in most instances, wholly unprepared to die. By your method, a style of wormless cider is constructed that would not fool anyone. It tastes a good deal like rain water that was rained about the first time that any raining was ever done, and was deprived of air ever since.

The closing chapter on the subject of "How to win the affections of the opposite sex at sixty yards," is first-rate. It is wonderful what triumph science and inventions have wrenched from obdurate conditions! Only a few years ago, a young man had to work hard for weeks and months in order to win the love of a noble young woman. Now, with your valuable and scholarly work, price twenty-five cents, he studies over the closing chapter an hour or two, then goes out into society and gathers in his victim. And yet I do not grudge the long, long hours I squandered in those years when peoplo were in heathenish darkness. I had no book like yours to tell me how to win the affections of the opposite sex. I could only blund r on, week after week and yet I do not regret it. It was just the school I needed. It did me good.

Your book will, no doubt, be a good thing for those who now grope, but I have groped so long that I have formed the habit and prefer it. Let me go right on groping. Those who desire to win the affections of the opposite sex at one sitting, will do well to send two bits for your great work, but I am in no hurry. My time is not valuable.

Preventing a Scandal.

BOYS should never be afraid or ashamed to do little odd jobs by which to acquire money. Too many boys are afraid, or at least seem to be embarrassed when asked to do chores, and thus earn small sums of money. In order to appreciate wealth we must earn it ourselves. That is the reason I labor. I do not need to labor. My parents are still living, and they certainly would not see me suffer for the necessities of life. But life in that way would not have the keen relish that it would if I earned the money myself.

Sawing wood used to be a favorite pastime with boys twenty years ago. I remember the first money I ever earned was by sawing wood. My brother and myself were to receive $5 for sawing five cords of wood. We allowed the job to stand, however, until the weather got quite warm, and then we decided to hire a foreigner who came along that way one glorious summer day when all nature seemed tickled and we knew that the fish would be apt to bite. So we hired the foreigner, and while he sawed, we would bet with him on various "dead sure things" until he got the wood sawed, when he went away owing us fifty cents.

We had a neighbor who was very wealthy. He noticed that we boys earned our own spending money, and he yearned to have his son try to ditto. So he told the boy that he was going away for a few weeks and that he would give him $2 per cord, or double price, to saw the wood. He wanted to teach the boy to earn and appreciate his money. So, when the old man went away, the boy secured a colored man to do the job at $1 per cord, by which process the youth made $10. This he judiciously invested in clothes, meeting his father at the train in a new summer suit and a speckled cane. The old man said he could see by the sparkle in the boy's clear, honest eyes, that healthful exercise was what boys needed.

When I was a boy I frequently acquired large sums of money by carrying coal up two flights of stairs for wealthy people who were too fat to do it themselves. This money I invested from time to time in side shows and other zoological attractions.

One day I saw a coal cart back up and unload itself on the walk in such a way as to indicate that the coal would have to be manually elevated inside the building. I waited till I nearly froze to death, for the owner to come along and solicit my aid. Finally he came. He smelled strong of carbolic acid, and I afterward learned that he was a physician and surgeon.

We haggled over the price for some time, as I had to carry the coal up two flights in an old waste paper basket and it was quite a task. Finally we agreed. I proceeded with the work. About dusk I went up the last flight of stairs with the last load. My feet seemed to weigh about nineteen pounds apiece and my face was very sombre.

In the gloaming I saw my employer. He was writing a prescription by the dim, uncertain light. He told me to put the last basketful in the little closet off the hall and then come and get my pay. I took the coal into the closet, but I do not know what I did with it. As I opened the door and stepped in, a tall skeleton got down off the nail and embraced me like a prodigal son. It fell on my neck and draped itself all over me. Its glittering phalanges entered the bosom of my gingham shirt and rested lightly on the pit of my stomach. I could feel the pelvis bone in the small of my back. The room was dark, but I did not light the gas. Whether it was the skeleton of a lady or gentleman, I never knew; but I thought, for the sake of my good name, I would not remain. My good name and a strong yearning for home were all that I had at that time.

So I went home. Afterwards, I learned that this physician got all his coal carried up stairs for nothing in this way, and he had tried to get rooms two flights further up in the building, so that the boys would have further to fall when they made their egress.

About Portraits.

HUDSON, WIS., August 25, 1885.

HON. WILLIAM F VILAS, Postmaster-General, Washington, D. C.

DEAR SIR.—For some time I have been thinking of writing to you and asking you how you were getting along with your department since I left it. I did not wish to write you for the purpose of currying favor with an administration against which I squandered a ballot last fall. Neither do I desire to convey the impression that I would like to open a correspondence with you for the purpose of killing time. If you ever feel like sitting down and answering this letter in an off-hand way it would please me very much, but do not put yourself out to do so. I wanted to ask you, however, how you like the pictures of yourself recently published by the patent insides. That was my principal object in writing. Having seen you before this great calamity befell you, I wanted to inquire whether you had really changed so much. As I remember your face, it was rather unusually intellectual and attractive for a great man. Great men are very rarely pretty. I guess that, aside from yourself, myself, and Mr. Evarts, there is hardly an eminent man in the country who would be considered handsome. But the engraver has done you a great injustice, or else you have sadly changed since I saw you. It hardly seems possible that your nose has drifted around to leeward and swelled up at the end, as the engraver would have us believe. I do not believe that in a few short months the look of firmness and conscious rectitude that I noticed could have changed to that of indecision and vacuity which we see in some of your late portraits as printed.

A NOSE ON THE BIAS.

I saw one yesterday, with your name attached to it, and it made my heart ache for your family. As a resident in your State I felt humiliated. Two of Wisconsin's ablest men have been thus slaughtered by the rude broad-axe of the engraver. Last fall, Senator Spooner, who is also a man with a first-class head and face, was libeled in this same reckless way. It makes me mad, and in that way impairs my usefulness. I am not a good citizen, husband or father when I am mad. I am a perfect simoom of wrath at such times, and I am not responsible for what I do.

Nothing can arouse the indignation of your friends, regardless of party, so much as the thought that while you are working so hard in the postoffice at Washington with your coat off, collecting box rent and making up the Western mail, the remorseless engraver and electrotyper are seeking to down you by making pictures of you in which you appear either as a dude or a tough.

While I have not the pleasure of being a member of your party, having belonged to what has been sneeringly alluded to as the g. o. p., I cannot refrain from expressing my sympathy at this time. Though we may have differed heretofore upon important questions of political economy, I cannot exult over these portraits. Others may gloat over these efforts to injure you, but I do not. I am not much of a gloater, anyhow.

I leave those to gloat who are in the gloat business.

Still, it is one of the drawbacks incident to greatness. We struggle hard through life that we may win the confidence of our fellow-men, only at last to have pictures of ourselves printed and distributed where they will injure us.

ASSORTED PHYSIOGNOMY.

I desire to add before closing this letter, Mr. Vilas, that with those who are acquainted with you and know your sterling worth, these portraits will make no difference. We will not allow them to influence us socially or politically What the effect may be upon offensive partisans who are total strangers to you, I do not know

My theory in relation to these cuts is, that they are combined and interchangeable, so that, with slight modifications, they are used for all great men. The cut, with the extras that go with it, consists of one head with hair (front view), one bald head (front view), one head with hair (side view), one bald head (side view), one pair eyes (with glasses), one pair eyes (plain), one Roman nose, one Grecian nose, one turn-up nose, one set whiskers (full), one moustache, one pair side-whiskers, one chin, one set large ears, one set medium ears, one set small ears, one set shoulders, with collar and necktie for above, one monkey-wrench, one set quoins, one galley, one oil-can, one screwdriver. These different features are then arranged so that a great variety of clergymen, murderers, senators, embezzlers, artists, dynamiters, humorists, arsonists, larcenists, poets, statesmen, base ball players, rinkists, pianists, capitalists, bigamists and sluggists are easily represented. No newspaper office should be without them. They are very simple, and any child can easily learn to operate it. They are invaluable in all cases, for no one knows at what moment a revolting crime may be committed by a comparatively unknown man, whose portrait you wish to give, and in this age of rapid political transformations, presentations and combinations, no enterprising paper should delay the acquisition of a combined portrait for the use of its readers.

Hoping that you are well, and that you will at once proceed to let no guilty man escape, I remain, yours truly, BILL NYE.

The Old South.

THE Old South Meeting House, in Boston, is the most remarkable structure in many respects to be found in that remarkable city. Always eager wherever I go to search out at once the gospel privileges, it is not to be wondered at, that I should have gone to the Old South the first day after I landed in Boston.

It is hardly necessary to go over the history of the Old South, except, perhaps, to refresh the memory of those who live outside of Boston. The Old South Society was organized in 1669, and the ground on which the old meeting-house now stands was given by Mrs. Norton, the widow of Rev. John Norton, since deceased. The first structure was of wood, and in 1729 the present brick building succeeded it. King's Handbook of Boston says: "It is one of the few historic buildings that have been allowed to remain in this iconoclastic age."

So it seems that they are troubled with iconoclasts in Boston, too. I thought I saw one hanging around the Old South on the day I was there, and had a good notion to point him out to the authorities, but thought it was none of my business.

I went into the building and registered, and then from force of habit or absent-mindedness handed my umbrella over the counter and asked how soon supper would be ready Everybody registers, but very few, I am told, ask how soon supper will be ready. The Old South is now run on the European plan, however.

The old meeting-house is chiefly remarkable for the associations that cluster around it. Two centuries hover about the ancient weather-vane and look down upon the visitor when the weather is favorable.

Benjamin Franklin was baptized and attended worship here, prior to his wonderful invention of lightning. Here on each succeeding Sabbath sat the man who afterwards snared the forked lightning with a string and put it in a jug for future generations. Here Whitefield preached and the rebels discussed the tyranny of the British king. Warren delivered his famous speech here upon the anniversary of the Boston massacre and the "tea party" organized in this same building. Two hundred years ago exactly, the British used the Old South as a military riding school, although a majority of the people of Boston were not in favor of it.

MR. FRANKLIN EXPERIMENTS.

It would be well to pause here and consider the trying situation in which our ancestors were placed at that time. Coming to Massachusetts as they did, at a time when the country was new and prices extremely high, they had hoped to escape from oppression and establish themselves so far away from the tyrant that he could not come over here and disturb them without suffering from the extreme nausea incident to a long sea voyage. Alas, however, when they landed at Plymouth rock there was not a decent hotel in the place. The same stern and rock-bound coast which may be discovered along the Atlantic sea-board to-day was there, and a cruel, relentless sky frowned upon their endeavors.

Where prosperous cities now flaunt to the sky their proud domes and floating debts, the rank jimson weed nodded in the wind and the pumpkin pie of to-day still slumbered in the bosom of the future. What glorious facts have, under the benign influence of fostering centuries, been born of apparent impossibility. What giant certainties have grown through these years from the seeds of doubt and discouragement and uncertainty! (Big firecrackers and applause.)

At that time our ancestors had but timidly embarked in the forefather business. They did not know that future generations in four-button cutaways would rise up and call them blessed and pass resolutions of respect on their untimely death. If they stayed at home the king taxed them all out of shape, and if they went out of Boston a few rods to get enough huckleberries for breakfast, they would frequently come home so full of Indian arrows that they could not get through a common door without great pain.

Such was the early history of the country where now cultivation and education and refinement run rampant and people sit up all night to print newspapers so that we can have them in the morning.

The land on which the Old South stands is very valuable for business purposes, and $400,000 will have to be raised in order to preserve the old landmark to future generations. I earnestly hope that it will be secured, and that the old meeting-house—dear not alone to the people of Boston, but to the millions of Americans scattered from sea to sea, who cannot forget where first universal freedom plumed its wings—will be spared to entertain within its hospitable walls, enthusiastic and reverential visitors for ages without end.

Knights of the Pen.

WHEN you come to think of it, it is surprising that so many newspaper men write so that any one but an expert can read it. The rapid and voluminous work, especially of daily journalism, knocks the beautiful business college penman, as a rule, higher than a kite. I still have specimens of my own handwriting that a total stranger could read.

I do not remember a newspaper acquaintance whose penmanship is so characteristic of the exacting neatness and sharp, clear cut style of the man, as is that of Eugene Field, of the Chicago *News.* As the "Nonpareil Writer" of the Denver *Tribune*, it was a mystery to me when he did the work which the paper showed each day as his own. You would sometimes find him at his desk, writing on large sheets of "print paper" with a pen and violet ink, in a hand that was as delicate as the steel plate of a bank note and the kind of work that printers would skirmish for. He would ask you to sit down in the chair opposite his desk, which had two or three old exchanges thrown on it. He would probably say, "Never mind those papers. I've read them. Just sit down on them if you want to." Encouraged by his hearty manner, you would sit down, and you would continue to sit down till you had protruded about three-fourths of your system through that hollow mockery of a chair. Then he would run to help you out and curse the chair, and feel pained because he had erroneously given you the ruin with no seat to it. He always felt pained over such things. He always suffered keenly and felt shocked over the accident until you had gone away, and then he would sigh heavily and "set" the chair again.

THE RUIN.

Frank Pixley, the editor of the San Francisco *Argonaut*, is not beautiful, though the *Argonaut* is. He is grim and rather on the Moses Montefiore style of countenance, but his hand-writing does not convey the idea of the man personally, or his style of dealing with the Chinese question. It is rather young looking, and has the uncertain manner of an eighteen-year-old boy.

Robert J. Burdette writes a small but plain hand, though he sometimes suffers from the savage typographical error that steals forth at such a moment as ye think not, and disfigures and tears and mangles the bright eyed children of the brain.

Very often we read a man's work and imagine we shall find him like it, cheery, bright and entertaining; but we know him and find that personally he is a refrigerator, or an egotist, or a man with a torpid liver and a nose like a rose geranium. You will not be disappointed in Bob Burdette, however, You think you will like him, and you always do. He will never be too famous to be a gentleman.

George W. Peck's hand is of the free and independent order of chirography. It is easy and natural, but not handsome. He writes very voluminously, doing his editorial writing in two days of the week, generally Friday and Saturday. Then he takes a rapid horse, a zealous bird dog and an improved double barrel duck destroyer and communes with nature.

Sam Davis, an old time Californian, and now in Nevada, writes the freest of any penman I know When he is deliberate, he may be betrayed into making a deformed letter and a crooked mark attached to it, which he characterizes as a word. He puts a lot of these together and actually pays postage on the collection under the delusion that it is a letter, that it will reach its destination, and that it will accomplish its object.

He makes up for his bad writing, however, by being an unpublished volume of old time anecdotes and funny experiences.

Goodwin, of the old *Territorial Enterprise*, and Mark Twain's old employer, writes with a pencil in a methodical manner and very plainly. The way he sharpens a "hard medium" lead pencil and skins the apostle of the so-called Church of Jesus Christ of Latter Day Saints, makes my heart glad. Hardly a day passes that his life is not threatened by the low browed thumpers of Mormondom, and yet the old war horse raises the standard of monogamy and under the motto, "One country, one flag and one wife at a time," he smokes his old meerschaum pipe and writes a column of razor blades every day. He is the buzz saw upon which polygamy has tried to sit. Fighting these rotten institutions hand to hand and fighting a religious eccentricity through an annual message, or a feeble act of congress, are two separate and distinct things.

If I had a little more confidence in my longevity than I now have, I would go down there to the Valley of the Jordan, and I would gird up my loins, and I would write with that lonely warrior at Salt Lake, and with the aid and encouragement of our brethren of the press who do not favor the right of one man to marry an old woman's home, we would rotten egg the bogus Temple of Zion till the civilized world, with a patent clothes pin on its nose, would come and see what was the matter.

I see that my zeal has led me away from my original subject, but I havn't time to regret it now.

The Wild Cow.

WHEN I was young and used to roam around over the country, gathering water-melons in the light of the moon, I used to think I could milk anybody's cow, but I do not think so now. I do not milk a cow now unless the sign is right, and it hasn't been right for a good many years. The last cow I tried to milk was a common cow, born in obscurity; kind of a self-made cow. I remember her brow was low, but she wore her tail high and she was haughty, oh, so haughty.

I made a common-place remark to her, one that is used in the very best of society, one that need not have given offence anywhere. I said "So"—and she "soed." Then I told her to "hist" and she histed. But I thought she overdid it. She put too much expression in it.

Just then I heard something crash through the window of the barn and fall with a dull, sickening thud on the outside. The neighbors came to see what it was that caused the noise. They found that I had done it in getting through the window.

I asked the neighbors if the barn was still standing. They said it was. Then I asked if the cow was injured much. They said she seemed to be quite robust. Then I requested them to go in and calm the cow a little, and see if they could get my plug hat off her horns.

I am buying all my milk now of a milkman. I select a gentle milkman who will not kick, and feel as though I could trust him. Then, if he feels as though he could trust me, it is all right.

Spinal Meningitis.

SO many people have shown a pardonable curiosity about the above named disease, and so few have a very clear idea of the thrill of pleasure it affords the patient, unless they have enjoyed it themselves, that I have decided to briefly say something in answer to the innumerable inquiries I have received.

Up to the moment I had a notion of getting some meningitis, I had never employed a physician. Since then I have been thrown in their society a great deal. Most of them were very pleasant and scholarly gentlemen, who will not soon be forgotten; but one of them doctored me first for pneumonia, then for inflammatory rheumatism, and finally, when death was contiguous, advised me that I must have change of scene and rest.

I told him that if he kept on prescribing for me, I thought I might depend on both. Change of physicians, however, saved my life. This horse doctor, a few weeks afterward, administered a subcutaneous morphine squirt in the arm of a healthy servant girl because she had the headache, and she is now with the rest of this veterinarian's patients in a land that is fairer than this.

She lived six hours after she was prescribed for. He gave her change of scene and rest. He has quite a thriving little cemetery filled with people who have succeeded in cording up enough of his change of scene and rest to last them through all eternity. He was called once to prescribe for a man whose head had been caved in by a stone match-box, and, after treating the man for asthma and blind staggers, he prescribed rest and change of scene for him, too. The poor asthmatic is now breathing the extremely rarified air of the New Jerusalem.

Meningitis is derived from the Latin *Meninges*, membrane, and—*itis*, an affix denoting inflammation, so that, strictly speaking, meningitis is the inflammation of a membrane, and when applied to the spine, or cerebrum, is called spinal meningitis, or cerebro-spinal meningitis, etc., according to the part of the spine or brain involved in the inflammation. Meningitis is a characteristic and result of so-called spotted fever, and by many it is deemed identical with it.

When we come to consider that the spinal cord, or marrow, runs down through the long, bony shaft made by the vertebræ, and that the brain and spine, though connected, are bound up in one continuous bony wall and covered with this inflamed membrane, it is not difficult to understand that the thing is very hard to get at. If your throat gets inflamed, a doctor asks you to run your tongue out into society about a yard and a half, and he pries your mouth open with one of Rogers Brothers' spoon handles. Then he is able to examine your throat as he would a page of the *Congressional Record*, and to treat it with some local application. When you have spinal meningitis, however, the doctor tackles you with bromides, ergots, ammonia, iodine, chloral hydrate, codi, bromide of ammonia, hasheesh, bismuth, valerianate of ammonia, morphine sulph., nux vomica, turpentine emulsion, vox humana, rex magnus, opium, cantharides, Dover's powders, and other bric-a-brac. These remedies are masticated and acted upon by the salivary glands, passed down the esophegus, thrown into the society of old gastric, submitted to the peculiar motion of the stomach and thoroughly chymified, then forwarded through the pyloric orifice into the smaller intestines, where they are touched up with bile, and later on handed over through the lacteals, thoracic duct, etc., to the vast circulatory system. Here it is yanked back and forth through the heart, lungs and capillaries, and if anything is left to fork over to the disease, it has to squeeze into the long, bony, air-tight socket that holds the spinal cord. All this is done without seeing the patient's spinal cord before or after taking. If it could be taken out, and hung over a clothes line and cleansed with benzine, and then treated with insect powder, or rolled in corn meal, or preserved in alcohol, and then put back, it would be all right; but you can't. You pull a man's spine out of his system and he is bound to miss it, no matter how careful you have been about it. It is difficult to keep house without the spine. You need it every time you cook a meal. If the spinal cord could be pulled by a dentist and put away in pounded ice every time it gets a hot-box, spinal meningitis would lose its stinger.

I was treated by thirteen physicians, whose names I may give in a future article. They were, as I said, men I shall long remember. One of them said very sensibly that meningitis was generally over-doctored. I told him that I agreed with him. I said that if I should have another year of meningitis and thirteen more doctors, I would have to postpone my trip to Europe, where I had hoped to go and cultivate my voice. I've got a perfectly lovely voice, if I could take it to Europe and have it sand-papered and varnished, and mellowed down with beer and bologna.

But I was speaking of my physicians. Some time I'm going to give their biographies and portraits, as they did those of Dr. Bliss, Dr. Barnes and others. Next year, if I can get railroad rates, I am going to hold a reunion of my physicians in Chicago. It will be a pleasant relaxation for them, and will save the lives of a large percentage of their patients.

Skimming the Milky Way.

THE COMET.

THE comet is a kind of astronomical parody on the planet. Comets look some like planets, but they are thinner and do not hurt so hard when they hit anybody as a planet does. The comet was so called because it had hair on it, I believe, but late years the bald-headed comet is giving just as good satisfaction everywhere.

The characteristic features of a comet are: A nucleus, a nebulous light or coma, and usually a luminous train or tail worn high. Sometimes several tails are observed on one comet, but this occurs only in flush times.

When I was young I used to think I would like to be a comet in the sky, up above the world so high, with nothing to do but loaf around and play with the little new-laid planets and have a good time, but now I can see where I was wrong. Comets also have their troubles, their perihilions, their hyperbolas and their parabolas. A little over 300 years ago Tycho Brahe discovered that comets were extraneous to our atmosphere, and since then times have improved. I can see that trade is steadier and potatoes run less to tows than they did before.

Soon after that they discovered that comets all had more or less periodicity. Nobody knows how they got it. All the astronomers had been watching them day and night and didn't know when they were exposed, but there was no time to talk and argue over the question. There were two or three hundred comets all down with it at once. It was an exciting time.

Comets sometimes live to a great age. This shows that the night air is not so injurious to the health as many people would have us believe. The great comet of 1780 is supposed to have been the one that was noticed about the time of Cæsar's death, 44 B. C., and still, when it appeared in Newton's time, seventeen hundred years after its first grand farewell tour, Ike said that it was very well preserved, indeed, and seemed to have retained all its faculties in good shape.

Astronomers say that the tails of all comets are turned from the sun. I do not know why they do this, whether it is etiquette among them or just a mere habit.

A later writer on astronomy said that the substance of the nebulosity and the tail is of almost inconceivable tenuity He said this and then death came to his relief. Another writer says of the comet and its tail that "the curvature of the latter and the acceleration of the periodic time in the case of Encke's comet indicate their being affected by a resisting medium which has never been observed to have the slightest influence on the planetary periods."

TYCHO BRAHE AT WORK.

I do not fully agree with the eminent authority, though he may be right. Much fear has been the result of the comet's appearance ever since the world began, and it is as good a thing to worry about as anything I know of. If we could get close to a comet without frightening it away, we would find that we could walk through it anywhere as we could through the glare of a torchlight procession. We should so live that we will not be ashamed to look a comet in the eye, however. Let us pay up our newspaper subscription and lead such lives that when the comet strikes we will be ready.

Some worry a good deal about the chances for a big comet to plow into the sun some dark, rainy night, and thus bust up the whole universe. I wish that was all I had to worry about. If any respectable man will agree to pay my taxes and funeral expenses, I will agree to do his worrying about the comet's crashing into the bosom of the sun and knocking its daylights out.

THE SUN.

This luminous body is 92,000,000 miles from the earth, though there have been mornings this winter when it seemed to me that it was further than that. A railway train going at the rate of 40 miles per hour would be 263 years going there, to say nothing of stopping for fuel or water, or stopping on side tracks to wait for freight trains to pass. Several years ago it was discovered that a slight error had been made in the calculations of the sun's distance from the earth, and, owing to a misplaced logarithm, or something of that kind, a mistake of 3,000,000 miles was made in the result. People cannot be too careful in such matters. Supposing that, on the strength of the information contained in the old time-table, a man should start out with only provisions sufficient to take him 89,000,000 miles and should then find that 3,0000,000 miles still stretched out ahead of him. He would then have to buy fresh figs of the train boy in order to sustain life. Think of buying nice fresh figs on a train that had been *en route* 250 years!

Imagine a train boy starting out at ten years of age, and perishing at the age of 60 years with only one-fifth of his journey accomplished. Think of five train boys, one after the other, dying of old age on the way, and the train at last pulling slowly into the depot with not a living thing on board except the worms in the "nice eating apples!"

The sun cannot be examined through an ordinary telescope with impunity. Only one man every tried that, and he is now wearing a glass eye that cost him $9.

If you examine the sun through an ordinary solar microscope, you discover that it has a curdled or mottled appearance, as though suffering from biliousness. It is also marked here and there by long streaks of light, called faculæ, which look like foam flecks below a cataract. The spots on the sun vary from minute pores the size of an ordinary school district to spots 100,000 miles in diameter, visible to the nude eye. The center of these spots is as black as a brunette cat, and is called the umbra, so called because it resembles an umbrella. The next circle is less dark, and called the penumbra, because it so closely resembles the penumbra.

There are many theories regarding these spots, but, to be perfectly candid with the gentle reader, neither Prof. Proctor nor myself can tell exactly what they are. If we could get a little closer, we flatter ourselves that we could speak more definitely. My own theory is they are either, first, open air caucuses held by the colored people of the sun; or, second, they may be the dark horses in the campaign; or, third, they may be the spots knocked off the defeated candidate by the opposition.

Frankly, however, I do not believe either of these theories to be tenable. Prof. Proctor sneers at these theories also on the ground that these spots do not appear to revolve so fast as the sun. This, however, I am prepared to explain upon the theory that this might be the result of delays in the returns.

However, I am free to confess that speculative science is filled with the intangible.

The sun revolves upon his or her axletree, as the case may be, once in 25 to 28 of our days, so that a man living there would have almost two years to pay a 30-day note. We should so live that when we come to die we may go at once to the sun.

Regarding the sun's temperature, Sir John Herschel says that it is sufficient to melt a shell of ice covering its entire surface to a depth of 40 feet. I do not know whether he made this experiment personally or hired a man to do it for him.

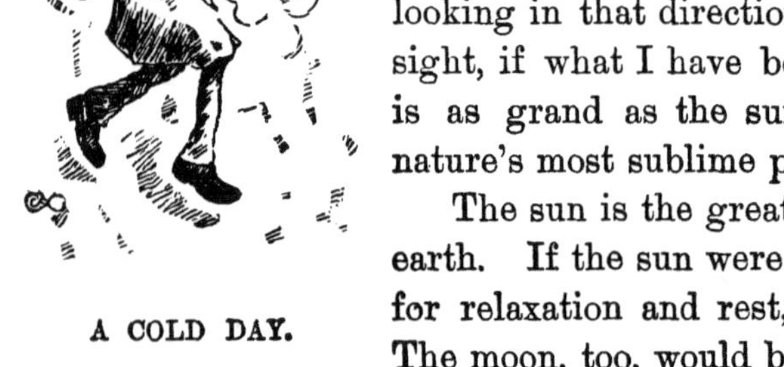

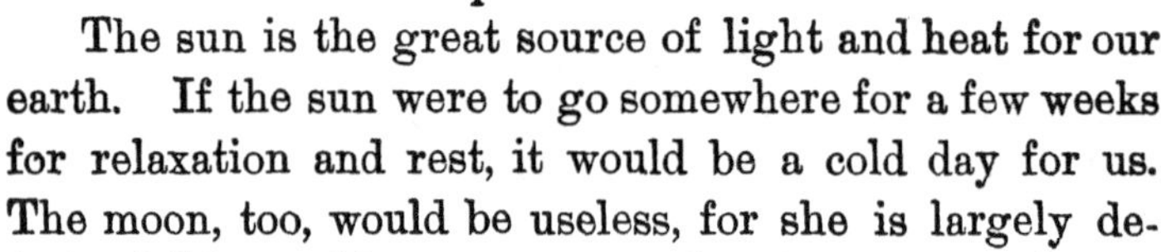

A COLD DAY.

The sun is like the star spangled banner—as it is "still there." You get up to-morrow morning just before sunrise and look away toward the east, and keep on looking in that direction, and at last you will see a fine sight, if what I have been told is true. If the sunrise is as grand as the sunset, it indeed must be one of nature's most sublime phenomena.

The sun is the great source of light and heat for our earth. If the sun were to go somewhere for a few weeks for relaxation and rest, it would be a cold day for us. The moon, too, would be useless, for she is largely dependent on the sun. Animal life would soon cease and real estate would become depressed in price. We owe very much of our enjoyment to the sun, and not many years ago there were a large number of people who worshiped the sun. When a man showed signs of emotional insanity, they took him up on the observatory of the temple and sacrificed him to the sun. They were a very prosperous and happy people. If the conqueror had not come among them with civilization and guns and grand juries they would have been very happy, indeed.

THE STARS.

There is much in the great field of astronomy that is discouraging to the savant who hasn't the time nor means to rummage around through the heavens. At times I am almost hopeless, and feel like saying to the great yearnful, hungry world: "Grope on forever. Do not ask me for another scientific fact. Find it out yourself. Hunt up your own new-laid planets, and let me have a rest. Never ask me again to sit up all night and take care of a new-born world, while you lie in bed and reck not."

I get no salary for examining the trackless void night after night when I ought to be in bed. I sacrifice my health in order that the public may know at once of the presence of a red-hot comet, fresh from the factory And yet, what thanks do I get?

Is it surprising that every little while I contemplate withdrawing from scientific research, to go and skin an eight-mule team down through the dim vista of relentless years?

Then, again, you take a certain style of star, which you learn from Professor Simon Newcomb is such a distance that it takes 50,000 years for its light to reach Boston. Now, we will suppose that after looking over the large stock of new and second-hand stars, and after examining the spring catalogue and price list, I decide that one of the smaller size will do me, and I buy it. How do I know that it was there when I bought it? Its cold and silent rays may have ceased 49,000 years before I was born and the intelligence be still on the way There is too much margin between sale and delivery Every now and then another astronomer comes to me and says. "Professor, I have discovered another new star and intend to file it. Found it last night about a mile and a half south of the zenith, running loose. Haven't heard of anybody who has lost a star of the fifteenth magnitude, about thirteen hands high, with light mane and tail, have you?" Now, how do I know that he has discovered a brand new star? How can I discover whether he is or is not playing an old, threadbare star on me for a new one?

We are told that there has been no perceptible growth or decay in the star business since man began to roam around through space, in his mind, and make figures on the barn door with red chalk showing the celestial time table.

No serious accidents have occurred in the starry heavens since I began to observe and study their habits. Not a star has waxed, not a star has waned to my knowledge. Not a planet has season-cracked or shown any of the injurious effects of our rigorous climate. Not a star has ripened prematurely or fallen off the trees. The varnish on the very oldest stars I find on close and critical examination to be in splendid condition. They will all no doubt wear as long as we need them, and wink on long after we have ceased to wink back.

In 1866 there appeared suddenly in the northern crown a star of about the third magnitude and worth at least $250. It was generally conceded by

A NIGHTLY VIGIL.

astronomers that this was a brand new star that had never been used, but upon consulting Argelander's star catalogue and price list it was found that this was not a new star at all, but an old, faded star of the ninth magnitude, with the front breadths turned wrong side out and trimmed with moonlight along the seams. After a few days of phenomenal brightness, it gently ceased to draw a salary as a star of the third magnitude, and walked home with an Uncle Tom's Cabin company.

It is such things as this that make the life of the astronomer one of constant and discouraging toil. I have long contemplated, as I say, the advisability of retiring from this field of science and allowing others to light the northern lights, skim the milky way and do other celestial chores. I would do it myself cheerfully if my health would permit, but for years I have realized, and so has my wife, that my duties as an astronomer kept me up too much at night, and my wife is certainly right about it when she says if I insist on scanning the heavens night after night, coming home late with the cork out of my telescope and my eyes red and swollen with these exhausting night vigils, I will be cut down in my prime. So I am liable to abandon the great labor to which I had intended to devote my life, my dazzling genius and my princely income. I hope that other savants will spare me the pain of another refusal, for my mind is fully made up that unless another skimmist is at once secured, the milky way will henceforth remain unskum.

A Thrilling Experience.

I HAD a very thrilling experience the other evening. I had just filled an engagement in a strange city, and retired to my cozy room at the hotel.

The thunders of applause had died away, and the opera house had been locked up to await the arrival of an Uncle Tom's Cabin Company The last loiterer had returned to his home, and the lights in the palace of the pork packer were extinguished.

No sound was heard, save the low, tremulous swash of the sleet outside, or the death-rattle in the throat of the bath-tub. Then all was still as the bosom of a fried chicken when the spirit has departed.

The swallow-tail coat hung limp and weary in the wardrobe, and the gross receipts of the evening were under my pillow. I needed sleep, for I was worn out with travel and anxiety, but the fear of being robbed kept me from repose. I know how desperate a man becomes when he yearns for another's gold. I know how cupidity drives a wicked man to mangle his victim, that he may win precarious prosperity, and how he will often take a short cut to wealth by means of murder, when, if he would enter politics, he might accomplish his purpose as surely and much more safely.

Anon, however, tired nature succumbed. I know I had succumbed, for the bell-boy afterward testified that he heard me do so.

The gentle warmth of the steam-heated room, and the comforting assurance of duty well done and the approval of friends, at last lulled me into a gentle repose.

Anyone who might have looked upon me, as I lay there in that innocent slumber, with the winsome mouth slightly ajar and the playful limbs cast wildly about, while a merry smile now and then flitted across the regular features, would have said that no heart could be so hard as to harbor ill for one so guileless and so simple.

I do not know what it was that caused me to wake. Some slight sound or other, no doubt, broke my slumber, and I opened my eyes wildly. The room was in semi-darkness.

Hark!

A slight movement in the corner, and the low, regular breathing of a human being! I was now wide awake. Possibly I could have opened my eyes wider, but not without spilling them out of their sockets.

Regularly came that soft, low breathing. Each time it seemed like a sigh of relief, but it did not relieve me. Evidently it was not done for that purpose. It sounded like a sigh of blessed relief, such as a woman might heave after she has returned from church and transferred herself from the embrace of her new Russia iron, black silk dress into a friendly wrapper.

Regularly, like the rise and fall of a wave on the summer sea, it rose and fell, while my pale lambrequin of hair rose and fell fitfully with it.

I know that people who read this will laugh at it, but there was nothing to laugh at. At first I feared that the sigh might be that of a woman who had entered the room through a transom in order to see me, as I lay wrapt in slumber, and then carry the picture away to gladden her whole life.

But no. That was hardly possible. It was cupidity that had driven some cruel villain to enter my apartments and to crouch in the gloom till the proper moment should come in which to spring upon me, throttle me, crowd a hotel pillow into each lung, and, while I did the Desdemona act, rob me of my hard-earned wealth.

Regularly still rose the soft breathing, as though the robber might be trying to suppress it. I reached gently under the pillow, and securing the money I put it in the pocket of my *robe de nuit.* Then, with great care, I pulled out a copy of Smith & Wesson's great work on "How to Ventilate the Human Form." I said to myself that I would sell my life as dearly as possible, so that whoever bought it would always regret the trade.

Then I opened the volume at the first chapter and addressed a thirty-eight calibre remark in the direction of the breath in the corner.

When the echoes had died away a sigh of relief welled up from the dark corner. Also another sigh of relief later on.

I then decided to light the gas and fight it out. You have no doubt seen a man scratch a match on the leg of his pantaloons. Perhaps you have also seen an absent-minded man undertake to do so, forgetting that his pantaloons were hanging on a chair at the other end of the room.

However, I lit the gas with my left hand and kept my revolver pointed toward the dark corner where the breath was still rising and falling.

People who had heard my lecture came rushing in, hoping to find that I had suicided, but they found that, instead of humoring the public in that way, I had shot the valve off the steam radiator.

It is humiliating to write the foregoing myself, but I would rather do so than have the affair garbled y careless hands.

Catching a Buffalo.

A PLEASING anecdote is being told through the press columns recently, of an encounter on the South Platte, which occurred some years ago between a Texan and a buffalo. The recital sets forth the fact that the Texans went out to hunt buffalo, hoping to get enough for a mess during the day. Toward evening they saw two gentlemen buffalo on a neighboring hill near the Platte, and at once pursued their game, each selecting an animal. They separated at once, Jack going one way galloping after his beast, while Sam went in the other direction. Jack soon got a shot at his game, but the bullet only tore a large hole in the fleshy shoulder of the bull and buried itself in the neck, maddening the animal to such a degree that he turned at once and charged upon horse and rider.

The astonished horse, with the wonderful courage, sagacity and *sang froid* peculiar to the broncho, whirled around two consecutive times, tangled his feet in the tall grass and fell, throwing his rider about fifty feet. He then rose and walked away to a quiet place, where he could consider the matter and give the buffalo an opportunity to recover.

The infuriated bull then gave chase to Jack, who kept out of the way for a few yards only, when, getting his legs entangled in the grass, he fell so suddenly that his pursuer dashed over him without doing him any bodily injury. However, as the animal went over his prostrate form, Jack felt the buffalo's tail brush across his face, and, rising suddenly, he caught it with a terrific grip and hung to it, thus keeping out of the reach of his enemy's horns, till his strength was just giving out, when Sam hove in sight and put a large bullet through the bull's heart.

This tale is told, apparently, by an old plainsman and scout, who reels it off as though he might be telling his own experience.

Now, I do not wish to seem captious and always sticking my nose into what is none of my business, but as a logical and zoological fact, I desire, in my cursory way, to coolly take up the subject of the buffalo tail. Those who have been in the habit of killing buffaloes, instead of running an account at the butcher shop, will remember that this noble animal has a genuine camel's hair tail about eight inches long, with a chenille tassel at the end, which he throws up into the rarified atmosphere of the far west, whenever he is surprised or agitated.

In passing over a prostrate man, therefore, I apprehend that in order to brush his face with the average buffalo tail, it would be necessary for him to sit down on the bosom of the prostrate scout and fan his features with the miniature caudal bud.

AN UNEQUAL MATCH.

The buffalo does not gallop an hundred miles a day, dragging his tail across the bunch grass and alkali of the boundless plains.

He snorts a little, turns his bloodshot eyes toward the enemy a moment and then, throwing his cunning little taillet over the dash-boardlet, he wings away in an opposite direction.

The man who could lie on his back and grab that vision by the tail would have to be moderately active. If he succeeded, however, it would be a question of the sixteenth part of a second only, whether he had his arms jerked out by the roots and scattered through space or whether he had strength of will sufficient to yank out the withered little frizz and hold the quivering ornament in his hands. Few people have the moral courage to follow a buffalo around over half a day holding on by the tail. It is said that a Sioux brave once tried it, and they say his tracks were thirteen miles apart. After merrily sauntering around with the buffalo one hour, during which time he crossed the territories of Wyoming and Dakota twice and surrounded the regular army three times, he became discouraged and died from the injuries he had received. Perhaps, however, it may have been fatigue.

It might be possible for a man to catch hold of the meager tail of a meteor and let it snatch him through the coming years.

It might be, that a man with a strong constitution could catch a cyclone and ride it bareback across the United States and then have a fresh one ready to ride back again, but to catch a buffalo bull in the full flush of manhood, as it were, and retain his tail while he crossed three reservations and two mountain ranges, requires great tenacity of purpose and unusual mental equipoise.

Remember, I do not regard the story I refer to as false, at least I do not wish to be so understood. I simply say that it recounts an incident that is rather out of the ordinary. Let the gentle reader lie down and have a Jack-rabbit driven across his face, for instance. The J Rabbit is as likely to brush your face with his brief and erect tail as the buffalo would be. Then carefully note how rapidly and promptly instantaneous you must be. Then closely attend to the manner in which you abruptly and almost simultaneously, have not retained the tail in your memory

A few people may have successfully seized the grieved and startled buffalo by the tail, but they are not here to testify to the circumstances. They are dead, abnormally and extremely dead.

John Adams.

AFTER viewing the birthplace of the Adamses out at Quincy I felt more reconciled to my own birthplace. Comparing the house in which I was born with those in which other eminent philanthropists and high-priced statesmen originated, I find that I have no reason to complain. Neither of the Adamses were born in a larger house than I was, and for general tone and eclat of front yard and cook-room on behind, I am led to believe that I have the advantage.

John Adams was born before John Quincy Adams. A popular idea seems to prevail in some sections of the Union that inasmuch as John Q. was bald-headed, he was the elder of the two; but I inquired about that while on the ground where they were both born, and ascertained from people who were familiar with the circumstances, that John was born first.

PRESIDENTIAL SIMPLICITY.

John Adams was the second president of the United States. He was a lawyer by profession, but his attention was called to politics by the passage of the stamp act in 1765. He was one of the delegates who represented Massachusetts in the first Continental Congress, and about that time he wrote a letter in which he said: "The die is now cast; I have passed the rubicon. Sink or swim, live or die, survive or perish with my country is my unalterable determination." Some have expressed the opinion that "the rubicon" alluded to by Mr. Adams in this letter was a law which he had succeeded in getting passed; but this is not true. The idea of passing the rubicon first originated with Julius Cæsar, a foreigner of some note who flourished a good deal B. C.

In June, 1776, Mr. Adams seconded a resolution, moved by Richard Henry Lee, that the United States "are, and of right ought to be, free and independent." Whenever Mr. Adams could get a chance to whoop for liberty now and forever, one and inseparable, he invariably did so.

In 1796, Mr. Adams ran for president. In the convention it was nip and tuck between Thomas Jefferson and himself, but Jefferson was understood to be a Universalist, or an Universalist, whichever would look the best in print, and so he only got 68 votes out of a possible 139. In 1800, however, Jefferson turned the tables on him, and Mr. Adams only received 65 to Jefferson's 73 votes.

Mr. Adams made a good president and earned his salary, though it wasn't so much of a job as it is now. When there was no Indian war in those days the president could put on an old blue flannel shirt and such other clothes as he might feel disposed to adopt, and fish for bull-heads in the Potomac and his nose peeled in the full glare of the fervid sun.

Now it is far different. By the time we get through with a president nowadays he isn't good for much. Mr. Hayes stood the fatigue of being president better, perhaps, than any other man since the republic became so large a machine. Mr. Hayes went home to Fremont with his mind just as fresh and his brain as cool as when he pulled up his coat tails to sit down in the presidential chair. The reason why Mr. Hayes saved his mind, his brain and his salary, was plain enough when we stop to consider that he did not use them much during his administration.

John Quincy Adams was the sixth president of the United States and the eldest son of John Adams. He was one of the most eloquent of orators, and shines in history as one of the most polished of our eminent and bald-headed Americans. When he began to speak, his round, smooth head, to look down upon it from the gallery, resembled a nice new billiard ball, but as he warmed up and became more thoroughly stirred, his intellectual dome changed to a delicate pink. Then, when he rose to the full height of his eloquent flight, and prepared to swoop down upon his adversaries and carry them into camp, it is said that his smooth intellectual rink was as red as the flush of rosy dawn on the 5th day of July.

He was educated both at home and abroad. That is the reason he was so polished. After he got so that he could readily spell and pronounce the most difficult words to be found in the large stores of Boston, he was sent to Europe, where he acquired several foreign tongues, and got so that he could converse with the people of Europe very fluently, if they were familiar with English as she is spoke.

John Quincy Adams was chosen president by the House of Representatives, there being no choice in the electoral contest, Adams receiving 84 votes, Andrew

Jackson 99, William H. Crawford 41, and Henry Clay 37. Clay stood in with Mr. Adams in the House of Representatives deal, it was said, and was appointed secretary of state under Mr. Adams as a result. This may not be true, but a party told me about it who got it straight from Washington, and he also told me in confidence that he made it a rule never to prevaricate.

Mr. Adams was opposed to American slavery, and on several occasions in Congress alluded to his convictions.

He was in Congress seventeen years, and during that time he was frequently on his feet attending to little matters in which he felt an interest, and when he began to make allusions, and blush all over the top of his head, and kick the desk, and throw ink-bottles at the presiding officer, they say that John Q. made them pay attention. Seward says, "with unwavering firmness, against a bitter and unscrupulous opposition, exasperated to the highest pitch by his pertinacity—amidst a perfect tempest of vituperation and abuse—he persevered in presenting his anti-slavery petitions, one by one, to the amount sometimes of 200 in one day" As one of his eminent biographers has truly said: "John Quincy Adams was indeed no slouch."

The Wail of a Wife.

"ETHEL" has written a letter to me and asked for a printed reply. Leaving off the opening sentences, which I would not care to have fall into the hands of my wife, her note is about as follows:

"————VT., Feb. 28, 1885.

"MY DEAR SIR: * * * * * * * * * * * * * * * * * [Tender part of letter omitted for obvious reasons.] Would it be asking too much for me to request a brief reply to one or two questions which many other married women as well as myself would like to have answered?

I have been married now for five years. To-day is the anniversary of my marriage. When I was single I was a teacher and supported myself in comfort. I had more pocket-money and dressed fully as well if not better than I do now. Why should girls who are abundantly able to earn their own livelihood struggle to become the slave of a husband and children, and tie themselves to a man when they might be free and happy?

I think too much is said by the men in a light and flippant manner about the anxiety of young ladies to secure a home and a husband, and still they do deserve a part of it, as I feel that I do now for assuming a great burden when I was comparatively independent and comfortable.

Now, will you suggest any advice that you think would benefit the yet unmarried and self-supporting girls who are liable to make the same mistake that I did, and thus warn them in a manner that would be so much more universal in its range, and reach so many more people than I could if I should raise my voice? Do this and you will be gratefully remembered by

ETHEL."

It would indeed be a tough, tough man who could ignore thy gentle plea, Ethel; tougher far than the pale, intellectual hired man who now addresses you in this private and underhanded manner, unknown to your husband. Please destroy this letter, Ethel, as soon as you see it in print, so that it will not fall into the hands of Mr. Ethel, for if it should, I am gone. If your husband were to run across this letter in the public press I could never look him in the eye again.

You say that you had more pocket-money before you were married than you have since, Ethel, and you regret your rash step. I am sorry to hear it. You also say that you wore better clothes when you were single than you do now. You are also pained over that. It seems that marriage with you has not paid any cash dividends. So that if you married Mr. Ethel as a financial venture, it was a mistake. You do not state how it has affected your husband. Perhaps he had more pocket-money and better clothes before he married than he has since. Sometimes two people do well in business by themselves, but when they go into partnership they bust higher than a kite, if you will allow me the free, English translation of a Roman expression which you might not fully understand if I should give it to you in the original Roman.

Lots of self-supporting young ladies have married and had to go very light on pin-money after that, and still they did not squeal, as you, dear Ethel. They did not marry for revenue only. They married for protection. (This is a little political bon mot which I thought of myself. Some of my best jokes this spring are jokes that I thought of myself.)

FOR REVENUE ONLY.

No, Ethel, if you married expecting to be a dormant partner during the day and then to go through Mr. Ethel's pantaloons pocket at night and declare a dividend, of course life is full of bitter, bitter regret and disappointment. Perhaps it is also for Mr. Ethel. Anyhow, I can't help feeling a pang of sympathy for him. You do not say that he is unkind or that he so far forgets himself as to wake you up in the morning with a harsh tone of voice and a yearling club. You do not say that he asks you for pocket-money, or, if so, whether you give it to him or not.

Of course I want to do what is right in the solemn warning business, so I will give notice to all simple young women who are now self-supporting and happy, that there is no statute requiring them to assume the burdens of wifehood and motherhood unless they prefer to do so. If they now have abundance of pin-money and new clothes, they may remain single if they wish without violating the laws of the land. This rule is also good when applied to young and self-supporting young men who wear good clothes and have funds in their pockets. No young man who is free, happy and independent, need invest his money in a family or carry a colicky child twenty-seven miles and two laps in one night unless he prefers it. But those who go into it with the right spirit, Ethel, do not regret it.

I would just as soon tell you, Ethel, if you will promise that it shall go no farther, that I do not wear as good clothes as I did before I was married. I don't have to. My good clothes have accomplished what I got them for. I played them for all they were worth, and since I got married the idea of wearing clothes as a vocation has not occurred to me.

Please give my kind regards to Mr. Ethel, and tell him that although I do not know him personally, I cannot help feeling sorry for him.

Bunker Hill.

LAST week for the first time I visited the granite obelisk known all over the civilized world as Bunker Hill monument. Sixty years ago, if my memory serves me correctly, General La Fayette, since deceased, laid the corner-stone, and Daniel Webster made a few desultory remarks which I cannot now recall. Eighteen years later it was formally dedicated, and Daniel spoke a good piece, composed mostly of things that he had thought up himself. There has never been a feature of the early history and unceasing struggle for American freedom which has so roused my admiration as this custom, quite prevalent among congressmen in those days, of writing their own speeches.

Many of Webster's most powerful speeches were written by himself or at his suggestion. He was a plain, unassuming man, and did not feel above writing his speeches. I have always had the greatest respect and admiration for Mr. Webster as a citizen, as a scholar and as an extemporaneous speaker, and had he not allowed his portrait to appear last year in the *Century*, wearing an air of intense gloom and a plug hat entirely out of style, my respect and admiration would have continued indefinitely

Bunker Hill monument is a great success as a monument, and the view from its summit is said to be well worth the price of admission. I did not ascend the obelisk, because the inner staircase was closed to visitors on the day of my visit and the lightning rod on the outside looked to me as though it had been recently oiled.

On the following day, however, I engaged a man to ascend the monument and tell me his sensations. He assured me that they were first-rate. At the feet of the spectator Boston and its environments are spread out in the glad sunshine. Every day Boston spreads out her environments just that way

Bunker Hill monument is 221 feet in height, and has been entirely paid for. The spectator may look at the monument with perfect impunity, without being solicited to buy some of its mortgage bonds. This adds much to the genuine thrill of pleasure while gazing at it.

There is a Bunker Hill in Macoupin County, Illinois, also in Ingham County, Michigan, and in Russell County, Kansas, but General Warren was not killed at either of these points.

One hundred and ten years ago, on the 17th day of the present month, one of America's most noted battles with the British was fought near where Bunker Hill monument now stands. In that battle the British lost 1,050 in killed and wounded, while the American loss numbered but 450. While the people of this country are showing such an interest in our war history, I am surprised that something has not been said about Bunker Hill. The Federal forces from Roxbury to Cambridge were under command of General Artemus Ward, the great American humorist. When the American humorist really puts on his war paint and sounds the tocsin, he can organize a great deal of mourning.

General Ward was assisted by Putnam, Starke, Prescott, Gridley and Pomeroy Colonel William Prescott was sent over from Cambridge to Charlestown for the purpose of fortifying Bunker Hill. At a council of war it was decided to fortify Breeds Hill, not so high but nearer to Boston than Bunker Hill. So a redoubt was thrown up during the night on the ground where the monument now stands.

The British landed a large force under Generals Howe and Pigot, and at 2 P M. the Americans were reinforced by Generals Warren and Pomeroy General Warren was of a literary turn of mind and during the battle took his hat off and recited a little poem beginning:

"Stand, the ground's your own, my braves!
Will ye give it up to slaves?"

A man who could deliver an impromptu and extemporaneous address like that in public, and while there was such a bitter feeling of hostility on the part of the audience, must have been a good scholar. In our great fratricidal strife twenty years ago, the inferiority of our generals in this respect was painfully noticeable. We did not have a commander who could address his troops in rhyme to save his neck. Several of them were pretty good in blank verse, but it was so blank that it was not just the thing to fork over to posterity and speak in school afterward.

Colonel Prescott's statue now stands where he is supposed to have stood when he told his men to reserve their fire till they saw the whites o enemy's eyes. Those who have examined the cast-iron flint-lock weapo in those days will admit that this order was wise. Those guns were ii to health, of course, when used to excess, but not necessarily or immediately fatal.

At the time of the third attack by the British, the Americans were out of ammunition, but they met the enemy with clubbed muskets, and it was found that one end of the rebel flint-lock was about as fatal as the other, if not more so.

Boston still meets the invader with its club. The mayor says to the citizens of Boston. "Wait till you can see the whites of the visitor's eyes, and then go for him with your clubs." Then the visitor surrenders.

I hope that many years may pass before it will again be necessary for us to soak this fair land in British blood. The boundaries of our land are now more extended, and so it would take more blood to soak it.

Boston has just reason to be proud of Bunker Hill, and it was certainly a great stroke of enterprise to have the battle located there. Bunker Hill is dear to every American heart, and there are none of us who would not have cheerfully gone into the battle then if we had known about it in time.

A Lumber Camp.

I HAVE just returned from a little impromptu farewell tour in the lumber camps toward Lake Superior. It was my idea to wade around in the snow for a few weeks and swallow baked beans and ozone on the ½ shell. The affair was a success. I put up at Bootjack camp on the raging Willow River, where the gay-plumaged chipmunk and the spruce gum have their home.

Winter in the pine woods is fraught with fun and frolic. It is more fraught with fatigue than funds, however. This winter a man in the Michigan and Wisconsin lumber camps could arise at 4:30 A. M., eat a patent pail full of dried apples soaked with Young Hyson and sweetened with Persian glucose, go out to the timber with a lantern, hew down the giants of the forest, with the snow up to the pit of his stomach, till the gray owl in the gathering gloom whooped and hooted in derision, and all for $12 per month and stewed prunes.

I did not try to accumulate wealth while I was in camp. I just allowed others to enter into the mad rush and wrench a fortune from the hand of fate while I studied human nature and the cook. I had a good many pleasant days there, too. I read such literary works as I could find around the camp and smoked the royal Havana smoking tobacco of the cookee. Those who have not lumbered much do not know much of true joy and sylvan smoking tobacco.

They are not using a very good grade of the weed in the lumber regions this winter. When I say lumber regions I do not refer entirely to the circumstances of a weak back. (Monkey-wrench, oil can and screwdriver sent with this joke; also rules for working it in all kinds of goods.) The tobacco used by the pine choppers of the nothern forest is called the Scandihoovian. I do not know why they call it that, unless it is because yon can smoke it in Wisconsin and smell it in Scandihoovia.

When night came we would gather around the blazing fire and talk over old times and smoke this tobacco. I smoked it till last week, then I bought a new mouth and resolved to lead a different life.

I shall never forget the evenings we spent together in that log shack in the heart of the forest. They are graven on my memory where time's effacing fingers can not monkey with them. We would most always converse. The crew talked the Norwegian language and I am using the English language mostly this winter. So each enjoyed himself in his own quiet way This seemed to throw the Norwegians a good deal together. It also threw me a good deal together. The Scandinavians soon learn our ways and our language, but prior to that they are quite clannish.

The cook, however, was an Ohio man. He spoke the Sandusky dialect with a rich, nut brown flavor that did me much good, so that after I talked with

I TOOK A PIE.

the crew a few hours in English, and received their harsh, corduroy replies in Norske, I gladly fled to the cook shanty There I could rapidly change to the smoothly flowing sentences peculiar to the Ohio tongue, and while I ate the common twisted doughnut of commerce, we would talk on and on of the pleasant days we had spent in our native land. I don't know how many hours I have thus spent, bringing the glad light into the eye of the cook as I spoke to him of Mrs. Hayes, an estimable lady, partially married, and now living at Fremont, Ohio.

I talked to him of his old home till the tears would unbidden start, as he rolled out the dough with a common Budweiser beer bottle, and shed the scalding into the flour barrel. Tears are always unavailing, but sometimes I think they are more so when they are shed into a barrel of flour. He was an easy weeper. He would shed tears on the slightest provocation, or anything else. Once I told him something so touchful that his eyes were blinded with tears for the nonce. Then I took a pie, and stole away so that he could be alone with his sorrow.

He used to grind the coffee at 2 A. M. The coffee mill was nailed up against a partition on the opposite side from my bed. That is one reason I did not stay any longer at the camp. It takes about an hour to grind coffee enough for thirty men, and as my ear was generally against the pine boards when the cook began, it ruffled my slumbers and made me a morose man.

We had three men at the camp who snored. If they had snored in my own language I could have endured it, but it was entirely unintelligible to me as it was. Still, it wasn't bad either. They snored on different keys, and still there was harmony in it—a kind of chime of imported snore as it were. I used to lie and listen to it for hours. Then the cook would begin his coffee mill overture and I would arise.

When I got home I slept from Monday morning till Washington's Birthday, without food or water.

My Lecture Abroad.

HAVING at last yielded to the entreaties of Great Britain, I have decided to make a professional farewell tour of England with my new and thrilling lecture, entitled "Jerked Across the Jordan, or the Sudden and Deserved Elevation of an American Citizen."

I have, therefore, already written some of the cablegrams which will be sent to the Associated Press, in order to open the campaign in good shape in America on my return.

Though I have been supplicated for some time by the people of England to come over there and thrill them with my eloquence, my thriller has been out of order lately, so that I did not dare venture abroad.

This lecture treats incidentally of the ease with which an American citizen may rise in the Territories, when he has a string tied around his neck, with a few personal friends at the other end of the string. It also treats of the various styles of oratory peculiar to America, with specimens of American oratory that have been pressed and dried especially for this lecture. It is a good lecture, and the few straggling facts scattered along through it don't interfere with the lecture itself in any way.

I shall appear in costume during the lecture.

At each lecture a different costume will be worn, and the costume worn at the previous lecture will be promptly returned to the owner.

Persons attending the lecture need not be identified.

Polite American dude ushers will go through the audience to keep the flies away from those who wish to sleep during the lecture.

Should the lecture be encored at its close, it will be repeated only once. This encore business is being overdone lately, I think.

Following are some of the cablegrams I have already written. If any one has any suggestions as to change, or other additional favorable criticisms, they will be gratefully received; but I wish to reserve the right, however, to do as I please about using them:

LONDON, ——, ——. —Bill Nye opened his foreign lecture engagement here last evening with a can-opener. It was found to be in good order. As soon as the doors were opened there was a mad rush for seats, during which three men were fatally injured. They insisted on remaining through the lecture, however, and adding to its horrors. Before 8 o'clock 500 people had been turned away. Mr. Nye announced that he would deliver a matinee this afternoon, but he has been petitioned by tradesmen to refrain from doing so, as it will paralyze the business interests of the city to such a degree that they offer to "buy the house," and allow the lecturer to cancel his engagement.

LONDON, ——, ——. —The great lecturer and contortionist, Bill Nye, last night closed his six weeks' engagement here with his famous lecture on "The Rise and Fall of the American Horse Thief," with a grand benefit and ovation. The elite of London was present, many of whom have attended every evening for six weeks to hear this same lecture. Those who can afford it will follow the lecturer back to America, in order to be where they can hear this lecture almost constantly

Mr. Nye, at the beginning of the season, offered a prize to anyone who should neither be absent nor tardy through the entire six weeks. After some hot discussion last evening, the prize was awarded to the janitor of the hall.

[Associated Press Cablegram.]

LONDON, ——, ——. —Bill Nye will sail for America to-morrow in the steamship Senegambia. On his arrival in America he will at once pay off the national debt and found a large asylum for American dudes whose mothers are too old to take in washing and support their sons in affluence.

The Miner at Home.

RECEIVING another notice of assessment on my stock in the Aladdin mine the other day, reminded me that I was still interested in a bottomless hole that was supposed at one time to yield funds instead of absorbing them. The Aladdin claim was located in the spring of '76 by a syndicate of journalists, none of whom had ever been openly accused of wealth. If we had been, we could have proved an alibi.

We secured a gang of miners to sink on the discovery, consisting of a Chinaman named How Long. How Long spoke the Chinese lauguage with great fluency Being perfectly familiar with that language, and a little musty in the trans-Missouri English, he would converse with us in his own language, sometimes by the hour, courteously overlooking the fact that we did not reply to him in the same tongue. He would converse in this way till he ran down, generally, and then he would refrain for a while.

Finally, How Long signified that he would like to draw his salary Of course he was ignorant of our ways, and as innocent of any knowledge of the intricate details peculiar to a mining syndicate as the child unborn. So he had gone to the president of our syndicate and had been referred to the superintendent, and he had sent How Long to the auditor, and the auditor had told him to go to the gang boss and get his time, and then proceed in the proper manner, after which, if his claim turned out to be all right, we would call a meeting of the syndicate and take early action in relation to it. By this, the reader will readily see that, although we were not wealthy, we knew how to do business just the same as though we had been a wealthy corporation.

How Long attended one of our meetings and at the close of the session made a few remarks. As near as I am able to recall his language, it was very much as follows:

"China boy no sabbe you dam slyndicate. You allee same foolee me too muchee. How Long no chopee big hole in the glound allee day for health. You Melican boy Laddee silver mine all same funny business. Me no likee slyndicate. Slyndicate heap gone all same woodbine. You sabbe me? How Long make em slyndicate pay tention. You April foolee me. You makee me tlired. You putee me too much on em slate. Slyndicate no good. Allee time stanemoff China boy. You allee time chin chin. Dlividend allee time heap gone."

Owing to a strike which then took place in our mine, we found that, in order to complete our assessment work, we must get in another crew or do the job ourselves. Owing to scarcity of help and a feeling of antagonism on the part of the laboring classes toward our giant enterprise, a feeling of hostility which naturally exists between labor and capital, we had to go out to the mine ourselves. We had heard of other men who had shoveled in their own mines and were afterward worth millions of dollars, so we took some bacon and other delicacies and hied us to the Aladdin.

I HAVE FORGOTTEN HIS FIRST REMARK.

Buck, our mining expert, went down first. Then he requested us to hoist him out again. We did so. I have forgotten what his first remark was when he got out of the bucket, but that don't make any difference, for I wouldn't care to use it here anyway.

It seems that How Long, owing to his heathenish ignorance of our customs and the unavoidable delay in adjusting his claim for work, labor and services, had allowed his temper to get the better of him, and he had planted a colony of American skunks in the shaft of the Aladdin.

That is the reason we left the Aladdin mine and no one jumped it. We had not done the necessary work in order to hold it, but when we went out there the following spring we found that no one had jumped it.

Even the rough, coarse miner, far from civilizing influences and beyond the reach of social advantages. recognizes the fact that this little, unostentatious animal plodding along through life in its own modest way, yet wields a wonderful influence over the destinies of man. So the Aladdin mine was not disturbed that summer.

We paid How Long, and in the following spring had a flattering offer for the claim if it assayed as well as we said it would, so Buck, our expert, went out to the Aladdin with an assayer and the purchaser. The assay of the Aladdin showed up very rich indeed, far above anything that I had ever hoped for, and so we made a sale. But we never got the money, for when the assayer got home he casually assayed his apparatus and found that his whole outfit had been salted prior to the Aladdin assay

I do not think our expert, Buck, would salt an assayer's kit, but he was charged with it at this time, and he said he would rather lose his trade than have trouble over it. He would rather suffer wrong than to do wrong, he said, and so the Aladdin came back on our hands.

It is not a very good mine if a man wants it as a source of revenue, but it makes a mighty good well. The water is cold and clear as crystal. If it stood in Boston, instead of out there in northern Colorado, where you can't get at it more than three months in the year, it would be worth $150. The great fault of the Aladdin mine is its poverty as a mine, and its isolation as a well.

An Operatic Entertainment.

LAST week we went up to the Coliseum, at Minneapolis, to hear Theodore Thomas' orchestra, the Wagner trio and Christine Nilsson. The Coliseum is a large rink just out of Minneapolis, on the road between that city and St. Paul. It can seat 4,000 people comfortably, but the management like to wedge 4,500 people in there on a warm day, and then watch the perspiration trickle out through the clapboards on the outside. On the closing afternoon, during the matinee performance, the building was struck by lightning and a hole knocked out of the Corinthian duplex that surmounts the oblique portcullis on the off side. The reader will see at once the location of the bolt.

The lightning struck the flag-staff, ran down the leg of a man who was repairing the electric light, took a chew of his tobacco, turned his boot wrong side out and induced him to change his sock, toyed with a chilblain, wrenched out a soft corn and roguishly put it in his ear, then ran down the electric light wire, a part of it filling an engagement in the Coliseum and the balance following the wire to the depot, where it made double-pointed toothpicks of a pole fifty feet high. All this was done very briefly Those who have seen lightning toy with a cottonwood tree, know that this fluid makes a specialty of it at once and in a brief manner. The lightning in this case, broke the glass in the skylight and deposited the broken fragments on a half dozen parquette chairs, that were empty because the speculators who owned them couldn't get but $50 apiece, and were waiting for a man to mortgage his residence and sell a team. He couldn't make the transfer in time for the matinee, so the seats were vacant when the lightning struck. The immediate and previous fluid then shot athwart the auditorium in the direction of the platform, where it nearly frightened to death a large chorus of children. Women fainted, ticket speculators fell $2 on desirable seats, and strong men coughed up a clove. The scene beggared description. I intended to have said that before, but forgot it. Theodore Thomas drew in a full breath, and Christine Nilsson drew her salary. Two thousand strong men thought of their wasted lives, and two thousand women felt for their back hair to see if it was still there. I say, therefore, without successful contradiction, that the scene beggared description. Chestnuts!

In the evening several people sang, "The Creation." Nilsson was Gabriel. Gabriel has a beautiful voice cut low in the neck, and sings like a joyous bobolink in the dew-saturated mead. How's that? Nilsson is proud and haughty in her demeanor, and I had a good notion to send a note up to her, stating that she needn't feel so lofty, and if she could sit up in the peanut gallery where I was and look at herself, with her dress kind of sawed off at the top, she would not be so vain. She wore a diamond necklace and silk skirt. The skirt was cut princesse, I think, to harmonize with her salary As an old neighbor of mine said when he painted the top board of his fence green, he wanted it "to kind of corroborate with his blinds." He's the same man who went to Washington about the time of the Guiteau trial, and said he was present at the "post mortise" examination. But the funniest thing of all, he said, was to see Dr. Mary Walker riding one of these "philosophers" around on the streets.

MAKING HIMSELF USEFUL.

But I am wandering. We were speaking of the Festival. Theodore Thomas is certainly a great leader. What a pity he is out of politics. He pounded the air all up fine there, Thursday I think he has 25 small-size fiddles, 10 medium-size, and 5 of those big, fat ones that a bald-headed man generally annoys. Then there were a lot of wind instruments, drums, et cetera. There were 600 performers on the stage, counting the chorus, with 4,500 people in the house and 3,000 outside yelling at the ticket office—also at the top of their voices—and swearing because they couldn't mortgage their immortal souls and hear Nilsson's coin silver notes. It was frightful. The building settled twelve inches in those two hours and a half, the electric lights went out nine times for refreshments, and, on the whole, the entertainment was a grand success. The first time the lights adjourned, an usher came in on the stage through a side entrance with a kerosene lamp. I guess he would have stood there and held it for Nilsson to sing by, if 4,500 people hadn't with one voice laughed him out into the starless night. You might as well have tried to light benighted Africa with a white bean. I shall never forget how proud and buoyant he looked as he sailed in with that kerosene lamp with a soiled chimney on it, and how hurt and grieved he seemed when he took it and groped his way out, while the Coliseum trembled with ill-concealed merriment. I use the term "ill-concealed merriment" with permission of the proprietors, for this season only.

Dogs and Dog Days.

I TAKE occasion at this time to ask the American people as one man, what are we to do to prevent the spread of the most insidious and disagreeable disease known as hydrophobia? When a fellow-being has to be smothered, as was the case the other day right here in our fair land, a land where tyrant foot hath never trod nor bigot forged a chain, we look anxiously into each other's faces and inquire, what shall we do?

Shall we go to France at a great expense and fill our systems full of dog virus and then return to our glorious land, where we may fork over that virus to posterity and thus mix up French hydrophobia with the navy-blue blood of free-born American citizens?

I wot not.

If I knew that would be my last wot I would not change it. That is just wot it would be.

But again.

What shall we do to avoid getting impregnated with the American dog and then saturating our systems with the alien dog of Paris?

It is a serious matter, and if we do not want to play the Desdemona act we must take some timely precautions. What must those precautions be?

Did it ever occur to the average thinking mind that we might squeeze along for weeks without a dog? Whole families have existed for years after being deprived of dogs. Look at the wealthy of our land. They go on comfortably through life and die at last with the unanimous consent of their heirs dogless.

Then why cannot the poor gradually taper off on dogs? They ought not to stop all of a sudden, but they could leave off a dog at a time until at last they overcame the pernicious habit.

I saw a man in St. Paul last week who was once poor, and so owned seven variegated dogs. He was confirmed in that habit. But he summoned all his will-power at last and said he would shake off these dogs and become a man. He did so, and to-day he owns a city lot in St. Paul, and seems to be the picture of health.

The trouble about maintaining a dog is that he may go on for years in a quiet, gentlemanly way, winning the regard of all who know him, and then all of a sudden he may hydrophobe in the most violent manner. Not only that, but he may do so while we have company. He may also bite our twins or the twins of our warmest friends. He may bite us now and we may laugh at it, but in five years from now, while we are delivering a humorous lecture, we may burst forth into the audience and bite a beautiful young lady in the parquet or on the ear.

It is a solemn thing to think of, fellow-citizens, and I appeal to those who may read this, as a man who may not live to see a satisfactory political reform—I appeal to you to refrain from the dog. He is purely ornamental. We may love a good dog, but we ought to love our children more. It would be a very, very noble and expensive dog that I would agree to feed with my only son.

I know that we gradually become attached to a good dog, but some day he may become attached to us, and what can be sadder than the sight of a leading citizen drawing a reluctant mad dog down the street by main strength and the seat of his pantaloons? (I mean his own, not the dog's pants. ☞ This joke will appear in book form in April. The book will be very readable, and there will be another joke in it also. eod tf.)

I have said a good deal about the dog, pro and con, and I am not a rabid dog abolitionist, for no one loves to have his clear-cut features licked by the warm, wet tongue of a noble dog any more than I do, but rather than see hydrophobia become a national characteristic or a leading industry here, I would forego the dog.

Perhaps all men are that way, however. When they get a little forehanded they forget that they were once poor, and owned dogs. If so, I do not wish to be unfair. I want to be just, and I believe I am. Let us yield up our dogs and take the affection that we would otherwise bestow on them on some human being. I have tried it and it works well. There are thousands of people in the world, of both sexes, who are pining and starving for the love and money that we daily shower on the dog.

If the dog would be kind enough to refrain from introducing his justly celebrated virus into the person of those only who kiss him on the cold, moist nose, it would be all right; but when a dog goes mad he is very impulsive, and he may bestow himself on an obscure man. So I feel a little nervous myself.

Christopher Columbus.

PROBABLY few people have been more successful in the discovering line than Christopher Columbus. Living as he did in a day when a great many things were still in an undiscovered state, the horizon was filled with golden opportunities for a man possessed of Mr. C.'s pluck and ambition. His life at first was filled with rebuffs and disappointments, but at last he grew to be a man of importance in his own profession, and the people who wanted anything discovered would always bring it to him rather than take it elsewhere.

And yet the life of Columbus was a stormy one. Though he discovered a continent wherein a millionaire attracts no attention, he himself was very poor.

Though he rescued from barbarism a broad and beautiful land in whose metropolis the theft of less than half a million of dollars is regarded as petty larceny, Chris himself often went to bed hungry. Is it not singular that the gray-eyed and gentle Columbus should have added a hemisphere to the history of our globe, a hemisphere, too, where pie is a common thing, not only on Sunday, but throughout the week, and yet that he should have gone down to his grave pieless!

Such is the history of progress in all ages and in all lines of thought and investigation. Such is the meagre reward of the pioneer in new fields of action.

I presume that America to-day has a larger pie area than any other land in which the Cockney English language is spoken. Right here where millions of native born Americans dwell, many of whom are ashamed of the fact that they were born here and which shame is entirely mutual between the Goddess of Liberty and themselves, we have a style of pie that no other land can boast of.

From the bleak and acid dried apple pie of Maine to the irrigated mince pie of the blue Pacific, all along down the long line of igneous, volcanic and stratified pie, America, the land of the freedom bird with the high instep to his nose, leads the world.

Other lands may point with undissembled pride to their polygamy and their cholera, but we reck not. Our polygamy here is still in its infancy and our leprosy has had the disadvantage of a cold, backward spring, but look at our pie.

Throughout a long and disastrous war, sometimes referred to as a fratricidal war, during which this fair land was drenched in blood, and also during which aforesaid war numerous frightful blunders were made which are fast coming to the surface—through the courtesy of participants in said war who have patiently waited for those who blundered to die off, and now admit that said participants who are dead did blunder exceedingly throughout all this long and deadly struggle for the supremacy of liberty and right—as I was about to say when my mind began to wobble, the American pie has shown forth resplendent in the full glare of a noonday sun or beneath the pale-green of the electric light, and she stands forth proudly to-day with her undying loyalty to dyspepsia untrammeled and her deep and deadly gastric antipathy still fiercely burning in her breast.

That is the proud history of American pie. Powers, principalities, kingdoms and hand-made dynasties may crumble, but the republican form of pie does not crumble. Tyranny may totter on its throne, but the American pie does not totter. Not a tot. No foreign threat has ever been able to make our common chicken pie quail. I do not say this because it is smart; I simply say it to fill up.

But would it not do Columbus good to come among us to-day and look over our free institutions? Would it not please him to ride over this continent which has been rescued by his presence of mind from the thraldom of barbarism and forked over to the genial and refining influences of prohibition and pie?

America fills no mean niche in the great history of nations, and if you listen carefully for a few moments you will hear some American, with his mouth full of pie, make that remark. The American is always frank and perfectly free to state that no other country can approach this one. We allow no little two-for-a-quarter monarchy to excel us in the size of our failures or in the calm and self-poised deliberation with which we erect a monument to the glory of a worthy citizen who is dead, and therefore politically useless.

The careless student of the career of Columbus will find much in these lines that he has not yet seen. He will realize when he comes to read this little sketch the pains and the trouble and the research necessary before such an article on the life and work of Columbus could be written, and he will thank me for it; but it is not for that that I have done it. It is a pleasure for me to hunt up and arrange historical and biographical data in a pleasing form for the student and savant. I am only too glad to please and gratify the student and the savant. I was that way myself once and I know how to sympathize with them.

P. S.—I neglected to state that Columbus was a married man. Still, he did not murmur or repine.

Accepting the Laramie Postoffice.

Office of DAILY BOOMERANG, LARAMIE CITY, WY., Aug. 9, 1882.

MY DEAR GENERAL.—I have received by telegraph the news of my nomination by the President and my confirmation by the Senate, as postmaster at Laramie, and wish to extend my thanks for the same.

I have ordered an entirely new set of boxes and postoffice outfit, including new corrugated cuspidors for the lady clerks.

I look upon the appointment, myself, as a great triumph of eternal truth over error and wrong. It is one of the epochs, I may say, in the Nation's onward march toward political purity and perfection. I do not know when I have noticed any stride in the affairs of state, which so thoroughly impressed me with its wisdom

A NEW OFFICE OUTFIT.

Now that we are co-workers in the same department, I trust that you will not feel shy or backward in consulting me at any time relative to matters concerning postoffice affairs. Be perfectly frank with me, and feel perfectly free to just bring anything of that kind right to me. Do not feel reluctant because I may at times appear haughty and indifferent, cold or reserved. Perhaps you do not think I know the difference between a general delivery window and a three-m quad, but that is a mistake.

My general information is far beyond my years.

With profoundest regard, and a hearty endorsement of the policy of the President and the Senate, whatever it may be,

I remain, sincerely yours, BILL NYE, P. M.

GEN. FRANK HATTON, Washington, D. C.

A Journalistic Tenderfoot.

MOST everyone who has tried the publication of a newspaper will call to mind as he reads this item, a similar experience, though, perhaps, not so pronounced and protuberant.

Early one summer morning a gawky young tenderfoot, both as to the West and the details of journalism, came into the office and asked me for a job as correspondent to write up the mines in North Park. He wore his hair longish and tried to make it curl. The result was a greasy coat collar and the general *tout ensemble* of the genus "smart Aleck." He had also clothed himself in the extravagant clothes of the dime novel scout and beautiful girl-rescuer of the Indian country. He had been driven west by a wild desire to hunt the flagrant Sioux warrior, and do a general Wild Bill business; hoping, no doubt, before the season closed, to rescue enough beautiful captive maidens to get up a young Vassar College in Wyoming or Montana.

I told him that we did not care for a mining correspondent who did not know a piece of blossom rock from a geranium. I knew it took a man a good many years to gain knowledge enough to know where to sink a prospect shaft even, and as to passing opinions on a vein, it would seem almost wicked and sacriligious to send a man out there among those old grizzly miners who had spent their lives in bitter experience, unless the young man could readily distinguish the points of difference between a chunk of free milling quartz and a fragment of bologna sausage.

He still thought he could write us letters that would do the paper some eternal good, and though I told him, as he wrung my hand and left, to refrain from writing or doing any work for us, he wrote a letter before he had reached the home station on the stage road, or at least sent us a long letter from there. It might have been written before he started, however.

The letter was of the "we-have-went" and "I-have-never-saw" variety, and he spelt curiosity "qrossity." He worked hard to get the word into his alleged letter, and then assassinated it.

Well, we paid no attention whatever to the letter, but meantime he got into the mines, and the way he dead-headed feed and sour mash, on the strength of his relations with the press, made the older miners weep.

Buck Bramel got a little worried and wrote to me about it. He said that our soft-eyed mining savant was getting us a good many subscribers, and writing up every little gopher hole in North Park, and living on Cincinnati quail, as we miners call bacon; but he said that none of these fine, blooming letters, regarding the assays on "The Weasel Asleep," "The Pauper's Dream," "The Mary Ellen" and "The Over Draft," ever seemed to crop out in the paper.

Why was it?

I wrote back that the white-eyed pelican from the buckwheat-enamelled plains of Arkansas had not remitted, was not employed by us, and that I would write and publish a little card of introduction for the bilious litterateur that would make people take in their domestic animals, and lock up their front fences and garden fountains.

COMMUNING WITH NATURE.

In the meantime they sent him up the gulch to find some "float." He had wandered away from camp thirty miles before he remembered that he didn't know what float looked like. Then he thought he would go back and inquire. He got lost while in a dark brown study and drifted into the bosom of the unknowable. He didn't miss the trail until a perpendicular wall of the Rocky Mountains, about 900 feet high, rose up and hit him athwart the nose.

He communed with nature and the coyotes one night and had a pretty tough time of it. He froze his nose partially off, and the coyotes came and gnawed his little dimpled toes. He passed a wretched night, and was greatly annoyed by the cold, which at that elevation sends the mercury toward zero all through the summer nights.

Of course he pulled the zodiac partially over him, and tried to button his alapaca duster a little closer, but his sleep was troubled by the sociability of the coyotes and the midnight twitter of the mountain lion. He ate moss agates rare and spruce gum for breakfast. When he got to the camp he looked like a forty-day starvationist hunting for a job.

They asked him if he found any float, and he said he didn't find a blamed drop of water, say nothing about float, and then they all laughed a merry laugh, and said that if he showed up at daylight the next morning within the limits of the park, the orders were to burn him at the stake.

The next morning neither he nor the best bay mule on the Troublesome was to be seen with naked eye. After that we heard of him in the San Juan country.

He had lacerated the finer feelings of the miners down there, and had violated the etiquette of San Juan, so they kicked a flour barrel out from under him one day when he was looking the other way, and being a poor tight-rope performer, he got tangled up with a piece of inch rope in such a way that he died of his injuries.

The Amateur Carpenter.

IN my opinion every professional man should keep a chest of carpenters' tools in his barn or shop, and busy himself at odd hours with them in constructing the varied articles that are always needed about the house. There is a great deal of pleasure in feeling your own independence of other trades, and more especially of the carpenter. Every now and then your wife will want a bracket put up in some corner or other, and with your new, bright saw and glittering hammer you can put up one upon which she can hang a cast-iron horse-blanket lambrequin, with inflexible water lilies sewed in it.

A man will, if he tries, readily learn to do a great many such little things and his wife will brag on him to other ladies, and they will make invidious comparisons between their husbands who can't do anything of that kind whatever, and you who are "so handy."

Firstly, you buy a set of amateur carpenter tools. You do not need to say that you are an amateur. The dealer will find that out when you ask him for an easy-running broad-ax or a green-gage plumb line. He will sell you a set of amateur's tools that will be made of old sheet-iron with basswood handles, and the saws will double up like a piece of stovepipe.

After you have nailed a board on the fence successfully, you will very naturally desire to do something much better, more difficult. You will probable try to erect a parlor table or rustic settee.

I made a very handsome bracket last week, and I was naturally proud of it. In fastening it together, if I hadn't inadvertently nailed it to the barn floor, I guess I could have used it very well, but in tearing it loose from the barn, so that the two could be used separately, I ruined a bracket that was intended to serve as the base, as it were, of a lambrequin which cost nine dollars, aside from the time expended on it.

During the month of March I built an ice-chest for this summer. It was not handsome, but it was roomy, and would be very nice for the season of 1886, I thought. It worked pretty well through March and April, but as the weather begins to warm up that ice-chest is about the warmest place around the house. There is actually a glow of heat around that ice-chest that I don't notice elsewhere. I've shown it to several personal friends. They seem to think it is not built tightly enough for an ice-chest. My brother looked at it yesterday, and said that his idea of an ice-chest was that it ought to be tight enough at least to hold the larger chunks of ice so that they would not escape through the pores of the ice-box. He says he never built one, but that it stood to reason that a refrigerator like that ought to be constructed so that it would keep the cows out of it. You don't want to have a refrigerator that the cattle can get through the cracks of and eat up your strawberries on ice, he says.

A neighbor of mine who once built a hen resort of laths, and now wears a thick thumb-nail that looks like a Brazil nut as a memento of that pullet corral, says my ice-chest is all right enough, only that it is not suited to this climate. He thinks that along Behring's Strait, during the holidays, my ice-chest would work like a charm. And even here, he thought, if I could keep the fever out of my chest there would be less pain.

I have made several other little articles of *vertu* this spring, to the construction of which I have contributed a good deal of time and two finger nails. I have also sawed into my leg two or three times. The leg, of course, will get well, but the pantaloons will not. Parties wishing to meet me in my studio during the morning hour will turn into the alley between Eighth and Ninth streets, enter the third stable door on the left, pass around behind my Gothic horse, and give the countersign and three kicks on the door in an ordinary tone of voice.

The Average Hen.

I AM convinced that there is great economy in keeping hens if we have sufficient room for them and a thorough knowledge of how to manage the fowl properly. But to the professional man, who is not familiar with the habits of the hen, and whose mind does not naturally and instinctively turn henward, I would say: Shun her as you would the deadly upas tree of Piscataquis county, Me.

Nature has endowed the hen with but a limited amount of brain-force. Any one will notice that if he will compare the skull of the average self-made hen with that of Daniel Webster, taking careful measurements directly over the top from one ear to the other, the well-informed brain student will at once notice a great falling-off in the region of reverence and an abnormal bulging out in the location of alimentiveness.

Now take your tape-measure and, beginning at memory, pass carefully over the occiputal bone to the base of the brain in the region of love of home and offspring and you will see that, while the hen suffers much in comparison with the statement in the relative size of sublimity, reflection, spirituality, time, tune, etc., when it comes to love of home and offspring she shines forth with great splendor.

The hen does not care for the sublime in nature. Neither does she care for music. Music hath no charms to soften her tough old breast. But she loves her home and her country. I have sought to promote the interests of the hen to some extent, but I have not been a marked success in that line.

I can write a poem in fifteen minutes. I always could dash off a poem whenever I wanted to, and a very good poem, too, for a dashed poem. I could write a speech for a friend in congress—a speech that would be printed in the Congressional Record and go all over the United States and be read by no one. I could enter the field of letters anywhere and attract attention, but when it comes to setting a hen I feel that I am not worthy. I never feel my utter unworthiness as I do in the presence of a setting hen.

When the adult hen in my presence expresses a desire to set I excuse myself and go away. That is the supreme moment when a hen desires to be alone. That is no time for me to introduce my shallow levity. I never do it

It is after death that I most fully appreciate the hen. When she has been cut down early in life and fried I respect her. No one can look upon the still features of a young hen overtaken by death in life's young morning, snuffed out as it were, like an old tin lantern in a gale of wind, without being visibly affected.

But it is not the hen who desires to set for the purpose of getting out an early edition of spring chickens that I am averse to. It is the aged hen, who is in her dotage, and whose eggs, also, are in their second childhood. Upon this hen I shower my anathemas. Overlooked by the pruning-hook of time, shallow in her remarks, and a wall-flower in society, she deposits her quota of eggs in the catnip conservatory, far from the haunts of men, and then in August, when eggs are extremely low and her collection of no value to any one but the antiquarian, she proudly calls attention to her summer's work.

This hen does not win the general confidence. Shunned by good society during life, her death is only regretted by those who are called upon to assist at her obsequies. Selfish through life, her death is regarded as a calamity by those alone who are expected to eat her.

And what has such a hen to look back upon in her closing hours? A long life, perhaps, for longevity is one of the characteristics of this class of hens; but of what has that life been productive? How many golden hours has she frittered away hovering over a porcelain door-knob trying to hatch out a litter of Queen Anne cottages. How many nights has she passed in solitude on her lonely nest, with a heart filled with bitterness toward all mankind, hoping on against hope that in the fall she would come off the nest with a cunning little brick block, perhaps.

THE RESULT OF PATIENCE.

Such is the history of the aimless hen. While others were at work she stood around with her hands in her pockets and criticised the policy of those who labored, and when the summer waned she came forth with nothing but regret to wander listlessly about and freeze off some more of her feet during the winter. For such a hen death can have no terrors.

Woodtick William's Story.

"WE had about as ornery and triflin' a crop of kids in Calaveras county, thirty years ago, as you could gather in with a fine-tooth comb and a brass band in fourteen States. For ways that was kittensome they were moderately active and abnormally protuberant. That was the prevailing style of Calaveras kid, when Mr. George W Mulqueen come there and wanted to engage the school at the old camp, where I hung up in the days when the country was new and the murmur of the six-shooter was heard in the land.

"George W Mulqueen was a slender young party from the effete East, with conscientious scruples and a hectic flush. Both of these was agin him for a promoter of school discipline and square root. He had a heap of information and big sorrowful eyes.

"So fur as I was concerned, I didn't feel like swearing around George or using any language that would sound irrelevant in a ladies' boodore; but as for the kids of the school, they didn't care a blamed cent. They just hollered and whooped like a passle of Sioux.

WINNING THEIR YOUNG LOVE.

"They didn't seem to respect literary attainments or expensive knowledge. They just simply seemed to respect the genius that come to that country to win their young love with a long-handled shovel and a blood-shot tone of voice. That's what seemed to catch the Calaveras kids in the early days.

"George had weak lungs, and they kept to work at him till they drove him into a mountain fever, and finally into a metallic sarcophagus.

"Along about the holidays the sun went down on George W Mulqueen's life, just as the eternal sunlight lit up the dewy eyes. You will pardon my manner, Nye, but it seemed to me just as if George had climbed up to the top of Mount Cavalry, or wherever it was, with that whole school on his back, and had to give up at last.

"It seemed kind of tough to me, and I couldn't help blamin' it onto the school some, for there was a half a dozen big snoozers that didn't go to school to learn, but just to raise Ned and turn up Jack.

"Well, they killed him, anyhow, and that settled it.

* * * * * * * * *

"The school run kind of wild till Feboowary, and then a husky young tenderfoot, with a fist like a mule's foot in full bloom, made an application for the place, and allowed he thought he could maintain discipline if they'd give him a chance. Well, they ast him when he wanted to take his place as tutor, and he reckoned he could begin to tute about Monday follering.

"Sunday afternoon he went up to the school-house to look over the ground, and to arrange a plan for an active Injin campaign agin the hostile hoodlums of Calaveras.

"Monday he sailed in about 9 A. M. with his grip-sack, and begun the discharge of his juties.

"He brought in a bunch of mountain-willers, and, after driving a big railroad-spike into the door-casing, over the latch, he said the senate and house would sit with closed doors during the morning session. Several large, white-eyed holy terrors gazed at him in a kind of dumb, inquiring tone of voice, but he didn't say much. He seemed considerably reserved as to the plan of the campaign. The new teacher then unlocked his alligator-skin grip, and took out a Bible and a new self-cocking weepon that had an automatic dingus for throwing out the empty shells. It was one of the bull-dog variety, and had the laugh of a joyous child.

"He read a short passage from the Scriptures, and then pulled off his coat and hung it on a nail. Then he made a few extemporaneous remarks, after which he salivated the palm of his right hand, took the self-cocking songster in his left, and proceeded to wear out the gads over the varied protuberances of his pupils.

"People passing by thought they must be beating carpets in the school-house. He pointed the gun at his charge with his left and manipulated the gad with his right duke. One large, overgrown Missourian tried to crawl out of the winder, but, after he had looked down the barrel of the shooter a moment, he changed his mind. He seemed to realize that it would be a violation of the rules of the school, so he came back and sat down.

"After he wore out the foliage, Bill, he pulled the spike out of that door, put on his coat and went away He never was seen there again. He didn't ask for any salary, but just walked off quietly, and that summer we accidently heard that he was George W. Mulqueen's brother."

In Washington.

I HAVE just returned from a polite and recherche party here. Washington is the hot-bed of gayety, and general headquarters for the recherche business. It would be hard to find a bontonger aggregation than the one I was just at, to use the words of a gentleman who was there, and who asked me if I wrote "The Heathen Chinee."

He was a very talented man, with a broad sweep of skull and a vague yearning for something more tangible—to drink. He was in Washington, he said, in the interests of Mingo county I forgot to ask him where Mingo county might be. He took a great interest in me, and talked with me long after he really had anything to say He was one of those fluent conversationalists frequently met with in society. He used one of these web-perfecting talkers—the kind that can be fed with raw Roman punch, and that will turn out punctuated talk in links, like varnished sausages. Being a poor talker myself, and rather more fluent as a listener, I did not interrupt him.

He said that he was sorry to notice how young girls and their parents came to Washington as they would to a matrimonial market.

I was sorry also to hear it. It pained me to know that young ladies should allow themselves to be bamboozled into matrimony. Why was it, I asked, that matrimony should ever single out the young and fair?

"Ah," said he, "it is indeed rough!"

He then breathed a sigh that shook the foilage of the speckled geranium near by, and killed an artificial caterpillar that hung on its branches.

"Matrimony is all right," said he, "if properly brought about. It breaks my heart, though, to notice how Washington is used as a matrimonial market. It seems to me almost as if these here young ladies were brought here like slaves and exposed for sale." I had noticed that they were somewhat exposed, but I did not know that they were for sale. I asked him if the waists of party dresses had always been so sadly in the minority, and he said they had.

I danced with a beautiful young lady whose trail had evidently caught in a doorway She hadn't noticed it till she had walked out partially through her costume.

I do not think a lady ought to give too much thought to her apparel; neither should she feel too much above her clothes. I say this in the kindest spirit, because I believe that man should be a friend to woman. No family circle is complete without a woman. She is like a glad landscape to the weary eye. Individually and collectively, woman is a great adjunct of civilization and progress. The electric light is a good thing, but how pale and feeble it looks by the light of a good woman's eyes. The telephone is a great invention. It is a good thing to talk at, and murmur into and deposit profanity in; but to take up a conversation, and keep it up, and follow a man out through the front door with it, the telephone has still much to learn from woman.

It is said that our government officials are not sufficiently paid; and I presume that is the case, so it became necessary to economize in every way; but, why should wives concentrate all their economy on the waist of a dress? When chest protectors are so cheap as they now are, I hate to see people suffer, and there is more real suffering, more privation and more destitution, pervading the Washington scapula and clavicle this winter than I ever saw before.

But I do not hope to change this custom, though I spoke to several ladies about it, and asked them to think it over. I do not think they will. It seems almost wicked to cut off the best part of a dress and put it at the other end of the skirt, to be trodden under feet of men, as I may say. They smiled good humoredly at me as I tried to impress my views upon them, but should I go there again next season and mingle in the mad whirl of Washington, where these fair women are also mingling in said mad whirl, I presume that I will find them clothed in the same gaslight waist, with trimmings of real vertebræ down the back.

Still, what does a man know about the proper costume of a woman? He knows nothing whatever. He is in many ways a little inconsistent. Why does a man frown on a certain costume for his wife, and admire it on the first woman he meets? Why does he fight shy of religion and Christianity and talk very freely about the church, but get mad if his wife is an infidel?

Crops around Washington are looking well. Winter wheat, crocusses and indefinite postponements were never in a more thrifty condition. Quite a number of people are here who are waiting to be confirmed. Judging from their habits, they are lingering around here in order to become confirmed drunkards.

I leave here to-morrow with a large, wet towel in my plug hat. Perhaps

I should have said nothing on this dress reform question while my hat is fitting me so immediately. It is seldom that I step aside from the beaten path of rectitude, but last evening, on the way home, it seemed to me that I didn't do much else but step aside. At these parties no charge is made for punch. It is perfectly free. I asked a colored man who was standing near the punch bowl, and who replenished it ever and anon, what the damage was, and he drew himself up to his full height.

Possibly I did wrong, but I hate to be a burden on anyone. It seemed odd to me to go to a first-class dance and find the supper and the band and the rum all paid for. It must cost a good deal of money to run this government.

My Experience as an Agriculturist.

DURING the past season I was considerably interested in agriculture. I met with some success, but not enough to madden me with joy. It takes a good deal of success to unscrew my reason and make it totter on its throne. I've had trouble with my liver, and various other abnormal conditions of the vital organs, but old reason sits there on his or her throne, as the case may be, through it all.

Agriculture has a charm about it which I can not adequately describe. Every product of the farm is furnished by nature with something that loves it, so that it will never be neglected. The grain crop is loved by the weevil, the Hessian fly and the chinch bug; the watermelon, the squash and the cucumber are loved by the squash bug; the potato is loved by the potato bug; the sweet corn is loved by the ant, thou sluggard; the tomato is loved by the cut-worm; the plum is loved by the curculio, and so forth, and so forth, so that no plant that grows need be a wall-flower. [Early blooming and extremely dwarf joke for the table. Plant as soon as there is no danger of frosts, in drills four inches apart. When ripe, pull it, and eat raw with vinegar. The red ants may be added to taste.]

Well, I began early to spade up my angle-worms and other pets, to see if they had withstood the severe winter. I found they had. They were unusually bright and cheerful. The potato bugs were a little sluggish at first, but as the spring opened and the ground warmed up they pitched right in, and did first-rate. Every one of my bugs in May looked splendidly I was most worried about my cut-worms. Away along in April I had not seen a cut-worm, and I began to fear they had suffered, and perhaps perished, in the extreme cold of the previous winter.

One morning late in the month, however, I saw a cut-worm come out from behind a cabbage stump and take off his ear muff. He was a little stiff in the joints, but he had not lost hope. I saw at once now was the time to assist him if I had a spark of humanity left. I searched every work I could find on agriculture to find out what it was that farmers fed their blamed cut-worms, but all scientists seemed to be silent. I read the agricultural reports, the dictionary, and the encyclopedia, but they didn't throw any light on the subject. I got wild. I feared that I had brought but one cut-worm through the winter, and I was liable to lose him unless I could find out what to feed him. I asked some of my neighbors, but they spoke jeeringly and sarcastically. I know now how it was. All their cut-worms had frozen down last winter, and they couldn't bear to see me get ahead.

THEY SPOKE JEERINGLY.

All at once, an idea struck me. I haven't recovered from the concussion yet. It was this: the worm had wintered under a cabbage stalk; no doubt he was fond of the beverage. I acted upon this thought and bought him two dozen red cabbage plants, at fifty cents a dozen. I had hit it the first pop. He was passionately fond of these plants, and would eat three in one night. He also had several matinees and sauerkraut lawn festivals for his friends, and in a week I bought three dozen more cabbage plants. By this time I had collected a large group of common scrub cut-worms, early Swedish cut-worms, dwarf Hubbard cut-worms, and short-horn cut-worms, all doing well, but still, I thought, a little hide-bound and bilious. They acted languid and listless. As my squash bugs, currant worms, potato bugs, etc., were all doing well without care, I devoted myself almost exclusively to my cut-worms. They were all strong and well, but they seemed melancholy with nothing to eat, day after day, but cabbages.

I therefore bought five dozen tomato plants that were tender and large. These I fed to the cut-worms at the rate of eight or ten in one night. In a week the cut-worms had thrown off that air of *ennui* and languor that I had formerly noticed, and were gay and light-hearted. I got them some more tomato plants, and then some more cabbage for change. On the whole I was as proud as any young farmer who has made a success of anything.

One morning I noticed that a cabbage plant was left standing unchanged. The next day it was still there. I was thunderstruck. I dug into the ground. My cut-worms were gone. I spaded up the whole patch, but there wasn't one. Just as I had become attached to them, and they had learned to look forward each day to my coming, when they would almost come up and eat a tomato-plant out of my hand, some one had robbed me of them. I was almost wild with despair and grief. Suddenly something tumbled over my foot. It was mostly stomach, but it had feet on each corner. A neighbor said it was a warty toad. He had eaten up my summer's work! He had swallowed my cunning little cut-worms. I tell you, gentle reader, unless some way is provided, whereby this warty toad scourge can be wiped out, I for one shall relinquish the joys of agricultural pursuits. When a common toad, with a sallow complexion and no intellect, can swallow up my summer's work, it is time to pause.

A New Autograph Album.

THIS autograph business is getting to be a little bit tedious. It is all one-sided. I want to get even some how, on some one. If I can't come back at the autograph fiend himself, perhaps I might make some other fellow creature unhappy. That would take my mind off the woes that are inflicted by the man who is making a collection of the autographs of "prominent men," and who sends a printed circular formally demanding your autograph, as the tax collector would demand your tax.

John Comstock, the President of the First National Bank, of Hudson, the other day suggested an idea. I gave him an autograph copy of my last great work, and he said. "Now, I'm a man of business. You gave me your autograph, I give you mine in return. That's what we call business." He then signed a brand new $5 national bank note, the cashier did ditto, and the two autographs were turned over to me.

Now, how would it do to make a collection of the signatures of the presidents and cashiers of national banks of the United States in the above manner? An album containing the autographs of these bank officials would not only be a handsome heirloom to fork over to posterity, but it would possess intrinsic value. In pursuance of this idea, I have been considering the advisability of issuing the following letter:

To the Presidents and Cashiers of the National Banks of the United States.

GENTLEMEN—I am now engaged in making a collection of the autographs of the presidents and cashiers of national banks throughout the Union, and to make the collection uniform, I have decided to ask for autographs written at the foot of the national currency bank note of the denomination of $5. I am not sectarian in my religious views, and I only suggest this denomination for the sake of uniformity throughout the album.

Card collections, cat albums and so forth, may please others, but I prefer to make a collection that shall show future ages who it was that built up our finances, and furnished the sinews of war. Some may look upon this move as a mercenary one, but with me it is a passion. It is not simply a freak, it is a desire of my heart.

In return I would be glad to give my own autograph, either by itself or attached to some little gem of thought which might occur to my mind at the time.

I have always taken a great interest in the currency of the country So far as possible I have made it a study. I have watched its growth, and noted with some regret its natural reserve. I may say that, considering meagre opportunities and isolated advantages afforded me, no one is more familiar with the habits of our national currency than I am. Yet, at times my laboratory has not been so abundantly supplied with specimens as I could have wished. This has been my chief drawback.

I began a collection of railroad passes some time ago, intending to file them away and pass the collection down through the dim vista of coming years, but in a rash moment I took a trip of several thousand miles, and those passes were taken up.

I desire, in conclusion, gentlemen, to call your attention to the fact that I have always been your friend and champion. I have never robbed the bank of a personal friend, and if I held your autographs I should deem you my personal friends, and feel in honor bound to discourage any movement looking toward an unjust appropriation of the funds of your bank. The autographs of yourselves in my possession, and my own in your hands, would be regarded as a tacit agreement on my part never to rob your bank. I would even be willing to enter into a contract with you not to break into your vaults, if you insist upon it. I would thus be compelled to confine myself to the stage coaches and railroad trains in a great measure, but I am getting now so I like to spend my evenings at home, anyhow, and if I do well this year, I shall sell my burglars' tools and give myself up to the authorities.

You will understand, gentlemen, the delicate nature of this request, I trust, and not misconstrue my motives. My intentions are perfectly honorable, and my idea in doing this is, I may say, to supply a long felt want.

Hoping that what I have said will meet with your approval and hearty co-operation, and that our very friendly business relations, as they have existed in the past, may continue through the years to come, and that your bank may wallow in success till the cows come home, or words to that effect, I beg leave to subscribe myself, yours in favor of one country, one flag and one bank account.

A Resign.

POSTOFFICE DIVAN, LARAMIE CITY, W T., Oct. 1, 1883.

TO THE PRESIDENT OF THE UNITED STATES:

SIR.—I beg leave at this time to officially tender my resignation as postmaster at this place, and in due form to deliver the great seal and the key to the front door of the office. The safe combination is set on the numbers 33, 66 and 99, though I do not remember at this moment which comes first, or how many times you revolve the knob, or which direction you should turn it at first in order to make it operate.

There is some mining stock in my private drawer in the safe, which I have not yet removed. This stock you may have, if you desire it. It is a luxury, but you may have it. I have decided to keep a horse instead of this mining stock. The horse may not be so pretty, but it will cost less to keep him.

You will find the postal cards that have not been used under the distributing table, and the coal down in the cellar. If the stove draws too hard, close the damper in the pipe and shut the general delivery window.

Looking over my stormy and eventful administration as postmaster here, I find abundant cause for thanksgiving. At the time I entered upon the duties of my office the department was not yet on a paying basis. It was not even self-sustaining. Since that time, with the active co-operation of the chief executive and the heads of the department, I have been able to make our postal system a paying one, and on top of that I am now able to reduce the tariff on average-sized letters from three cents to two. I might add that this is rather too too, but I will not say anything that might seem undignified in an official resignation which is to become a matter of history.

Through all the vicissitudes of a tempestuous term of office I have safely passed. I am able to turn over the office to-day in a highly improved condition, and to present a purified and renovated institution to my successor.

Acting under the advice of Gen. Hatton, a year ago, I removed the feather bed with which my predecessor, Deacon Hayford, had bolstered up his administration by stuffing the window, and substituted glass. Finding nothing in the book of instructions to postmasters which made the feather bed a part of my official duties, I filed it away in an obscure place and burned it in effigy, also in the gloaming. This act maddened my predecessor to such a degree, that he then and there became a candidate for justice of the peace on the Democratic ticket. The Democratic party was able, however, with what aid it secured from the Republicans, to plow the old man under to a great degree.

STRICT ATTENTION TO BUSINESS.

It was not long after I had taken my official oath before an era of unexampled prosperity opened for the American people. The price of beef rose to a remarkable altitude, and other vegetables commanded a good figure and a ready market. We then began to make active preparations for the introduction of the strawberry-roan two-cent stamps and the black-and-tan postal note. One reform has crowded upon the heels of another, until the country is to-day upon the foam-crested wave of permanent prosperity

Mr. President, I cannot close this letter without thanking yourself and the heads of departments at Washington for your active, cheery and prompt co-operation in these matters. You can do as you see fit, of course, about incorporating this idea into your Thanksgiving proclamation, but rest assured it would not be ill-timed or inopportune. It is not alone a credit to myself. It reflects credit upon the administration also.

I need not say that I herewith transmit my resignation with great sorrow and genuine regret. We have toiled on together month after month, asking for no reward except the innate consciousness of rectitude and the salary as fixed by law. Now we are to separate. Here the roads seem to fork, as it were, and you and I, and the cabinet, must leave each other at this point.

You will find the key under the door-mat, and you had better turn the cat out at night when you close the office. If she does not go readily, you can make it clearer to her mind by throwing the cancelling stamp at her.

If Deacon Hayford does not pay up his box-rent, you might as well put his mail in the general delivery, and when Bob Head gets drunk and insists on a letter from one of his wives every day in the week, you can salute him through the box delivery with an old Queen Anne tomahawk, which you will find near the Etruscan water-pail. This will not in any manner surprise either of these parties.

Tears are unavailing. I once more become a private citizen, clothed only with the right to read such postal cards as may be addressed to me personally, and to curse the inefficiency of the postoffice department. I believe the voting class to be divided into two parties, viz Those who are in the postal service, and those who are mad because they cannot receive a registered letter every fifteen minutes of each day, including Sunday.

Mr. President, as an official of this Government I now retire. My term of office would not expire until 1886. I must, therefore, beg pardon for my eccentricity in resigning. It will be best, perhaps, to keep the heart-breaking news from the ears of European powers until the dangers of a financial panic are fully past. Then hurl it broadcast with a sickening thud.

My Mine.

I HAVE decided to sacrifice another valuable piece of mining property this spring. It would not be sold if I had the necessary capital to develop it. It is a good mine, for I located it myself. I remember well the day I climbed up on the ridge-pole of the universe and nailed my location notice to the eaves of the sky

It was in August that I discovered the Vanderbilt claim in a snow-storm. It cropped out apparently a little southeast of a point where the arc of the orbit of Venus bisects the milky way, and ran due east eighty chains, three links and a swivel, thence south fifteen paces and a half to a blue spot in the sky, thence proceeding west eighty chains, three links of sausage and a half to a fixed star, thence north across the lead to place of beginning.

The Vanderbilt set out to be a carbonate deposit, but changed its mind. I sent a piece of the cropping to a man over in Salt Lake, who is a good assayer and quite a scientist, if he would brace up and avoid humor. His assay read as follows to-wit:

SALT LAKE CITY, U. T., August 25, 1877.

MR. BILL NYE:—Your specimen of ore No. 35832, current series, has been submitted to assay and shows the following result:

Metal.	Ounces.	Value per ton.
Gold	--	--
Silver	--	--
Railroad iron	1	--
Pyrites of poverty	9	--
Parasites of disappointment	90	--

MCVICKER, Assayer.

NOTE.—I also find that the formation is igneous, prehistoric and erroneous. If I were you I would sink a prospect shaft below the vertical slide where the old red brimstone and preadamite slag cross-cut the malachite and intersect the schist. I think that would be schist about as good as anything you could do. Then send me specimens with $2 for assay and we shall see what we shall see.

Well, I didn't know he was "an humorist," you see, so I went to work on the Vanderbilt to try and do what Mac. said. I sank a shaft and everything else I could get hold of on that claim. It was so high that we had to carry water up there to drink when we began and before fall we had struck a vein of the richest water you ever saw. We had more water in that mine than the regular army could use.

When we got down sixty feet I sent some pieces of the pay streak to the assayer again. This time he wrote me quite a letter, and at the same time inclosed the certificate of assay.

SALT LAKE CITY, U. T., October 3, 1877.

MR. BILL NYE:—Your specimen of ore No. 36132, current series, has been submitted to assay and shows the following result:

Metal.	Ounces.	Value per ton.
Gold	--	--
Silver	--	--
Stove polish	trace	.01
Old gray whetstone	trace	.01
Bromide of axle grease	stain	--
Copperas	trace	5c worth
Blue vitrol	trace	5c worth

McVICKER, Assayer.

In the letter he said there was, no doubt, something in the claim if I could get the true contact with calcimine walls denoting a true fissure. He thought I ought to run a drift. I told him I had already run adrift.

Then he said to stope out my stove polish ore and sell it for enough to go on with the development. I tried that, but capital seemed coy. Others had been there before me and capital bade me soak my head and said other things which grated harshly on my sensitive nature.

The Vanderbilt mine, with all its dips, spurs, angles, variations, veins, sinuosities, rights, titles, franchises, prerogatives and assessments is now for sale. I sell it in order to raise the necessary funds for the development of the Governor of North Carolina. I had so much trouble with water in the Vanderbilt, that I named the new claim the Governor of North Carolina, because he was always dry.

Mush and Melody.

LATELY I have been giving a good deal of attention to hygiene—in other people. The gentle reader will notice that, as a rule, the man who gives the most time and thought to this subject is an invalid himself; just as the young theological student devotes his first sermon to the care of children, and the ward politician talks the smoothest on the subject of how and when to plant ruta-bagas or wean a calf from the parent stem.

Having been thrown into the society of physicians a great deal the past two years, mostly in the role of patient, I have given some study to the human form; its structure and idiosyncracies, as it were. Perhaps few men in the same length of time have successfully acquired a larger or more select repertoire of choice diseases than I have. I do not say this boastfully. I simply desire to call the attention of our growing youth to the glorious possibilities that await the ambitious and enterprising in this line.

Starting out as a poor boy, with few advantages in the way of disease, I have resolutely carved my way up to the dizzy heights of fame as a chronic invalid and drug-soaked relic of other days. I inherited no disease whatever. My ancestors were poor and healthy. They bequeathed me no snug little nucleus of fashionable malaria such as other boys had. I was obliged to acquire it myself. Yet I was not discouraged. The results have shown that disease is not alone the heritage of the wealthy and the great. The poorest of us may become eminent invalids if we will only go at it in the right way But I started out to say something on the subject of health, for there are still many common people who would rather be healthy and unknown than obtain distinction with some dazzling new disease.

Noticing many years ago that imperfect mastication and dyspepsia walked hand in hand, so to speak, Mr. Gladstone adopted in his family a regular mastication scale; for instance, thirty-two bites for steak, twenty-two for fish, and so forth. Now I take this idea and improve upon it. Two statesmen can always act better in concert if they will do so.

With Mr. Gladstone's knowledge of the laws of health and my own musical genius, I have hit on a way to make eating not only a duty, but a pleasure. Eating is too frequently irksome. There is nothing about it to make it attractive.

What we need is a union of mush and melody, if I may be allowed that expression. Mr. Gladstone has given us the graduated scale, so that we know just what metre a bill of fare goes in as quick as we look at it. In this way the day is not far distant when music and mastication will march down through the dim vista of years together.

The Baked Bean Chant, the Vermicelli Waltz, the Mush and Milk March, the sad and touchful Pumpkin Pie Refrain, the gay and rollicking Oxtail Soup Gallop, and the melting Ice Cream Serenade will yet be common musical names.

Taking different classes of food, I have set them to music in such a way that the meal, for instance, may open with a Soup Overture, to be followed by a Roast Beef March in C, and so on, closing with a kind of Mince Pie La Somnambula pianissimo in G. Space, of course, forbids an extended description of this idea as I propose to carry it out, but the conception is certainly grand. Let us picture the jaws of a whole family moving in exact time to a Strauss waltz on the silent remains of the late lamented hen, and we see at once how much real pleasure may be added to the process of mastication.

The Blase Young Man.

I HAVE just formed the acquaintance of a *blase* young man. I have been on an extended trip with him. He is about twenty-two years old, but he is already weary of life. He was very careful all the time never to be exuberant. No matter how beautiful the landscape, he never allowed himself to exube.

Several times I succeeded in startling him enough to say "Ah!" but that was all. He had the air all the time of a man who had been reared in luxury and fondled so much in the lap of wealth that he was weary of life, and yearned for a bright immortality. I have often wished that the pruning-hook of time would use a little more discretion. The *blase* young man seemed to be tired all the time. He was weary of life because life was hollow

He seemed to hanker for the cool and quiet grave. I wished at times that the hankering might have been more mutual. But what does a cool, quiet grave want of a young man who never did anything but breathe the nice pure air into his froggy lungs and spoil it for everybody else?

This young man had a large grip-sack with him which he frequently consulted. I glanced into it once while he left it open. It was not right, but I did it. I saw the following articles in it:

31 Assorted Neckties.
1 pair Socks (whole).
1 pair do. (not so whole).
17 Collars.
1 Shirt.
1 quart Cuff-Buttons.
1 suit discouraged Gauze Underwear.
1 box Speckled Handkerchiefs.
1 box Condition Powders.
1 Toothbrush (prematurely bald).
1 copy Martin F Tupper's Works.
1 box Prepared Chalk.
1 Pair Tweezers for encouraging Moustache to come out to breakfast.
1 Powder Rag.
1 Gob ecru-colored Taffy
1 Hair-brush, with Ginger Hair in it.
1 Pencil to pencil Moustache at night.
1 Bread and Milk Poultice to put on Moustache on retiring, so that it will not forget to come out again the next day.
1 Box Trix for the breath.
1 Box Chloride of Lime to use in case breath becomes unmanageable.
1 Ear-spoon (large size).
1 Plain Mourning Head for Cane.
1 Vulcanized Rubber Head for Cane (to bite on).

1 Shoe-horn to use in working Ears into Ear-Muffs.
1 Pair Corsets.
1 Dark-brown Wash for Mouth, to be used in the morning.
1 Large Box *Ennui*, to be used in Society
1 Box Spruce Gum, made in Chicago and warranted pure.
1 Gallon Assorted Shirt Studs.
1 Polka-dot Handkerchief to pin in side pocket, but not for nose.
1 Plain Handkerchief for nose.
1 Fancy Head for Cane (morning).
1 Fancy Head for Cane (evening).
1 Picnic Head for Cane.
1 Bottle Peppermint.
1 do. Catnip.
1 Waterbury Watch.
7 Chains for same.
1 Box Letter Paper.
1 Stick Sealing Wax (baby blue).
1 do " (Bismarck brindle).
1 do " (mashed gooseberry).
1 Seal for same.
1 Family Crest (wash-tub rampant on a field calico).

HE IS NIX BONUM.

There were other little articles of virtu and bric-a-brac till you couldn't rest, but these were all that I could see thoroughly before he returned from the wash-room.

I do not like the *blase* young man as a traveling companion. He is *nix bonum*. He is too *E pluribus* for me. He is not *de trop* or *sciatica* enough to suit my style.

If he belonged to me I would picket him out somewhere in a hostile Indian country, and then try to nerve myself up for the result.

It is better to go through life reading the signs on the ten-story buildings and acquiring knowledge, than to dawdle and "Ah!" adown our pathway to the tomb and leave no record for posterity except that we had a good neck to pin a necktie upon. It is not pleasant to be called green, but I would rather be green and aspiring than *blase* and hide-bound at nineteen.

Let us so live that when at last we pass away our friends will not be immediately and uproariously reconciled to our death.

History of Babylon.

THE history of Babylon is fraught with sadness. It illustrates, only too painfully, that the people of a town make or mar its success rather than the natural resources and advantages it may possess on the start. Thus Babylon, with 3,000 years the start of Minneapolis, is to-day a hole in the ground, while Minneapolis socks her XXXX flour into every corner of the globe, and the price of real estate would make a common dynasty totter on its throne.

Babylon is a good illustration of the decay of a town that does not keep up with the procession. Compare her to-day with Kansas City While Babylon was the capital of Chaldea, 1,270 years before the birth of Christ, and Kansas City was organized so many years after that event that many of the people there have forgotten all about it, Kansas City has doubled her population in ten years, while Babylon is simply a gothic hole in the ground.

Why did trade and emigration turn their backs upon Babylon and seek out Minneapolis, St. Paul, Kansas City and Omaha? Was it because they were blest with a bluer sky or a more genial sun? Not by any means. While Babylon lived upon what she had been and neglected to advertise, other towns with no history extending back into the mouldy past, whooped with an exceeding great whoop and tore up the ground and shed printers' ink and showed marked signs of vitality. That is the reason that Babylon is no more.

This life of ours is one of intense activity. We cannot rest long in idleness without inviting forgetfulness, death and oblivion. "Babylon was probably the largest and most magnificent city of the ancient world." Isaiah, who lived about 300 years before Herodotus, and whose remarks are unusually free from local or political prejudice, refers to Babylon as "the glory of kingdoms, the beauty of the Chaldic's excellency," and, yet, while Cheyenne has the electric light and two daily papers, Babylon hasn't got so much as a skating rink.

A city fourteen miles square with a brick wall around it 355 feet high, she has quietly forgotten to advertise, and in turn she, also, is forgotten.

Babylon was remarkable for the two beautiful palaces, one on each side of the river, and the great temple of Belus. Connected with one of these palaces was the hanging garden, regarded by the Greeks as one of the seven wonders of the world, but that was prior to the erection of the Washington monument and civil service reform.

This was a square of 400 Greek feet on each side. The Greek foot was not so long as the modern foot introduced by Miss Mills, of Ohio. This garden was supported on several tiers of open arches, built one over the other, like the walls of a classic theatre, and sustaining at each stage, or story, a solid platform from which the arches of the next story sprung. This structure was also supported by the common council of Babylon, who came forward with the city funds, and helped to sustain the immense weight.

It is presumed that Nebuchadnezzar erected this garden before his mind became affected. The tower of Belus, supposed by historians with a good memory to have been 600 feet high, as there is still a red chalk mark in the sky where the top came, was a great thing in its way. I am glad I was not contiguous to it when it fell, and also that I had omitted being born prior to that time.

"When we turn from this picture of the past," says the historian, Rawlinson, referring to the beauties of Babylon, "to comtemplate the present condition of these localities, we are at first struck with astonishment at the small traces which remain of so vast and wonderful a metropolis. The broad walls of Babylon are utterly broken down. God has swept it with the besom of destruction,"

One cannot help wondering why the use of the besom should have been abandoned. As we gaze upon the former site of Babylon we are forced to admit that the new besom sweeps clean. On its old site no crumbling arches or broken columns are found to indicate her former beauty. Here and there huge heaps of debris alone indicate that here Godless wealth and wicked, selfish, indolent, enervating, ephemeral pomp, rose and defied the supreme laws to which the bloated, selfish millionaire and the hard-handed, hungry laborer alike must bow, and they are dust to-day.

Babylon has fallen. I do not say this in a sensational way or to depreciate the value of real estate there, but from actual observation, and after a full investigation, I assert without fear of successful contradiction, that Babylon has seen her best days. Her boomlet is busted, and, to use a political phrase, her oriental hide is on the Chaldean fence.

Such is life. We enter upon it reluctantly; we wade through it doubtfully, and die at last timidly. How we Americans do blow about what we can do before breakfast, and, yet, even in our own brief history, how we have demonstrated what a little thing the common two-legged man is. He rises up rapidly to acquire much wealth, and if he delays about going to Canada he goes to Sing Sing, and we forget about him. There are lots of modern Babylonians in New York City to-day, and if it were my business I would call their attention to it. The assertion that gold will procure all things has been so common and so popular that too many consider first the bank account, and after that honor, home, religion, humanity and common decency. Even some of the churches have fallen into the notion that first comes the tall church, then the debt and mortgage, the ice cream sociable and the kingdom of Heaven. Cash and Christianity go hand in hand sometimes, but Christianity ought not to confer respectability on anbody who comes into the church to purchase it.

I often think of the closing appeal of the old preacher, who was more earnest than refined, perhaps, and in winding up his brief sermon on the Christian life, said: "A man may lose all his wealth and get poor and hungry and still recover, he may lose his health and come down clost to the dark stream and still git well again, but, when he loses his immortal soul it is good-bye John."

Lovely Horrors.

I DROPPED in the other day to see New York's great congress of wax figures and soft statuary carnival. It is quite a success. The first thing you do on entering is to contribute to the pedestal fund. New York this spring is mostly a large rectangular box with a hole in the top, through which the genial public is cordially requested to slide a dollar to give the goddess of liberty a boom.

I was astonished and appalled at the wealth of apertures in Gotham through which I was expected to slide a dime to assist some deserving object. Every little while you run into a free-lunch room where there is a model ship that will start up and operate if you feed it with a nickle. I never visited a town that offered so many inducements for early and judicious investments as New York.

But we were speaking of the wax works. I did not tarry long to notice the presidents of the United States embalmed in wax, or to listen to the band of lutists who furnished music in the winter garden. I ascertained where the chamber of horrors was located, and went there at once. It is lovely I have never seen a more successful aggregation of horrors under one roof and at one price of admission.

If you want to be shocked at cost, or have your pores opened for a merely nominal price, and see a show that you will never forget as long as you live, that is the place to find it. I never invested my money so as to get so large a return for it, because I frequently see the whole show yet in the middle of the night, and the cold perspiration ripples down my spinal column just as it did the first time I saw it.

The chamber of horrors certainly furnishes a very durabl show. I don't think I was ever more successfully or economically horrified.

I got quite nervous after a while, standing in the dim religious light watching the lovely horrors. But it is the saving of money that I look at most. I have known men to pay out thousands of dollars for a collection of delirium tremens and new-laid horrors no better than these that you get on week days for fifty cents and on Sundays for two bits. Certainly New York is the place where you get your money's worth.

There are horrors there in that crypt that are well worth double the price of admission. One peculiarity of the chamber of horrors is that you finally get nervous when anyone touches you, and you immediately suspect that he is a horror who has come out of his crypt to get a breath of fresh air and stretch his legs.

That is the reason I shuddered a little when I felt a man's hand in my pocket. It was so unexpected, and the surroundings were such that I must have appeared startled. The man was a stranger to me, though I could see that he was a perfect gentleman. His clothes were superior to mine in every way, and he had a certain refinement of manners which betrayed his ill-concealed Knickerbocker lineage high.

HE WAS GREATLY ANNOYED.

I said, "Sir, you will find my fine cut tobacco in the other pocket." This startled him so that he wheeled about and wildly dashed into the arms of a wax policeman near the door. When he discovered that he was in the clutches of a suit of second-hand clothes filled with wax, he seemed to be greatly annoyed and strode rapidly away.

I returned to view a chaste and truthful scene where one man had successfully killed another with a club. I leaned pensively against a column with my own spinal column, wrapped in thought.

Pretty soon a young gentleman from New Jersey with an Adam's apple on him like a full-grown yam, and accompanied by a young lady also from the mosquito jungles of Jersey, touched me on the bosom with his umbrella and began to explain me to his companion.

"This," said the Adam's apple with the young man attached to it, "is Jesse James, the great outlaw chief from Missouri. How life-like he is. Little would you think, Emeline that he would as soon disembowel a bank, kill th entire board of directors of a railroad company and ride off the rolling stock, as you would wrap yourself around a doughnut. How tender and kind he looks. He not only looks gentle and peaceful, but he looks to me as if he wasn't real bright."

"THIS IS JESSE JAMES."

I then uttered a piercing shriek and the young man from New Jersey went away Nothing is so embarrassing to an eminent man as to stand quietly near and hear people discuss him.

But it is remarkable to see people get fooled at a wax show. Every day a wax figure is taken for a live man, and live people are mistaken for wax. I took hold of a waxen hand in one corner of the winter garden to see if the ring was a real diamond, and it flew up and took me across the ear in such a life-like manner that my ear is still hot and there is a roaring in my head that sounds very disagreeable, indeed.

The Bite of a Mad Dog.

A "FAMILY PHYSICIAN," published in 1883, says, for the bite of a mad dog "Take ash-colored ground liverwort, cleaned, dried, and powdered, half an ounce; of black pepper, powdered, a quarter of an ounce. Mix these well together, and divide the powder into four doses, one of which must be taken every morning, fasting, for four mornings successively in half an English pint of cow's milk, warm. After these four doses are taken, the patient must go into the cold bath, or a cold spring or river, every morning, fasting, for a month. He must be dipped all over, but not stay in (with his head above water) longer than half a minute if the water is very cold. After this he must go in three times a week for a fortnight longer. He must be bled before he begins to take the medicine."

It is very difficult to know just what is best to do when a person is bitten by a mad dog, but my own advice would be to kill the dog. After that feel of the leg where bitten, and ascertain how serious the injury has been. Then go home and put on another pair of pantaloons, throwing away those that have been lacerated. Parties having but one pair of pantaloons will have to sequester themselves or excite remarks. Then take a cold bath, as suggested above, but do not remain in the bath (with the head above water) more than half an hour. If the head is under water, you may remain in the bath until the funeral, if you think best.

When going into the bath it would be well to take something in your pocket to bite, in case the desire to bite something should overcome you. Some use a common shingle-nail for this purpose, while others prefer a personal friend. In any event, do not bite a total stranger on an empty stomach. It might make you ill.

Never catch a dog by the tail if he has hydrophobia. Although that end of the dog is considered the most safe, you never know when a mad dog may reverse himself.

If you meet a mad dog on the street, do not stop and try to quell him with a glance of the eye. Many have tried to do that, and it took several days to separate the two and tell which was mad dog and which was queller.

The real hydrophobia dog generally ignores kindness, and devotes himself mostly to the introduction of his justly celebrated virus. A good thing to do on observing the approach of a mad dog is to flee, and remain fled until he has disappeared.

Hunting mad dogs in a crowded street is great sport. A young man with a new revolver shooting at a mad dog is a fine sight. He may not kill the dog, but he might shoot into a covey of little children and possibly get one.

It would be a good plan to have a balloon inflated and tied in the back yard during the season in which mad dogs mature, and get into it on the approach of the infuriated animal (get into the balloon, I mean, not the dog).

This plan would not work well, however, in case a cyclone should come at the same time. When we consider all the uncertainties of life, and the danger from hydrophobia, cyclones and breach of promise, it seems sometimes as though the penitentiary was the only place where a man could be absolutely free from anxiety.

If you discover that your dog has hydrophobia, it is absolutely foolish to try to cure him of the disease. The best plan is to trade him off at once for anything you can get. Do not stop to haggle over the price, but close him right out below cost.

Do not tie a tin can to the tail of a mad dog. It only irritates him, and he might resent it before you get the can tied on. A friend of mine, who was a practical joker, once sought to tie a tin can to the tail of a mad dog on an empty stomach. His widow still points with pride to the marks of his teeth on the piano. If mad dogs would confine themselves exclusively to practical jokers, I would be glad to endow a home for indigent mad dogs out of my own private funds.

Arnold Winkelreid.

THIS great man lived in the old romantic days when it was a common thing for a patriot to lay down his life that his country might live. He knew not fear, and in his noble heart his country was always on top. Not alone at election did Arnold sacrifice himself, but on the tented field, where the buffalo grass was soaked in gore, did he win for himself a deathless name. He was as gritty as a piece of liver rolled in the sand. Where glory waited, there you would always find Arnold Winkelreid at the bat, with William Tell on deck.

CLEAR THE TRACK.

One day the army of the tyrant got a scoop on the rebel mountaineers and it looked bad for the struggling band of chamois shooters. While Arnold's detachment didn't seem to amount to a hill of beans, the hosts of the tyrannical Austrian loomed up like six bits and things looked forbidding. It occurred to Colonel Winkelreid that the correct thing would be to break through the war front of the enemy, and then, while in his rear, crash in his cranium with a cross gun while he was looking the other way. Acting on this thought, he asked several of his most trusted men to break through the Austrian line, so that the balance of the command could pass through and slaughter enough of the enemy for a mess, but these men seemed a little reticent about doing so, owing to the inclemency of the weather and the threatening aspect of the enemy. The armed foe swarmed on every hillside and their burnished spears glittered below in the cañon. You couldn't throw a stone in any directicn without hitting a phalanx. It was a good year for the phalanx business.

Then Arnold took off his suspenders, and, putting a fresh chew of tobacco in among his back teeth, he told his men to follow him and he would show them his little racket. Marching up to the solid line of lances, he gathered an armful and put them in the pit of his stomach, and, as he sank to the earth, he spoke in a shrill tone of voice to posterity, saying, "Clear the track for Liberty" He then died.

His remains looked like a toothpick holder.

But he made way for Liberty, and his troops were victorious.

At the inquest it was shown that he might have recovered, had not the spears sat so hard on his stomach.

Probably A. Winkelreid will be remembered with gratitude long after the name of the Sweet Singer of Michigan shall have rotted in oblivion. He recognized and stuck to his proper spear. (This is a little mirthful deviation of my own.)

I can think of some men now, even in this $ age of the world, who could win glory by doing as A. W did. They could offer themselves up. They could suffer for the right and have their names passed down to posterity, and it would be perfectly splendid.

But the heroes of to-day are different. They are just as courageous, but they take a wheelbarrow and push it from New York to San Francisco, or they starve forty days and forty nights and then eat watermelon and lecture, or they eat 800 snipe in 800 years, or get an inspiration and kill somebody with it.

The heroes of our day do not wear peaked hats and shoot chamois, and sass tyrants and knock the worm out of an apple at fifty-nine yards rise with a cross gun, as Tell did, but they know how to be loved by the people and get half of the gate money They are brave, but not mortally.. The heroes of our day all die of old age or political malaria.

Murray and the Mormons.

GOV MURRAY, the gritty Gentile governor of Utah, would be noticed in a crowd. He is very tall, yet well proportioned, square-built and handsome. He was called fine looking in Kentucky, but the narrow-chested apostle of the abnormally connubial creed does not see anything pretty about him. Murray moves about through Salt Lake City in a cool, self-possessed kind of way that is very annoying to the church. Full-bearded, with brown moustache and dark hair parted a little to leeward of center; clothed in a diagonal Prince Albert coat, a silk hat and other clothes, he strolls through Zion like a man who hasn't got a yelping majority of ignorant lepers, led by a remorseless gang of nickel-plated apostles, thirsting for his young blood. I really believe he don't care a continental. The days of the avenging angel and the meek-eyed Danite, carrying a large sock loaded with buckshot, are over, perhaps; but only those who try to be Gentiles in a land of polygamous wives and anonymous white-eyed children, know how very unpopular it is. Judge Goodwin, of the Tribune, feels lonesome if he gets through the day without a poorly spelled, spattered, daubed and profane valentine threatening his life. The last time I saw him he showed me a few of them. They generally referred to him as a blankety blank "skunk," and a "hound of hell." He said he hoped I wound pardon him for the apparent egotism, but he felt as though the Tribune was attracting attention almost every day Some of these little billet-doux invited him to call at a trysting place on Tribune avenue and get his alleged brains scattered over a vacant lot. Most all of them threatened him with a rectangular head, a tin ear, or a watch pocket under the eye. He didn't seem to care much. He felt pleased and proud. Goodwin was always pleased with things that other men didn't like much. In the old days, when he and Mark Twain and Dan DeQuille were together, this was noticed in him. Gov. Murray is the same way. He feels the public pulse, and says to himself: "Sometime there's going to be music here by the entire band, and I desire to be where I shan't miss a note."

There are people who think the Mormons will not fight. Perhaps not. They won't if they are let alone, and allowed to fill the sage brush and line the banks of the Jordan with juvenile *nom de plumes.* They are peaceful while they may populate Utah and invade adjoining territoties with their herds of ostensible wives and prattling progeny; while they can bring in every year via Castle Garden and the stock yards palace emigrant car, thousands of proselyted paupers from every pest house of Europe, and the free-love idiots of America. But when Murray gets an act of congress at his back and a squad of nervy, gamy, law-abiding monogamous assistants appointed by the president under that act of congress to knock crosswise and crooked the Jim Crow revelations of Utah and Mormondom, you will see the fur fly, and the fragrant follower of a false prophet will rise up William Riley and the regular army will feel lonesome. I asked a staff officer in one of the territories last summer what would be the result if the Mormons, with their home drill and their arms and their devotion to home and their fraudulent religion, should awake Nicodemas and begin to massacre the Gentiles, and the regular army should be sent over the Wasatch range to quell the trouble.

"Why," said he, "the white-eyed followers of Mormonism would kill the regular army with clubs. You can wear out a tribe of hostile Indians when the grass gives out and the antelope hunts the foothills, but the Mormons make everything they eat, drink and wear. They don't care whether there's tariff or free trade. They can make everything from gunpowder to a knit undershirt, from a $250 revelation to a hand-made cocktail. When a church gets where it can make such cooking whisky as the Mormons do, it is time to call for volunteers and put down the hydra-headed monster."

If congress don't step on a technicality and fall down, it looks like amusement ahead, and if a District of Columbia rule, or martial law, or tocsin of war is the result, Gov. Murray is a good style of war governor. He isn't the kind of a man to put on his wife's gossamer cloak and meander over into Montana. He would give the matter his attention, and you would find him in the neighborhood when the national government decided to sit down on disorderly conduct in Utah. The first lever to be used will be the great wealth of which the Mormon church and its members privately are possessed. Then the oleaginous prophet will get a revelation to gird up his loins and to load the double-barrel shotgun, and fire the culverin, and to knock monogamy into a cocked hat. Money first and massacre second. They can draw on their revelation supply house at three days, any time, for authority to fill the irrigation ditches of Zion with the blood of the Gentile and feed his vital organs to the coyote.

About Geology.

GEOLOGY is that branch of natural science which treats of the structure of the earth's crust and the mode of formation of its rocks. It is a pleasant and profitable study, and to the man who has married rich and does not need to work, the amusement of busting geology with the Bible, or busting the Bible with geology is indeed a great boon.

Geology goes hand in hand with zoology, botany, physical geography and other kindred sciences. Taxidermy, chiropody and theology are not kindred sciences.

Geologists ascertain the age of the earth by looking at its teeth and counting the wrinkles on its horns. They have learned that the earth is not only of great age, but that it is still adding to its age from year to year.

It is hard to say very much of a great science in so short an article, and that is one great obstacle which I am constantly running against as a scientist.

I once prepared a paper in astronomy entitled "The Chronological History and Habits of the Spheres." It was very exhaustive and weighed four pounds. I sent it to a scientific publication that was supposed to be working for the advancement of our race. The editor did not print it, but he wrote me a crisp and saucy postal card, requesting me to call with a dray and remove my stuff before the board of health got after it. In five short years from that time he was a corpse. As I write these lines, I learn with ill-concealed pleasure that he is still a corpse. An awful dispensation of Providence, in the shape of a large, wilted cucumber, laid hold upon his vitals and cursed him with an inward pain. He has since had the opportunity, by actual personal observation, to see whether the statements by me relating to astronomy were true. His last words were: "Friends, Romans and countrymen, beware of the q-cumber. It will w up." It was not original, but it was good.

The four great primary periods of the earth's history are as follows, viz, to-wit:

1. The Eozoic or dawn of life.
2. The Palæozoic or period of ancient life.
3. The Mesozoic or middle period of life.
4. The Neozoic or recent period of life.

These are all subdivided again, and other words more difficult to spell are introduced into science, thus crowding out the vulgar herd who cannot afford to use the high priced terms in constant conversation.

Old timers state that the primitive condition of the earth was extremely damp. With the onward march of time, and after the lapse of millions of years, men found that they could get along with less and less water, until at last we see the pleasant, blissful state of things. Aside from the use of water at our summer resorts, that fluid is getting to be less and less popular. And

THE MASTODON.

even here at these resorts it is generally flavored with some foreign substance.

The earth's crust is variously estimated in the matter of thickness. Some think it is 2,500 miles thick, which would make it safe to run heavy trains across the earth anywhere on top of a second mortgage, while other scientists say that if we go down one-tenth of that distance we will reach a place where the worm dieth not. I do not wish to express an opinion as to the actual depth or thickness of the earth's crust, but I believe that it is none too thick to suit me.

Thickness in the earth's crust is a mighty good fault. We estimate the age of certain strata of the earth's formation by means of a union of our knowledge of plant and animal life, coupled with our geological research and a good memory. The older scientists in the field of geology do not rely solely upon the tracks of the hadrasaurus or the cornucopia for their data. They simply use these things to refresh their memory

I wish that I had time and space to describe some of the beautiful bacteria and gigantic worms that formerly inhabited the earth. Such an aggregation of actual, living Silurian monsters, any one of which would make a man a fortune to-day, if it could be kept on ice and exhibited for one season only. You could take a full grown mastodon to-day, and with no calliope, no lithographs, no bearded lady, no clown with four pillows in his pantaloons and no iron-jawed woman, you could go across this continent and successfully compete with the skating rink.

There would be but one difficulty Your expenses would not be heavy The mastodon would be willing to board around, and no one would feel like turning a mastodon out of doors if he seemed to be hungry; but he might get away from you and frolic away so far in one night that you couldn't get him for a day or two, even if you sent a detective for him.

If I had a mastodon I would rather take him when he was young, and then I could make a pet of him, so that he could come and eat out of my hand without taking the hand off at the same time. A large mastodon weighing a hundred tons or so is awkward, too. I suppose that nothing is more painful than to be stepped on by an adult mastodon.

I hope at some future time to write a paper for the Academy of Science on the subject of "Deceased Fauna, Fossiliferous Debris and Extinct Jokes," showing how, when and why these early forms of animal life came to be extinct.

A Wallula Night.

I HAVE just returned after a short tour in the far West. I made the tour with my new lecture, which I am delivering this winter for the benefit, and under the auspices, of a young man who was a sufferer in the great rise-up-William-Riley-and-come-along-with-me cyclone, which occurred at Clear Lake, in this State, a year ago last September.

In said cyclone, said young man was severely caressed by the elements, and tipped over in such a way as to shatter the right leg, just below the gambrel joint. I therefore started out to deliver a few lectures for his benefit, and in so doing have made a 4,000 mile trip over the Northern Pacific railway, and the Oregon River and Navigation company's road. On the former line the passenger is fed by means of the dining-car, a very good style of entertainment, indeed, and well worthy of the age in which we live; but at Wallula Junction I stopped over to catch a west-bound Oregon Railway and Navigation train.

That was where I fooled myself. I should have taken my valise and a rubber door mat from the sleeping-car, and crawled into the lee of a snow fence for the night. I did not give the matter enough thought. I just simply went into the hotel and registered my name as a man would in other hotels. This house was kept, or retained, I should say, by a relative of the late Mr. Shylock. You have heard, no doubt, how some of the American hotels have frowned on Mr. Shylock's relatives. Well, Mr. Shylock's family got even with the whole American people the night I stopped in No. 2, second floor of the Abomination of Desolation. As a representative of the American people, I received for my nation, vicariously, the stripes intended for many generations.

No. 2 is regarded as a room by people who have not been in it. By those who have, it is looked upon as a morgue.

When I stepped into it, I noticed an odor of the dead past. It made me shudder my overshoes off. The first thing that attracted my attention after I was left alone, was the fact that other people had occupied this room before I had, and, although they were gone, they had left a kind of an air of inferiority that clung to the alleged apartment, an air of plug tobacco and perspiration, if you will pardon the expression.

They had also left a pair of Venetian pantaloons. From this clue, my active brain at once worked out the problem and settled the fact that the party who had immediately preceded me was a man. Long and close study of the habits and characteristics of humanity has taught me to reason out these matters, and to reach accurate conclusions with astonishing rapidity

He was not only a man, but he was a short man, with parenthetical legs and a thoughtful droop to the seat of his pants. I also discovered that more of this man's life had been expended in sitting on a pitch pine log than in prayer.

One of his front teeth was gone, also. This I learned from a large cast of his mouth, shown on the end of a plug of tobacco still left in the pocket.

In Wallula there is a marked feeling of childlike trust and confidence between people. It is a feature of Wallula society, I may say. The people of the junction trust strangers to a remarkable extent. In what other town in this whole republic would a pair of pantaloons be thus left in the complete power of a total stranger, a stranger, too, to whom pantaloons were a great boon? I could easily have caught those pantaloons off the nail, thrust them into my bosom, and fled past the drowsy night clerk, out into the great, sheltering arms of the silent night, but I did not.

IN SUSPENSE.

Anon through the long hours I would awake and listen fitfully to the wail of damned souls, as it seemed to me, the wail of those who tried to stay there a week, and had starved to death. Here was their favorite wailing place. Here was the place where damned souls seemed to throw aside all restraint and have a good time. I tried to keep out the sound by stuffing the pillow in my ear, but what is a cheap hotel pillow in a man's ear, if he wants to keep the noise out.

So I lay there and listened to the soft sigh of the bath tub, the loud, defiant challenge of the athletic butler down stairs, the last weak death rattle in the throat of the coffee pot in the dining room, and the wail of the damned souls who had formerly stopped at this hotel, but who had been rescued at last, and had hilariously gone to perdition, only to come back at night and torment the poor guest by bragging over the superiority of hell as a refuge from the Wallula hotel.

Now and then in the night I would almost yield to a wild impulse and catch those pantaloons off the hook, to rush out and go to Canada with them, and then I would softly go through the pockets and hang them back again.

It was an awful night. When morning dawned at last, and I took the pillow out of my ear and looked in the delirious and soap-spattered mirror, I saw that my beautiful hair, which had been such a source of pride to me ten years ago, had disappeared in places. I paid my bill, called the attention of the landlord to the fact that I had not taken those pantaloons nor betrayed his trust, and then I went away.

Flying Machines.

A LONG and exhaustive examination of the history of flying machines enables me to give briefly some of the main points of a few, for the benefit of those who may be interested in this science. I give what I do in order to prepare the public to take advantage of the different methods, and be ready at once to fly as soon as the weather gets pleasant.

A Frenchman invented a flying-machine, or dofunny, as we scientists would term it, in 1600 and something, whereby he could sail down from the wood-shed and not break his neck. He could not rise from the ground like a lark and trill a few notes as he skimmed through the sky, but he could fall off an ordinary hay stack like a setting hen, with the aid of his wings. His name was Besnier.

One hundred and twenty-five years after that a prisoner at Vienna, named Jacob Dagen, told the jailer that he could fly. The jailer seemed incredulous, and so Jake constructed a pair of double barrel umbrellas, that worked by hand, and fluttered with his machine into the air fifty feet. He came down in a direct line, and in doing so ran one of the umbrellas through his thorax. I am glad it is not the custom now to wear an umbrella in the thorax.

In England, during the present century, several inventors produced flying machines, but in an evil hour agreed to rise on them themselves, and so they died from their injuries. Some came down on top of the machines, while others preceded their inventions by a few feet, but the result was the same. The invention of flying machines has always been handicapped, as it were, by this fact. Men invent a flying machine and then try to ride it and show it off, and thus they are prevented by death from perfecting their rolling stock and securing their right of way.

In 1842, Mr. William Henderson got out a "two-propeller" machine, and tried to incorporate a company to utilize it for the purpose of carrying letters, running errands, driving home the cows, lighting the Northern Lights and skimming the cream off the Milky Way, but it didn't seem to compete very successfully with other modes of travel, and so Mr. Henderson wrapped it up in an old tent and put it away in the hay-mow.

In 1853, Mr. J H. Johnson patented a balloon and parachute dingus which worked on the principle of a duck's foot in the mud. I use scientific terms because I am unable to express myself in the common language of the vulgar herd. This machine had a tail which, under great excitement, it would throw over the dash board as it bounded through the air.

Probably the biggest thing in its way under this head was the revival of flying under the presidency of the Duke of Argyle, the society being called the Aeronautical Society of Great Britain. This society made some valuable calculations and experiments in the interest of aerostation, adding much to our scientific knowledge, and filling London with cripples.

In 1869, Mr. Joseph T. Kaufman invented and turned loose upon the people of Glasgow an infernal machine intended to soar considerably in a quiet kind of way and to be propelled by steam. It looked like the bird known to ornithology as the *flyupithecrick*, and had an air brake, patent coupler, buffer and platform. It was intended to hold two men on ice and a rosewood casket with silver handles. It was mounted on wheels, and, as it did not seem to skim through the air very much, the people of Glasgow hitched a clothes line to it and used it for a band wagon.

Rufus Porter invented an aerial dewdad ten years ago in Connecticut, where so many crimes have been committed since Mark Twain moved there. This was called the "aeraport," and looked like a seed wart floating through space. This engine was worked by springs connected with propellers. A saloon was suspended beneath it, I presume on the principle that when a man is intoxicated he weighs a pound less. This machine flew around the rotunda of the Merchants' Exchange, in New York City, eleven times, like a hen with her head cut off, but has not been on the wing much since then.

Other flying machines have been invented, but the air is not peopled with them as I write. Most of them have folded their pinions and sought the seclusion of a hen-house. It is to be hoped that very soon some such machine will be perfected, whereby a man may flit from the fifth story window of the Grand Pacific Hotel, in Chicago, to Montreal before breakfast, leaving nothing in his room but the furniture and his kind regards.

Such an invention would be hailed with much joy, and the sale would be enormous. Now, however, the matter is still in its infancy. The mechanical birds invented for the purpose of skimming through the ether blue, have not skum. The machines were built with high hopes and a throbbing heart, but the aforesaid ether remains unskum as we go to press. The Milky Way is in the same condition, awaiting the arrival of the fearless skimmer. Will men ever be permitted to pierce the utmost details of the sky and ramble around among the stars with a gum overcoat on? Sometimes I trow he will, and then again I ween not.

Asking for a Pass.

THE general passenger agent of a prominent road leading out of Chicago toward the south, tells me that he is getting a good many letters lately asking for passes, and he complains bitterly over the awkward and unsatisfactory style of the correspondence. Acting on this suggestion and though a little late in the day, perhaps, I have erected the following as a guide to those who contemplate writing under similar circumstances:

Office of THE EVENING SQUEAL,
January 14, 1886.

GENERAL PASSENGER AGENT, GREAT NORTH AMERICAN GITTHERE R. R., CHICAGO, ILL.

DEAR SIR.—I desire to know by return mail whether or no you would be pleased to swap transportation for kind words. I am the editor of "The Squeal," published at this place. It is a paper pure in tone, world wide in its scope and irresistible in the broad sweep of its mighty arm.

THE PRESS.

I desire to visit the great exposition at New Orleans this winter, and would be willing to yield you a few words of editorial opinion, set in long primer type next to pure reading matter, and without advertising marks.

My object in thus addressing you is two-fold. I have always wanted to do your road a kind act that would put it on its feet, but I have never before had the opportunity. This winter I feel just like it, and am not willing, but anxious. Another object, though trivial, perhaps, to you, is vital to me. If I do not get the pass, I am afraid I shall not reach there till the exposition is over. You can see for yourself how important it is that I should have transportation. Day after day the president will come on to the grounds and ask if I am there. Some official will salute him and answer sadly, "No, your highness, he has not yet arrived, but we look for him soon. He is said to be stuck in a mud hole somewhere in Egypt." Then the exposition will drag on again.

STUCK IN A MUD HOLE.

You may make the pass read, "For self, Chicago to New Orleans and return," and I will write the editorial, or you may make it read, "Self and wife" and I will let you write it yourself. Nothing is too good for my friends. When a man does me a kind act or shows signs of affection, I just allow him to walk all over me and make himself perfectly free with the policy of my paper.

The "Evening Squeal" has been heard everywhere. We send it to the four winds of Heaven, and its influence is felt wherever the English language is respected. And yet, if you want to belong to my coterie of friends, you can make yourself just as free with its editorial columns as you would if you owned it.

And yet "The Squeal" is a bad one to stir up. I shudder to think what the result would be if you should incur the hatred of "The Squeal." Let us avoid such a subject or the possibility of such a calamity

"The Squeal" once opposed the candidacy of a certain man for the office of school district clerk, and in less than four years he was a corpse! Struck down in all his wanton pride by one of the popular diseases of the day.

My paper at one time became the foe of a certain road which tapped the great cranberry vineyards of northern Minnesota, and that very fall the cranberries soured on the vines!

I might go on for pages to show how the pathway of "The Squeal" has been strewn with the ruins of railroads, all prosperous and happy till they antagonized us and sought to injure us.

I believe that the great journals and trunk lines of the land should stand in with one another. If you have the support and moral encouragement of the press you will feel perfectly free to run over any one who gets on your track. Besides, if I held a pass over your road I should feel very much reserved about printing the details of any accident, delay or washout along your line. I aim to mould public opinion, but a man can subsidize and corrupt me if he goes at it right. I write this to kind of give you a pointer as to how you can go to work to do so if you see fit.

Should you wish to pervert my high moral notions in relation to railways, please make it good for thirty days, as it may take me a week or so to mortgage my property and get ready to go in good style. I will let you know on what day I will be in New Orleans, so that you can come and see me at that time. Should you have difficulty in obtaining an audience with me, owing to the throng of crowned heads, just show this autograph letter to the doorkeeper, and he will show you right in. Wipe your boots before entering.

Yours truly, DANIEL WEBSTER BRIGGS,
Editor of "The Squeal."

It is my opinion that no railroad official, however disobliging, would hesitate a moment about which way he would swing after reading an epistle after this pattern. Few, indeed, are the men who would be impolitic enough to incur the displeasure of such a paper as I have artfully represented "The Squeal" to be.

Words About Washington.

THE name of George Washington has always had about it a glamour that made him appear more in the light of a god than a tall man with large feet and a mouth made to fit an old-fashioned, full-dress pumpkin pie. I use the word glamour, not so much because I know what glamour means, but because I have never used it before, and I am getting a little tired of the short, easy words I have been using so long.

George Washington's face has beamed out upon us for many years now, on postage stamps and currency, in marble, and plaster, and bronze, in photographs of original portraits, paintings, and stereoscopic views. We have seen him on horseback and on foot, on the war-path and on skates, cussing his troops for their shiftlessness, and then in the solitude of the forest, with his snorting war-horse tied to a tree, engaged in prayer.

We have seen all these pictures of George, till we are led to believe that he did not breathe our air or eat American groceries. But George Washington was not perfect. I say this after a long and careful study of his life, and I do not say it to detract the very smallest iota from the proud history of the Father of his Country. I say it simply that the boys of America who want to become George Washingtons will not feel so timid about trying it.

When I say that George Washington, who now lies so calmly in the lime-kiln at Mount Vernon, could reprimand and reproach his subordinates at times, in a way to make the ground crack open and break up the ice in the Delaware a week earlier than usual, I do not mention it in order to show the boys of our day that profanity will make them resemble George Washington. That was one of his weak points, and no doubt he was ashamed of it, as he ought to have been. Some poets think that if they get drunk, and stay drunk, they will resemble Edgar A. Poe and George D. Prentice. There are lawyers who play poker year after year, and get regularly skinned, because they have heard that some of the able lawyers of the past century used to come home at night with poker chips in their pockets.

Whisky will not make a poet, nor poker a great pleader. And yet I have seen poets who relied solely on the potency of their breath, and lawyers who knew more of the habits of a bob-tail flush than they ever did of the statutes in such case made and provided.

George Washington was always ready. If you wanted a man to be first in war, you could call on George. If you desired an adult who would be first baseman in time of peace, Mr. Washington could be telephoned at any hour of the day or night. If you needed a man to be first in the hearts of his countrymen, George's postoffice address was at once secured.

Though he was a great man, he was once a poor boy. How often we hear that in America! It is the place where it is a positive disadvantage to be born wealthy. And yet, sometimes I wish they had experimented a little that way on me. I do not ask now to be born rich, of course, because it is too late; but it seems to me that, with my natural good sense and keen insight into human nature, I could have struggled along under the burdens and cares of wealth with great success. I do not care to die wealthy, but if I could have been born wealthy, it seems to me I would have been tickled almost to death.

I love to believe that true greatness is not accidental. To think and to say that greatness is a lottery is pernicious. Man may be wrong sometimes in his judgment of others, both individually and in the aggregate, but he who gets ready to be a great man will surely find the opportunity.

Many who read the above paragraph will wonder who I got to write it for me, but they will never find out.

In conclusion, let me say that George Washington was successful for three reasons. One was that he never shook the confidence of his friends. Another was that he had a strong will without being a mule. Some people cannot distinguish between being firm and being a big blue jackass.

Another reason why Washington is loved and honored to-day, is that he died before we had a chance to get tired of him. This is greatly superior to the method adopted by many modern statesmen, who wait till their constituency weary of them and then reluctantly and tardily die.

The Board of Trade.

I WENT into the Chicago Board of Trade awhile ago to see about buying some seed wheat for sowing on my farm next spring. I heard that I could get wheat cheaper there than anywhere else, so I went over. The members of the Board seemed to be all present. They were on the upper floor of the house, about three hundred of them, I judge, engaged in conversation. All of them were conversing when I entered, with the exception of a sad-looking man who had just been squeezed into a corner and injured, I was told. I told him that arnica was as good as anything I knew of for that, but he seemed irritated, and I strode majestically away. Probably he thought I had no business to speak to him without an introduction, but I never stand on ceremony when I see anyone in pain.

INDULGING IN CONVERSATION.

I got a ticket when I went in, and began to look around for my wheat. I didn't see any at first. I then asked one of the conversationalists how wheat was.

"Oh, wheat's pretty steady just now, 'specially October, but yesterday we thought the bottom had dropped out. Perfect panic in No. 2, red; No. 2, Chicago Spring, 73⅞. Dull, my Christian friend, dull is no name for it. More fellers got pinched yesterday than would patch purgatory fifteen miles. What you doing, buying or selling?"

"Buying."

"Better let me sell you some choice Chicago Spring way down. Get some man you know on the Board to make the trade for you."

"Well, if you've got something good and cheap, and that you know will grow, I'd like to look at it," I said.

He took me over by the door where there was a dishpan full of wheat, and asked me how that struck me. I said it looked good and asked him how much he could spare of it at 73. He said he had 50,000 bushels that he wasn't using, and he thought he could get me another 50,000 of a friend, if I wanted it. I said no, 100,000 bushels was more than I needed. I told him that if he would let me have that dishpan full, one-half cash and the balance in installments, I might trade with him, but I didn't want him to sell me his last bushel of wheat and rob himself.

"Very likely you've got a family," said I, "and you musn't forget that we've got a long, cold, hard winter ahead of us. Hang on to your wheat. Don't let Tom, Dick and Harry come along and chisel you out of your last kernel, just to be neighborly"

I remained in the room an hour and a half, the cynosure of all eyes. There is a great deal of sociability there. Three hundred men all talking diagonally at each other at the same time, reminds me of a tete-a-tete I once had with a warm personal friend, who was a boiler-maker. He invited me to come around to the shop and visit him. He said we could crawl down through the manhole into the boiler and have a nice visit while he worked.

I remember of following him down through the hole into the boiler; then they began to head boiler rivets, and I knew nothing more till I returned to consciousness the next day to find myself in my own luxuriously-furnished apartments.

The family physician was holding my hand. My wife asked: "Is he conscious yet, do you think, doctor?"

"Yes," he replied, "your husband begins to show signs of life. He may live for many years, but his intellect seems to have been mislaid during his illness. Do you know whether the cat has carried anything out of this room lately?"

Then my wife said: "Yes, the cat did get something out of this room only the other day and ate it. Poor thing!"

The Cow-Boy.

SO much amusing talk is being made recently anent the blood-bedraggled cow-boy of the wild West, that I rise as one man to say a few things, not in a dictatorial style, but regarding this so-called or so esteemed dry land pirate who, mounted on a little cow-pony and under the black flag, sails out across the green surge of the plains to scatter the rocky shores of Time with the bones of his fellow-man.

A great many people wonder where the cow-boy, with his abnormal thirst for blood, originated. Where did this young Jesse James, with his gory record and his dauntless eye, come from? Was he born in a buffalo wallow at the foot of some rock-ribbed mountain, or did he first breathe the thin air along the brink of an alkali pond, where the horned toad and the centipede sang him to sleep, and the tarantula tickled him under the chin with its hairy legs?

Careful research and cold, hard statistics show that the cow-boy, as a general thing, was born in an unostentatious manner on the farm. I hate to sit down on a beautiful romance and squash the breath out of a romantic dream, but the cow-boy who gets too much moist damnation in his system, and rides on a gallop up and down Main street shooting out the lights of the beautiful billiard palaces, would be just as unhappy if a mouse ran up his pantaloon-leg as you would, gentle reader. He is generally a youth who thinks he will not earn his twenty-five dollars per month if he does not yell, and whoop, and shoot, and scare little girls into St. Vitus's dance. I've known more cow-boys to injure themselves with their own revolvers than to injure anyone else. This is evidently because they are more familiar with the hoe than they are with the Smith & Wesson.

One night, while I had rooms in the business part of a Territorial city in the Rocky Mountain cattle country, I was awakened at about one o'clock A. M. by the most blood-curdling cry of "Murder" I ever heard. It was murder with a big "M." Across the street, in the bright light of a restaurant, a dozen cow-boys with broad sombreros and flashing silver braid, huge leather chaperajas, Mexican spurs and orange silk neckties, and with flashing revolvers, were standing. It seemed that a big, red-faced Captain Kidd of the band, with his skin full of valley tan, had marched into an ice-cream resort with a self-cocker in his hand, and ordered the vanilla coolness for the gang. There being a dozen young folks at the place, mostly male and female, from a neighboring hop, indulging in cream, the proprietor, a meek Norwegian with thin white hair, deemed it rude and outre to do so. He said something to that effect, whereat the other eleven men of alcoholic courage let off a yell that froze the cream into a solid glacier, and shook two kerosene lamps out of their sockets in the chandeliers.

HE YELLED MURDER.

Thereupon, the little Y. M. C. A. Norwegian said.

"Gentlemans, I kain't neffer like dot squealinks and dot kaind of a tings, and you fellers mit dot ledder pantses on and dot funny glose and such a tings like dot, better keep kaind of quiet, or I shall call up the policemen mit my delephone."

Then they laughed at him, and cried yet again with a loud voice.

This annoyed the ice-cream agriculturist, and he took the old axe-handle that he used to jam the ice down around the freezer with, and peeled a large area of scalp off the leader's dome of thought, and it hung down over his eyes, so that he could not see to shoot with any degree of accuracy.

After he had yelled "Murder!" three or four times, he fell under an ice-cream table, and the mild-eyed Scandinavian broke a silver-plated castor over the organ of self-esteem, and poured red pepper, and salt, and vinegar, and Halford sauce and other relishes, on the place where the scalp was loose.

This revived the brave but murderous cow-gentleman, and he begged that he might be allowed to go away.

The gentle Y. M. C. A. superintendent of the ten-stamp ice-cream freezers then took the revolvers away from the bold buccaneer, and kicked him out through a show-case, and saluted him with a bouquet of July oysters that suffered severely from malaria.

All cow-boys are not sanguinary; but out of twenty you will generally find one who is brave when he has his revolvers with him; but when he forgot and left his shooters at home on the piano, the most tropical violet-eyed dude can climb him with the butt-end of a sunflower, and beat his brains out and spatter them all over that school district.

In the wild, unfettered West, beware of the man who never carries arms, never gets drunk and always minds his own business. He don't go around shooting out the gas, or intimidating a kindergarten school; but when a brave frontiersman, with a revolver in each boot and a bowie down the back of his neck, insults a modest young lady, and needs to be thrown through a plate-glass window and then walked over by the populace, call on the silent man who dares to wear a clean shirt and human clothes.

Stirring Incidents at a Fire.

LAST night I was awakened by the cry of fire. It was a loud, hoarse cry, such as a large, adult man might emit from his window on the night air. The town was not large, and the fire department, I had been told, was not so effective as it should have been.

For that reason I arose and carefully dressed myself, in order to assist, if possible. I carefully lowered myself from my room, by means of a staircase which I found concealed in a dark and mysterious corner of the passage.

On the streets all was confusion. The hoarse cry of fire had been taken up by others, passed around from one to another, till it had swollen into a dull roar. The cry of fire in a small town is always a grand sight.

All along the street in front of Mr. Pendergast's roller rink the blanched faces of the people could be seen. Men were hurrying to and fro, knocking the bystanders over in their frantic attempts to get somewhere else. With great foresight, Mr. Pendergast, who had that day finished painting his roller rink a dull-roan color, removed from the building the large card which bore the legend:

* *

FRESH PAINT !

* *

so that those who were so disposed might feel perfectly free to lean up against the rink and watch the progress of the flames.

Anon the bright glare of the devouring element might have been seen bursting through the casement of Mr. Cicero Williams's residence, facing on the alley west of Mr. Pendergast's rink. Across the street the spectator whose early education had not been neglected could distinctly read the sign of our esteemed fellow-townsman, Mr. Alonzo Burlingame, which was lit up by the red glare of the flames so that the letters stood out plainly as follows:

ALONZO BURLINGAME,

DEALER IN SOFT AND HARD COAL, ICE-CREAM, WOOD, LIME, CEMENT, PERFUMERY, NAILS, PUTTY, SPECTACLES, AND HORSE RADISH.

CHOCOLATE CARAMELS AND TAR ROOFING.

GAS FITTING AND UNDERTAKING IN ALL ITS BRANCHES.
HIDES, TALLOW, AND MAPLE SYRUP.
FINE GOLD JEWELRY, SILVERWARE, AND SALT.
GLUE, CODFISH, AND GENT'S NECKWEAR.
UNDERTAKER AND CONFECTIONER.
☞DISEASES OF HORSES AND CHILDREN A SPECIALTY.

JNO. WHITE, PTR.

The flames spread rapidly, until they threatened the Palace rink of our esteemed fellow-townsman, Mr. Pendergast, whose genial and urbane manner has endeared him to all.

With a degree of forethought worthy of a better cause, Mr. Leroy W Butts suggested the propriety of calling out the hook and ladder company, an organization of which every one seemed to be justly proud. Some delay ensued in trying to find the janitor of Pioneer Hook and Ladder Company No. 1's building, but at last he was secured, and, after he had gone home for the key, Mr. Butts ran swiftly down the street to awaken the foreman, but, after he had dressed himself and inquired anxiously about the fire, he said that he was not foreman of the company since the 2d of April.

Meantime the firefiend continued to rise up ever and anon on his hind feet and lick up salt-barrel after salt-barrel in close proximity to the Palace rink, owned by our esteemed fellow-citizen, Mr. Pendergast. Twice Mr. Pendergast was seen to shudder, after which he went home and filled out a blank which he forwarded to the insurance company.

Just as the town seemed doomed, the hook and ladder company came rushing down the street with their navy-blue hook and ladder truck. It is indeed a beauty, being one of the Excelsior noiseless hook and ladder factory's best instruments, with tall red pails and rich blue ladders.

Some delay ensued, as several of the officers claimed that under a new by-law passed in January they were permitted to ride on the truck to fires. This having been objected to by a gentleman who had lived in Chicago several years, a copy of the by-laws was sent for and the dispute summarily settled. The company now donned its rubber overcoats with great coolness and proceeded at once to deftly twist the tail of the firefiend.

It was a thrilling sight as James McDonald, a brother of Terrance McDonald, Trombone, Ind., rapidly ascended one of the ladders in the full glare of the devouring element and fell off again.

Then a wild cheer arose to a height of about nine feet, and all again became confused.

It was now past 11 o'clock, and several of the members of the hook and ladder company who had to get up early the next day in order to catch a train excused themselves and went home to seek much-needed rest.

Suddenly it was discovered that the brick livery stable of Mr. Abraham McMichaels, a nephew of our worthy assessor, was getting hot. Leaving the Palace rink to its fate, the hook and ladder company directed its attention to the brick barn, and, after numerous attempts, at last succeeded in getting its large iron prong fastened on the second story window-sill, which was pulled out. The hook was again inserted, but not so effectively, bringing down at this time an armful of hay and part of an old horse blanket. Another courageous jab was made with the iron hook, which succeeded in pulling out about 5 cents worth of brick. This was greeted by a wild burst of applause from the bystanders, during which the hook and ladder company fell over each other and added to the horror of the scene by a mad burst of pale-blue profanity.

It was not long before the stable was licked up by the firefiend, and the hook and ladder company directed its attention toward the undertaking, embalming, and ice-cream parlors of our highly esteemed fellow-townsman, Mr. A. Burlingame. The company succeeded in pulling two stone window-sills out of this building before it burned. Both times they were encored by the large and aristocratic audience.

Mr. Burlingame at once recognized the efforts of the heroic firemen by tapping a keg of beer, which he distributed among them at 25 cents per glass.

This morning a space forty-seven feet wide, where but yesterday all was joy and prosperity and beauty, is covered over with blackened ruins. Mr. Pendergast is overcome by grief over the loss of his rink, but assures us that if he is successful in getting the full amount of his insurance he will take the money and build two rinks, either one of which will be far more imposing than the one destroyed last evening.

A movement is on foot to give a literary and musical entertainment at Burley's hall, to raise funds for the purchase of new uniforms for the "fire laddies," at which Mrs. Butts has consented to sing "When the Robins Nest Again," and Miss Mertie Stout will recite "'Ostler Jo," a selection which never fails to offend the best people everywhere. Twenty-five cents for each offense.

☞ Let there be a full house.

The Little Barefoot Boy.

WITH the moist and misty spring, with the pink and white columbine of the wildwood and the breath of the cellar and the incense of burning overshoes in the back yard, comes the little barefoot boy with fawn colored hair and a droop in his pantaloons. Poverty is not the grand difficulty with the little barefoot boy of spring. It is the wild, ungovernable desire to wiggle his toes in the ambient air, and to soothe his parboiled heels in the yielding mud.

I see him now in my mind's eye, making his annual appearance like a rheumatic housefly, stepping high like a blind horse. He has just left his shoes in the woodshed and stepped out on the piazza to proclaim that violet-eyed spring is here. All over the land the gladiolus bulb and the ice man begin to swell. The south wind and the new-born calf at the barn begin to sigh. The oak tree and the dude begin to put on their spring apparel. All nature is gay. The thrush is warbling in the asparagus orchard, and the prima donna does her throat up in a red flannel rag to wait for another season.

All these things indicate spring, but they are not so certain and unfailing as the little barefoot boy whose white feet are thrust into the face of the approaching season. Five months from now those little dimpled feet, now so bleached and tender, will look like a mudturtle's back and the superior and leading toe will have a bandage around it, tied with a piece of thread.

Who would believe that the budding hoodlum before us, with the yellow chilblain on his heel and the early spring toad in his pocket, which he will present to the timid teacher as a testimonial of his regard this afternoon, may be the Moses who will lead the American people forty years hence into the glorious sunlight of a promised land.

He may possibly do it, but he doesn't look like it now.

Yet John A. Logan and Samuel J. Tilden were once barefooted boys, with a suspender apiece. It doesn't seem possible, does it?

How can we imagine at this time Julius Cæsar and Hannibal Hamlin and Lucretia Borgia at some time or other stubbed their bare toes against a root and filled the horizon with pianissimo wails. The barefoot boy of spring will also proceed to bathe in the river as soon as the ice and the policeman are out. He will choose a point on the boulevard, where he can get a good view of those who pass, and in company with eleven other little barefoot boys, he will clothe himself in an Adam vest, a pair of bare-skin pantaloons, a Greek slave overcoat and a yard of sunlight, and gaze earnestly at those who go by on the other side. Up and down the bank, pasting each other with mud, the little barefoot boys of spring chase each other, with their vertebræ sticking into

A TESTIMONIAL OF REGARD.

the warm and sleepy air, while down in the marsh, where the cat-tails and the broad flags and the peach can and the deceased horse grow, the bull-frog is twittering to his mate.

Later on, the hoarse voice of a rude parental snorter is heard approaching, and twelve slim Cupids with sunburned backs are inserted into twelve little cotton shirts and twelve despondent pairs of pantaloons hang at half-mast to twelve home-made suspenders, and as the gloaming gathers about the old home, twelve boys back up against the ice-house to cool off, while the enraged parent hangs up the buggy whip in the old place.

Favored a Higher Fine.

WILL. TAYLOR, the son of the present American Consul at Marseilles, was a good deal like other boys while at school in his old home, at Hudson, Wis. One day he called his father into the library, and said:

"Pa, I don't like to tell you, but the teacher and I have had trouble."

"What's the matter now?"

"Well, I cut one of the desks a little with my knife, and the teacher says I've got to pay a dollar or take a lickin' "

"Well, why don't you take the licking and say nothing more about it? I can stand considerable physical pain, so long as it visits our family in that form. Of course, it is not pleasant to be flogged, but you have broken a rule of the school, and I guess you'll have to stand it. I presume that the teacher will in wrath remember mercy, and avoid disabling you so that you can't get your coat on any more."

"But, pa, I feel mighty bad about it already, and if you'd pay my fine I'd never do it again. I know a good deal more about it now, and I will never do it again. A dollar ain't much to you, pa, but it's a heap to a boy that hasn't got a cent. If I could make a dollar as easy as you can, pa, I'd never let my little boy get flogged that way just to save a dollar. If I had a little feller that got licked bekuz I didn't put up for him, I'd hate the sight of money always. I'd feel as if every dollar in my pocket had been taken out of my little kid's back."

"Well, now, I'll tell you what I'll do. I'll give you a dollar to save you from punishment this time, but if anything of this kind ever occurs again I'll hold you while the teacher licks you, and then I'll get the teacher to hold you while I lick you. That's the way I feel about that. If you want to go around whittling up our educational institutions you can do so; but you will have to purchase them afterward yourself. I don't propose to buy any more damaged school furniture. You probably grasp my meaning, do you not? I send you to school to acquire an education, not to acquire liabilities, so that you can come around and make an assessment on me. I feel a great interest in you, Willie, but I do not feel as though it should be an assessable interest. I want to go on, of course, and improve the property, but when I pay my dues on it I want to know that it goes toward development work. I don't want my assessments to go toward the purchase of a school-desk with American hieroglyphics carved on it.

"I hope that you will bear this in your mind, my son, and beware. It will be greatly to your interest to beware. If I were in your place I would put in a large portion of my time in the beware business."

The boy took the dollar and went thoughtfully away to school, and no more was ever said about the matter until Mr. Taylor learned casually several months later that the Spartan youth had received the walloping and filed away the dollar for future reference. The boy was afterward heard to say that he favored a much heavier fine in cases of that kind. One whipping was sufficient, he said, but he favored a fine of $5. It ought to be severe enough to make it an object.

"I Spy."

DEAR reader, do you remember the boy of your school who did the heavy falling through the ice and was always about to break his neck, but managed to live through it all? Do you call to mind the youth who never allowed anybody else to fall out of a tree and break his collar bone when he could attend to it himself? Every school has to secure the services of such a boy before it can succeed, and so our school had one. When I entered the school I saw at a glance that the board had neglected to provide itself with a boy whose duty it was to nearly kill himself every few days in order to keep up the interest, so I applied for the position. I secured it without any trouble whatever. The board understood at once from my bearing that I would succeed. And I did not betray the trust they had reposed in me.

BRINGING IN THE REMAINS.

Before the first term was over I had tried to climb two trees at once and been carried home on a stretcher; been pulled out of the river with my lungs full of water, and artificial respiration resorted to; been jerked around over the north half of the county by a fractious horse whose halter I had tied to my leg, and which leg is now three inches longer than the other; together with various other little early eccentricities which I cannot at this moment call to mind. My parents at last got so that along about 2 o'clock P M. they would look anxiously out of the window and say, "Isn't it about time for the boys to get here with William's remains? They generally get here before 2 o'clock."

One day five or six of us were playing "I spy" around our barn. Everybody knows how to play "I spy." One shuts his eyes and counts 100, for instance, while the others hide. Then he must find the rest and say "I spy" so-and-so and touch the "goal" before they do. If anybody beats him to the goal the victim has to "blind" over again.

Well, I knew the ground pretty well, and could drop twenty feet out of the barn window and strike on a pile of straw so as to land near the goal, touch it, and let the crowd in free without getting found out. I did this several times and got the blinder, James Bang, pretty mad. After a boy has counted 500 or 600, and worked hard to gather in the crowd, only to get jeered and laughed at by the boys, he loses his temper. It was so with James Cicero Bang. I knew that he almost hated me, and yet I went on. Finally, in the fifth ballot, I saw a good chance to slide down and let the crowd in again as I had done on former occasions. I slipped out of the window and down the side of the barn about two feet, when I was detained unavoidably There was a "batten" on the barn that was loose at the upper end. I think I was wearing my father's vest on that day, as he was away from home, and I frequently wore his clothes when he was absent. Anyhow the vest was too large, and when I slid down that loose board ran up between the vest and my person in such a way as to suspend me about eighteen feet from the ground, in a prominent but very uncomfortable position.

I remember it quite distinctly James C. Bang came around where he could see me. He said: "I spy Billy Nye and touch the goal before him." No one came to remove the barn. No one came to sympathize with me in my great sorrow and isolation. Every little while James C. Bang would come around the corner and say: "Oh, I see ye. You needn't think you're out of sight up there. I can see you real plain. You better come down and blind. I can see ye up there!"

I tried to unbotton my vest and get down there and lick James, but it was of no use. It was a very trying time. I can remember how I tried to kick myself loose, but failed. Sometimes I would kick the barn and sometimes I would kick a large hole in the horizon. Finally I was rescued by a neighbor who said he didn't want to see a good barn kicked into chaos just to save a long-legged boy that wasn't worth over six bits.

It affords me great pleasure to add that while I am looked up to and madly loved by every one that does not know me, Jas. C. Bang is brevet president of a fractured bank, taking a lonely bridal tour by himself in Europe and waiting for the depositors to die of old age.

The mills of the gods grind slowly, but they most generally get there with both feet. (Adapted from the French by permission.)

Mark Antony.

MARCUS ANTONIUS, commonly called Mark Antony, was a celebrated Roman general and successful politician, who was born in 83 B. C. His grandfather, on his mother's side, was L. Julius Cæsar, and it is thought that to Mark's sagacity in his selection of a mother, much of his subsequent success was due.

Young Antony was rather gay and festive during his early years, and led a life that in any city but Rome would have occasioned talk. He got into a great many youthful scrapes, and nothing seemed to please him better than to repeatedly bring his father's gray hairs down in sorrow to the grave. Debauchery was a matter to which he gave much thought, and many a time he was found consuming the midnight oil while pursuing his studies in this line.

At that time Rome was well provided for in the debauchery department, and Mr. Antony became a thorough student of the entire curriculum.

About 57 B. C. he obtained command of the cavalry of Gambinino in Syria and Egypt. He also acted as legate for Cæsar in Gaul about 52 B. C., as nearly as I can recall the year. I do not know exactly what a legate is, but it had something to do with the Roman ballet, I understand, and commanded a good salary.

He was also elected, in 50, B. C., as Argus and Tribune—acting as Tribune at night and Argus during the day time, I presume, or he may have been elected Tribune and ex-officio Argus. He was more successful as Tribune than he was in the Argus business.

Early in 49, B. C., he fled to Cæsar's camp, and the following year was appointed commander-in-chief. He commanded the left wing of the army at the battle of Pharsalia, and years afterward used to be passionately fond of describing it and explaining how he saved the day, and how everybody else was surprised but him, and how he was awakened by hearing one of the enemy's troops, across the river, stealthily pulling on his pantaloons.

Antony married Fulvia, the widow of a successful demagogue named P. Clodius. This marriage could hardly be regarded as a success. It would have been better for the widow if she had remained Mrs. P Clodius, for Mark Antony was one of those old-fashioned Romans who favored the utmost latitude among men, but heartily enjoyed seeing an unfaithful woman burned at the stake. In those days the Roman girl had nothing to do but live a pure and blameless life, so that she could marry a shattered Roman rake who had succeeded in shunning a blameless life himself, and at last, when he was sick of all kinds of depravity and needed a good, careful wife to take care of him, would come with his dappled, sin-sick soul and shattered constitution, and his vast acquisitions of debts, and ask to be loved by a noble young woman. Nothing pleased a *blase* Roman so well as to have a young and beautiful girl, with eyes like liquid night, to take the job of reforming him. I frequently get up in the night to congratulate myself that I was not born, 2,000 years ago, a Roman girl.

The historian continues to say, that though Mr. Antony continued to live a life of licentious lawlessness, that occasioned talk even in Rome, he was singularly successful in politics.

He was very successful at funerals, also, and his off-hand obituary works were sought for far and wide. His impromptu remarks at the grave of Cæsar, as afterward reported by Mr. Shakespeare, from memory, attracted general notice and made the funeral a highly enjoyable affair. After this no assassination could be regarded as a success, unless Mark Antony could be secured to come and deliver his justly celebrated eulogy.

About 43, B. C., Antony, Octavius and Lepidus formed a co-partnership under the firm name and style of Antony, Octavius & Co., for the purpose of doing a general, all-round triumvirate business and dealing in Roman republican pelts. The firm succeeded in making republicanism extremely odious, and for years a republican hardly dared to go out after dark to feed the horse, lest he be jumped on by a myrmidon and assassinated. It was about this time that Cicero had a misunderstanding with Mark's myrmidons and went home packed in ice.

Mark Antony, when the firm of Antony, Octavius & Co. settled up its affairs, received as his share the Asiatic provinces and Egypt. It was at this time that he met Cleopatra at an Egyptian sociable and fell in love with her. Falling in love with fair women and speaking pieces over new-made graves seemed to be Mark's normal condition. He got into a quarrel with Octavius and settled it by marrying Octavia, Octavius' sister, but this was not a love match, for he at once returned to Cleopatra, the author of Cleopatra's needle and other works.

This love for Cleopatra was no doubt the cause of his final overthrow, for he frequently went over to see her when he should have been at home killing invaders. He ceased to care about slashing around in carnage, and preferred to turn Cleopatra's music for her while she knocked out the teeth of her old upright piano and sang to him in a low, passionate, *vox humana* tone.

So, at last, the great cemetery declaimer and long distance assassin, Mark Antony, was driven out of his vast dominions after a big naval defeat at Actium, in September, 31 B. C., retreated to Alexandria, called for more reinforcements and didn't get them. Deserted by his fleet, and reduced to a hand-me-down suit of clothes and a two-year-old plug hat, he wrote a poetic wail addressed to Cleopatra and sent it to the Alexandria papers; then, closing the door and hanging up his pantaloons on a nail so as to reduce the sag in the knees, he blew out the gas and climbed over the high board fence which stands forever between the sombre present and the dark blue, mysterious ultimatum.

Man Overbored.

"SPEAKING about prohibition," said Misery Brown one day, while we sat lying on the dump of the *Blue Tail Fly*, "I am prone to allow that the more you prohibit, the more you—all at once—discover that you have more or less failed to prohibit.

"Now, you can win a man over to your way of thinking, sometimes, but you musn't do it with the butt-end of a telegraph-pole. You might convert him that way, perhaps, but the mental shock and phrenological concussion of the argument might be disastrous to the convert himself.

"A man once said to me that rum was the devil's drink, that Satan's home was filled with the odor of hot rum, that perdition was soaked with spiced rum and rum punch. 'You wot not,' said he, 'the ruin rum has rot. Why, Misery Brown,' said he, 'rum is my *bete noir.*' I said I didn't care what he used it for, he'd always find it very warming to the system. I told him he could use it for a hot *bete noir*, or a *blanc mange*, or any of those fancy drinks; I didn't care.

"But the worst time I ever had grappling with the great enemy, I reckon, was in the later years of the war, when I pretty near squashed the rebellion. Grim-visaged war had worn me down pretty well. I played the big tuba in the regimental band, and I began to sigh for peace.

"We had been on the march all summer, it seemed to me. We'd travel through dust ankle-deep all day that was just like ashes, and halt in the red-hot sun five minutes to make coffee. We'd make our coffee in five minutes, and sometimes we'd make it in the middle of the road; but that's neither here nor there.

"We finally found out that we would make a stand in a certain town, and that the Q. M. had two barrels of old and reliable whisky in store. We also found out that we couldn't get any for medical purposes nor anything else

All we could do was to suffer on and wait till the war closed. I didn't feel like postponing the thing myself, so I began to investigate. The great foe of humanity was stored in a tobacco-house, and the Q. M. slept three nights between the barrels. The chances for a debauch looked peaked and slim in the extreme. However, there was a basement below, and I got in there one night with a half-inch auger, and two wash-tubs. Later on there was a sound of revelry by night. There was considerable 'on with the dance, let joy be unconfined.'

"The next day there was a spongy appearance to the top of the head, which seemed to be confined to our regiment, as a result of the sudden giving way, as it were, of prohibitory restrictions. It was a very disagreeable day, I remember. All nature seemed clothed in gloom, and R. E. Morse, P D. Q., seemed to be in charge of the proceedings. Redeyed Regret was everywhere.

"We then proceeded to yearn for the other barrel of woe, that we might pile up some more regret, and have enough misery to last us through the balance of the campaign. We acted on this suggestion, and, with a firm resolve and the same half-inch auger, we stole once more into the basement of the tobacco-house.

"I bored nineteen consecutive holes in the atmosphere, and then an intimate friend of mine bored twenty-seven distinct holes in the floor, only to bore through the bosom of the night. Eleven of us spent the most of the night boring into the floor, and at three o'clock A. M. it looked like a hammock, it was so full of holes. The quartermaster slept on through it all. He slept in a very audible tone of voice, and every now and then we could hear him slumbering on.

"At last we decided that he was sleeping middling close to that barrel, so we began to bore closer to the snore. It was my turn to bore, I remember, and I took the auger with a heavy heart. I bored through the floor, and for the first time bored into something besides oxygen. It was the quartermaster. A wild yell echoed through the southern confederacy, and I pulled out my auger. It had on the point a strawberry mark, and a fragment of one of those old-fashioned woven wire gray shirts, such as quartermasters used to wear.

"I remember that we then left the tobacco-house. In the hurry we forgot two wash-tubs, a half-inch auger, and 980,361 new half-inch auger holes that had never been used."

"Done it A-Purpose."

AT Greeley a young man with a faded cardigan jacket and a look of woe got on the train, and as the car was a little crowded he sat in the seat with me. He had that troubled and anxious expression that a rural young man wears when he first rides on the train. When the engine whistled he would almost jump out of that cardigan jacket, and then he would look kind of foolish, like a man who allows his impulses to get the best of him. Most everyone noticed the young man and his cardigan jacket, for the latter had arrived at the stage of droopiness and jaded-across-the-shoulders look that the cheap knit jacket of commerce acquires after awhile, and it had shrunken behind and stretched out in front so that the horizon, as you stood behind the young man, seemed to be bound by the tail of this garment, which started out at the pocket with good intentions and suddenly decided to rise above the young man's shoulder blades.

He seemed so diffident and so frightened among strangers, that I began to talk with him.

"Do you live at Greeley?" I inquired.

"No, sir," he said, in an embarrassed way, as most anyone might in the presence of greatness. "I live on a ranch up the Pandre. I was just at Greeley to see the circus."

I thought I would play the tenderfoot and inquiring pilgrim from the cultured East, so I said: "You do not see the circus often in the West, I presume, the distance is so great between towns and the cost of transportation is so great?"

"No, sir. This is the first circus I ever was to. I have never saw a circus before."

"How did you like it?"

"O, tip-top. It was a good thing. I'd like to see it every day if I could. I laughed and drank lemonade till I've got my cloze all pinned up with pins, and I'd as soon tell you, if you wont give it away, that my pants is tied on me with barbed fence wire."

"Probably that's what gives you that anxious and apprehensive look?"

"Yes, sir. If I look kind of doubtless about something, its because I'm afraid my pantaloons will fall off on the floor and I will have to borrow a roller towel to wear home."

"How did you like the animals?"

"I liked that part of the Great Moral Aggregation the best of all. I have not saw such a sight before. I could stand there and watch that there old scaly elephant stuff hay into his bosom with his long rubber nose for hours. I'd read a good deal first and last about the elephant, the king of beasts, but I had never yet saw one. Yesterday father told me there hadn't been much joy into my young life, and so he gave me a dollar and told me to go over to the circus and have a grand time. I tell you, I just turned myself loose and gave myself up to pleasure."

I WAS A POOR CONVERSATIONALIST.

"What other animals seemed to please you?" I asked, seeing that he was getting a little freer to talk.

"Oh, I saw the blue-nosed babboon from Farther India, and the red-eyed sandhill crane from Maddygasker, I think it was, and the sacred Jack-rabbit from Scandihoovia, and the lop-eared layme from South America. Then there was the female acrobat with her hair tied up with red ribbon. It's funny about them acroba wimmen. They get big pay, but they never buy cloze with their money Now, the idea of a woman that gets $2 or $3 a day, for all I know, coming out there before 2,000 total strangers, wearing a pair of Indian war clubs and a red ribbon in her hair. I tell you, pardner, them acrobat prima donnars are mighty stingy with their money, or else they're mighty economical with their cloze."

"Did you go into the side show?"

"No, sir. I studied the oil paintings on the outside, but I didn't go in. I met a handsome looking man there near the side show, though, that seemed to take an interest in me. There was a lottery along with the show and he wanted me to go and throw for him."

"Capper, probably?"

"Perhaps so. Anyhow, he gave me a dollar and told me to go and throw for him."

"Why didn't he throw for himself?"

"O, he said the lottery man knew him and wouldn't let him throw."

"Of course. Same old story. He saw you were a greeney and got you to throw for him. He stood in with the game so that you drew a big prize for the capper, created a big excitement, and you and the crowd sailed in and lost all the money you had. I'll bet he was a man with a velvet coat, and a moustache dyed a dead black and waxed as sharp as a cambric needle."

"Yes; that's his description to a dot. I wonder if he really did do that a-purpose."

"Well, tell us about it. It does me good to hear a blamed fool tell how he lost his money Don't you see that your awkward ways and general greenness struck the capper the first thing, and you not only threw away your own money, but two or three hundred other wappy-jawed pelicans saw you draw a big prize and thought it was yours, then they deposited what little they had and everything was lovely."

"Well, I'll tell you how it was, if it'll do any good and save other young men in the future. You see this capper, as you call him, gave me a $1 bill to throw for him, and I put it into my vest pocket so, along with the dollar bill father gave me. I always carry my money in my right hand vest pocket. Well, I sailed up to the game, big as old Jumbo himself, and put a dollar into the game. As you say, I drawed a big prize, $20 and a silver cup. The man offered me $5 for the cup and I took it."

"Then it flashed over my mind that I might have got my dollar and the other feller's mixed, so I says to the proprietor, 'I will now invest a dollar for a gent who asked me to draw for him.'

"Thereupon I took out the other dollar, and I'll be eternally chastised if I didn't draw a brass locket worth about two bits a bushel."

I didn't say anything for a long time. Then I asked him how the capper acted when he got his brass locket.

"Well, he seemed pained and grieved about something, and he asked me if I hadn't time to go away into a quiet place where we could talk it over by ourselves; but he had a kind of a cruel, insincere look in his eye, and I said no, I believed I didn't care to, and that I was a poor conversationalist, anyhow; and so I came away, and left him looking at his brass locket and kicking holes in the ground and using profane language.

"Afterward I saw him talking to the proprietor of the lottery, and I feel, somehow, that they had lost confidence in me. I heard them speak of me in a jeering tone of voice, and one said as I passed by: 'There goes the meek-eyed rural convict now,' and he used a horrid oath at the same time.

"If it hadn't been for that one little quincidence, there would have been nothing to mar the enjoyment of the occasion."

Picnic Incidents.

CAMPING out in summer for several weeks is a good thing generally. Freedom from social restraint and suspenders is a great luxury for a time, and nothing purifies the blood quicker, or makes a side of bacon taste more like snipe on toast, than the crisp ozone that floats through the hills and forests where man can monkey o'er the green grass without violating a city ordinance.

The picnic is an aggravation. It has just enough of civilization to be a nuisance, and not enough barbarism to make life seem a luxury. If our aim be to lean up against a tree all day in a short seersucker coat and ditto pantaloons that segregated while we were festooning the hammock, the picnic is the thing. If we desire to go home at night with a jelly symphony on each knee and a thousand-legged worm in each ear, we may look upon the picnic as a success.

But to those who wish to forget the past and live only in the booming present, to get careless of gain and breathe brand-new air that has never been used, to appease an irritated liver, or straighten out a torpid lung, let me say, pick out a high, dry clime, where there are trout enough to give you an excuse for going there, take what is absolutely necessary and no more, and then stay there long enough to have some fun.

If we picnic, we wear ourselves out trying to have a good time, so that we can tell about it when we get back, but we do not actually get acquainted with each other before we have to quit and return.

To camp, is to change the whole programme of life, and to stop long enough in the never-ending conflict for dollars and distinction, to get a full breath and look over the field. Still, it is not always smooth sailing. To camp, is sometimes to show the material of which we are made. The dude at home is the dude in camp, and wherever he goes he demonstrates that he was made for naught. I do not know what a camping party would do with a dude unless they used him to bait a bear trap with, and even then it would be taking a mean advantage of the bear. The bear certainly has some rights which we are bound in all decency to respect.

James Milton Sherrod said he had a peculiar experience once while he was in camp on the Poudre in Colorado.

"We went over from Larmy," said he, "in July, eight years ago—four of us. There was me and Charcoal Brown, and old Joe and young Joe Connoy. We had just got comfortably down on the Lower Fork, out of the reach of everybody and sixty miles from a doctor, when Charcoal Brown got sick. Wa'al, we had a big time of it. You can imagine yourself somethin' about it. Long in the night Brown began to groan and whoop and holler, and I made a diagnosis of him. He didn't have much sand anyhow. He was tryin' to git a pension from the government on the grounds of desertion and failure to provide, and some such a blame thing or another, so I didn't feel much sympathy fur him. But when I lit the gas and examined him, I found that he had a large fever on hand, and there we was without a doggon thing in the house but a jug of emigrant whiskey and a paper of condition powders fur the mule. I was a good deal rattled at first to know what the dickens to do fur him. The whiskey wouldn't do him any good, and, besides, if he was goin' to have a long spell of sickness we needed it for the watchers.

MAKING USE OF A DUDE.

"Wa'al, it was rough. I'd think of a thousand things that was good fur fevers, and then I'd remember that we hadn't got 'em. Finally old Joe says to me, 'James, why don't ye soak his feet?' says he. 'Soak nuthin',' says I; 'what would ye soak 'em in?' We had a long-handle frying-pan, and we could heat water in it, of course, but it was too shaller to do any good, anyhow; so we abandoned that synopsis right off. First I thought I'd try the condition powders in him, but I hated to go into a case and prescribe so recklessly Finally I thought of a case of rheumatiz that I had up in Bitter Creek years ago, and how the boys filled their socks full of hot ashes and put 'em all over me till it started the persbyterian all over me and I got over it.

CHARCOAL BROWN'S REPROACHES.

So we begun to skirmish around the tent for socks, and I hope I may be tee-totally skun if there was a blame sock in the whole syndicate. Ez fur me, I never wore 'em, but I did think young Joe would be fixed. He wasn't though. Said he didn't want to be considered proud and high strung, so he left his socks at home.

"Then we begun to look around and finally decided that Brown would die pretty soon if we didn't break up the fever, so we concluded to take all the ashes under the camp-fire, fill up his cloze, which was loose, tie his sleeves at the wrists, and his pants at the ankles, give him a dash of condition powders and a little whiskey to take the taste out of his mouth, and then see what ejosted nature would do.

So we stood Brown up agin a tree and poured hot ashes down his back till he begun to fit his cloze pretty quick, and then we laid him down in the tent and covered him up with everything we had in our humble cot. Everything worked well till he begun to perspirate, and then there was music, and don't you forget it. That kind of soaked the ashes, don't you see, and made a lye that would take the peelin' off a telegraph pole.

"Charcoal Brown jest simply riz up and uttered a shrill whoop that jarred the geology of Colorado, and made my blood run cold. The goose flesh riz on old Joe Connoy till you could hang your hat on him anywhere. It was awful.

"Brown stood up on his feet, and threw things, and cussed us till we felt ashamed of onrselves. I've seen sickness a good deal in my time, but—I give it to you straight—I never seen an invalid stand up in the loneliness of the night, far from home and friends, with the concentrated lye oozin' out of the cracks of his boots, and reproach people the way Charcoal Brown did us.

"He got over it, of course, before Christmas, but he was a different man after that. I've been out campin' with him a good many times sence, but he never complained of feelin' indisposed. He seemed to be timid about tellin' us even if he was under the weather, and old Joe Connoy said mebbe Brown was afraid we would prescribe fur him or sumthin'."

Nero.

NERO, who was a Roman Emperor from 54 to 68 A. D., was said to have been one of the most disagreeable monarchs to meet that Rome ever had. He was a nephew of Culigula, the Emperor, on his mother's side, and a son of Dominitius Ahenobarbust, of St. Lawrence county The above was really Nero's name, but in the year 50, A. D., his mother married Claudius and her son adopted the name of Nero Claudius Cæsar Drusus Germanicus. This name he was in the habit of wearing during the cold weather, buttoned up in front. During the hot weather, Nero was all the name he wore. In 53, Nero married Octavia, daughter of Claudius, and went right to housekeeping. Nero and Octavia did not get along first-rate. Nero soon wearied of his young wife and finally transferred her to the New Jerusalem.

In 54, Nero's mother, by concealing the rightful heir to the throne for several weeks and doctoring the returns, succeeded in getting the steady job of Emperor for Nero at a good salary

His reign was quite stormy and several long, bloody wars were carried on during that period. He was a good vicarious fighter and could successfully hold a man's coat all day, while the man went to the front to get killed. He loved to go out riding over the battle fields, as soon as it was safe, in his gorgeously bedizened band chariot and he didn't care if the wheels rolled in gore up to the hub, providing it was some other man's gore. It gave him great pleasure to drive about over the field of carnage and gloat over the dead. Nero was not a great success as an Emperor, but as a gloater he has no rival in history

Nero's reign was characterized, also, by the great conflagration and Roman fireworks of July, 64, by which two-thirds of the city of Rome was destroyed. The emperor was charged with starting this fire in order to get the insurance on a stock of dry goods on Main street.

Instead of taking off his crown, hanging it up in the hall and helping to put out the fire, as other Emperors have done time and again, Nero took his violin up stairs and played, "I'll Meet You When the Sun Goes Down." This occasioned a great deal of adverse criticism on the part of those who opposed the administration. Several persons openly criticised Nero's policy and then died.

A man in those days, would put on his overcoat in the morning and tell his wife not to keep dinner waiting. "I am going down town to criticise the Emperor a few moments," he would say "If I do not get home in time for dinner, meet me on the 'evergreen shore.'"

Nero, after the death of Octavia, married Poppæa Sabina. She died afterward at her husband's earnest solicitation. Nero did not care so much about being a bridegroom, but the excitement of being a widower always gratified and pleased him.

He was a very zealous monarch and kept Rome pretty well stirred up during his reign. If a man failed to show up anywhere on time, his friends would look sadly at each other and say, "Alas, he has criticised Nero."

A man could wrestle with the yellow fever, or the small-pox, or the Asiatic cholera and stand a chance for recovery, but when he spoke sarcastically of Nero, it was good-bye John.

When Nero decided that a man was an offensive partisan, that man would generally put up the following notice on his office door:

"Gone to see the Emperor in relation to charge of offensive partisanship. Meet me at the cemetery at 2 o'clock."

Finally, Nero overdid this thing and ran it into the ground. He did not want to be disliked and so, those who disliked him were killed. This made people timid and muzzled the press a good deal.

The Roman papers in those days were all on one side. They did not dare to be fearless and outspoken, for fear that Nero would take out his ad. So they would confine themselves to the statement that: "The genial and urbane Afranius Burrhus had painted his new and *recherche* picket fence last week," or "Our enterprising fellow townsman, Cæsar Kersikes, will remove the tail of his favorite bulldog next week, if the weather should be auspicious," or "Miss Agrippina Bangoline, eldest daughter of Romulus Bangoline, the great Roman rinkist, will teach the school at Eupatorium, Trifoliatum Holler, this summer. She is a highly accomplished young lady, and a good speller."

Nero got more and more fatal as he grew older, and finally the Romans began to wonder whether he would not wipe out the Empire before he died. His back yard was full all the time of people who had dropped in to be killed, so that they could have it off their minds.

Finally, Nero himself yielded to the great strain that had been placed upon him and, in the midst of an insurrection in Gaul, Spain and Rome itself, he fled and killed himself.

The Romans were very grateful for Nero's great crowning act in the killing line, but they were dissatisfied because he delayed it so long, and therefore they refused to erect a tall monument over his remains. While they admired the royal suicide and regarded it as a success, they censured Nero's negligence and poor judgment in suiciding at the wrong end of his reign.

I have often wondered what Nero would have done if he had been Emperor of the United States for a few weeks and felt as sensitive to newspaper criticism as he seems to have been. Wouldn't it be a picnic to see Nero cross the Jersey ferry to kill off a few journalists who had adversely criticised his course? The great violin virtuoso and light weight Roman tyrant would probably go home by return mail, wrapped in tinfoil, accompanied by a note of regret from each journalist in New York, closing with the remark, that "in the midst of life we are in death, therefore now is the time to subscribe."

Squaw Jim.

"JIM, you long-haired, backslidden Caucasian nomad, why don't you say something? Brace up and tell us your experience. Were you kidnapped when you were a kid and run off into the wild wickyup of the forest, or how was it that you came to leave the Yankee reservation and eat the raw dog of the Sioux?"

We were all sitting around the roaring fat-pine fire at the foot of the cañon, and above us the full moon was filling the bottom of the black notch in the mountains, where God began to engrave the gulch that grew wider and deeper till it reached the valley where we were.

Squaw Jim was tall, silent and grave. He was as dignified as the king of clubs, and as reticent as the private cemetery of a deaf and dumb asylum. He didn't move when Dutch Joe spoke to him, but he noticed the remark, and after awhile got up in the firelight, and later on the silent savage made the longest speech of his life.

"BOYS, YOU CALL ME SQUAW JIM."

"Boys, you call me Squaw Jim, and you call my girl a half breed. I have no other name than Squaw Jim with the pale faced dude and the dyspeptic sky pilot who tells me of his God. You call me Squaw Jim because I've married a squaw and insist on living with her. If I had married Mist-of-the-Waterfall, and had lived in my tepee with her summers, and wintered at St. Louis with a wife who belonged to a tall peaked church, and who wore her war paint, and her false scalp-lock, and her false heart into God's wigwam, I'd be all right, probably. They would have laughed about it a little among the boys, but it would have been "wayno" in the big stone lodges at the white man's city.

"I loved a pale faced girl in Connecticut forty years ago. She said she did me, but she met with a change of heart and married a bare-back rider in a circus. Then she ran away with the sword swallower of the side show, and finally broke her neck trying to walk the tight rope. The jury said if the rope had been as tight as she was it might have saved her life.

"Since then I've been where the sun and the air and the soil were free. It kind of soothed me to wear moccasins and throw my biled shirt into the Missouri. It took the fever of jealousy and disappointment out of my soul to sleep in the great bosom of the unhoused night. Soon I learned how to parley-vous in the Indian language, and to wear the clothes of the red man. I married the squaw girl who saved me from the mountain fever and my foes. She did not yearn for the equestrian of the white man's circus. She didn't know how to raise XxYxZ to the nth power, but she was a wife worthy of the President of the United States. She was way off the trail in matters of etiquette, but she didn't know what it was to envy and hate the pale faced squaw with the sealskin sacque and the torpid liver, and the high-priced throne of grace. She never sighed to go where they are filling up Connecticut's celestial exhibit with girls who get mysteriously murdered and the young men who did it go out lecturing. You see I keep posted.

"Boys, you kind of pity me, I reckon, and say Squaw Jim might have been in Congress if he'd stayed with his people and wore night shirts and pared his claws, but you needn't.

"My wife can't knock the tar out of a symphony on the piano, but she can mop the dew off the grass with a burglar, and knock out a dude's eyes at sixty yards rise.

"My wife is a little foggy on the winter style of salvation, and probably you'd stall her on how to drape a silk velvet overskirt so it wouldn't hang one-sided, but she has a crude idea of an every day, all wool General Superintendent of the Universe and Father of all-Humanity, whether they live under a horse blanket tepee or a Gothic mortgage. She might look out of place before the cross, with her chilblains and her childlike confidence, among the Tom cat sealskin sacques of your camel's hair Christianity, but if the world was supplied with Christians like my wife, purgatory would make an assignment, and the Salvation Army would go home and hoe corn. Sabe?

Squaw Jim's Religion.

REFERRING to religious matters, the other day, Sqaw Jim said: "I was up at the Post yesterday to kind of rub up against royalty, and refresh my memory with a few papers. I ain't a regular subscriber to any paper, for I can't always get my mail on time. We're liable to be here, there and everywhere, mebbe at some celebrated Sioux watering place and mebbe on the warpath, so I can't rely on the mails much, but I manage, generally, to get hold of a few old papers and magazines now and then. I don't always know who's president before breakfast the day after election, but I manage to skirmish around and find out before his term expires.

"Now, speaking about the religion of the day, or, rather, the place where it used to be, it seems to me as if there's a mistake somewhere. It looks as if religion meant greenness, and infidelity meant science and smartness, according to the papers. I'm no scientist myself. I don't know evolution from the side of a house. As an evolver I couldn't earn my board, probably, and I wouldn't know a protoplasm from a side of sole leather; but I know when I get to the end of my picket rope, and I know just as sure where the knowable quits and the unknowable begins as anybody I mean I can crawl into a prairie dog hole, and pull the hole in and put it in my pocket, in my poor, weak way, just as well as a scientist can. If a man offered to trade me a spavined megatherium for a foundered hypothesis, I couldn't know enough about either of the blamed brutes to trade and make a profit. I never run around after delightful worms and eccentric caterpillers. I have so far controlled myself and escaped the habit, but I am able to arrive at certain conclusions. You think that because I am the brother-in-law to an Indian outbreak, I don't care whether Zion languishes or not; but you are erroneous. You make a very common mistake.

"Mind you, I don't pretend to be up on the plan of salvation, and so far as vicarious atonement goes, I don't even know who is the author of it, but I've got a kind of hand-made religion that suits me. It's cheap, and portable, and durable, and stands our severe northern climate first rate. It ain't the protuberant kind. It don't protude into other people's way like a sore thumb. All-wool religion don't go around with a chip on it's shoulder looking for a personal deal.

"If I had time and could move my library around with me during our summer tour, I might monkey with speculative science and expose the plan of creation, but as it is now, I really haven't time.

"I say this, however, friends, Romans and backsliders: I think sometimes when my little half-breed girl comes to me in the evening in her night dress, and kneels by me with her little brown face in between my knees, and with my hard hands in her unbraided hair, that she's got something better than speculative science.

"When she says.

'Now I lay me down to sleep.
I pray the Lord my soul to keep;
If I should die before I wake,
I pray the Lord my soul to take:
This I ask for Jesus' sake;'

MOVING HIS LIBRARY.

and I know that a million more little angels are saying that same thing, at that same hour, to that same imaginary God, I say to myself, if that is a vain, empty infatuation, blessed be that holy infatuation.

"If that's a wild and crazy delusion, let me be always deluded. If forty millions of chubby little angels bow their dimpled knees every evening to a false and foolish tradition, let me do so, too. If I die, then I will be in good company, even if I go no farther than the clouds of the valley.

One Kind of Fool.

A YOUNG man, with a plated watch-chain that would do to tie up a sacred elephant, came into Denver the other day from the East, on the Julesburg Short line, and told the hotel clerk that he had just returned from Europe, and was on his way across the continent with the intention of publishing a book of international information. He handed an oilcloth grip across the counter, registered in a bold, bad way and with a flourish that scattered the ink all over the clerk's white shirt front.

He was assigned to a quiet room on the fifth floor, that had been damaged by water a few weeks before by the fire department. After an hour or two spent in riding up and down the elevator and ringing for things that didn't cost anything, he oiled his hair and strolled into the dining-room with a severe air, and sat down opposite a big cattle man, who never oiled his hair or stuck his nose into other people's business.

The European traveler entered into conversation with the cattle man. He told him all about Paris and the continent, meanwhile polishing his hands on the tablecloth and eating everything within reach. While he ate another man's dessert, he chatted on gaily about Cologne and pitied the cattle man who had to stay out on the bleak plains and watch the cows, while others paddled around Venice and acquired information in a foreign land.

At first the cattle man showed some interest in Europe, but after awhile he grew quiet and didn't seem to enjoy it. Later on the European tourist, with soiled cuffs and auburn mane, ordered the waiters around in a majestic way, to impress people with his greatness, tipped over the vinegar cruet into the salt and ate a slice of boiled egg out of another man's salad.

Casually a tall Kansas man strolled in and asked the European tourist what he was doing in Denver. The cattle man, who, by the way, has been abroad five or six times and is as much at home in Paris as he is in Omaha, investigated the matter, and learned that the fresh French tourist had been herding hens on a chicken ranch in Kansas for six years, and had never seen blue water. He then took a few personal friends to the dining-room door, and they watched the alleged traveler. He had just taken a long, refreshing drink from the finger bowl of his neighbor on the left and was at that moment, trying to scoop up a lump of sugar with the wrong end of the tongs.

There are a good many fools who drift around through the world and dodge the authorities, but the most disastrous ass that I know is the man who goes West with two dollars and forty cents in his pocket, without brains enough to soil the most delicate cambric handkerchief, and tries to play himself for a savant with so much knowledge that he has to shed information all the time to keep his abnormal knowledge from hurting him.

John Adams' Diary.

DECEMBER 3, 1764.—I am determined to keep a diary, if possible, the rest of my life. I fully realize how difficult it will be to do so. Many others of my acquaintance have endeavored to maintain a diary, but have only advanced so far as the second week in January. It is my purpose to write down each evening the events of the day as they occur to my mind, in order that in a few years they may be read and enjoyed by my family. I shall try to deal truthfully with all matters that I may refer to in these pages, whether they be of national or personal interest, and I shall seek to avoid anything bitter or vituperative, trying rather to cool my temper before I shall submit my thoughts to paper.

"WHERE'S THE PIE?"

DECEMBER 4.—This morning we have had trouble with the hired girl. It occurred in this wise: We had fully two-thirds of a pumpkin pie that had been baked in a square tin. This major portion of the pie was left over from our dinner yesterday, and last night, before retiring to rest, I desired my wife to suggest something in the cold pie line, which she did. I lit a candle and explored the pantry in vain. The pie was no longer visible. I told Mrs. Adams that I had not been successful, whereupon we sought out the hired girl, whose name is Tootie Tooterson, a foreign damsel, who landed in this country Nov. 7, this present year. She does not understand our language, apparently, especially when we refer to pie. The only thing she does without a strong foreign accent is to eat pumpkin pie and draw her salary. She landed on our coast six weeks ago, after a tedious voyage across the heaving billows. It was a close fight between Tootie and the ocean, but when they quit, the heaving billows were one heave ahead by the log.

Miss Tooterson landed in Massachusetts in a woolen dress and hollow clear down into the ground. A strong desire to acquire knowledge and cold, hand-made American pie seems to pervade her entire being.

She has only allowed Mrs. Adams and myself to eat what she did not want herself.

Miss Tooterson has also introduced into my household various European eccentricities and strokes of economy which deserve a brief notice here. Among other things she has made pie crust with castor oil in it, and lubricated the pancake griddle with a pork rind that I had used on my lame neck. She is thrifty and saving in this way, but rashly extravagant in the use of doughnuts, pie and Medford rum, which we keep in the house for visitors who are so unfortunate as to be addicted to the doughnut, pie or rum habit.

It is discouraging, indeed, for two young people like Mrs. Adams and myself, who have just begun to keep house, to inherit a famine, and such a robust famine, too. It is true that I should not have set my heart upon such a transitory and evanescent terrestrial object like a pumpkin pie so near to T. Tooterson, imported pie soloist, doughnut mastro and feminine virtuoso, but I did, and so I returned from the pantry desolate.

A PIE SOLOIST.

I told Abigail that unless we poisoned a few pies for Tootie the Adams family would be a short-lived race. I could see with my prophetic eye that unless the Tootersons yielded the Adamses would be wiped out. Abigail would not consent to this, but decided to relieve Miss Tooterson from duty in this department, so this morning she went away. Not being at all familiar with the English language, she took four of Abigail's sheets and quite a number of towels, handkerchiefs and collars. She also erroneously took a pair of my night-shirts in her poor, broken way Being entirely ignorant of American customs, I presume that she will put a belt around them and wear them externally to church. I trust that she will not do this, however, without mature deliberation.

IGNORANT OF AMERICAN CUSTOMS.

I also had a bottle of lung medicine of a very powerful nature which the doctor had prepared for me. By some oversight, Miss Tooterson drank this the first day that she was in our service. This was entirely wrong, as I did not intend to use it for the foreign trade, but mostly for home consumption.

This is a little piece of drollery that I thought of myself. I do not think that a joke impairs the usefulness of a diary, as some do. A diary with a joke in it is just as good to fork over to posterity as one that is not thus disfigured. In fact, what has posterity ever done for me that I should hesitate about socking a little humor into a diary? When has posterity ever gone out of its way to do me a favor? Never! I defy the historian to show a single instance where posterity has ever been the first to recognize and remunerate ability.

John Adams' Diary.

(No. 2.)

DECEMBER 6.—It is with great difficulty that I write this entry in my diary, for this morning Abigail thought best for me to carry the oleander down into the cellar, as the nights have been growing colder of late.

I do not know which I dislike most, foreign usurpation or the oleander. I have carried that plant up and down stairs every time the weather has changed, and the fickle elements of New England have kept me rising and falling with the thermometer, and whenever I raised or fell I most always had that scrawny oleander in my arms.

Richly has it repaid us, however, with its long, green, limber branches and its little yellow nubs on the end. How full of promises to the eye that are broken to the heart. The oleander is always just about to meet its engagements, but later on it peters out and fails to materialize.

I do not know what we would do if it were not for our house plants. Every fall I shall carry them cheerfully down cellar, and in the spring I will bring up the pots for Mrs. Adams to weep softly into. Many a night at the special instance and request of my wife I have risen, clothed in one simple, clinging garment, to go and see if the speckled, double and twisted Rise-up-William-Riley geranium was feeling all right.

Last summer Abigail brought home a slip of English ivy. I do not like things that are English very much, but I tolerated this little sickly thing because it seemed to please Abigail. I asked her what were the salient features of the English ivy. What did the English ivy do? What might be its specialty? Mrs. Adams said that it made a specialty of climbing. It was a climber from away back. "All right," I then to her did straightway say, "let her climb. It was a good early climber. It climbed higher than Jack's beanstalk. It climbed the golden stair. Most of our plants are actively engaged in descending the cellar stairs or in ascending the golden stair most all the time.

I descended the stairs with the oleander this morning, though the oleander got there a little more previously than I did. Parties desiring a good, second-hand oleander tub, with castors on it, will do well to give us a call before going elsewhere. Purchasers desiring a good set of second-hand ear muffs for tulips will find something to their advantage by addressing the subscriber.

We also have two very highly ornamental green dogoods for ivy vines to ramble over. We could be induced to sell these dogoods at a sacrifice, in order to make room for our large stock of new and attractive dogoods. These articles are as good as ever. We bought them during the panic last fall for our vines to climb over, but, as our vines died of membranous croup in November, these dogoods still remain unclum. ☞Second-hand dirt always on hand. Ornamental geranium stumps at bed-rock prices. Highest cash prices paid for slips of black-and-tan foliage plants. We are headquarters for the century plant that draws a salary for ninety-nine years and then dies.

I do not feel much like writing in my diary to-day, but the physician says that my arm will be better in a day or two, so that it will be more of a pleasure to do business.

We are still without a servant girl, so I do some of the cooking. I make a fire each day and boil the teakettle. People who have tried my boiled teakettle say it is very fine.

Some of my friends have asked me to run for the Legislature here next election. Somehow I feel that I might, in public life, rise to distinction some day, and perhaps at some future time figure prominently in the affairs of a one-horse republic at a good salary.

I have never done anything in the statesman line, but it does not look difficult to me. It occurs to me that success in public life is the result of a union of several great primary elements, to-wit:

Firstly—Ability to whoop in a felicitous manner.

Secondly—Promptness in improving the proper moment in which to whoop.

Thirdly—Ready and correct decision in the matter of which side to whoop on.

Fourthly—Ability to cork up the whoop at the proper moment and keep it in a cool place till needed.

And this last is one of the most important of all. It is the amateur statesman who talks the most. Fearing that he will conceal his identity as a fool, he babbles in conversation and slashes around in his shallow banks in public.

As soon as I get the house plants down cellar and get their overshoes on for the winter, I will more seriously consider the question of our political affairs here in this new land where we have to tie our scalps on at night and where every summer is an Indian summer.

John Adams' Diary.

(No. 3.)

DECEMBER 10.—I have put in a long and exhausting day in the court to-day in the case of Merkins vs. Merkins, a suit for divorce in which I am the counsel for the plaintiff, Eliza J Merkins.

The case itself is a peculiarly trying one, and the plaintiff adds to its horrors by consulting me when I want to do something else. I took her case at an agreed price, and so Mrs. Merkins is trying to get her money's worth by consulting me in a way I abhor. She has consulted me in every mood and tense that I know of; at my office, on the street, in church, at the festive board and at different funerals to which we both happened to be called. Mrs. Merkins has hung like a pall over several Massachusetts funerals which otherwise had every symptom of success.

I am a great admirer of woman as a woman, but as a client in a suit for divorce she has her peculiarities. I have seen Eliza in every phase of the case. She has been calm and tearful, stormy and snorting, low-spirited and red-nosed, violent and menacing, resigned but sobby, trustful and confidential, high strung and haughty, crushed and weepy.

She makes a specialty of shedding the red-hot scalding tear wherever she can obtain permission to do so. She has wept in my wood-box, in my new spittoon, on my desk and on my birthday I told her that I wished she would please weep on something else. There were enough objects in nature upon which a poor woman who wept constantly and had no other visible means of support could shed the wild torrents of her grief, without weeping on my anniversary. A man wants to keep his birthday as dry as possible. He hates to have it wept on by a client who has jewed him down to half price, and then insisted on coming in to sob with him in the morning before he has swept the office floor.

One time she came and sobbed on my shoulder. Her tears are of the warm, damp kind, and feel disagreeable as they roll down the neck of a comparative stranger, who never can be aught but a friend. She rested her bonnet on my bosom while she wept, and I then discovered that she has been in the habit of wearing this bonnet while cooking her buckwheat pancakes. I presume she keeps her bonnet on all the time, so that she may be ready to dash out and consult me at all times without delay Still, she ought not to do it, for when she leans her head on the bosom of her counsel in order to consult him, he detects the odor of the early sausage and the fleeting pancake.

A TENDER CASE.

You may bust such a bonnet and crush it if you will,
But the scent of the pancake will cling round it still.

As soon as I saw that her object was to lean up against me and not only convulse herself with sobs, but that she intended to jar me also with her great woe, I told her that I would have to request her to avaunt. I then, as she did not act upon my suggestion, avaunted her myself. I avaunted her into a chair with a sickening thud.

She then burst forth in a torrent of vituperation. When the abnormal sobber is suddenly corked up, these sobs rankle in the system and burst forth in the shape of vituperation. In the course of her remarks, she stated in a violent manner that she would denounce me throughout the country and retain other counsel. I told her I wished she would, as my sympathies were with Mr. Merkins. I told her that she must either pay me a larger fee or I should insist on her weeping in the alley before she came up.

She then took her departure with a rising inflection. On the following day, however, I found her at the office door, and she stood near and consulted me again, while I took up the ashes and started a fire in the stove.

Her case is quite peculiar.

She wants a divorce from her husband on the grounds of cruelty to animals, or something of that kind, and when she first told me about it I thought she had a case, but when we came to trial I found that she had had every reason to believe that if she could be segregated from Mr. Merkins she could at once become the bride of a gentleman who ploughed the raging main.

Just as we went to the jury to-day with the case, she heard casually that the gentleman who had been in the main-ploughing business had just married without her knowledge or consent.

"Heap Brain."

MUCH trouble has been done by a long haired phrenologist in the West who has, during his life, felt of over a hundred thousand heads. A comparison of a large number of charts given in these cases shows that so far no head examined would indicate anything less than a member of the lower house of congress. Artists, orators, prima-donnas and statesmen are plenty, but there are no charts showing the natural-born farmer, carpenter, shoemaker or chambermaid.

A FUTURE PRESIDENT.

That is the reason butter is so high west of the Missouri river to-day, while genius actually runs riot.

What this day and age of the world needs, is a phrenologist who will paw around among the intellectual domes of free-born American citizens, and search out a few men who can milk a cow in a cool and unimpassioned tone of voice.

It is true that every man in America is a sovereign, but he had better not overdo it. The man who sits up nights to be a sovereign and allows the calves to eat his brown-eyed beans, is not leading his fellow men up to a higher and nobler life. The sovereign business can be run in the ground if we are not careful.

Very likely the white-eyed boy with the hickory dado along the base of his overalls is the boy who in future years is to be the president of the United States. But do not, oh, do not trow, fair young reader, that every Albino youth in our broad land who wears an isosceles triangle in navy blue flannel athwart his system, is going to be the chief magistrate of this mighty republic.

We need statesmen and orators and artists very much; but the world at this moment also needs several athletic parties with the horse-sense adequate to produce flour and other vegetables necessary to feed the aforesaid statesmen, orators, etc., etc.

Let me say a word to the bright-eyed youth of America. Let me murmur in your ear this never dying truth: When a long-haired crank asks you a dollar to tell you, you are a young Demosthenes, stand up and look yourself over at a distance before you swallow it all.

There is no use talking, we have got to procure provisions in some manner, and in order to do so the natural-born bone and muscle of the country must go at and promote the growth of such things, or else we artists, poets and statesmen, will have to take off our standing collars and do it ourselves.

Phrenology is a good thing, no doubt, if we can purify it. So long as it does not become the slave of capital, there is nothing about phrenology that is going to do harm; but when it becomes the creature of the trade dollar, it looks as though the country would be filled up with wild-eyed genius that hasn't had a square meal for two weeks. The time will surely come when America will demand less statesmanship and more flour, when less statistics and a purer, nobler and more progressive style of beefsteak will demand our attention.

I had hoped that phrenology would step in and start this reform; but so far it has not, within the range of my observation. It may be, however, that the mental giant bump translator with whom I came in contact was not a fair representative. Still, he has been in the business for over thirty years, and some of our most polished criminals have passed under his hands.

An erroneous phrenologist once told me that I would shine as a revivalist, and said that I ought to marry a tall blonde with a nervous, sanguinary temperament. Then he said, "One dollar, please," and I said, "All right, gentle scientist with the tawny mane, I will give you the dollar and marry the tall blonde with the bank account and bilious temperament, when you give me a chart showing me how to dispose of a brown-eyed brunette with a thoughtful cast of countenance, who married me in an unguarded moment two years ago."

He looked at me in a reproachful kind of way, struck at me with a chair in an absent-minded manner and stole away.

The Approaching Humorist.

THE following letter has been received, and, as it encloses no unsmirched postage stamp to insure a private reply, I take great pleasure in answering it in these pages:

CHRISTIANA, KAS., Sept. 22nd, 1884.

DEAR SIR.—I am studying for a Humorist. Could you help me to some of the JOLIEST Books that are written? With some of the best Jokes of the Day &c &c &c.

Also what it would be best for me to do for to become an Humorist

I am said to be a Natural Born Humorist by my friends and all I need is Cultivation to make my mark

Please reply by return mail

Kindly Yours HERMAN A. H.

For some time I have been grieving over the dearth of humor in America, and wondering who the great coming humorist was to be. Several papers have already deplored the lack of humor in our land, but they have not been able to put their finger on the approaching humorist of the age. Just as we had begun to despair, however, here he comes, quietly and unostentatiously, modestly and ungrammatically. Unheralded and silently, like Maud S. or any other eminent man, he slowly rises above the Kansas horizon, and tells us that it will be impossible to conceal his identity any longer. He is the approaching humorist of the nineteenth century.

It is a serious matter, Herman, to prescribe a course of study that will be exactly what you need to bring you out. Perhaps you might do well to take a Kindergarten course in spelling and the rudiments of grammar; still, that is not absolutely necessary. A friend of mine named Billings has done well as a humorist, though his knowledge of spelling seems to be pitiably deficient. Grammar is convenient where a humorist desires to put on style or show off before crowned heads, but it is not absolutely indispensable.

Regarding the "Joliest Books" necessary for your perusal, in order to chisel your name on the eternal tablets of fame, tastes will certainly differ. I am almost sorry that you wrote to me, because we might not agree. You write like one of these "Joly" humorists such as people employ to go along with a picnic and be the life of the party, and whose presence throughout the country has been so depressing. If one may be allowed to judge of your genius by the few autograph lines forwarded, you belong to that class of brain-workers upon whom devolves the solemn duty of pounding sand. If you are really a brain-worker, will you kindly inform the writer whose brain you are working now, and how you like it as far as you have gone?

American humor has burst forth from all kinds of places, nearly. The various professions have done their share. One has risen from a tramp until he is wealthy and dyspeptic, and another was blown up on a steamboat before he knew that he was a humorist.

Suppose you try that, Herman. M. Quad, one of the very successful humorists of the day, both in a literary and financial way, was blown up by a steamboat before he bloomed forth into the full flush and power of success. Try that, Herman. It is a severe test, but it is bound to be a success. Even if it should be disastrous to you, it will be rich in its beneficial results to those who escape.

What We Eat.

ON 3d street, St. Paul, there stands a restaurant that has outside as a sign, under a glass case, a rib roast, a slice of ham and a roast duck that I remembered distinctly having seen there in 1860 and before the war. I asked an epicure the other day if he thought it right to keep those things there year after year when so many were starving throughout the length and breadth of the land. He then straightway did take me up close so that I could see that the food was made of plaster and painted, as hereinbefore set forth and by me translated, as Walt Whitman would say.

A day or two afterward, at a rural hotel, I struck some of that same roast beef and ham. I thought that the sign had been put on the table by mistake, and I made bold to tell the proprietor about it, on the ground that "any neglect or impertinence on the part of servants should be reported at the office." He received the information with great rudeness and a most disagreeable air.

There are two kinds of guests who live at the average hotel. One is the party who gets up and walks over the whole *corps de hote*, from the bald-headed proprietor to the bootblack, while the other is the meek and mild-eyed man, doomed to sit at the table and bewail the flight of time and the horrors of starvation while waiting for the relief party to come with his food.

I belong to the latter class. Born, as I was, in a private family, and early acquiring the habit of eating food that was intended to assuage hunger mostly, it takes me a good while to accustom myself to the style of dyspeptic microbe used simply to ornament a bill of fare. Of course it is maintained by some hotel men that food solely for eating purposes is becoming obsolete and *outre*, and that the stuff they put on their bills of fare is just as good to pour down the back of a guest as diet that is cooked for the common, low, perverted taste of people who have no higher aspiration than to eat their food.

Of course the genial, urbane and talented reader will see at once the style of hotel I am referring to. It is the hotel that apes the good hotel and prints a bill of fare solely as a literary effort. That is the hotel where you find the moth-eaten towel and the bed-ridden coffee. There is where you get butter that runs the elevator day times and sleeps on the flannel cakes at night.

It is there that you meet the weary and way-worn steak that bears the toothprints of other guests who are now in a land where the early-rising chambermaid cannot enter.

I also refer to the hotel where the bellboy is simply an animated polisher of banisters, and otherwise extremely useless. It is likewise the house where the syrup tastes like tincture of rhubarb, and the pancakes taste like a hektograph.

The traveling man will call to mind the hotel to which I refer, and he will instantly name it and tell you that he has never spent the Sabbath there.

I honestly believe that some hotel men lose money and custom by trying to issue a large blanket-sheet bill of fare every day, when a more modest list containing two or three things that a human being could eat with impunity would be far more acceptable, healthy and remunerative.

Some people can live on cracked wheat, bran and skimmed milk, no matter where they go, and so they always seem to be perfectly happy; but, while simplicity is my watchword, and while I am Old Simplicity himself, as it were, I haven't been constructed with stomachs enough to successfully wrestle with these things. I like a few plain dishes with victuals on them, cooked by a person who has had some experience in that line before. I am not so especially tied to high prices and finger-bowls, for I have risen from the common people, and during the first eighteen years of my life I had to dress myself. I was not always the pampered child of enervating luxury that I now am, by any means. So I can subsist for weeks on good, plain food, and never murmur or repine; but where the mistake at some hotels seems to have been made, is in trying to issue a bill of fare every day that will attract the attention of literary minds and excite the curiosity of linguists instead of people who desire to assuage an internal craving for grub.

I use the term grub in its broadest and most comprehensive sense.

So, if I may take the liberty to do so, let me exhort the landlord who is gradually accumulating indebtedness and remorse, to use a plainer, less elaborate, but more edible list of refreshments. Otherwise his guests will all die young.

Let him discard the seamless waffle and the kiln-dried hen. Let him abstain from the debris known as cottage pudding, that being its alias, while the doctors recognize it as old Gastric Disturbance. Too much of our hotel food tastes like the second day of January or the fifth day of July. That's the whole thing in a few words, and unless the good hotels are nearer together we shall have to multiply our cemetery facilities.

Poor hotels are responsible for lots of drunkards every year. The only time I am tempted to soak my sorrows in rum is after I have read a delusive bill of fare and eaten a broiled barn-hinge with gravy on it that tasted like the broth of perdition. It is then that the demon of intemperance and colic comes to me and, in siren tones, says: "Try our bourbon, with 'Polly Narius' on the side."

Care of House Plants.

STERN winter is the season in which to keep the eye peeled for the fragile little house plant. It is at that time that the coarse and brutal husband carries the Scandinavian flower known as the Ole Ander, part way down the cellar, and allows it to fall the rest of the way. I carried a large Ole Ander up and down stairs for nine years, until the spring of 1880. That was rather a backward spring, and a pale red cow, with one horn done up in a French twist, ate the most of it as it stood on the porch.

CARRYING OUT THE OLE ANDER.

This cow was a total stranger to me. I had never done anything for her by which to win her esteem. It shows how Providence works through the humblest means sometimes to accomplish a great good.

I have tried many times to find the postoffice address of that lonely cow, so I might comfort her declining years, but she seemed to have melted away into the bosom of space, for I cannot find her. Anyone knowing the whereabouts of a pale red cow, with one horn done up in a French twist, and wearing a look of settled melancholy, will please communicate the same to me, as we have another Ole Ander that will just about fit her, I think, by spring.

Bulbs may be wrapped in cotton and put in a cool place in the fall, and fed to the domestic animals in the spring. Geraniums should put on their buffalo overcoats about the middle of November in our rigid northern clime, and in the spring they will have the same luxuriant foliage as the tropical hat-rack. Vines may be left in the room during the winter until the furnace slips a cog and then you can pull them down and feed them to the family horses. In changing your plants from the living rooms or elsewhere to the cellar in the fall, take great care to avoid injury to the pot. I have experienced some very severe winters in my life, but I have never seen the mercury so low that a flower-pot couldn't struggle through and look fresh and robust in the spring. The longevity of the pot is surprising when we consider how much death there is all about it. I had a large brown flower-pot once that originally held the germ of a calla lily. This lily emerged from the soil with the light of immortality

WREAKING VENGEANCE.

in its eye. It got up to where we began to be attached to it, and then it died. Then we put a plant in its place which was given us by a friend. I do not remember now what this plant was called, but I know it was sent to us wrapped up in a piece of moist brown paper, and half an hour later a dray drove up to the house with the name of the plant itself. In the summer it required very little care, and in the winter I would cover the little thing up with its name, and it would be safe till spring. One evening we had a free-for-all *musicale* at my house, and a corpulent friend of mine tried to climb it, and it died. (Tried to climb the plant, not the *musicale.*) The plant yielded to the severe climb it. This joke now makes its *debut* for the first time before the world. Anyone who feels offended with this joke may wreak his vengeance on a friend of mine named Sullivan, who is passionately fond of having people wreak their vengeance on him. People having a large amount of unwreaked vengeance on hand will do well to give him a call before purchasing elsewhere.

A Peaceable Man.

WILL L. VISSCHER always made a specialty of being a peaceable man. He would make most any sacrifice in order to secure general amnesty I've known him to go around six blocks out of his way, to avoid a stormy interview with a belligerant dog. He was always very tender-hearted about dogs, especially the open-faced bulldog.

But he had a queer experience years ago, in St. Jo, Missouri. He had been city editor of the Kansas City *Journal* for some time, but one evening, while in the composing-room, the foreman told him that the place for the city editor was down stairs, in his office. He therefore ordered Visscher to go down there. Visscher said he would do so later on, after he got fatigued with the composing-room and wanted change of scene.

The foreman thereupon jumped on Mr. Visscher with a small pica wrought iron side stick. Visscher allowed that he was a peaceable man, but entered into the general chaos of double-leaded editorial, and hair and brass dashes, and dashes for liberty and heterogeneous "pi," and foot-sticks and teeth, with great zeal. He succeeded in putting a large doric head on the foreman, and although he was a peaceable man, he went down to the office and got his discharge for disturbing the discipline of the office.

He went to St. Jo the same day, and celebrated his *debut* into the town by a little game of what is known as "draw." He was fortunate in "filling his hand," and while he was taking in the stakes, a young man from Arkansas, who was in the game, nipped a two-dollar note in a quiet kind of way, which, however, was detected by Mr. V., who mentioned the matter at the time. This maddened the Arkansas man, and later on he put one of his long arms around Mr. Visscher so as to pinion him, and then smote him across the brow with an instrument, known to science as "the brass knucks." This irritated Mr. Visscher, and as soon as he had returned to consciousness he remarked that, although it was rather an up-hill job in Missouri, he was trying to be a peaceable man. He then broke the leg of a card-table over the head of the Arkansas man, and went to the doctor to get his own brow sewed on again.

While he was sitting in the doctor's office a friend of the Arkansas man came in and asked him to please stand up while he knocked him down. Visscher opened a little dialogue with the man, and drew him into conversation till he could open a case of surgical instruments near by, then he took out one of those knives that the surgeons use in removing the viscera from the leading gentleman at a post mortem.

"Now," said he, sharpening the knife on the stove-pipe and handing down a jar containing alcohol with a tumor in it, "I am a peaceful man and don't want any fuss; but if you insist on a personal encounter, I will slice off fragments of your physiognomy at my leisure, and for twenty minutes I will fill this office with your favorite features. I make a specialty of being a peaceable man, remember; but if you'll just say the word, I'll put overcoat button-holes and eyelet-holes and crazy-quilts all over your system. If I've got to kill off the poker-players of St. Jo before I can have any fun, I guess I might as well be-in on you as on any one I know."

HE WAS A PEACEABLE MAN.

He then made a stab at the man and pinned his coat-tail to the door-frame. Fear loaned the bad man strength, and, splitting the coat-tail, he fled, taking little mementoes of the tumor-jar and shedding them in his flight.

When Mr. Visscher went up to the *Herald* office soon after to get a job, he was introduced casually to the foreman, who said:

"Ah, this is the young man who licks the foreman of the paper he works on, is it? I am glad to meet you, Mr. Visscher. I am looking for a white-eyed son of a sea-cook who goes around over Missouri thumping the foremen of our leading journals. Come out into the ante-room, Mr. Visscher, till I jar your back teeth loose and send you to the morgue in a gunny-sack." Mr. Visscher repeated that he was trying to live in Missouri and be a peceable man, but that if there was anything that he could do to make it pleasant for the foreman, he would cheerfully do it.

Mr. Visscher was a small man, but when he felt aggrieved about anything he was very harassing to his adversary. They "clinched" and threw each other back and forth across the hall with great vigor. When they stopped for breath, the foreman's coat was pulled over his head and the bosom of Mr. Visscher's shirt was hanging on the gas-jet. There were also two front teeth on the floor unaccounted for.

Visscher pinned on his shirt-bosom and said he was a peaceable man, but if the custom seemed to demand four fights in one day, he would try to conform to any local usage of the city. Wherever he went, he wanted to fall right into line and be one of the party.

When he got well he was employed on the *Herald*, and for four years edited the amnesty column of the paper successfully.

Biography of Spartacus.

SPARTACUS, whose given name seems to have been torn off in its passage down through the corridors of time, was born in Thrace and educated as a shepherd. While smearing the noses of the young lambs with tar one spring, in order to prevent the snuffles among them, he thought that he would become a robber. It occurred to him that this calling was the only one he knew of that seemed to be open to the young man without means.

He had hardly got started, however, in the "hold up" industry, when he was captured by the Romans, sold at cost and trained as a gladiator, in a school at Capua. Here he succeeded in stirring up a conspiracy and uniting two hundred or more of the grammar department of the school in a general ruction, as it was then termed.

The scheme was discovered and only seventy of the number escaped, headed by Spartacus. These snatched cleavers from the butcher shops, pickets from the Roman fences and various other weapons, and with them fought their way to the foot hill where they met a wagon train loaded with arms and supplies. They secured the necessary weapons whereby to go into a general war business and established themselves in the crater of Mount Vesuvius.

Spartacus was a man of wonderful carriage and great physical strength. It had always been his theory that a man might as well die of old age as to feed himself to a Roman menagerie. He maintained that he would rather die in a general free fight, where he had a chance, than to be hauled around over the arena by one leg behind a Numidian lion.

So he took his little band and fought his way to Vesuvius. There they had a pleasant time camping out nights and robbing the Roman's daytimes. The excitement of sleeping in a crater, added a wonderful charm to their lives. While others slept cold in Capua, Spartacus cuddled up to the crater and kept comfortable.

For a long time the little party had it all their own way They sniffed the air of freedom and lived on Roman spring chicken on the half shell, and it beat the arena business all hollow.

At last, however, an army of 3,000 men was sent against them, and Spartacus awoke one morning to find himself blocked up in his crater. For a time the outlook was not cheering. Spartacus thought of telegraphing the war department for reinforcements, but finally decided not to do so.

Finally, with ladders made of wild vines, the little garrison slipped out through what had seemed an impassable fissure in the crater, got in the rear of the army and demolished it completely. That's the kind of man that Spartacus was. Fighting was his forte.

Spartacus was also a good public speaker. One of his addresses to the gladiators has been handed down to posterity through the medium of the Fifth Reader, a work that should be in every household. In his speech he states that he was not always thus. But since he is thus, he believes that he has not yet been successfully outthussed by any body.

He speaks of his early life in the citron groves of Syrsilla, and how quiet and reserved he had been, never daring to say "gosh" within a mile of the house; but finally how the Romans landed on his coast and killed off his family. Then he desired to be a fighter. He had killed more lions than any other man in Italy. He kept a big crew of Romans busy, winter and summer, catching fresh lions for him to stick. He had killed a large number of men also. At one matinee for ladies and children he had killed a prominent man from the north, and had done it so fluently that he was encored three times. The stage manager then came forward and asked that the audience would please refrain from another encore as he had run out of men, but if the ladies and children would kindly attend on the following Saturday he hoped to be prepared with a good programme. In fact, he had just heard from his agent who wrote him that they had purchased two big lions and also had a robust gladiator up a tree. He hoped that he could get into town in a day or two with both attractions.

Spartacus finally stood at the head of an army of 100,000 men, all starting out from the little band of 70 that cut loose from Capua with borrowed cleavers and axhandles. This war lasted but two years, during which time Spartacus made Rome howl. Spartacus had too much sense to attack Rome. But at last his army was betrayed and disorganized. With nothing but death or capture for him, he rode out between the two contending armies, shot his war horse in order to save expenses, and on foot rushed into the thickest of the fight. This was positively his last appearance. He killed a large number of people, but at last he yielded to the great pressure that was brought to bear upon him and died.

Probably no man not actually engaged in the practice of medicine ever killed so many people as Spartacus. He did not kill them because he disliked them personally, but because he thought it advisable to do so. Had he lived till the present time he would have done well as a lecturer. "Ten Years in the Arena, with Illustrations," would draw first-rate at this time among a certain class of people. The large number of people still living in this country, who will lay aside their work and go twenty miles to attend a funeral, no matter whose funeral it is, would, no doubt, enjoy a bull fight or the calm and refining joy that hovered over the arena. Those who have paid $175,000 to see Colonel John L. Sullivan disfigure a friend, would, no doubt, have made it $350,000 if the victim could have been killed and dragged around over the ring by the leg.

Two thousand years have not refined us so much that we need be puffed up with false pride about it.

Concerning Book Publishing.

"AMATEUR" writes me that he is about to publish a book, and asks me if I will be kind enough to suggest some good, reliable publisher for him.

This would suggest that "Amateur" wishes to confer his book on some deserving publisher with a view to building him up and pouring a golden stream of wealth into his coffers. "Amateur" already, in his mind's eye, sees the eager millions of readers knocking each other down and trampling upon one another in the mad rush for his book. In my mind, I see his eye, lighted up with hope, and, though he lives in New Jersey, I fancy I can hear his quickened breath as his bosom heaves.

WISHES TO CONFER HIS BOOK ON SOME DESERVING PUBLISHER.

Evidently he has never published a book. There is a good deal of fun ahead of him that he does not wot of. I used to think that when I got the last page of my book ready for press, the front yard would be full of publishers tramping down the velvet lawn and the meek-eyed pansies in their crazy efforts to get hold of the manuscript, but when I had written the last word of my first volume of soul-throb, and had opened the casement to look out on the howling, hungry mob of publishers, with check-books in one hand and a pillow-case full of scads in the other, I was a little puzzled to notice the abrupt and pronounced manner in which they were not there.

All of us have to struggle before we can catch the eye of the speaker.

Milton didn't get one-fiftieth as much for "Paradise Lost" as I got for my first book, and yet you will find people to-day who claim that if Milton had lived he could have knocked the socks off of me with one hand tied behind him. Recollect, however, that I am not here to open a discussion on this matter. Everyone is entitled to his own opinion in relation to authors. People cannot agree on the relative merits of literature. Now, for instance, last summer I met a man over in South Park, Col., who could repeat page after page of Shakespeare, and yet, when I asked him if he was familiar with the poems of the "Sweet Singer of Michigan," he turned upon me a look of stolid vacancy, and admitted that he had never heard of her in his life.

A Calm.

THE old Greeley Colony in Colorado, a genuine oasis in the desert, with its huge irrigating canals of mountain water running through the mighty wheat fields, glistening each autumn at the base of the range, affords a good deal that is curious, not only to the mind of the gentleman from the States, but even to the man who lives at Cheyenne, W. T., only a few hours' journey to the north.

You could hardly pick out two cities so near each other and yet so unlike as Cheyenne and Greeley The latter is quiet, and even accused of being dull, and yet everybody is steadily getting rich. It is a town of readers, thinkers and mental independents. It is composed of the elements of New England shrewdness and Western push, yet Greeley as compared with Cheyenne would be called a typical New England town in the midst of the active, fluctuating, booming West.

Cheyenne is not so tame. With few natural advantages the reputation of Cheyenne is that, in commercial parlance, she is "A 1" for promptness in paying her debts and absence of failures. There is more wealth there in proportion to the number of inhabitants than elsewhere in the civilized world, no doubt. The people take special pleasure in surprising Eastern people who visit them by a reception very often that they will long remember for cordiality, hospitality, and even magnificence.

Still I didn't start out to write up either Cheyenne or Greeley I intended to mention casually Dr. Law, of the latter place, who acted as my physician for a few months and coaxed me back from the great hereafter. I had been under the hands of a physician just before, who was also coroner, and who, I found afterward, was trying to treat me professionally as long as the lamp held out to burn, intending afterward to sit upon me officially He had treated me professionally until he was about ready to summon his favorite coroner's jury. Then I got irritated and left the county of his jurisdiction.

Learning that Dr. Law was relying solely on the practice of medicine for a livelihood, I summoned him, and after explaining the great danger that stood in the way of harmonizing the practice of medicine and the official work of the inquest business, I asked him if he had any business connection with any undertaking establishment or *hic jacet* business, and learning from him that he had none, I engaged him to solder up my vertebræ and reorganize my spinal duplex.

Sometimes it isn't entirely the medicine you swallow that paralyzes pain so much as it is the quiet magnetism of a good story and the snap of a pleasant eye. I had one physician who tried to look joyous when he came into the room, but he generally asked me to run my tongue out till he could see where it was tied on, then he would feel my pulse with his cold finger and time it with a $6 watch, and after that he would write a new prescription for horse medicine and heave a sigh, look at me as he might if it had been the last time he ever expected to see me on earth, and then he would sigh and go away. When he came back he generally looked shocked and grieved to find me alive. This was the *pro tem* physician and *ex-officio* coroner. I always felt as though I ought to apologize to him for clinging to life so, when no doubt he had the jury in the hall waiting to "view" me.

Dr. Law used to tell me of the early history of the Greeley Colony, and how the original cranks of the community used to be in session most of the time, and how they sometimes neglected to do their planting to do legislating, and how they overdid the council work and neglected to "bug" their potatoes. I remember, also, of his description of how the crew, working on the original big irrigating canal, struck when it was about half done, and swore that from the Poudre the ditch was going to run up hill, and would, therefore, be a failure. The engineer didn't know at first what was best to do with the beligerent laborers, but finally he took the leader away from the rest of the crew and said, "Now, I tell you this in confidence, because of course I know perfectly well that the stockholders may kick on it if they hear it, but I'm building the blamed thing as level as I can and putting one end of it in the Poudre and one end in the Platte. Now, if I'm building it up hill the water'll run down from the Platte into the Poudre, and if not it'll run from the Poudre into the Platte. Sabe?"

The ditch was built, and now a deep, still river runs from the Poudre to the Platte, according to advertisement.

Greeley is also noted for its watchmakers. I sent my watch to the first one I heard of, and he said it needed cleaning. He cleaned it. I paid him $2 and took it home, when it ran two hours and then suspended. Then I took it to another watchmaker who said that the first man had used machine oil on its works, and had heated the wheels so as to gum the oil on the cogs. He would have to eradicate the cooked oil from the watch, and it would cost me $3. I paid it, and joyfully took the watch home. The next day I found that it had gained time enough to pay for itself. By noon, it had fatigued itself so that it was losing terribly, and by the day following had folded its still hands across its pale face in the sleep that knows no waking. I took it to the third and last jeweler in the town. Everyone said he was a good workman, but a trifle slow. In the afternoon I went in to see how he was getting along with it. He was sitting at his bench with a dice cup in his eye, apparently looking into the digestive economy of the watch.

I looked at him some time, not wishing to disturb him and interfere with his diagnosis. He did not move or say anything. Several people came in to trade and get the correct time, but he paid no attention to them.

I got tired and changed from one foot to the other several times. Then I asked him how he got along, or something of that kind, but he never opened his head. He was the most preoccupied watch savant I ever saw. No outside influence could break up his chain of thought when he got after a diseased watch.

I finally got around on the outside of the shop and looked in the window, where I could get a good view of his face

He was asleep.

The Story of a Struggler.

MY name is Kaulbach. William J. Kaulbach is my name, and I am spending the summer in Canada. I may remain here during the winter, also. My parents are very poor. They had never been wealthy, and at the time of my birth they were even less wealthy than they had been before. As soon as I was born the poverty of my parents attracted my attention. I decided at once to relieve their distress. I intended to aid them from my own pocket, but found upon examination that I had no funds in my pocket; also, no pocket; also, no place to put a pocket if I had brought one with me. So my parents continued to be poor, and to put by a little poverty for a rainy day. I was sole heir to the poverty they had acquired in all these years.

Nature did not do much for me in the way of beauty, either. I was quite plain when born and may still be identified by that peculiarity. Plainness with me is not only a characteristic, but it is a passion. My whole being is wrapped up in it. My hair is a sort of neutral brindle, such as grows upon the top of a retired hair trunk, and my freckles are olive green, fading into a delicate, crushed-bran color. They are very large, and actually pain me at times.

My teacher tried to encourage me by telling me of other poor boys who had grown up to be president of the United States, and he tried to get me to consent to having my name used as a candidate; but I refrained from doing so. I knew that, although I was deserving of the place, I could not endure the bitterness of a campaign, and that the illustrated papers would enlarge upon my personal appearance and bring out my freckles till you could hang your hat on them.

So I grew up to be a stage robber.

When I have my mask on my freckles do not show. I lectured on phrenology at first to get means to prosecute my studies as a stage robber, and when I had perfected myself as a burglar I went abroad to study the methods of the Italian banditti. I was two years under the teaching of the old masters, and acquired great fluency as a robber while there. I studied from nature all the time, and some of my best work was taken from life. I had an opportunity to observe all the methods of the most celebrated garroting maestro and stilletto virtuoso. He was an enthusiast and thoroughly devoted to his art. He had a large price on his head, also. Aside from that he went bareheaded winter and summer.

MAKING HIS DEBUT.

Finally I returned to my own native land, poor, but fired with a mighty ambition. I went west and proceeded at once to *debut.* I went west to hold up the country I was very successful, indeed, and have had my hands in the pockets of our most eminent men.

We were isolated from society a good deal, but we met the better class of people now and then in the course of our business. I did not like so much night work, and sometimes we had to eat raw pork because we did not wish to build a fire that would attract mosquitoes and sheriffs. So we were liable more or less to trichina and insomnia, but still we were free from sewer gas and poll tax. We did not get our mail with much regularity, but we got a lick at some mighty fine scenery.

But all this is only incidental. What I desired to say was this: Fame and distinction come high, and when we have them in our grasp at last we find that they bring their resultant sorrows. I worked long and hard for fame, and sat up nights and rode through alkali dust for thousands of miles, that I might be known as the leading robber of the age in which I lived, only to find at last that my great fame was the source of my chief annoyance. It made me so widely known that I felt, as Christine Nilsson says, "as though I lived in a glass case." Everyone wanted to see me. Everyone wanted my autograph. Everyone wanted my skeleton to hang up in the library.

I could have traveled with a show and drawn a large salary, but I hated to wear a boiler iron overcoat all through the hot weather, after having lived so wild and free. But all this attention worried me so that I could not sleep, and many a night I would arise from the lava bed on which I had reclined, and putting on my dressing-gown and slippers, I would wander about under the stars and wish that I could be an unknown boy again in my far away home. But I could not. I often wished that I could die a natural death, but that was out of the question.

Finally, it got so that I did not dare to take a chew of tobacco, unless I did so under an assumed name. I hardly dared to let go of my six-shooter long enough to wipe my nose, for fear that someone might get the drop on me.

That is the reason why I came to Canada. Here among so many criminals, I do not attract attention, but I use a *nom de plume* all the time, even here, and all these hot nights, while others take off their clothing, I lie and swelter in my heavy winter *nom de plume*.

The Old Subscriber.

AT this season of the year, we are forcibly struck with the earnest and honest effort that is being made by the publisher of the American newspaper. It is a healthy sign and a hopeful one for the future of our country. It occurs to me that with the great advancement of the newspaper, and the family paper, and the magazine, we do not expect leaders and statesmen to think for us so much as we did fifty years ago. We do not allow the newspaper to mold us so much as we did. We enjoy reading the opinion of a bright, brave, and cogent editor because we know that he sits where he can acquire his facts in a few hours from all quarters of the globe, and speak truly to his great audience in relation to those facts, but we have ceased to allow even that man to think for us.

What then is to be the final outcome of all this? Is it not that the average American is going to use, and is using, his thinker more than he ever did before? Will not that thinker then, like the muscle of the blacksmith's arm, or the mule's hind foot, grow to a wondrous size as a result? Most assuredly.

The day certainly is not far distant, when the American can not only outfight, out-row, out-bat, out-run, out-lie, and out-sail all other nationalities; but he will also be able to out-think them. We already point with pride to some of the wonderful thoughts that our leading thinkists, with their thinkers, have thunk. There are native born Americans now living, who have thought of things that would make the head of the amateur thinker ache for a week.

All this is largely due to the free use of the newspaper as a home educator. The newspaper is growing more and more ubiquitous, if I may be allowed the expression. Many poor people, who, a few years ago, could not afford the newspaper, now have it scolloped and put it on their pantry shelves every year.

But I did not start out to enlarge upon the newspaper. I would like to say a word or two more, however, on that general subject. Very often we hear some wise man with the responsibility of the universe on his sholders, the man who thinks he is the censor of the human race now, and that he will be foreman of the grand jury on the Judgment Day—we hear this kind of man say every little while.

"We've got too many papers. We are loaded down with reading matter. Can't read all my paper every day. Lots of days I throw my paper aside before I get it all read through, and never have a chance to finish it. All that is dead loss."

It is, of course, a dead loss to that kind of a man. He is the kind of man that expects his family to begin at one side of the cellar and eat right straight across it—cabbages, potatoes, turnips, pickles, apples, pumpkins, etc., etc.,—without stopping to discriminate. There are none too many papers, so far as the subscriber is concerned. Looking at it from the publisher's standpoint sometimes, there are too many.

To the man who has inherited too large, wide, sinewy hands, and a brain that under the microscope looks like a hepatized lung, it seems some days as though the field had been over-crowded when he entered it. To the young man who was designed to maul rails or sock the fence-post into the bosom of the earth, and who has evaded that sphere of action and disregarded the mandate to maul rails, or to take a coal-pick and toy with the bowels of the earth, hoping to win an easier livelihood by feeding sour paste to village cockroaches, and still poorer pabulum to his subscribers, the newspaper field seems to be indeed jam full.

But not so the man who is tall enough to see into the future about nine feet. He still remembers that he must live in the hearts of his subscribers, and he makes their wants his own. He is not to proud to listen to suggestions from the man who works. He recognizes that it is not the man with the diamond-mounted stomach who has contributed most to his success, but the man who never dips into society much with the exception of his family, perhaps, and that ought to be good society. A man ought not to feel too good to associate with his wife and children. Generally my sympathies are with his wife and children, if they have to associate with him very much.

But if I could ever get down to it, I would like to say a word on behalf of the old subscriber. Being an old subscriber myself, I feel an interest in his cause; and as he rarely rushes into print except to ask why the police contrive to keep aloof from anything that might look like a fight, or to inquire why the fire department will continue year after year to run through the streets killing little children who never injured the department in any way, just so that they will be in time to chop a hole in the roof of a house that is not on fire, and pour some water down into the library, then whoop through an old tin dipper a few times and go away—as the old subscriber does not generally say much in print except on the above subjects, I make bold to say on his behalf that as a rule, he is not treated half as well as the prodigal son, who has been spending his substance on a rival paper, or stealing his news outright from the old subscriber.

Why should we pat the new subscriber on the back, and give him a new album that will fall to pieces whenever you laugh in the same room? Why should you forget the old love for the new? Do we not often impose on the old subscriber by giving up the space he has paid for to flaming advertisements to catch the coy and skittish gudgeon who still lurks outside the fold? Do we not ofttimes offer a family Bible for a new subscriber when an old subscriber may be in a lost and undone state?

Do we not again and again offer to the wife of our new subscriber a beautiful, plain gold ring, or a lace pin for a year's subscription and $1, while the wife of our old subscriber is just in the shank of a long, hard, cold winter, without a ring or a pin to her back?

We ought to remember that the old subscriber came to us with his money when we most needed it. He bore with us when we were new in the business, and used such provincialisms as "We have saw" and "If we had knew." He bore with us when the new column rules were so sharp that they chawed the paper all up, and the office was so cold, waiting for wood to come in on subscription, that the "color" was greasy and reluctant. He took our paper and paid for it, while the new subscriber was in the penitentiary for all we know. He made a mild kick sometimes when he "didn't git his paper reggler;" but he paid on the first day of January every year in advance, out of an old calfskin wallet that opened out like a concertina, and had a strap that went around it four times, and looked as shiny, and sweaty, and good-natured as the razor-strop that might have been used by Noah.

The old subscriber never asked any rebate, or requested a prize volume of poetry with a red cover, because he had paid for another year; but he simply warmed his numb fingers, so that he could loosen his overalls and lower one side enough to let his hand into the pocket of his best pantaloons underneath, and there he always found the smooth wallet, and inside of it there was always a $2 bill, that had been put there to pay for the paper. Then the old subscriber would warm his hands some more, ask "How's tricks?" but never begin to run down the paper, and then he would go away to work for another year.

I want to say that this country rests upon a great, solid foundation of old, paid-up subscribers. They are the invisible, rock-ribbed resting-place for the dazzling superstructure and the slim and peaked spire. Whether we procure a new press or a new dress, a new contributor or a new printers' towel, we must bank on the old subscriber; for the new one is fickle, and when some other paper gives him a larger or a redder covered book, he may desert our standard. He yearns for the flesh-pots and the new scroll saws of other papers. He soon wearies of a uniformly good paper, with no chance to draw a town lot or a tin mine — in Montana.

THE RIGHT SORT OF SUBSCRIBER.

Let us, therefore, brethren of the press, cling to the old subscriber as he has clung to us. Let us say to him, on this approaching Christmas Eve, "Son, thou art always with me, and all that I have is thine. It was meet that we should make merry, that this, thy brother, who had been a subscriber for our vile contemporary many years, but is alive again, and during a lucid interval has subscribed for our paper; but, after all, we would not go to him if we wanted to borrow a dollar. Remember that you still have our confidence, and when we want a good man to indorse our note at the bank, you will find that your name in our memory is ever fresh and green."

Looking this over, I am struck with the amount of stuff I have successfully said, and yet there is a paucity of ideas. Some writers would not use the word paucity in this place without first knowing the meaning of it, but I am not that way. There are thousands of words that I now use freely, but could not if I postponed it until I could learn their meaning. Timidity keeps many of our authors back, I think. Many are more timid about using big words than they are about using other people's ideas.

A friend of mine wanted to write a book, but hadn't the time to do it. So he asked me if I wouldn't do it for him. He was very literary, he said, but his business took up all his time, so I asked him what kind of a book he wanted. He said he wanted a funny book, with pictures in it and a blue cover. I saw at once that he had fine literary taste and delicate discrimination, but probably did not have time to give it full swing. I asked him what he thought it would be worth to write such a book. "Well," he said, he had always supposed that I enjoyed it myself, but if I thought I ought to have pay besides, he would be willing to pay the same as he did for his other writing—ten cents a folio.

He is worth $50,000, because he has documentary evidence to show that a man who made that amount out of deceased hogs, had the misfortune to be his father and then die.

It was a great triumph to be born under such circumstances, and yet the young man lacks the mental stamina necessary to know how to successfully eat common mush and milk in such a low key that will not alarm the police.

I use this incident more as an illustration than anything else. It illustrates how anything may be successfully introduced into an article of this kind without having any bearing whatever upon it.

I like to close a serious essay, or treatise, with some humorous incident, like the clown in the circus out West last summer, who joked along through the performance all the afternoon till two or three children went into convulsions, and hypochondria seemed to reign rampant through the tent. All at once a bright idea struck him. He climbed up on the flying trapeze, fell off, and broke his neck. He was determined to make that audience laugh, and he did it at last. Every one felt repaid for the trouble of going to the circus.

My Dog.

HAVE owned quite a number of dogs in my life, but they are all dead now. Last evening I visited my dog cemetery—just between the gloaming and the shank of the evening. On the biscuit-box cover that stands at the head of a little mound fringed with golden rod and pickle bottles, the idler may still read these lines, etched in red chalk by a trembling hand:

LITTLE KOSCIUSKO,
——NOT DEAD,——
BUT JERKED HENCE
By Request.
S. Y. L.
(See you Later.)

I do not know why he was called Kosciusko. I do not care. I only know that his little grave stands out there while the gloaming gloams and the soughing winds are soughing.

Do you ask why I am alone here and dogless in this weary world?

I will tell you, anyhow. It will not take long, and it may do me good:

Kosciusko came to me one night in winter, with no baggage and unidentified. When I opened the door he came in as though he had left something in there by mistake and had returned for it.

He stayed with us two years as a watch-dog. In a desultory way, he was a good watch-dog. If he had watched other people with the same unrelenting scrutiny with which he watched me, I might have felt his death more keenly than I do now.

The second year that little Kosciusko was with us, I shaved off a full beard one day while down town, put on a clean collar and otherwise disguised myself, intending to surprise my wife.

Kosciusko sat on the front porch when I returned. He looked at me as the cashier of a bank does when a newspaper man goes in to get a suspiciously large check cashed. He did not know me. I said, "Kosciusko, have you forgotten your master's voice?"

He smiled sarcastically, showing his glorious wealth of mouth, but still sat there as though he had stuck his tail into the door-steps and couldn't get it out.

So I waived the formality of going in at the front door, and went around to the portcullis, on the off side of the house, but Kosciusko was there when I arrived. The cook, seeing a stranger lurking around the manor house, encouraged Kosciusko to come and gorge himself with a part of my leg, which he did. Acting on this hint I went to the barn. I do not know why I went to the barn, but somehow there was nothing in the house that I wanted. When

THE COMBAT.

a man wants to be by himself, there is no place like a good, quiet barn for thought. So I went into the barn, about three feet prior to Kosciusko.

Noticing the stairway, I ascended it in an aimless kind of way, about four steps at a time. What happened when we got into the haymow I do not now recall, only that Kosciusko and I frolicked around there in the hay for some time. Occasionally I would be on top, and then he would have all the delegates, until finally I got hold of a pitchfork, and freedom shrieked when Kosciusko fell. I wrapped myself up in an old horse-net and went into the house. Some of my clothes were afterward found in the hay, and the doctor pried a part of my person out of Kosciusko's jaws, but not enough to do me any good.

I have owned, in all, eleven dogs, and they all died violent deaths, and went out of the world totally unprepared to die.

A Picturesque Picnic.

RAILROADS have made the Rocky Mountain country familiar and contiguous, I may say, to the whole world; but the somber cañon, the bald and blackened cliff, the velvety park and the snowy, silent peak that forever rests against the soft, blue sky, are ever new The foamy green of the torrent has whirled past the giant walls of nature's mighty fortress myriads of years, perhaps, and the stars have looked down into the great heart of earth for centuries, where the silver thread of streams, thousands of feet below, has been patiently carving out the dark cañon where the eagle and the solemn echo have their home.

I said this to a gentleman from Leadville a short time ago as we toiled up Kenoska Hill, between Platte cañon and the South Park, on the South Park and Pacific Railway. He said that might be true in some cases and even more so, perhaps, depending entirely on whether it would or not.

I do not believe at this moment that he thoroughly understood me. He was only a millionaire and his soul, very likely, had never throbbed and thrilled with the mysterious music nature yields to her poet child.

He could talk on and on of porphyry walls and contact veins, gray copper and ruby silver, and sulphurets and pyrites of iron, but when my eye kindled with the majestic beauty of these eternal battlements and my voice trembled a little with awe and wonder; while my heart throbbed and thrilled in the midst of nature's eloquent, golden silence, this man sat there like an Etruscan ham and refused to throb or thrill. He was about as unsatisfactory a throbber and thriller as I have met for years.

At an elevation of over 10,000 feet above high water mark, Fahrenheit, the South Park, a hundred miles long, surrounded by precipitous mountains or green and sloping foot-hills, burst upon us. In the clear, still air, a hundred miles away, at Pueblo, I could hear a promissory note and cut-throat mortgage drawing three per cent. a month. So calm and unruffled was the rarified air that I fancied I could hear the thirteenth assessment on a share of stock at Leadville toiling away at the bottom of a two hundred and fifty foot shaft.

Colorado air is so pure that men in New York have, in several instances, heard the dull rumble of an assessment working as far away as the San Juan country.

At Como, in the park, I met Col. Wellington Wade, the Duke of Dirty Woman's Ranch, and barber extraordinary to old Stand-up-and-Yowl, chief of the Piebiters.

Colonel Wade is a reformed temperance lecturer. I went to his shop to get shaved, but he was absent. I could smell hair oil through the keyhole, but the Colonel was not in his slab-inlaid emporium. He had been preparing another lecture on temperance, and was at that moment studying the habits of his adversary at a neighboring gin palace. I sat down on the steps and devoured the beautiful landscape till he came. Then I sat down in the chair, and he hovered over me while he talked about an essay he had written on the flowing bowl. His arguments were not so strong as his breath seemed to be. I asked him if he wouldn't breathe the other way awhile and let me sober up. I learned afterward that although his nose was red, his essay was not.

He would shave me for a few moments, and then he would hone the razor on his breath and begin over again. I think he must have been pickling his lungs in alcohol. I never met a more pronounced gin cocktail symphony and bologna sausage study in my life.

I think Sir Walter Scott must have referred to Colonel Wade when he said, "Breathes there a man with soul so dead?" Colonel Wade's soul might not have been dead, but it certainly did not enjoy perfect health.

I went over the mountains to Breckenridge the next day, climbed two miles perpendicularly into the sky, rode on a special train one day, a push car the next and a narrow-gauge engine the next. Saw all the beauty of the country, in charge of Superintendent Smith, went over to Buena Vista and had a congestion of the spine and a good time generally. You can leave Denver on a morning train and see enough wild, grand, picturesque loveliness before supper, to store away in your heart and hang upon the walls of memory, to last you all through your busy, humdrum life, and it is a good investment, too.

Taxidermy.

THIS name is from two Greek words which signify "arrangement" and "skin," so that the ancient Greeks, no doubt, regarded taxidermy as the original skin-game of that period. Taxidermy did not flourish in America prior to the year 1828. At that time an Englishman named Scudder established a museum and general repository for upholstered beasts.

Since then the art has advanced quite rapidly. To properly taxiderm, requires a fine taste and a close study of the subject itself in life, akin to the requirements necessary in order to succeed as a sculptor. I have seen taxidermed animals that would not fool anybody. I recall, at this time especially, a mountain lion, stuffed after death by a party who had not made this matter a subject of close study The lion was represented in a crouching attitude, with open jaws and red gums. As time passed on and year succeeded year, this lion continued to crouch. His tail became less rampant and drooped like a hired man on a hot day. His gums became less fiery red and his reddish skin hung over his bones in a loose and distraught manner, like an old buffalo robe thrown over the knees of a vinegary old maid. Spiders spun their webs across his dull, white fangs. Mice made their nests in his abdominal cavity. His glass eye became hopelessly strabismussed, and the moths left him bald-headed on the stomach. He was a sad commentary on the extremely transitory nature of all things terrestrial and the hollowness of the stuffed beast.

I had a stuffed bird for a long time, which showed the cunning of the stuffer to a great degree. It afforded me a great deal of unalloyed pleasure, because I liked to get old hunters to look at it and tell me what kind of a bird it was. They did not generally agree. A bitter and acrimonious fight grew out of a discussion in relation to this bird. A man from Vinegar Hill named Lyons and a party called Soiled Murphy (since deceased), were in my office one morning—Mr. Lyons as a witness, and Mr. Murphy in his great specialty as a drunk and disorderly. We had just disposed of the case, and had just stepped down from the bench, intending to take off the judicial ermine and put some more coal in the stove, when the attention of Soiled Murphy was attracted to the bird. He allowed that it was a common "hell-diver with an ab normal head," while Lyons claimed that it was a kingfisher.

The bird had a duck's body, the head of a common eagle and the feet of a sage hen. These parts had been adjusted with great care and the tail loaded with lead somehow, so that the powerful head would not tip the bird up behind. With this *rara avis*, to use a foreign term, I loved to amuse and instruct old hunters, who had been hunting all their lives for a free drink, and hear them tell how they had killed hundred of these birds over on the Poudre in an early day, or over near Elk Mountain when the country was new.

So Lyons claimed that he had killed millions of these fowls, and Soiled Murphy, who was known as the tomato can and beer-remnant savant of that country, said that before the Union Pacific Railroad got into that section, these birds swarmed around Hutton's lakes and lived on horned toads.

The feeling got more and more partisan till Mr. Lyons made a pass at Soiled Murphy with a large red cuspidor that had been presented to me by Valentine Baker, a dealer in abandoned furniture and mines. Mr. Murphy then welted Lyons over the head with the judicial scales. He then adroitly caught a lump of bituminous coal with his countenance and fell to the floor with a low cry of pain.

I called in an outside party as a witness, and in the afternoon both men were convicted of assault and battery. Soiled Murphy asked for a change of venue on the ground that I was prejudiced. I told him that I did not allow anything whatever to prejudice me, and went on with the case.

This great taxidermic masterpiece led to other assaults afterward, all of which proved remunerative in a small way. My successor claimed that the bird was a part of the perquisites of the office, and so I had to turn it over with the docket.

I also had a stuffed weasel from Cummins City that attracted a great deal of attention, both in this country and in Europe. It looked some like a weasel and some like an equestrian sausage with hair on it.

The Ways of Doctors.

"THERE'S a big difference in doctors, I tell you," said an old-timer to me the other day. "You think you know something about 'em, but you are still in the fluff and bloom, and kindergarten of life, Wait till you've been through what I have."

"Where, for instance?" I asked him.

"Well, say nothing about anything else, just look at the doctors we had in the war. We had a doctor in our regiment that looked as if he knew so much that it made him unhappy. I found out afterward that he ran a kind of cow foundling asylum, in Utah before the war, and when he had to prescribe for a human being, it seemed to kind of rattle him.

"I fell off'n my horse early in the campaign and broke my leg, I rickolect, and he sot the bone. He thought that a bone should be sot similar to a hen. He made what he called a good splice, but the break was above the knee, and he got the cow idea into his head in a way that set the knee behind. That was bad.

"I told him one day that he was a blamed fool. He gave me a cigar and told me I must be a mind reader.

HE GAVE ME A CIGAR.

"For several weeks our colonel couldn't eat anything, and seemed to feel kind of billious. He didn'tknow what the trouble was till he went to the doctor. He looked at the colonel a few moments, examined his tongue, and told him right off that he had lost his cud.

"He bragged a good deal on his diagnosis. He said he'd like to see the disease he couldn't diagnose with one hand tied behind him.

"He was always telling me how he had resuscitated a man they hung over at T— City in the early day. He was hung by mistake, it seemed. It was a

BURIED WITH MILITARY HONORS.

dark night and the Vigilance committee was in something of a hurry, having another party to hang over at Dirty Woman's ranch that night, and so they erroneously hung a quiet young feller from Illinois, who had been sent west to cure a case of bronchitis. He was right in the middle of an explanation when the head vigilanter kicked the board from under him and broke his neck.

"All at once, some one said: 'My God, we have made a ridiculous blunder. Boys, we can't be too careful about hanging total strangers. A few more such breaks as these, and people from the States will hesitate about coming here to make their homes. We have always claimed that this was a good country for bronchitis, but if we write to Illinois and tell this young feller's parents the facts, we needn't look for a very large hegira from Illinois next season. Doc., can't you do anything for the young man?'

"Then this young physician stepped forward, he says, and put his knee on the back of the boy's neck, give it a little push, at the same time pulled the head back with a snap that straightened the neck, and the young feller, who was in the middle of a large word, something like 'contumely,' when the barrel tipped over, finished out the word and went right on with the explanation. The doctor said he lived a good many years, and was loved and esteemed by all who knew him.

"The doctor was always telling of his triumphs in surgery He did save a good many lives, too, toward the close of the war. He did it in an odd way, too.

"He had about one year more to serve, and, with his doctoring on one side and the hostility of the enemy on the other, our regiment was wore-down to about five hundred men. Everybody said we couldn't stand it more than another year. One day, however, the doctor had just measured a man for a porus plaster, and had laid the stub of his cigar carefully down on the top of a red powder-keg, when there was a slight atmospheric disturbance, the smell of burnt clothes, and our regiment had to apply for a new surgeon.

"The wife of our late surgeon wrote to have her husband's remains forwarded to her, but I told her that it would be very difficult to do so, owing to the nature of the accident. I said, however, that we had found an upper set of store teeth imbedded in a palmetto tree near by, and had buried them with military honors, erecting over the grave a large board, on which was inscribed the name and age of the deceased and this inscription:

"*Not dead, but spontaneously distributed. Gone to meet his glorified throng of patients. Ta, ta. vain world.*"

Absent Minded.

I REMEMBER an attorney, who practiced law out West years ago, who used to fill his pipe with brass paper fasteners, and try to light it with a ruling pen about twice a day. That was his usual average.

He would talk in unknown tongues, and was considered a thorough and revised encyclopedia on everything from the tariff on a meerschaum pipe to the latitude of Crazy Woman's Fork west of Greenwich, and yet if he went to the postoffice he would probably mail his pocketbook and carefully bring his letter back to the office.

One day he got to thinking about the Monroe doctrine, or the sudden and horrible death of Judas Iscariot, and actually lost his office. He walked up and down for an hour, scouring the town for the evanescent office that had escaped his notice while he was sorrowing over the shocking death of Judas, or Noah's struggles against malaria and a damp, late spring.

Martin Luther Brandt was the name of this eccentric jurist. He got up in the night once, and dressed himself, and taking a night train in that dreamy way of his, rode on to Denver, took the Rio Grande train in the morning and drifted away into old Mexico somewhere. He must have been in that same old half comatose state when he went away, for he made a most ludicrous error in getting his wife in the train. When he arrived in old Mexico he found that he had brought another man's wife, and by some strange oversight had left his own at home with five children. It hardly seems possible that a man could be so completely enveloped in a brown study that he would err in the matter of a wife and five children, but such was the case with Martin Luther. Martin Luther couldn't tell you his own name if you asked him suddenly, so as to give him a nervous shock.

This dreamy, absent-minded, wool-gathering disease is sometimes contagious. Pretty soon after Martin Luther struck Mexico the malignant form of brown study broke out among the greasers, and an alarming mania on the somnambulistic order seemed to follow it. A party of Mexican somnambuloes one night got together, and while the disease was at its height tied Martin Luther to the gable of a 'dobe hen palace. His soul is probably at this moment floundering around through space, trying to find the evergreen shore.

An old hunter, who was a friend of mine, had this odd way of walking aimlessly around with his thoughts in some other world.

I used to tell him that some day he would regret it, but he only laughed and continued to do the same fool thing.

Last fall he saw a grizzly go into a cave in the upper waters of the Platte, and strolled in there to kill her. As he has not returned up to this moment, I am sure he has erroneously allowed himself to get mixed up as to the points of the compass, and has fallen a victim to this fatal brown study. Some think that the brown study had hair on it.

Woman's Wonderful Influence.

"WOMAN wields a wonderful influence over man's destinies," said Woodtick William, the other day, as he breathed gently on a chunk of blossom rock and then wiped it carefully with the tail of his coat.

"Woman in most cases is gentle and long suffering, but if you observe close for several consecutive weeks you will notice that she generally gets there with both feet.

"I've been quite a student of the female mind myself. I have, therefore, had a good deal of opportunity to compare the everedge man with the everedge woman as regards ketchin' on in our great general farewell journey to the tomb.

"Woman has figgered a good deal in my own destinies. My first wife was a large, powerful woman, who married me before I hardly knew it. She married me down near Provost, in an early day. Her name was Lorena. The name didn't seem to suit her complexion and phizzeek as a general thing. It was like calling the fat woman in the museum Lily. Lorena was a woman of great

"YOU GO ON WITH YOUR PETITION."

strength of purpose. She was also strong in the wrists. Lorena was of foreign extraction, with far-away eyes and large, earnest red hands. You ought to have saw her preserve order during the hour for morning prayers. I had a hired man there in Utah, in them days, who was inclined to be a scoffer at our plain home-made style of religion. So I told Lorena that I was a little afraid that Orlando Whoopenkaugh would rise up suddenly while I was at prayer and spatter my thinker all over the cook stove, or create some other ruction that would cast a gloom over our devotions.

"Lorena said: 'Never mind, William. You are more successful in prayer, while I am more successful in disturbances. You go on with your petition, and I will preserve order."

"Lorena saved my life once in a singular manner. Being a large, powerful woman, of course she no doubt preserved me from harm a great many times; but on this occasion it was a clear case.

"I was then sinking on the Coopon claim, and had got the prospect shaft down a couple of hundred foot and was drifting for the side wall with indifferent success. We was working a day shift of six men, blasting, hysting and a little timbering. I was in charge of the crew and eastern capital was furnishing the ready John Davis, if you will allow me that low term.

LORENA JUMPING NINE FEET HIGH.

"Lorena and me had been a little edgeways for several days, owing to a little sassy remark made by her and a retort on my part in which I thoughtlessly alluded to her brother, who was at that time serving out a little term for life down at Canyon City, and who, if his life is spared, is at it yet. If I wanted to make Lorena jump nine feet high and holler, all I had to do was just to allude in a jeering way to her family record. So she got madder and madder, till at last it ripened into open hostility, and about noon on the 13th day of September Lorena attacked me with a large butcher knife and drove me into the adjoining county. She told me, also, that if I ever returned to Provost she would cut me in two right between the pancreas and the watch pocket and feed me to the hens.

"I thought if she felt that way about it I would not return. I felt so hurt and so grieved about it that I never stopped till I got to Omaha. Then I heard how Lorena, as a means in the hands of Providence, had saved my unprofitable life.

"When she got back to the house and had put away her butcher knife, a man came rushing in to tell her that the boys had struck a big pay streak of water, and that the whole crew in the Coopon was drowned, her husband among the rest.

"Then it dawned on Lorena how she had saved me, and for the first time in her life she burst into tears. People who saw her said her grief was terrible. Tears are sad enough when shed by a man, but when we see a strong woman bowed in grief, we shudder.

"No one who has never deserted his wife at her urgent request can fully realize the pain and anguish it costs. I have been married many times since, but the sensation is just the same to-day as it was the first time I ever deserted my wife.

"As I said, though, a woman has a wonderful influence over a man's whole life. If I had a chance to change the great social fabric any, though, I should ask woman to be more thoughtful of her husband, and, if possible, less severe. I would say to woman, be a man. Rise above these petty little tyrannical ways. Instead of asking your husband what he does with every cent you give him, learn to trust him. Teach him that you have confidence in him. Make him think you have anyway, whether you have or not. Do not seek to get a whif, of his breath every ten minutes to see whether he has been drinking or not. If you keep doing that you will sock him into a drunkard's grave, sure pop. He will at first lie about it, then he will use disinfectants for the breath, and then he will stay away till he gets over it. The timid young man says, 'Pass the cloves, please. I've got to get ready to go home pretty soon.' The man whose wife really has fun with him says, 'Well, boys, good-night. I'm sorry for you.' Then he goes home.

"Very few men have had the opportunities for observation in a matrimonial way that I have, William. You see, one man judges all the wives in Christendom by his'n. Another does ditto, and so it goes. But I have made matrimony a study. It has been a life-work for me. Others have simply dabbled into it. I have studied all its phases and I am an expert. So I say to you that woman, in one way or another, either by strategy and winnin' ways or by main strength and awkwardness, is absolutely sure to wield an all-fired influence over poor, weak man, and while grass grows and water runs, pardner, you will always find her presiding over man's destinies and his ducats."

Causes for Thanksgiving.

WE are now rapidly approaching the date of our great national thanksgiving. Another year has almost passed by on the wings of tireless time.

Since last we gathered about the festive board and spattered the true inwardness of the family gobbler over the table cloth, remorseless time, who knows not the weight of weariness, has sought out the good, the true and the beautiful, as well as the old, the sinful and the tough, and has laid his heavy hand upon them. We have no more fitting illustration of the great truth that death prefers the young and tender than the deceased turkey upon which we are soon to operate. How still he lies, mowed down in life's young morn to make a yankee holiday.

How changed he seems! Once so gay and festive, now so still, so strangely quiet and reserved. How calmly he lies, with his bare limbs buried in the lurid atmosphere like those of a hippytehop artist on the west side.

Soon the amateur carver will plunge the shining blade into the unresisting bird, and the air will be filled with stuffing and half smothered profanity. The Thanksgiving turkey is a grim humorist, and nothing pleases him so well as to hide his joint in a new place and then flip over and smile when the student misses it and buries the knife in the bosom of a personal friend. Few men can retain their *sang froid* before company when they have to get a step ladder and take down the second joint and the merry thought from the chandelier while people are looking at them.

And what has the past year brought us? Speaking from a Republican standpoint, it has brought us a large wad of dark blue gloom. Speaking from a Democratic standpoint, it has been very prolific of fourth-class postoffices worth from $200 down to $1.35 per annum. Politically, the past year has been one of wonderful changes. Many have, during the year just past, held office for the first time. Many, also, have gone out into the cold world since last Thanksgiving and seriously considered the great problem of how to invest a small amount of actual perspiration in plain groceries.

Many who considered the life of a politician to be one of high priced food and inglorious ease, have found, now that they have the fruit, that it is ashes on their lips.

Our foreign relations have been mutually pleasant, and those who dwell across the raging main, far removed from the refining influences of our prohibitory laws, have still made many grand strides toward the amelioration of our lost and undone race. Many foreigners who have never experienced the pleasure of drinking mysterious beverages from gas fixtures and burial caskets in Maine, or from a blind pig in Iowa, or a Babcock fire extinguisher in Kansas, still enjoy life by bombarding the Czar as he goes out after a scuttle of coal at night, or by putting a surprise package of dynamite on the throne of a tottering dynasty, where said tottering dynasty will have to sit down upon it and then pass rapidly to another sphere of existence.

Many startling changes have taken place since last November. The political fabric in our own land has assumed a different hue, and men who a year ago were unnoticed and unknown are even more so now. This is indeed a healthy sign. No matter what party or faction may be responsible for this, I say in a wholly non-partisan spirit, that I am glad of it.

I am glad to notice that, owing to the active enforcement of the Edmunds bill in Utah, polygamy has been made odorous. The day is not far distant when Utah will be admitted as a State and her motto will be "one country, one flag, and one wife at a time." Then will peace and prosperity unite to make the modern Zion the habitation of men. The old style of hand-made valley tan will give place to a less harmful beverage, and we will welcome the new sister in the great family circle of States, not clothed in the disagreeable endowment robe, but dressed up in the Mother Hubbard wrapper, with a surcingle around it, such as the goddess of liberty wears when she has her picture taken.

Crops throughout the northwest have been fairly good, though the gain yield has been less in quantity and inferior in quality to that of last year. A Democratic administration has certainly frowned upon the professional, partisan office seekers, but it has been unable to stay the onward march of the chintz bug or to produce a perceptible falling off in pip among the yellow-limbed fowls. While Jeffersonian purity and economy have seemed to rage with great virulence at Washington, in the northwest heaves and botts among horses and common, old-fashioned hollow horn among cattle have been the prevailing complaints.

And yet there is much for which we should be thankful. Many broad-browed men who knew how a good paper ought to be conducted, but who had no other visible means of support, have passed on to another field of labor, leaving the work almost solely in the hands of the vast army of novices who at the present are at the head of journalism throughout the country, and who sadly miss those timely words of caution that were wont to fall from the lips of those men whose spirits are floating through space, finding fault with the arrangement of the solar system.

The fool-killer, in the meantime, has not been idle. With his old, rusty, unloaded musket, he has gathered in enough to make his old heart swell with pride, and to this number he has added many by using "rough on rats," a preparation that never killed anything except those that were unfortunate enough to belong to the human family.

Still the fool-killer has missed a good many on account of the great rush of business in his line, and I presume that no one has a greater reason to be thankful for this oversight than I have.

Farming in Maine.

THE State of Maine is a good place in which to experiment with prohibition, but it is not a good place to farm it in very largely.

In the first place, the season is generally a little reluctant. When I was up near Moosehead Lake, a short time ago, people were driving across that body of water on the ice with perfect impunity. That is one thing that interferes with the farming business in Maine. If a young man is sleigh-riding every night till midnight, he don't feel like hoeing corn the following day. Any man who has ever had his feet frost-bitten while bugging potatoes, will agree with me that it takes away the charm of pastoral pursuits. It is this desire to amalgamate dog days and Santa Claus, that has injured Maine as an agricultural hot-bed.

A DAY-DREAM.

Another reason that might be assigned for refraining from agricultural pursuits in Maine, is that the agitator of the soil finds when it is too late that soil itself, which is essential to the successful propagation of crops, has not been in use in Maine for years. While all over the State there is a magnificent stone foundation on which a farm might safely rest, the superstructure, or farm proper, has not been secured.

If I had known when I passed through Minnesota and Illinois what a soil famine there was in Maine, I would have brought some with me. The stone crop this year in Maine will be very great. If they do not crack open during the dry weather, there will be a great many. The stone bruise is also looking unusually well for this season of the year, and chilblains were in full bloom when I was there.

In the neighborhood of Pittsfield, the country seems to run largely to cold water and chattel mortgages. Some think that rum has always kept Maine back, but I claim that it has been wet feet. In another article I refer to the matter of rum in Maine more fully.

The agricultural resources of Pittsfield and vicinity are not great, the principal exports being spruce gum and Christmas trees. Here also the huckleberry hath her home. But the country seems to run largely to Christmas trees. They were not yet in bloom when I visited the State, so it was too early to gather popcorn balls and Christmas presents.

Here, near Pittsfield, is the birthplace of the only original wormless dried apple pie, with which we generally insult our gastric economy when we lunch along the railroad. These pies, when properly kiln-dried and rivetted, with German silver monogram on top, if fitted out with Yale time lock, make the best fire and burglar-proof wormless pies of commerce. They take the place of civil war, and as a promoter of intestine strife they have no equal.

The farms in Maine are fenced in with stone walls. I do not know way this is done, for I did not see anything on these farms that anyone would naturally yearn to carry away with him.

I saw some sheep in one of these enclosures. Their steel-pointed bills were lying on the wall near them, and they were resting their jaws in the crisp, frosty morning air. In another enclosure a farmer was planting clover seed with a hypodermic syringe, and covering it with a mustard plaster. He said that last year his clover was a complete failure because his mustard plasters were no good. He had tried to save money by using second-hand mustard plasters, and of course the clover seed, missing the warm stimulus, neglected to rally, and the crop was a failure.

Here may be noticed the canvas-back moose and a strong antipathy to good rum. I do not wonder that the people of Maine are hostile to rum—if they judge all rum by Maine rum. The moose is one of the most gamey of the finny tribe. He is caught in the fall of the year with a double-barrel shotgun and a pair of snow-shoes. He does not bite unless irritated, but little boys should not go near the female moose while she is on her nest. The masculine moose wears a harelip, and a hat rack on his head to which is attached a placard on which is printed.

☞ PLEASE KEEP OFF THE GRASS. ☜

This shows that the moose is a humorist.

Doosedly Dilatory.

SINCE the investigation of Washington pension attorneys, it is a little remarkable how scarce in the newspapers is the appearance of advertisements like this.

PENSIONS! Thousands of soldiers of the late war are still entitled to pensions with the large accumulations since the injury was received. We procure pensions, back pay, allowances. Appear in the courts for non-resident clients in United States land cases, etc. Address Skinnem & Co., Washington, D. C.

I didn't participate in the late war, but I have had some experience in putting a few friends and neighbors on the track of a pension. Those who have tried it will remember some of the details. It always seemed to me a little more difficult somehow for a man who had lost both legs at Antietam, than for the man who got his nose pulled off at an election three years after the war closed. It, of course, depended a good deal on the extemporaneous affidavit qualifications of the applicant. About five years ago an acquaintance came to me and said he wanted to get a pension from the government, and that he hadn't the first idea about the details. He didn't know whether he should apply to the President or to the Secretary of State. Would I "kind of put him onto the racket." I asked him what he wanted a pension for, and he said his injury didn't show much, but it prevented his pursuit of kopecks and happiness. He had nine children by his first wife, and if he could get a pension he desired to marry again.

As to the nature of his injuries, he said that at the battle of Fair Oaks he supported his command by secreting himself behind a rail fence and harassing the enemy from time to time, by a system of coldness and neglect on his part. While thus employed in breaking the back of the Confederacy, a solid shot struck a crooked rail on which he was sitting, in such a way as to jar his spinal column. From this concussion he had never fully recovered. He didn't notice it any more while sitting down and quiet, but the moment he began to do manual labor or to stand on his feet too long, unless he had a bar or something to lean up against, he felt the cold chill run up his back and life was no object.

I told him that I was too busy to attend to it, and asked him why he didn't put his case in the hands of some Washington attorney, who could be on the ground and attend to it. He decided that he would, so he wrote to one of these philanthropists whom we will call Fitznoodle. I give him the *nom de plume* of Fitznoodle to nip a $20,000 libel suit in the bud. Well, Fitznoodle sent back some blanks for the claimant to sign, by which he bound himself, his heirs, executors, representatives and assigns, firmly by these presents to pay to said Fitznoodle, the necessary fees for postage, stationery, car fare, concert tickets, and office rent, while said claim was in the hands of the pension department. He said in a letter that he would have to ask for $2, please, to pay for postage. He inclosed a circular in which he begged to refer the claimant to a reformed member of the bar of the District of Columbia, a backslidden foreign minister and three prominent men who had been dead eleven years by the watch. In a postscript he again alluded to the $2 in a casual way, waved the American flag two times, and begged leave to subscribe himself once more. "Yours Fraternally and professionally, Good Samaritan Fitznoodle, Attorney at Law, Solicitor in Chancery, and Promotor of Even-handed Justice in and for the District of Columbia." The claimant sent his $2, not necessarily for publication, but as a guaranty of good faith.

Later on Mr. Fitznoodle said that the first step would be to file a declaration enclosing $5 and the names of two witnesses who were present when the claimant was born, and could identify him as the same man who enlisted from Emporia in the Thirteenth Kansas Nighthawks. Five dollars must be enclosed to defray the expenses of a trip to the office of the commissioner of pensions, which trip would naturally take in eleven saloons and ten cents in car fare. "P S.—Attach to the declaration the signature and seal of a notary public of pure character, $5, the certificate of the clerk of a court of record as to the genuineness of the signature of the notary public, his term of appointment and $5." These documents were sent, after which there was a lull of about three months. Then the swelling in Mr. Fitznoodle's head had gone down a little, but there was still a seal brown taste in his mouth. So he wrote the claimant that it would be necessary to jog the memory of the department about $3 dollars worth; and to file collateral testimony setting forth that claimant was a native born American or that he had declared his intention to become a citizen of the United States, that he had not formed nor expressed an opinion for or against the accused, which the testimony would not eradicate, that he would enclose $3, and that he had never before applied for a pension. After awhile a circular from the pension end of the department was received, stating that the claimant's application had been received, filed and docketed No. 188,935,-062½, on page 9,847 of book G, on the thumb-hand side as you come in on the New York train. On the strength of this document the claimant went to the grocery and bought an ecru-colored ham, a sack of corn meal and a pound of tobacco. In June Mr. Fitznoodle sent a blank to be filled out by the claimant, stating whether he had or had not been baptized prior to his enlistment; and, if so, to what extent, and how he liked it so far as he had gone. This was to be sworn to before two witnesses, who were to be male, if possible, and if not, the department would insist on their being female. These witnesses must swear that they had no interest in the said claim, or anything else. On receipt of this, together with $5 in postoffice money order or New York draft, the document would be filed and, no doubt, acted upon at once. In July, a note came from the attorney saying that he regretted to write that the pension department was now 250,000 claims behind, and if business was taken up in its regular order, the claim under discussion might not be reached for between nine and ten years. However, it would be possible to "expedite" the claim, if $25 could be remitted for the purpose of buying a spike-tail coat and plug hat, in which to appear before the commissioner of pensions and mash him flat on the shape of the attorney. As the claimant didn't know much of the practical working of the machinery of government, he swallowed this pill and remitted the $25. Here followed a good deal of red tape and international monkeying during which the claimant was alternately taking an oath to support the constitution of the United States, and promising to support the constitution and by-laws of Mr. Fitznoodle. The claimant was constantly assured that his claim was a good one and on these autograph letters written with a type-writer, the war-born veteran with a concussed vertebra, bought groceries and secured the funds to pay his assessments.

For a number of years I heard nothing of the claim, but a few months ago, when Mr. Fitznoodle was arrested and jerked into the presence of the grand jury, a Washington friend wrote me that the officers found in his table a letter addressed to the man who was jarred in the rear of the Union army;

and in which (the letter, I mean), he alluded to the long and pleasant correspondence which had sprung up between them as lawyer and client, and regretting that, as the claim would soon be allowed, their friendly relations would no doubt cease, would he please forward $13 to pay freight on the pension money, and also a lock of his hair that Mr. Fitznoodle could weave into a watchchain and wear always. As the claimant does not need the papers, he probably thinks by this time that Mr. Good Samaritan Fitznoodle has been kidnapped and thrown into the moaning, hungry sea.

Every Man His Own Paper-Hanger.

IT would please me very much, at no distant day, to issue a small book filled with choice recipes and directions for making home happy I have accumulated an immense assortment of these things, all of general use and all excellent in their way, because they have been printed in papers all over the country—papers that would not be wrong. Some of these recipes I have tried.

I have tried the recipe for paste and directions for applying wall paper, as published recently in an agricultural paper to which I had become very much attached.

This recipe had all the characteristics of an ingenuous and honest document. I cut it out of the paper and filed it away where I came very near not finding it again. But I was unfortunate enough to find it after a long search.

The scheme was to prepare a flour paste that would hold forever, and at the same time make the paper look smooth and neat to the casual observer. It consisted of so many parts flour, so many parts hot water and so many parts common glue. First, the walls were to be sized, however. I took a common tape measure and sized the walls.

Then I put a dishpan on the cook stove, poured in the flour, boiling water and glue. This rapidly produced a dark brown mess of dough, to which I was obliged to add more hot water. It looked extremely repulsive to me, but it looked a good deal better than it smelled.

I did not have much faith in it, but I thought I would try it. I put some of it on a long strip of wall paper and got up on a chair to apply it. In the excitement of trying to stick it on the wall as nearly perpendicular as possible, I lost my balance while still holding the paper and fell in such a manner as to wrap four yards of bronze paper and common flour paste around my wife's head, with the exception of about four feet of the paper which I applied to an oil painting of a Gordon Setter in a gilt frame.

I decline to detail the dialogue which then took place between my wife and myself. Whatever claim the public may have on me, it has no right to demand this. It will continue to remain sacred. That is, not so very sacred of course, if I remember my exact language at the time, but sacredly secret from the prying eyes of the public.

It is singular, but it is none the less the never dying truth, that the only time that paste ever stuck anything at all, was when I applied it to my wife and that picture. After that it did everything but adhere. It gourmed and it gummed everything, but that was all.

I LOST MY BALANCE.

The man who wrote the recipe may have been stuck on it, but nothing else ever was.

Finally a friend came along who helped me pick the paper off the dog and soothe my wife. He said that what this paste needed was more glue and a quart of molasses. I added these ingredients, and constructed a quart of chemical molasses which looked like crude ginger bread in a molten state.

Then, with the aid of my friend, I proceeded to paper the room. The paper would seem to adhere at times, and then it would refrain from adhering. This was annoying, but we succeeded in applying the paper to the walls in a way that showed we were perfectly sincere about it. We didn't seek to mislead anybody or cover up anything. Any one could see where each roll of paper tried to be amicable with its neighbor—also where we had tried the laying on of hands in applying the paper.

We got all the paper on in good shape—also the bronze. But they were in different places. The paper was on the walls, but the bronze was mostly on our clothes and on our hands. I was very tired when I got through, and I went to bed early, hoping to get much needed rest. In the morning, when I felt fresh and rested, I thought that the paper would look better to me.

There is where I fooled myself. It did not look better to me. It looked worse.

All night long I could occasionally hear something crack like a Fourth of July. I did not know at the time what it was, but in the morning I discovered.

It seems that, during the night, that paper had wrinkled itself up like the skin on the neck of a pioneer hen after death. It had pulled itself together with so much zeal that the room was six inches smaller each way and the carpet didn't fit.

There is only one way to insure success in the publication of recipes. They must be tried by the editor himself before they are printed. If you have a good recipe for paste, you must try it before you print it. If you have a good remedy for botts, you must get a botty horse somewhere and try the remedy before you submit it. If you think of publishing the antidote for a certain poison, you should poison some one and try the antidote on him, in order to test it, before you bamboozle the readers of your paper.

This, of course, will add a good deal of extra work for the editor, but editors need more work. All they do now is to have fun with each other, draw their princely salaries, and speak sarcastically of the young poet who sings,

> "You have came far o'er the sea,
> And I've went away from thee."

Sixty Minutes in America.

THE following selections are from the advance sheets of a forthcoming work with the above title, to be published by M. Foll de Roll. It is possible that other excerpts will be made from the book, in case the present harmonious state of affairs between France and America is not destroyed by my style of translation.

In the preface M. Foll de Roll says: "France has long required a book of printed writings about that large, wide land of whom we listen to so much and yet so little *sabe*, as the piquant Californian shall say. America is considerable. America I shall call vast. She care nothing how high freedom shall come; she must secure him. She exclaims to all people: 'You like freedom pretty well, but you know nothing of it. We throw away every day more freedom than you shall see all your life. Come to this place when you shall run out of freedom. We make it. Do not ask us for money, but if you want personal liberty, please look over our vast stock before you elsewhere go.'

"So everybody goes to America, where he shall be free to pay cash for what the American has for sale.

"In this book will be found everything that the French people want to know of that singular land, for did I not cross it from New Jersey City, the town where all the New York people have to go to get upon the cars, through to the town of San Francisco?

"For years the writer of this book has had it in his mind to go across America, and then tell the people of France, in a small volume costing one franc, all about the grotesque land of the freedom bird."

* * * * * * * * *

In the opening chapter he alludes to New York casually, and apologizes for taking up so much space.

"When you shall land in New York, you shall feel a strange sensation. The stomach is not so what we should call 'Rise up William Riley,' to use an

Americanism which will not bear translation. I ride along the Rue de Twenty-three, and want to eat everything my eyes shall fall upon.

"I stay at New York all night, and eat one large supper at 6 o'clock, and again at 9. At 12 I awake and eat the inside of my hektograph, and then lie down once more to sleep. The hektograph will be henceforth, as the American shall say, no good, but what is that when a man is starving in a foreign land?

"I leave New York in the morning on the Ferry de Pavonia, a steamer that goes to New Jersey City Many people go to New York to buy food and clothes. Then you shall see them return to the woods, where they live the rest of the time. Some of the females are quite *petite* and, as the Americans have it, 'scrumptious.' One stout girl at New Jersey City, I was told, was 'all wool and a yard wide.'

"The relations between New York and New Jersey City are quite amicable, and the inhabitants seem to spend much of their time riding to and fro on the Ferry de Pavonia and other steamers. When I talked to them in their own language they would laugh with great glee, and say they could not parley voo Norwegian very good.

"The Americans are very fond of witnessing what may be called the *tournament de slug.* In this, two men wearing upholstered mittens shake hands, and then one strikes at the other with his right hand, so as to mislead him, and, while he is taking care of that, the first man hits him with his left and knocks out some of his teeth. Then the other man spits out his loose teeth and hits his antagonist on the nose, or feeds him with the thumb of his upholstered mitten for some time. Half the gate money goes to the hospital where these men are in the habit of being repaired.

"One of these men, who is now the champion scrapper, as one American author has it, was once a poor boy, but he was proud and ambitious. So he practiced on his wife evenings, after she had washed the dishes, until he found that he could 'knock her out,' as the American has it. Then he tried it on other relatives, and step by step advanced till he could make almost any man in America cough up pieces of this upholstered mitten which he wears in public.

"In closing this chapter on New York, I may say that I have not said so much of the city itself as I would like, but enough so that he who reads with care may feel somewhat familiar with it. New York is situated on the east side of America, near New Jersey City. The climate is cool and frosty a part of the year, but warm and temperate in the summer months. The surface is generally level, but some of the houses are quite tall.

"I would not advise Frenchmen to go to New York now, but rather to wait until the pedestal of M. Bartholdi's Statue of Liberty has been paid for. Many foreigners have already been earnestly permitted to help pay for this pedestal."

Rev. Mr. Hallelujah's Hoss.

THERE are a good many difficult things to ride, I find, beside the bicycle and the bucking Mexican plug. Those who have tried to mount and successfully ride a wheelbarrow in the darkness of the stilly night will agree with me.

You come on a wheelbarrow suddenly when it is in a brown study, and you undertake to straddle it, so to speak, and all at once you find the wheelbarrow on top. I may say, I think, safely, that the wheelbarrow is, as a rule, phlegmatic and cool; but when a total stranger startles it, it spreads desolation and destruction on every hand.

This is also true of the perambulator, or baby-carriage. I undertook to evade a child's phæton, three years ago last spring, as it stood in the entrance to a hall in Main street. The child was not injured, because it was not in the carriage at the time; but I was not so fortunate. I pulled pieces of perambulator out of myself for two weeks with the hand that was not disabled.

How a sedentary man could fall through a child's carriage in such a manner as to stab himself with the awning and knock every spoke out of three wheels, is still a mystery to me, but I did it. I can show you the doctor's bill now.

The other day, however, I discovered a new style of riding animal. The Rev. Mr. Hallelujah was at the depot when I arrived, and was evidently waiting for the same Chicago train that I was in search of. Rev Mr. Hallelujah had put his valise down near an ordinary baggage-truck which leaned up against the wall of the station building.

He strolled along the platform a few moments, communing with himself and agitating his mind over the subject of Divine Retribution, and then he went up and leaned against the truck. Finally, he somehow got his arms under the handles of the truck as it stood up between his back and the wall. He still continued to think of the plan of Divine Retribution, and you could have seen his lips move if you had been there.

Pretty soon some young ladies came along, rosy in winter air, beautiful beyond compare, frosty crystals in their hair; smiled they on the preacher there.

He returned the smile and bowed low. As he did so, as near as I can figure it out, he stepped back on the iron edge of the truck that the baggage-man generally jabs under the rim of an iron-bound sample-trunk when he goes to load it. Anyhow, Mr. Hallelujah's feet flew toward next spring. The truck started across the platform with him and spilled him over the edge on the track ten feet below. So rapid was the movement that the eye with difficulty followed his evolutions. His valise was carried onward by the same wild avalanch, and "busted" open before it struck the track below.

A RAPID MOVEMENT.

I was surprised to see some of the articles that shot forth into the broad light of day Among the rest there was a bran fired new set of ready-made teeth, to be used in case of accident. Up to that moment I didn't know that Mr. Hallelujah used the common tooth of commerce. These teeth slipped out of the valise with a Sabbath smile and vulcanized rubber gums.

In striking the iron track below, the every-day set which the Rev. Mr. Hallelujah had in use became loosened, and smiled across the road-bed and right of way at the bran fired new array of incisors, cuspids, bi-cuspids and molars that flew out of the valise. Mr. Hallelujah got up and tried to look merry, but he could not smile without his teeth. The back seams of his Newmarket coat were more successful, however.

Mr. Hallelujah's wardrobe and a small boy were the only objects that dared to smile.

Somnambulism and Crime.

A RECENT article in the London *Post* on the subject of somnambulism, calls to my mind several little incidents with somnambulistic tendencies in my own experience.

This subject has, indeed, attracted my attention for some years, and it has afforded me great pleasure to investigate it carefully

Regarding the causes of dreams and somnambulism, there are many theories, all of which are more or less untenable. My own idea, given, of course, in a plain, crude way, is that thoughts originate on the inside of the brain and then go at once to the surface, where they have their photographs taken, with the understanding that the negatives are to be preserved. In this way the thought may afterward be duplicated back to the thinker in the form of a dream, and, if the impulse be strong enough, muscular action and somnambulism may result.

On the banks of Bitter Creek, some years ago, lived an open-mouthed man, who had risen from affluence by his unaided effort until he was entirely free from any incumbrance in the way of property. His mind dwelt on this matter a great deal during the day Thoughts of manual labor flitted through his mind, but were cast aside as impracticable. Then other means of acquiring property suggested themselves. These thoughts were photographed on the delicate negative of the brain, where it is a rule to preserve all negatives. At night these thoughts were reversed within the think resort, if I may be allowed that term, and muscular action resulted. Yielding at last to the great desire for possessions and property the somnambulist groped his way to the corral of a total stranger, and selecting a choice mule with great dewy eyes and real camel's hair tail, he fled. On and on he pressed, toward the dark, uncertain west, till at last rosy morn clomb the low, outlying hills and gilded the gray outlines of the sage-brush. The coyote slunk back to his home, but the somnambulist did not.

He awoke as day dawned, and, when he found himself astride the mule of another, a slight shudder passed the entire length of his frame. He then fully realized that he had made his debut as a somnambulist. He seemed to think that he who starts out to be a somnambulist should never turn back. So he pressed on, while the red sun stepped out into the awful quiet of the dusty waste and gradually moved up into the sky, and slowly added another day to those already filed away in the dark maw of ages.

* * * * * * * * *

Night came again at last, and with it other somnambulists similar to the first, only that they were riding on their own beasts. Some somnambulists ride their own animals, while others are content to bestride the steeds of strangers.

The man on the anonymous mule halted at last at the mouth of a deep canon. He did so at the request of other somnambulists. Mechanically he got down from the back of the mule and stood under a stunted mountain pine.

After awhile he began to ascend the tree by means of his neck. When he had reached the lower branch of the tree he made a few gestures with his feet by a lateral movement of the legs. He made several ineffectual efforts to kick some pieces out of the horizon, and then, after he had gently oscilliated a few times, he assumed a pendent and perpendicular position at right angles with the limb of the tree.

The other somnambulists then took the mule safely back to his corral, and the tragedy of a night was over.

The London *Post* very truly says that where somnambulism can be proved it is a good defense in a criminal action. It was so held in this case.

Various methods are suggested for rousing the somnambulist, such as tickling the feet, for instance; but in all my own experience, I never knew of a more radical or permanent cure than the one so imperfectly given above. It might do in some cases to tickle the feet of a somnambulist discovered in the act of riding away on an anonymous mule, but how could you successfully tickle the soles of his feet while he is standing on them? In such cases, the only true way would be to suspend the somnambulist in such a way as to give free access to the feet from below, and, at the same time, give him a good, wide horizon to kick at.

Modern Architecture.

IT may be premature, perhaps, but I desire to suggest to anyone who may be contemplating the erection of a summer residence for me, as a slight testimonial of his high regard for my sterling worth and symmetrical escutcheon—a testimonial more suggestive of earnest admiration and warm personal friendship than of great intrinsic value, etc., etc., etc., that I hope he will not construct it on the modern plan of mental hallucination and morbid delirium tremens peculiar to recent architecture.

Of course, a man ought not to look a gift house in the gable end, but if my friends don't know me any better than to build me a summer cottage and throw in odd windows that nobody else wanted, and then daub it up with colors they have bought at auction and applied to the house after dark with a shot-gun, I think it is time that we had a better understanding.

THE ARCHITECT.

Such a structure does not come within either of the three classes of renaissance. It is neither Florentine, Roman, or Venetian. Any man can originate such a style if he will only drink the right kind of whiskey long enough and then describe the feelings to an amanuensis.

Imagine the sensation that one of these modern, sawed-off cottages would create a hundred years from now, if it should survive! But that is impossible. The only cheering feature of the whole matter is that these creatures of a disordered imagination must soon pass away, and the bright sunlight of hard horse sense shine in through the shattered dormers and gables and gnawed-off architecture of the average summer resort.

A friend of mine a few days ago showed me his new house with much pride. He asked me what I thought of it. I told him I liked it first-rate. Then I went home and wept all night. It was my first falsehood.

The house, taken as a whole, looked to me like a skating rink that had started out to make money, and then suddenly changed its mind and resolved to become a tannery Then ten feet higher it lost all self-respect and blossomed into a full-blown drunk and disorderly, surrounded by the smokestack of a foundry and the bright future of thirty days ahead with the chain gang. That's the way it looked to me.

The roofs were made of little odds and ends of misfit rafters and distorted shingles that somebody had purchased at a sheriff's sale, and the rooms and stairs were giddy in the extreme.

I went in and rambled around among the cross-eyed staircases and other night-mares till reason tottered on her throne. Then I came out and stood on the architectural wart, called the side porch, to get fresh air. This porch was painted a dull red, and it had wooden rosettes at the corners that looked like a new carbuncle on the nose of a social wreck.

Farther up on the demoralized lumber pile I saw, now and then, places where the workman's mind had wandered and he had nailed on his clapboards wrong side up, and then painted them with Paris green that he had intended to use on something else.

It was an odd looking structure, indeed. If my friend got all the material for nothing from people who had fragments of paint and lumber left over after they failed, and then if the workmen constructed it of night for mental relaxation and intellectual repose, without charge, of course the scheme was a financial success, but architecturally the house is a gross violation of the statutes in such cases made and provided, and against the peace and dignity of the State.

There is a look of extreme poverty about the structure which a man might struggle for years to acquire and then fail. No one could look upon it without a feeling of heartache for the man who built that house, and probably struggled on year after year, building a little at a time as he could steal the lumber, getting a new workman each year, building a knob here and a protuberance there, putting in a three-cornered window at one point and a yellow tile or a wad of broken glass and other debris at another, patiently filling in around the ranch with any old rubbish that other people had got through with, painting it as he went along, taking what was left in the bottom of the pots after his neighbors had painted their bob-sleds or their tree boxes—little favors thankfully received—and then surmounting the whole pile with a potpourri of roof, and grand farewell incubus of humps and hollows for the rain to wander through and seek out the different cells where the lunatics live who inhabit it.

I did tell my friend one thing that I thought would improve the looks of his house. He asked me eagerly what it could be. I said it would take a man of great courage to do it for him. He said he didn't care for that. He would do it himself. If it only needed one thing he would never rest till he had it, whatever that might be.

Then I told him that if he had a friend—one he could trust—who would steal in there some night while the family were away, and scratch a match on the leg of his breeches, or on the breeches of any other gentleman who happened to be present, and hold it where it would ignite the alleged house, and then remain near there to see that the fire department did not meddle with it, he would confer a great favor on one who would cheerfully retaliate in kind on call.

Letter to a Communist.

DEAR SIR.—Your courteous letter of the 1st instant, in which you cordially consent to share my wealth and dwell together with me in fraternal sunshine, is duly received. While I dislike to appear cold and distant to one who seems so yearnful and so clinging, and while I do not wish to be regarded as purse-proud or arrogant, I must decline your kind offer to whack up. You had not heard, very likely, that I am not now a Communist. I used to be, I admit, and the society no doubt neglected to strike my name off the roll of active members. For a number of years I was quite active as a Communist. I would have been more active, but I had conscientious scruples against being active in anything then.

While you may be perfectly sincere in your belief that the great capitalists like Mr. Gould and Mr. Vanderbilt should divide with you, you will have great difficulty in making it perfectly clear to them. They will probably demur and delay, and hem and haw, and procrastinate, till finally they will get out of it in some way. Still, I do not wish to throw cold water on your enterprise. If the other capitalists look favorably on the plan, I will cheerfully co-operate with them. You go and see what you can do with Mr. Vanderbilt, and then come to me.

You go on at some length to tell me how the most of the wealth is in the hands of a few men, and then you attack those men and refer to them in a way that makes my blood run cold. You tell the millionaires of America to beware, for the hot breath of a bloody-handed Nemesis is already in the air.

You may say to Nemesis, if you please, that I have a double-barreled shotgun standing at the head of my bed every night, and that I am in the Nemesis business. You also refer to the fact that the sleuth-hounds of eternal justice are camped on the trail of the pampered millionaire, and you ask us to avaunt. If you see the other sleuth-hounds of your society within a week or two, I wish you would say to them that at a regular meeting of the millionaires of this country, after the minutes of the previous meeting had been read and approved, we voted almost unanimously to discourage any sleuth-hound that we

PRACTICAL COMMUNISM.

found camped on our trail after ten o'clock, P M. Sleuth-hounds who want to ramble over our trails during office hours may do so with the utmost impunity, but after ten o'clock we want to use our trails for other purposes. No man wants to go to the great expense of maintaining a trail winter and summer, and then leave it out nights for other people to use and return it when they get ready

I do not censure you, however. If you could convince every one of the utility of Communism, it would certainly be a great boon—to you. To those who are now engaged in feeding themselves with flat beer out of a tomato can, such a change as you suggest would fall like a ray of sunshine in a rat-hole, but alas! it may never be. I tried it awhile, but my efforts were futile. The effect of my great struggle seemed to be that men's hearts grew more and more stony, and my pantaloons got thinner and thinner on the seat, 'till it seemed to me that the world never was so cold. Then I made some experiments in manual labor. As I began to work harder and sit down less, I found that the world was not so cold. It was only when I sat down a long time that I felt how cold and rough the world really was.

Perhaps it is so with you. Sedentary habits and stale beer are apt to make us morbid. Sitting on the stone door sills of hallways and public buildings during cold weather is apt to give you an erroneous impression of life.

Of course I am willing to put my money into a common fund if I can be convinced that it is best. I was an inside passenger on a Leadville coach some years ago, when a few of your friends suggested that we all put our money into a common fund, and I was almost the first one to see that they were right. They went away into the mountains to apportion the money they got from our party, but I never got any dividend. Probably they lost my post-office address.

The Warrior's Oration.

WARRIORS! We are met here to-day to celebrate the white man's Fourth of July. I do not know what the Fourth of July has done for us that we should remember his birthday, but it matters not. Another summer is on the wane, and so are we. We are the wall-eyed waners from Wanetown. We have monopolized the wane business of the whole world.

Autumn is almost here, and we have not yet gone upon the war path. The pale face came among us with the corn planter and the Desert Land Act, and we bow before him.

What does the Fourth of July signify to us? It is a hollow mockery! Where the flag of the white man now waves in the breeze, a few years ago the scalp of our foe was hanging in the air. Now my people are seldom. Some are dead and others drunk.

Once we chased the deer and the buffalo across the plains, and lived high. Now we eat the condemned corned beef of the oppressor. and weep over the graves of our fallen braves. A few more moons and I, too, shall cross over to the Happy Reservation.

Once I could whoop a couple of times and fill the gulch with warlike athletes. Now I may whoop till the cows come home and only my sickly howl comes back to me from the hillsides. I am as lonely as the greenback party. I haven't warriors enough to carry one precinct.

Where are the proud chieftains of my tribe? Where are Old Weasel Asleep and Orlando the Hic Jacet Promoter? Where are Prickly Ash Berry and The Avenging Wart? Where are The Roman-nosed Pelican and Goggle-eyed Aleck, The-man-who-rides-the-blizzard-bareback?

They are extremely gone. They are extensively whence. Ole Blackhawk, in whose veins flows the blood of many chiefs, is sawing wood for the Belle of the West deadfall for the whiskey He once rode the war pony into the fray and buried his tomahawk in the phrenology of his foe. Now he straddles the saw-buck and yanks the woodsaw athwart the bosom of the basswood chunk.

My people once owned this broad land; but the Pilgrim Fathers (where are they?) came and planted the baked bean and the dried apple, and my tribe vamoosed. Once we were a nation. Now we are the tin can tied to the American eagle.

WARRIORS! This should be a day of jubilee, but how can the man rejoice who has a boil on his nose? How can the chief of a once proud people shoot firecrackers and dance over the graves of his race? How can I be hilarious with the victor, on whose hands are the blood of my children?

If we had known more of the white man, we would have made it red hot for him four hundred years ago when he came to our coast. We fed him and clothed him as a white-skinned curiosity then, but we didn't know there were so many of him. All he wanted then was a little smoking tobacco and love. Now he feeds us on antique pork, and borrows our annuities to build a Queen Anne wigwam with a furnace in the bottom and a piano in the top.

WARRIORS! My words are few. Tears are idle and unavailing. If I had scalding tears enough for a millsite, I would not shed a blamed one. The warrior suffers, but he never squeals. He accepts the position and says nothing. He wraps his royal horse blanket around his Gothic bones and is silent.

But the pale face cannot tickle us with a barley straw on the Fourth of July and make us laugh. You can kill the red man, but you cannot make him hilarious over his own funeral. These are the words of truth, and my warriors will do well to paste them in their plug hats for future reference.

The Holy Terror.

WHILE in New England trying in my poor, weak way to represent the "rowdy west," I met a sad young man who asked me if I lived in Chi-eene. I told him that if he referred to Cheyenne, I had been there off and on a good deal.

He said he was there not long ago, but did not remain. He bought some clothes in Chicago, so that he could appear in Chi-eene as a "holy terror" when he landed there, and thus in a whole town of "holy terrors" he would not attract attention.

I am not, said he, by birth or instinct, a holy terror, but I thought I would like to try it a little while, anyhow. I got one of those Chicago sombreros with a gilt fried cake twisted around it for a band. Then I got a yellow silk handkerchief on the ten cent counter to tie around my neck. Then I got a suit of smoke-tanned buckskin clothes and a pair of moccasins. I had never seen a bad, bad man from Chi-eene, but I had seen pictures of them and they all wore moccasins. The money that I had left I put into a large revolver and a butcher knife with a red Morocco sheath to it. The revolver was too heavy for me to hold in one hand and shoot, but by resting it on a fence I could kill a cow easy enough if she wasn't too blamed restless.

I went out to the stock yards in Chicago one afternoon and practiced with my revolver. One of my thumbs is out there at the stock yards now.

At Omaha I put on my new suit and sent my human clothes home to my father. He told me when I came away that when I got out to Wyoming, probably I wouldn't want to attract attention by wearing clothes, and so I could send my clothes back to him and he would be glad to have them.

At Sidney I put on my revolver and went into the eating house to get my dinner. A tall man met me at the door and threw me about forty feet in an oblique manner. I asked him if he meant anything personal by that and he said not at all, not at all. I then asked him if he would not allow me to eat my dinner and he said that depended on what I wanted for my dinner. If I would lay down my arms and come back to the reservation and remain neutral to the Government and eat cooked food, it would be all right, but if I insisted on eating raw dining-room girls and scalloped young ladies, he would bar me out.

We landed at Chi-eene in the evening. They had hacks and 'busses and carriages till you couldn't rest, all standing there at the depot, and a large colored man in a loud tone of voice remarked: "INTEROCEAN HO-TEL! ! ! !"

I went there myself, It had doors and windows to it, and carpets and gas.

A REAL COWBOY.

The young man who showed me to my room was very polite to me. He seemed to want to get acquainted. He said:

"You are from New Hampshire, are you not?"

I told him not to give it away, but I was from New Hampshire. Then I asked him how he knew.

He said that several New Hampshire people had been out there that summer, and they had worn the same style of revolver and generally had one thumb done up in a rag. Then he said that if I came from New Hampshire he would show me how to turn off the gas.

He also took my revolver down to the office with him and put it in the safe, because he said someone might get into my room in the night and kill me with it if he left it here. He was a perfect gentleman.

They have a big opera house there in Chi-eene, and while I was there they had the Eyetalian opera singers, Patty and Nevady there. The streets were lit up with electricity, and people seemed to kind of politely look down on me, I thought. Still, they acted as if they tried not to notice my clothes and dime museum hat.

They seemed to look at me as if I wasn't to blame for it, and as if they felt sorry for me. If I'd had my United States clothes with me, I could have had a good deal of fun in Chi-eene, going to the opera and the lectures, and concerts, et cetera. But finally I decided to return, so I wrote to my parents how I had been knocked down and garroted, and left for dead with one thumb shot off, and they gladly sent the money to pay funeral expenses.

With this I got a cut-rate ticket home and surprised and horrified my parents by dropping in on them one morning just after prayers. I tried to get there prior to prayers, but was side-tracked by my father's new anti-tramp bull dog.

Boston Common and Environs.

STROLLING through the Public Garden and the famous Boston Common, the untutored savage from the raw and unpolished West is awed and his wild spirit tamed by the magnificent harmony of nature and art. Everywhere the eye rests upon all that is beautiful in nature, while art has heightened the pleasing effect without having introduced the artistic jim-jams of a lost and undone world.

It is a delightful place through which to stroll in the gray morning while the early worm is getting his just deserts. There, in the midst of a great city, with the hum of industry and the low rumble of the throbbing Boston brain dimly heard in the distance, nature asserts herself, and the weary, sad-eyed stranger may ramble for hours and keep off the grass to his heart's content.

Nearly every foot of Boston Common is hallowed by some historical incident. It is filled with reminiscences of a time when liberty was not overdone in this new world, and the tyrant's heel was resting calmly on the neck of our forefathers.

In the winter of 1775-6, over 110 years ago, as the ready mathematician will perceive, 1,700 redcoats swarmed over Boston Common. Later on the local antipathy to these tourists became so great that they went away. They are still fled. A few of their descendants were there when I visited the Common, but they seemed amicable and did not wear red coats. Their coats this season are made of a large check, with sleeves in it. Their wardrobe generally stands a larger check than their bank account.

The fountains in the Common and the Public Garden attract the eye of the stranger, some of them being very beautiful. The Brewer fountain on Flagstaff hill, presented to the city by the late Gardner Brewer, is very handsome. It was cast in Paris, and is a bronze copy of a fountain designed by Lienard of that city. At the base there are figures representing Neptune with his fabled pickerel stabber, life size; also Amphitrite, Acis and Galatea. Surviving relatives of these parties may well feel pleased and gratified over the life-like expression which the sculptor has so faithfully reproduced.

But the Coggswell fountain is probably the most eccentric squirt, and one which at once rivets the eye of the beholder. I do not know who designed it, but am told that it was modeled by a young man who attended the codfish autopsy at the market daytimes and gave his nights to art.

The fountain proper consists of two metallic bullheads rampart. They stand on their bosoms, with their tails tied together at the top. Their mouths are abnormally distended, and the water gushes forth from their tonsils in a beautiful stream.

The pose of these classical codfish or bullheads is sublime. In the spirited Græco-Roman tussle which they seem to be having, with their tails abnormally elevated in their artistic catch-as-catch-can or can-can scuffle, the designer has certainly hit upon a unique and beautiful impossibility.

Each bullhead also has a tin dipper chained to his gills, and through the live-long day, till far into the night, he invites the cosmopolitan tramp to come and quench his never-dying thirst.

The frog pond is another celebrated watering place. I saw it in the early part of May, and if there had been any water in it, it would have been a fine sight. Nothing contributes to the success of a pond like water.

I ventured to say to a Boston man that I was a little surprised to find a little frog pond containing neither frogs or pond, but he said I would find it all right if I would call around during office hours.

While sitting on one of the many seats which may be found on the Common one morning, I formed the acquaintance of a pale young man, who asked me if I resided in Boston. I told him that while I felt flattered to think that I could possibly fool anyone, I must admit that I was only a pilgrim and a stranger.

He said that he was an old resident, and he had often noticed that the people of the Hub always Spoke to a Felloe till he was tired. I afterward learned that he was not an actual resident of Boston, but had just completed his junior year at the State asylum for the insane. He was sent there, it seems, as a confirmed case of unjustifiable Punist. Therefore the governor had Punist him accordingly This is a specimen of our capitalized joke with Queen Anne do-funny on the corners. We are shipping a great many of them to England this season, where they are greedily snapped up and devoured by the crowned heads. It is a good hot weather joke, devoid of mental strain, perfectly simple and may be laughed at or not without giving the slightest offense.

Drunk in a Plug Hat.

THIS world is filled with woe everywhere you go. Sorrow is piled up in the fence corners on every road. Unavailing regret and red-nosed remorse inhabit the cot of the tie-chopper as well as the cut-glass cage of the millionaire. The woods are full of disappointment. The earth is convulsed with a universal sob, and the roads are muddy with tears. But I do not call to mind a more touching picture of unavailing misery and ruin, and hopeless chaos, than the plug hat that has endeavored to keep sober and maintain self-respect while its owner was drunk. A plug hat can stand prosperity, and shine forth joyously while nature smiles. That's the place where it seems to thrive. A tall silk hat looks well on a thrifty man with a clean collar, but it cannot stand dissipation.

I once knew a plug hat that had been respected by everyone, and had won its way upward by steady endeavor. No one knew aught against it till one evening, in an evil hour, it consented to attend a banquet, and all at once its joyous career ended. It met nothing but distrust and cold neglect everywhere, after that.

Drink seems to make a man temporarily unnaturally exhilerated. During that temporary exhileration he desires to attract attention by eating lobster salad out of his own hat, and sitting down on his neighbor's.

The demon rum is bad enough on the coatings of the stomach, but it is even more disastrous to the tall hat. A man may mix up in a crowd and carry off an overdose of valley tan in a soft hat or a cap, but the silk hat will proclaim it upon the house-tops, and advertise it to a gaping, wondering world. It has a way of getting back on the rear elevation of the head, or over the bridge of the nose, or of hanging coquettishly on one ear, that says to the eagle-eyed public: "I am chockfull."

I cannot call to mind a more powerful lecture on temperance, than the silent pantomime of a man trying to hang his plug hat on an invisible peg in his own hall, after he had been watching the returns, a few years ago. I saw that he was excited and nervously unstrung when he came in, but I did not fully realize it until he began to hang his hat on the smooth wall.

At first he laughed in a good-natured way at his awkwardness, and hung it up again carefully; but at last he became irritated about it, and almost forgot himself enough to swear, but controlled himself. Finding, however, that it refused to hang up, and that it seemed rather restless, anyhow, he put it in the corner of the hall with the crown up, pinned it to the floor with his umbrella, and heaved a sigh of relief. Then he took off his overcoat and, through a clerical error, pulled off his dress-coat also. I showed him his mistake and offered to assist him back into his apparel, but he said he hadn't got so old and feeble yet that he couldn't dress himself.

A POWERFUL LECTURE.

Later on he came into the parlor, wearing a linen ulster with the belt drooping behind him like the broken harness hanging to a ship-wrecked and stranded mule. His wife looked at him in a way that froze his blood. This startled him so that he stepped back a pace or two, tangled his feet in his surcingle, clutched wildly at the empty gas-light, but missed it and sat down in a tall majolica cuspidor.

There were three games of whist going on when he fell, and there was a good deal of excitement over the playing, but after he had been pulled out of the American tear jug and led away, everyone of the twelve whist-players had forgotten what the trump was.

They say that he has abandoned politics since then, and that now he don't care whether we have any more November elections or not. I asked him once if he would be active during the next campaign, as usual, and he said he thought not. He said a man couldn't afford to be too active in a political campaign. His constitution wouldn't stand it.

At that time he didn't care much whether the American people had a president or not. If every public-spirited voter had got to work himself up into a state of nervous excitability and prostration where reason tottered on its throne, he thought that we needed a reform.

Those who wished to furnish reasons to totter on their thrones for the National Central Committee at so much per tot, could do so; he, for one, didn't propose to farm out his immortal soul and plug hat to the party, if sixty million people had to stand four years under the administration of a setting hen.

Spring.

SPRING is now here. It has been here before, but not so much so, perhaps, as it is this year. In spring the buds swell up and bust. The "violets" bloom once more, and the hired girl takes off the double windows and the storm door. The husband and father puts up the screen doors, so as to fool the annual fly when he tries to make his spring debut. The husband and father finds the screen doors and windows in the gloaming of the garret. He finds them by feeling them in the dark with his hands. He finds the rafters, also, with his head. When he comes down, he brings the screens and three new intellectual faculties sticking out on his brow like the button on a barn door.

Spring comes with joyous laugh, and song, and sunshine, and the burnt sacrifice of the over-ripe boot and the hoary overshoe. The cowboy and the new milch cow carol their roundelay. So does the veteran hen. The common egg of commerce begins to come forth into the market at a price where it can bo secured with a step-ladder, and all nature seems tickled.

There are four seasons—spring, summer, autumn and winter. Spring is the most joyful season of the year. It is then that the green grass and the lavender pants come forth. The little robbins twitter in the branches, and the horny-handed farmer goes joyously afield to till the soil till the cows come home.—*Virgil.*

We all love the moist and fragrant spring. It is then that the sunlight waves beat upon the sandy coast, and the hand-maiden beats upon the sandy carpet. The man of the house pulls tacks out of himself and thinks of days gone by, when you and I were young, Maggie. Who does not leap and sing in his heart when the dandelion blossoms in the low lands, and the tremulous tail of the lambkin agitates the balmy air?

The lawns begin to look like velvet and the lawn-mower begins to warm its joints and get ready for the approaching harvest. The blue jay fills the forest with his classical and extremely *au revoir* melody, and the curculio crawls out of the plum-tree and files his bill. The plow-boy puts on his father's boots and proceeds to plow up the cunning little angle worm. Anon, the black-bird alights on the swaying reeds, and the lightning-rod man alights on the farmer with great joy and a new rod that can gather up all the lightning in two States and put it in a two-gallon jug for future use.

Who does not love spring, the most joyful season of the year? It is then that the spring bonnet of the workaday world crosses the earth's orbit and makes the bank account of the husband and father look fatigued. The low shoe and the low hum of the bumble-bee are again with us. The little striped hornet heats his nose with a spirit lamp and goes forth searching for the man with the linen pantaloons. All nature is full of life and activity. So is the man with the linen pantaloons. Anon, the thrush will sing in the underbrush, and the prima donna will do up her voice in a red-flannel rag and lay it away.

I go now into my cellar to bring out the gladiola bulb and the homesick turnip of last year. Do you see the blue place on my shoulder? That is where I struck when I got to the foot of the cellar stairs. The gladiola bulbs are looking older than when I put them away last fall. I fear me they will never again bulge forth. They are wrinkled about the eyes and there are lines of care upon them. I could squeeze along two years without the gladiola and the oleander in the large tub. If I should give my little boy a new hatchet and he should cut down my beautiful oleander, I would give him a bicycle and a brass band and a gold-headed cane.

O spring, spring,
You giddy young thing.*

---

*From poems of passion and one thing another, by the author of this sketch.

The Duke of Rawhide.

"I BELIEVE I've got about the most instinct bulldog in the United States," said Cayote Van Gobb yesterday. "Other pups may show cuteness aud cunning, you know, but my dog, the Duke of Rawhide Buttes, is not only generally smart, but he keeps up with the times. He's not only a talented cuss, but his genius is always fresh and original."

"What are some of his specialties, Van?" said I.

"Oh, there's a good many of 'em, fust and last. He never seems to be content with the achievements that please other dogs. You watch him and you'll see that his mind is active all the time. When he is still he's working up some scheme or another, that he will ripen and fructify later on.

"For three year's I've had a watermelon patch and run it with more or less success, I reckon. The Duke has tended to 'em after they got ripe, and I was going to say that it kept his hands pretty busy to do it, but, to be more accurate, I should say that it kept his mouth full. Hardly a night after the melons got ripe and in the dark of the moon, but the Dude would sample a cowboy or a sheep-herder from the lower Poudre. Watermelons were generally worth ten cents a pound along the Union Pacific for the first two weeks, and a fifty-pounder was worth $5. That made it an object to keep your melons, for in a good year you could grow enough on ten acres to pay off the national debt.

"Well, to return to my subject. Duke would sleep days during the season and gather fragments of the rear breadths of Western pantaloons at night. One morning Duke had a piece of fancy cassimere in his teeth that I tried to pry out and preserve, so that I could identify the owner, perhaps, but he wouldn't give it up. I coaxed him and lammed him across the face and eyes with an old board, but he wouldn't give it to me. Then I watched him. I've been watchin' him ever since. He took all these fragments of goods I found, over into the garret above the carriage shed.

"Yesterday I went in there and took a lantern with me. There on the floor the Duke of Rawhide had arranged all the samples of Rocky Mountain pantaloons with a good deal of taste, and I don't suppose you'd believe it, but that blamed pup is collecting all these little scraps to make himself a crazy quilt.

"You can talk about instinct in animals, but, so far as the Duke of Rawhide Buttes is concerned, it seems to me more like all-wool genius a yard wide."

Etiquette at Hotels.

ETIQUETTE at hotels is a subject that has been but lightly treated upon by our modern philosophy, and yet it is a subject that lies very near to every American heart. Had I not already more reforms on hand than I can possibly successfully operate I would gladly use my strong social influence and trenchant pen in that direction. Etiquette at hotels, both on the part of the proprietor, and his hirelings, and the guest, is a matter that calls loudly for improvement.

The hotel waiter alone, would well repay a close study From the tardy and polished loiterer of the effete East, to the off-hand and social equal of the budding West, all waiters are deserving of philosophical scrutiny I was thrown in contact with a waiter in New York last summer, whose manners were far more polished than my own. Every time I saw him standing there with his immediate pantaloons and swallow-tail coat, and the far-away, chastened look of one who had been unfortunate, but not crushed, I felt that I was unworthy to be waited upon by such a blue-blooded thoroughbred, and I often wished that we had more such men in Congress. And when he would take my order and go away with it, and after the meridian of my life had softened into the mellow glory of the sere and yellow leaf, when he came back, still looking quite young, and never having forgotten me, recognizing me readily after the long, dull, desolate years, I was glad, and I felt that he deserved something more than mere empty thanks and I said to him: "Ah, sir, you still remember me after years of privation and suffering. When every one else in New York has forgotten me, with the exception of the confidence man, you came to me with the glad light of recognition in your clear eye. Would you be offended if I gave you this trifling testimonial of my regard?" at the same time giving him my note at thirty days.

I wanted him to have something by which to always remember me, and I guess he has.

Speaking of waiters, reminds me of one at Glendive, Montana. We had to telegraph ahead in order to get a place to sleep, and when we registered the landlord shoved out an old double-entry journal for us to record our names and postoffice address in. The office was the bar and before we could get our rooms assigned us, we had to wait forty-five minutes for the landlord to collect pay for thirteen drinks and lick a personal friend. Finally, when he got around to me, he told me that I could sleep in the night bar-tender's bed, as he would be up all night, and might possibly get killed and never need it again, anyhow. It would cost me $4 cash in advance to sleep one night in the bar-tender's bed, he said, and the house was so blamed full that he and his wife had got to wait till things kind of quieted down, and then they would have to put a mattress on the 15 ball pool table and sleep there.

I called attention to my valuable valise that had been purchased at great cost, and told him that he would be safe to keep that behind the bar till I paid; but he said he wasn't in the second-hand valise business, and so I paid in advance. It was humiliating, but he had the edge on me.

At the tea table I noticed that the waiter was a young man who evidently had not been always thus. He had the air of one who yearns to have some one tread on the tail of his coat. Meekness, with me, is one of my characteristics. It is almost a passion. It is the result of personal injuries received in former years at the hands of parties who excelled me in brute force and who succeeded in drawing me out in conversation, as it were, till I made remarks that were injudicious.

So I did not disagree with this waiter, although I had grounds. When he came around and snorted in my ear, "Salt pork, antelope and cold beans," at the same time leaning his full weight on my back, while he evaded the revenue laws by retailing his breath to the guests without a license, I thought I would call for what he had the most of, so I said if he didn't mind and it wouldn't be too much trouble, I would take cold beans.

I will leave it to the calm, impassionate and unpartisan reader to state whether that remark ought to create ill-feeling. I do not think it ought. However, he was irritable, and life to him seemed to be cold and dark. So he went to the general delivery window that led into the cold bean laboratory, and remarked in a hoarse, insolent, and ironical tone of voice:

"Nother damned suspicious looking character wants cold beans."

Fifteen Years Apart.

THE American Indian approximates nearer to what man should be—manly, physically perfect, grand in character, and true to the instincts of his conscience—than any other race of beings, civilized or uncivilized. Where do we hear such noble sentiments or meet with such examples of heroism and self-sacrifice as the history of the American Indian furnishes? Where shall we go to hear again such oratory as that of Black Hawk and Logan? Certainly the records of our so-called civilization do not furnish it, and the present century is devoid of it.

They were the true children of the Great Spirit. They lived nearer to the great heart of the Creator than do their pale-faced conquerors of to-day who mourn over the lost and undone condition of the savage. Courageous, brave and the soul of honor, their cruel and awful destruction from the face of the earth is a sin of such magnitude that the relics and the people of America may well shrink from the just punishment which is sure to follow the assassination of as brave a race as ever breathed the air of Heaven.

AT FIFTEEN.

I wrote the above scathing rebuke of the American people when I was 15 years of age. I ran across the dissertation yesterday. As a general rule, it takes a youth 15 years of age to arraign Congress and jerk the administration bald-headed. The less he knows about things generally, the more cheerfully will he shed information right and left.

At the time I wrote the above crude attack upon the government, I had not seen any Indians, but I had read much. My blood boiled when I thought of the wrongs which our race had meted out to the red man. It was at the time when my blood was just coming to a boil that I penned the above paragraph. Ten years later I had changed my views somewhat, relative to the Indian, and frankly wrote to the government of the change. When I am doing the administration an injustice, and I find it out, I go to the president candidly, and say: "Look here, Mr. President, I have been doing you a wrong. You were right and I was erroneous. I am not pig-headed and stubborn. I just admit fairly that I have been hindering the administration, and I do not propose to do so any more."

So I wrote to Gen. Grant and told him that when I was 15 years of age I wrote a composition at school in which I had arraigned the people and the administration for the course taken toward the Indians. Since that time I had seen some Indians in the mountains—at a distance—and from what I had seen of them I was led to believe that I had misjudged the people and the executive. I told him that so far as possible I would like to repair the great wrong so done in the ardor of youth and to once more sustain the arm of the government.

He wrote me kindly and said he was glad that I was friendly with the government again, and that now he saw nothing in the way of continued national prosperity. He said he would preserve my letter in the archives as a treaty of peace between myself and the nation. He said only the day before he had observed to the cabinet that he didn't care two cents about a war with foreign nations, but he would like to be on a peace footing with me. The country could stand outside interference better than intestine hostility. I do not know whether he meant anything personal by that or not. Probably not.

He said he remembered very well when he first heard that I had attacked the Indian policy of the United States in one of my school essays. He still called to mind the feeling of alarm and apprehension which at that time pervaded the whole country. How the cheeks of strong men had blanched and the Goddess of Liberty felt for her back hair and exchanged her Mother Hubbard dress for a new cast-iron panoply of war and Roman hay knife. Oh, yes, he said, he remembered it as though it had been yesterday

Having at heart the welfare of the American people as he did, he hoped that I would never attack the republic again.

And I never have. I have been friendly, not only personally, but officially, for a good while. Even if I didn't agree with some of the official acts of the president I would allow him to believe that I did rather than harrass him with cold, cruel and adverse criticism. The abundant success of this policy is written in the country's wonderful growth and prosperous peace.

Dessicated Mule.

THE red-eyed antagonist of truth is not found alone in the ranks of the newspaper phalanx. You run up against him in all walks of life. He flourishes in all professions, and he is ready at all times to entertain. There is quite a difference between a malicious falsehood and the different shades of parables, fables with a moral, Sabbath-school books, newspaper sketches, and anecdotes told to entertain.

A malicious lie is injurious personally. A business lie is a falsehood for revenue only But the yarns that are spun around camp-fires, in mining and logging camps, to while away a dull evening, are not within the jurisdiction of the criminal code or the home missionary

On the train, yesterday several old lumbermen were telling about hard roads and steep hills, engineering skill, and so forth. Finally they told about "snubbing" a loaded team down bad hills, and one man said

"You might 'snub' down a cheap hill, but you couldn't do it on our road. We tried it. Couldn't do a thing. Finally we got to building snow-sheds and hauling sand. You build a snow-shed that covers the grade, then fill the road in with two feet of loose sand, and you're O. K, We did that last winter, and when you drive a four-horse load of logs down through them long snow-sheds on bare ground, mind ye, and the bobs go plowing through the sand, the sled-shoes will make the fire fly so that you can read the President's message at midnight."

Then an old man who went to Pike's Peak during the excitement and returned afterward, woke up and yawned two or three times, and said they used to have some trouble, a good many years ago, getting over the range where the South Park road now goes from Chalk Creek Cañon through Alpine Tunnel to the Gunnison.

"We tried 'snubbing' and everything we could think of, but it was N. G.

"Finally we got hold of a new kind of 'snub' that worked pretty well. We had a long table made a-purpose, that would reach to the foot of the hill from the top, and we'd tie a three-ton load to the end at the top of the hill; then we would hitch six mules to the end at the foot of the hill. Well, the principle of the thing was, that as the load went down on the Gunnison side it would pull the mules up the opposite side, tails first."

"How did it work?"

"Oh, it worked all right if the mules and the load balanced; but one day we put on a light mule named Emma Abbott, and the load got a start down the Gunnison side that made that old cable sing. The wagon tipped over and concussed a keg of blasting powder, and that obliterated the rest of the goods.

"But the air on the other side was full of mules. You ought to seen 'em come up that hill!

"It takes considerable of a crisis to affect the natural reserve of six mules; but when they saw how it was, they backed up that mountain with great enthusiasm. They didn't touch the ground but once in three thousand feet, but they struck the canopy of heaven several times.

"When the sky cleared up, we made a careful inventory of the stock.

"We had a second-hand three-inch cable and some desiccated mule. We never went to look for the wagon; but when the weather got warm, the Coyotes helped us find Emma Abbott.

"She was hanging by the ear in the crotch of an old hemlock tree.

"Life was extinct.

"We found a few more of the mules, but they were fractional.

"Emma Abbott was the only complete mule we found."

Time's Changes.

I FIXED myself and went out trout fishing on the only original Kinnickinnick river last week. It was a kind of Rip Van Winkle picnic and farewell moonlight excursion home. I believe that Rip Van Winkle, however, confined himself to hunting mostly with an old musket that was on the retired list when Rip took his sleepy drink on the Catskills. If he could have gone with me fishing last week over the old trail, digging angle-worms at the same old place where I left the spade sticking in the grim soil twenty years ago—if we could have waded down the Kinnickinnick together with high rubber boots on, and got nibbles and bites at the same places, and found the same old farmers with nearly a quarter of a century added to their lives and glistening in their hair, we would have had fun no doubt on that day, and a headache on the day following. This affords me an opportunity to say that trout may be caught successfully without a corkscrew. I have tried it. I've about decided that the main reason why so many large lies are told about the number of trout caught all over the country, is that at the moment the sportsman pulls his game out of the water, he labors under some kind of an optical illusion, by reason of which he sees about nine trout where he ought to see only one.

I wish I had as many dollars as I have soaked deceased angle-worms in that same beautiful Kinnickinnick. There was a little stream made into it that we called Tidd's creek. It is still there. This stream runs across Tidd's farm, and Tidd twenty years ago wouldn't allow anybody to fish in the creek. I can still remember how his large hand used to feel, as he caught me by the nape of the neck and threw me over the fence with my amateur fishing tackle and a willow "stringer" with eleven dried, stiff trout on it. Last week I thought I would try Tidd's creek again. It was always a good place to fish, and I felt the same old excitement, with just enough vague forebodings in it to make it pleasant. Still, I had grown a foot or so since I used to fish there, and perhaps I could return the compliment by throwing the old gentleman over his own fence, and then hiss in ear "R-r-r-r-e-v-e-n-g-e!!!"

I BECAME MORE FEARLESS.

I had got pretty well across the "lower forty" and had about decided that Tidd had been gathered to his fathers, when I saw him coming with his head up like a steer in the corn. Tidd is a blacksmith by trade, and he has an arm with hair on it that looks like Jumbo's hind leg. I felt the same old desire to climb the fence and be alone. I didn't know exactly how to work it. Then I remembered how people had remarked that I had changed very much in twenty years, and that for a homely boy I had grown to be a remarkably picturesque-looking man. I trusted to Tidd's failing eyesight and said:

"How are you?"

He said, "How are you?" That did not answer my question, but I didn't mind a little thing like that.

Then he said: "I sposed that every pesky fool in this country knew I don't allow fishing on my land."

"That may be," says I, "but I ain't fishing on your land. I always fish in a damp place if I can. Moreover, how do I know this is your land? Carrying the argument still further, and admitting that every peesky fool knows that you didn't allow fishing here, I am not going to be called a pesky fool with impunity, unless you do it over my dead body." He stopped about ten rods away and I became more fearless. "I don't know who you are," said I, as I took off my coat and vest and piled them up on my fish basket, eager for the fray. "You claim to own this farm, but it is my opinion that you are the hired man, puffed up with a little authority You can't order me off this ground till you show me a duly certified abstract of title and then identify yourself. What protection does a gentleman have if he is to be kicked and cuffed about by Tom, Dick and Harry, claiming they own the whole State. Get out! Avaunt! If you don't avaunt pretty quick [illegible] you and sell you to a medical college."

He stood in dumb amazement a moment, then he said he would go and get his deed and his shotgun. I said shotguns suited me exactly, and I told him to bring two of them loaded with giant powder and barbed wire. I would not live alway. I asked not to stay. When he got behind the corn-crib I climbed the fence and fled with my ill-gotten gains.

The blacksmith in his prime may lick the small boy, but twenty years changes their relative positions. Possibly Tidd could tear up the ground with me now, but in ten more years, if I improve as fast as he fails, I shall fish in that same old stream again.

Letter From New York.

DEAR FRIEND.—Being Sunday, I take an hour to write you a letter in regard to this place. I came here yesterday without attracting undue attention from people who lived here. If they was surprised, they concealed it from me.

I've camped out on the Chug years ago, and went to sleep with no live thing near me except my own pony, and woke up with the early song of the coyote, and have been on the lonesome plain for days where it seemed to me that a hostile would be mighty welcome if he would only say something to me, but I was never so lonesome as I was here in this big town last night, although it is the most thick settled place I was ever at.

I was so kind of low and depressed that I strolled in to the bar at last, allowing that I could pound on the counter and call up the boys and get acquainted a little with somebody, just as I would at Col. Luke Murrin's, at Cheyenne; but when I waved to the other parties, and told them to rally round the foaming beaker, they apologized, and allowed they had just been to dinner.

Just been to dinner, and there it was pretty blamed near dark! Then I asked 'em to take a cigar, but they mostly cackillated they had no occasion.

I was mad, but what could I do? They was too many for me, and I couldn't cœrce the white livered aristocratic mob, for quicker'n scat they could have hollored into a little cupboard they had there in the corner, and in less'n two minits they'd of had the whole police department and the hook and ladder company down there after me with a torch-light procession.

So I swallowed my wrath and a tame drink of cultivated whiskey with Apollo Belvidere on the side, and went out into the auditorium of the hotel.

Here I was very unhappy, being, as the editor of the Green River *Gazette* would say, "the cynosure of all eyes."

I would rather not be a cynosure, even at a good salary; so I thought I would ask the proprietor to build a fire in my room. I went up to the recorder's office, where the big hotel autograft album is, and asked to see the proprietor.

A good-looking young man came forward and asked me what he could do for me. I said if it wouldn't be too much trouble, I wisht he would build a little fire in my room, and I would pay him for it; or, if he would show me where the woodpile was, I would build the fire myself—I wasn't doing anything special at that time.

He then whistled through his teeth and crooked his finger in a shrill tone of voice to a young party who was working for him, and told him to "build a fire in four-ought-two."

I then sat down in the auditorium and read out of a railroad tract, which undertook to show that a party that undertook to ride over a rival road, must do so because life was a burden to him, and facility, and comfort, and safety, and such things no object whatever. But still I was very lonely, and felt as if I was far, far away from home.

I couldn't have been more uncomfortable if I'd been a young man I saw twenty-five years ago on the old overland trail. He had gone out to study the Indian character, and to win said Indian to the fold. When I next saw him he was twenty miles farther on. He had been thrown in contact with said Indian in the meantime. I judged he had been making a collection of Indian arrows. He was extremely no more. He looked some like Saint Sebastian, and some like a toothpick-holder.

I was never successfully lost on the plains, and so I started out after supper to find my room. I found a good many other rooms, and tried to get into them, but I did not find four-ought-two till a late hour; then I subsidized the night patrol on the third floor to assist me.

This is a nice place to stop, but it is a little too rich for my blood, I guess Not so much as regards price, but I can see that I am beginning to excite curiosity among the boarders. People are coming here to board just because I am here, and it is disagreeable. I do not court notoriety. I have always lived in a plain way, and I would give a dollar if people would look the other way while I eat my pie. Yours truly, E. O. D.

To E. Wm. Nye, Esq.

P. S.—This is not a dictated letter. I left my stenograffer and revolver at Pumpkin Buttes. E. O. D.

Crowns and Crowned Heads.

DURING the hot weather very few crowns are worn this season, and a few hints as to the care of the crown itself may not be out of place.

The crown should not be carelessly hung on the hat rack in the royal hall for the flies to roost upon, but it should be thoroughly cleaned and put away as soon as the weather becomes too hot to wear it comfortably.

Great care should be used in cleaning a gold-plated crown, to avoid wearing out the plate. Take a good stiff tooth brush, with a little soapsuds, and clean the crown thoroughly at first, drying it on a clean towel and taking care not to drop it on the floor and thus knock the moss-agate diadem loose. Next, get a sleeve of the royal undershirt, or, in case you can not procure one readily, the sleeve of a duke or right-bower may be used. Soak this in vinegar, and, with a coat of whiting, polish the crown thoroughly, wrap it in cotton-flannel and put in the bureau. Sometimes, the lining of the crown becomes saturated with hair-oil from constant use and needs cleaning. In such cases the lining may be removed, boiled in concentrated lye two hours, or until tender, and then placed on the grass to bleach in the sun.

Most crowns are size six-and-seven-eighths, and they are therefore frequently too large for the number six head of royalty. In such cases a newspaper may be folded lengthwise and laid inside the sweat-band of the crown, thus reducing the size and preventing any accident by which his or her majesty might lose the crown in the coal-bin while doing chores.

After the Fourth of July and other royal holidays, this newspaper may be removed, and the crown will be found none too large for the imperial dome of thought.

Sceptres may be cleaned and wrapped in woolen goods during the hot months. The leg of an old pair of pantaloons makes a good retort to run a sceptre into while not in use. Never try to kill flies or drive carpet tacks with the sceptre. It is an awkward tool at best, and you might easily knock a thumb nail loose. Great care should also be taken of the royal robe. Do not use it for a lap robe while dining, nor sleep in it at night. Nothing looks more repugnant than a king on the throne, with little white feathers all over his robe.

It is equally bad taste to govern a kingdom in a maroon robe with white horse hairs all over it.

I once knew a king who invariably curried his horses in his royal robes; and if the steeds didn't stand around to suit him, he would ever and anon welt them in the pit of the stomach with his cast-iron sceptre, It was greatly to the

A HARD-WORKING MONARCH.

interest of his horses not to incur the royal displeasure, as the reader has no doubt already surmised.

The robe of the king should only be worn while his majesty is on the throne. When he comes down at night, after his day's work, and goes out after his coal and kindling-wood, he may take off his robe, roll it up carefully, and stick it under the throne, where it will be out of sight. Nothing looks more untidy than a fat king milking a bobtail cow in a Mother Hubbard robe trimmed with imitation ermine.

My Physician.

[AN OPEN LETTER.]

DEAR SIR: I have seen recently an open letter addressed to me, and written by you in a vein of confidence and strictly sub rosa. What you said was so strictly confidential, in fact, that you published the letter in New York, and it was copied through the press of the country. I shall, therefore, endeavor to be equally careful in writing my reply.

You refer in your kind and confidential note to your experience as an invalid, and your rapid recovery after the use of red-hot Mexican pepper tea in a molten state.

But you did not have such a physician as I did when I had spinal meningitis. He was a good doctor for horses and blind staggers, but he was out of his sphere when he strove to fool with the human frame. Change of scene and rest were favorite prescriptions of his. Most of his patients got both, especially eternal rest. He made a specialty of eternal rest.

He did not know what the matter was with me, but he seemed to be willing to learn.

My wife says that while he was attending me I was as crazy as a loon, but that I was more lucid than the physician. Even with my little, shattered wreck of mind, tottering between a superficial knowledge of how to pound sand and a wide, shoreless sea of mental vacuity, I still had the edge on my physician, from an intellectual point of view. He is still practicing medicine in a quiet kind of way, weary of life, and yet fearing to die and go where his patients are.

He had a sabre wound on one cheek that gave him a ferocious appearance. He frequently alluded to how he used to mix up in the carnage of battle, and how he used to roll up his pantaloons and wade in gore. He said that if the tocsin of war should sound even now, or if he were to wake up in the night and hear war's rude alarum, he would spring to arms and make tyranny tremble till its suspender buttons fell off.

Oh, he was a bad man from Bitter Creek.

One day I learned from an old neighbor that this physician did not have anything to do with preserving the Union intact, but that he acquired the scar on his cheek while making some experiments as a drunk and disorderly He would come and sit by my bedside for hours, waiting for this mortality to put on immortality, so that he could collect his bill from the estate, but one day I arose during a temporary delirium, and extracting a slat from my couch I smote him across the pit of the stomach with it, while I hissed through my clenched teeth:

"Physician, heal thyself."

I then tottered a few minutes, and fell back into the arms of my attendants. If you do not believe this, I can still show you the clenched teeth. Also the attendants.

I had a hard time with this physician, but I still live, contrary to his earnest solicitations.

"PHYSICIAN, HEAL THYSELF."

I desire to state that should this letter creep into the press of the country, and thus become in a measure public, I hope that it will create no ill-feeling on your part.

Our folks are all well as I write, and should you happen to be on Lake Superior this winter, yachting, I hope you will drop in and see us. Our latch string is hanging out most all the time, and if you will pound on the fence I will call off the dog.

I frequently buy a copy of your paper on the streets. Do you get the money?

Are you acquainted with the staff of *The Century*, published in New York? I was in *The Century* office several hours last spring, and the editors treated me very handsomely, but, although I have bought the magazine ever since, and read it thoroughly, I have not seen yet where they said that "they had a pleasant call from the genial and urbane William Nye." I do not feel offended over this. I simply feel hurt.

Before that I had a good notion to write a brief epic on the "Warty Toad," and send it to *The Century* for publication, but now it is quite doubtful.

The Century may be a good paper, but it does not take the press dispatches, and only last month I saw in it an account of a battle that to my certain knowledge occurred twenty years ago.

All About Oratory.

TWENTY centuries ago last Christmas there was born in Attica, near Athens, the father of oratory, the greatest orator of whom history has told us. His name was Demosthenes. Had he lived until this spring, he would have been 2,270 years old; but he did not live. Demosthenes has crossed the mysterious river. He has gone to that bourne whence no traveler returns.

Most of you, no doubt, have heard about it. On those who may not have heard it, the announcement will fall with a sickening thud.

This sketch is not intended to cast a gloom over your hearts. It was designed to cheer those who read it and make them glad they could read.

Therefore, I would have been glad if I could have spared them the pain which this sudden breaking of the news of the death of Demosthenes will bring. But it could not be avoided. We should remember the transitory nature of life, and when we are tempted to boast of our health, and strength, and wealth, let us remember the sudden and early death of Demosthenes.

Demosthenes was not born an orator. He struggled hard and failed many times. He was homely, and he stammered in his speech; but before his death they came to him for hundreds of miles to get him to open their county fairs, and jerk the bird of freedom bald-headed on the Fourth of July.

When Demosthenes' father died, he left fifteen talents to be divided between Demosthenes and his sister. A talent is equal to about $1,000. I often wish I had been born a little more talented.

Demosthenes had a short breath, a hesitating speech, and his manners were very ungraceful. To remedy his stammering, he filled his mouth full of pebbles and howled his sentiments at the angry sea. However, Plutarch says that Demosthenes made a gloomy fizzle of his first speech. This did not discourage him. He finally became the smoothest orator in that country, and it was no uncommon thing for him to fill the First Baptist Church of Athens full. There are now sixty of his orations extant, part of them written by Demosthenes and part of them written by his private secretary.

When he started in, he was gentle, mild and quiet in his manner; but later on, carrying his audience with him, he at last became enthusiastic. He thundered, he roared, he whooped, he howled, he jarred the windows, he sawed the air, he split the horizon with his clarion notes, he tipped over the table, kicked the lamps out of the chandeliers and smashed the big bass viol over the chief fiddler's head.

Oh, Demosthenes was business when he got started. It will be a long time before we see another off-hand speaker like Demosthenes, and I, for one, have never been the same man since I learned of his death.

"Such was the first of orators," says Lord Brougham. "At the head of all the mighty masters of speech, the adoration of ages has consecrated his place, and the loss of the noble instrument with which he forged and launched his thunders, is sure to maintain it unapproachable forever."

I have always been a great admirer of the oratory of Demosthenes, and those who have heard both of us, think there is a certain degree of similarity in our style.

And not only did I admire Demosthenes as an orator, but as a man; and, though I am no Vanderbilt, I feel as though I would be willing to head a subscription list for the purpose of doing the square thing by his sorrowing wife, if she is left in want, as I understand that she is.

I must now leave Demosthenes and pass on rapidly to speak of Patrick Henry.

Mr. Henry was the man who wanted liberty or death. He preferred liberty, though. If he couldn't have liberty, he wanted to die, but he was in no great rush about it. He would like liberty, if there was plenty of it; but if the British had no liberty to spare, he yearned for death. When the tyrant asked him what style of death he wanted, he said that he would rather die of extreme old age. He was willing to wait, he said. He didn't want to go unprepared, and he thought it would take him eighty or ninety years more to prepare, so that when he was ushered into another world he wouldn't be ashamed of himself.

One hundred and ten years ago, Patrick Henry said: "Sir, our chains are forged. Their clanking may be heard on the plains of Boston. The war is inevitable, and let it come. I repeat it, sir, let it come!"

In the spring of 1860, I used almost the same language. So did Horace Greeley. There were four or five of us who got our heads together and decided that the war was inevitable, and consented to let it come.

Then it came. Whenever there is a large, inevitable conflict loafing around waiting for permission to come, it devolves on the great statesmen and bald-headed *literati* of the nation to avoid all delay. It was so with Patrick Henry. He permitted the land to be deluged in gore, and then he retired. It is the duty of the great orator to howl for war, and then hold some other man's coat while he fights.

Strabismus and Justice.

OVER in St. Paul I met a man with eyes of cadet blue and a terra cotta nose. His eyes were not only peculiar in shape, but while one seemed to constantly probe the future, the other was apparently ransacking the dreamy past. While one rambled among the glorious possibilities of the remote yet golden ultimately, the other sought the somber depths of the previously

He told me that years ago he had a mild case of strabismus and that both eyes seemed to glare down his nose till he got restless and had them operated on. Those were the days when they used to fasten a crochet hook under the internal rectus muscle and cut it a little with a pair of optical sheep shears. The effect of this course was to allow the eye to drift back to a direct line; but this man fell into the hands of a drunken surgeon who cut the muscle too much, and thereby weakened it so that it gradually swung past the point it ought to have stopped at, and he saw with horror that his eye was going to turn out and protrude, as it were, so that a man could hang his hat on it. The other followed suit, and the two orbs that had for years looked along the bridge of the terra cotta nose, gradually separated, and while one looked toward next Christmas with fond anticipations, the other loved to linger over the remembrances of last fall.

This thing continued till he had to peer into the future with his off eye closed, and vice versa.

It is needless to say that he hungered for the blood of that physician and surgeon. He tried to lay violent hands on him and wipe up the ground with him and wear him out across a telegraph pole. But the authorities always prevented the administration of swift and lawful justice.

Time passed on, till one night the abnormal wall-eyed man loosened a board in the sidewalk up town so that the physician and surgeon caught his foot in it and caused an oblique fracture of the scapula, pied his dura mater, busted his cornucopia and wrecked his sarah-bellum.

Perhaps I am in error as to some of these medical terms and their orthography, but that is about the way the man with the divergent orbs told it to me.

The physician and surgeon was quite a ruin. He had to wear clapboards on himself for months, and there were other doctors, and laudable pus and threatened gangrene and doctors' bills, with the cemetery looming up in the near future. Day after day he took his own anti-febrile drinks, and rammed his busted system full of iron and strychnine and beef tea and dover's powders and hypodermic squirt till he wished he could die, but death would not come. He pawed the air and howled. They fed him his own nux vomica, tincture of rhubarb and phosphates and gruel, and brought him back to life with a crooked collar bone, a shattered shoulder blade and a look of woe.

Then he sued the town for $50,000 damages because the sidewalk was imperfect, and the wild-eyed man with the inflamed nose got on the jury.

I will not explain how it was done, but there was a verdict for defendant with costs on the Esculapian wreck. The man with the crooked vision is not handsome, but he is very happy. He says the mills of the gods grind slowly, but they pulverize middling fine.

A Spencerian Ass.

AFTER I had accumulated a handsome competence as city editor of the old Morning *Sentinel* at Laramie City, and had married and gone to housekeeping with a gas stove and other luxuries, my place on the *Sentinel* was taken by a newspaper man named Hopkins, who had just graduated from a business college, and who brought a nice glazed grip sack and a diploma with him that had never been used.

Hopkins wrote a fine Spencerian hand and wore a black and tan dog whereever he went. The boys were willing to overlook his copper-plate hand, but they drew the line at the dog. He not only wrote in beautiful style, but he copied his manuscript, so that when it went in to the printer it was as pretty as a wedding invitation.

HE THREW ME OUT.

Hopkins ran the city page nine days, and then he came into the city hall where I was trying a simple drunk and bade me adieu.

I just say this to show how difficult it is for a fine penman to get ahead as a journalist. Of course good, readable writers like Knox and John Hancock may become great, but they have to be men of sterling ability to start with.

I have some of the most bloodcurdling horrors preserved for the purpose of showing Hopkins' wonderful and vivid style. I will throw them in.

"A little son of our esteemed fellow townsman, J. H. Hayford, suffered greatly last evening with virulent colic, but this A. M., as we go to press, is sleeping easily."

Think of shaking the social foundations of a mountain mining and stock town with such grim, nervous prostrators as that! The next day he startled Southern Wyoming and Northern Colorado and Utah with the maddening statement that "our genial friend, Leopold Gussenhoven's fine, yellow dog, Florence Nightingale, had been seriously threatened with insomnia."

That was the style of mental calisthenics he gave us in a town where death by opium and ropium was liable to occur, and where five men with their Mexican spurs on climbed one telegraph pole in one night and sauntered into the remote indefinitely. Hopkins told me that he had tried to do what was right, but that he had not succeeded very well. He wrung my hand and said:

"I have tried hard to make the *Sentinel* fill a long want felt, but I have not been fortunate. The foreman over there is a harsh man. He used to come in and intimate in a frowning and erect tone of voice, that if I did not produce that copy p. d. q., or some other abbreviation or other, that he would bust my crust, or words of like import.

"Now that's no way to talk to a man of a nervous temperament who is engaged in copying a list of hotel arrivals, and shading the capitals as I was. In the business college it was not that way. Everything was quiet, and there was nothing to jar a man like that.

"Of course I would like to stay on the *Sentinel* and draw the princely salary, but there are two hundred reasons why I cannot do it. So far as the physical effort is concerned, I could draw the salary with one hand tied behind me, but there is too much turmoil and mad haste in daily journalism to suit me, and another thing, the proprietor of the *Sentinel* this morning stole up behind me and struck me over the head with a wrought-iron side stick weighing ten pounds. If I had not concealed a coil spring in my plug hat, the blow would have been deleterious to me.

"Then he threw me out of the door against a total stranger, and flung pieces of coal at me and called me a copper-plate ass, and said that if I ever came into the office again he would assassinate me.

"That is the principal reason why I have severed my connection with the *Sentinel*."

As he said this, Mr. Hopkins took out a polka-dot handkerchief, wiped away a pearly tear the size of a walnut, wrung my hand, also the polka-dot wipe, and stole out into the great, horrid hence.

Anecdotes of Justice.

THE justice of the peace is sometimes a peculiarity, and if someone does not watch him he will exceed his jurisdiction. It took a constable, a sheriff, a prosecuting attorney and a club to convince a Wyoming justice of the peace that he had no right to send a man to the penitentiary for life. Another justice in Utah sentenced a criminal to be hung on the following Friday between twelve and one o'clock of said day, but he couldn't enforce the sentence. A Wisconsin justice of the peace granted a divorce and in two weeks married the couple over again—ten dollars for the divorce and two dollars for the relapse. Another Badger justice bound a young man over to appear and answer at the next term of the Circuit Court for the crime of chastity, and the evidence was entirely circumstantial, too.

Another one, when his first case came up, jerked a candle box around behind the dining-room table, put his hat on the back of his head, borrowed a chew of tobacco from the prisoner and said: "Now, boys, the court's open. The first feller that says a word unless I speak to him will get paralyzed. Now tell your story" Then each witness and the defendant reeled off his yarn without being sworn. The justice fined the defendant ten dollars and made the complaining witness pay half the costs. The justice then took the fine and put it in his pocket, adjourned court, and in an hour was so full that it took six men to hold his house still long enough for him to get into the doors.

A North Park justice of the peace and under-sheriff formed a partnership years ago for the purpose of supplying people with justice at New York prices, and by doing a strictly cash business they dispensed with a good deal of justice, such as it was.

It was a misdemeanor to kill game and ship it out of the State, and as there was a good deal killed there, consisting of elk, antelope and black tail deer especially, and as it could not be hauled out of the Park at that season without going across the Wyoming line and back again into the State of Colorado, the under-sheriff would load himself down with warrants, signed in blank, and station himself on horseback at the foot of the pass to the North. He would then arrest everybody indiscriminately who had any fraction of a deer, antelope or elk on his wagon, try the case then and there, put on a fine of $25 to $75, which if paid never reached the treasury, and then he would wait for another victim. The average man would rather pay the fine than go back a hundred miles through the mountains to stand trial, so the under-sheriff and justice thrived for some time. But one day the under-sheriff served his patent automatic warrant on a young man who refused to come down. The officer then drew one of those large baritone instruments that generally has a coward at one end and a corpse at the other. He pointed this at the young man and assessed a fine of $50 and costs. Instead of paying this fine, the youth, who was quite nimble, but unarmed, knocked the bogus officer down with the butt end of his six-mule whip, took his self-cocking credentials away and lit out. In less than a week the justice and his copper were in the refrigerator.

I was once a justice of the peace, and a good many funny little incidents occurred while I held that office. I do not allude to my official life here in order to call attention to my glowing career, for thousands of others, no doubt, could have administered the affairs of the office as well as I did, but rather to speak of one incident which took place while I was a J. P

One night after I had retired and gone to sleep a milkman, called Bill Dunning, rang the bell and got me out of bed. Then he told me that a man who owed him a milk bill of $35 was all loaded up and prepared to slip across the line overland into Colorado, there to grow up with the country and acquire other indebtedness, no doubt. Bill desired an attachment for the entire wagon-load of goods and said he had an officer at hand to serve the writ.

"But," said I, as I wrapped a "welcome" husk door mat around my glorious proportions, "how do you know while we converse together he is not winging his way down the valley of the Paudre?"

"Never mind that, jedge," says William. "You just fix the dockyments and I'll tend to the defendant."

In an hour Bill returned with $35 in cash for himself and the entire costs of the court, and as we settled up and fixed the docket I asked Bill Dunning how he detained the defendant while we made out the affidavit bond and writ of attachment.

"You reckollect, jedge," says William, "that the waggin wheel is held onto the exle with a big nut. No waggin kin go any length of time without that there nut onto the exle. Well, when I diskivered that what's-his-name was packed up and the waggin loaded, I took the liberty to borrow one o' them there nuts fur a kind of momento, as it were, and I kept that in my pocket till we served the writ and he paid my bill and came to his milk, if you'll allow me that expression, and then I says to him, 'Pardner,' says I, 'you are going far, far away where I may never see you again. Take this here nut,' says I, 'and put it onto the exle of the oft hind wheel of your waggin, and whenever you look at it hereafter, think of poor old Bill Dunning, the milkman.'"

The Chinese God.

I PRESUME that I shall not be accused of sacrilege in referring to the Chinese god as an inferior piece of art. Viewed simply from an artistic and economical standpoint, it seems to me that the Chimaman should have less pride in his bow-legged and inefficient god than in any other national institution.

I do not wish to be understood as interfering with any man's religious views; but when polygamy is made a divine decree, or a bass-wood deity is whittled out and painted red, to look up to and to worship, I cannot treat that so-called religious belief with courtesy and reverence. I am quite liberal in all religious matters. People have noticed that and remarked it, but the Oriental god of commerce seems to me to be greatly over-rated. He seems to lack that genuine decision of character which should be a feature of an over-ruling power.

I ask the phrenologist to come with me and examine the head of the alleged Josh, and to state whether or not he believes that the properly balanced head of a successful god should not have a more protuberant knob of spirituality, and a less pronounced alimentiveness. Should the bump of combativeness hang out over the ear, while time, tune and calculation are noticeably reticent? I certainly wot not.

Again, how can the physiognomy of the Celestial Josh be consistent with a moral and temperate god? The low brow would not indicate a pronounced omniscience, and the Jumbo ears and the copious neck would not impress me with the idea of purity and spirituality.

It is, no doubt, wrong to attack sacred matters for the purpose of gaining notoriety; but I believe I am right, when I assert that the Chinese god must go. We should not be Puritanical, but we might safely draw the line at the bow-legged and sedentary goddess of leprosy

If Confucius bowed the suppliant knee to that goggle-eyed jim-jam Josh, I am grieved to know it. If such was the case, the friends of Confucius should keep the matter from me. I cannot believe that the great philosopher wallowed in the dust at the feet of such a polka-dot carricature of a gorilla's horrid dream.

I bought a Chinese god once, for four bits. He was not successful in the profession which he aimed to follow. Whatever he may have been in China, he was not a very successful god in the English language. I put him upon

THE DOG EXITS.

the mantel, and the clock stopped, the servant girl sent in her resignation, and a large dog jumped through the parlor-window. All this happened within two hours from the time I erected the lop-eared, knocked-kneed and club-footed Oolong in my household.

Perhaps this may have been largely due to my ignorance of his habits. Possibly if I had been more familiar with his eccentricities, it would have been all right; but as it was, there was no book of instructions given with him, and I couldn't seem to make him work.

During the week following, the prospect shaft of the New Jerusalem mine struck a subterranean gulf-stream and water-logged the stock, a tall yellow dog, under the weight of a great woe, picked out my cistern to suicide in, and I skated down the cellar-stairs on my my shoulder-blades and the phrenological location known as Love of Home, in such a terrible manner as to jar the foundations of the earth, and kick a large hole out of the bosom of the night.

I then met with a change of heart, and overthrew the warty heathen god, and knocked him galley west. My hens at once began to watch the produce market, and, noticing the high price of eggs, commenced to orate with great zeal instead of standing around with their hands in their pockets. I saw the new moon over my right shoulder, and all nature seemed gay once more.

The above are a few of my reasons for believing that the Chinese god is either greatly over-estimated, or else shippers and producers are flooding the market with fraudulent gods.

A Great Spiritualist.

I HAVE an uncle who is a physician, and a very busy one at that. He is a very active man, and allows himself very little relaxation indeed. How many times he has said to me, "Well, I can't stand here and fool away my time with you. I've got a typhoid fever patient down in the lower end of town who will get well if I don't get over there this forenoon."

He never allows himself any relaxation to speak of, except to demonstrate the truth of spiritualism. He does love to monkey with the supernatural, and he delights in getting hold of some skeptical friend and convincing him of the presence of spirits beyond a doubt. I've known him to ignore two cases of croup and one case of twins to attend a seance and help convince a doubting Thomas on the spirit question.

I believe that he and I, together with a little time in which to prepare, could convince the most skeptical. He says that with a friend to assist him, who is *en rapport*, and who has a little practice, he can reach the stoniest heart. He is a very susceptible medium indeed, and created a great furore in his own town. He said it was a great comfort to him to converse with his former patients, and he felt kind of attached to them, so that he hated to be separated from them, even in death.

Spiritualism had quite a run in his neighborhood at one time, as I have said. Even his own family yielded to the convincing proof and the astounding phenomena. If his wife hadn't found some of his spiritual tracks down cellar, she would have remained firm, no doubt, but the doctor forgot and left his step-ladder down there, and that showed where the hole in the floor opened into his mysterious cabinet.

He said if he had been a little more careful, no doubt he could have convinced anybody of the presence of spirits or anything else. He said he didn't intend to give up as long as there was anything left in the cellar.

He had such unwavering confidence in the phenomena that all he asked of anybody was faith and a buckskin string about two feet long.

He and his brother, a reformed member of Congress, read the inmost thoughts of a skeptical friend all one evening by the aid of supernatural powers and a tin tube. The reformed member of Congress acted as medium, and the doctor, who was unfortunately and ostensibly called away into the country early in the evening, remained at the window outside, where he could read the queries written by the victim on a slip of paper. Then he would run around the house and murmur the same through a tin tube at another window by the medium's ear.

It was astounding. The skeptical man would write some deep question on a slip of paper, and after the medium had felt of his brow, and groaned a few hollow groans, and rolled his eyes up, he would answer it without having been within twenty feet of the question or the questioner. The victim said he would never doubt again.

What a comfort it was to know that immortality was an established fact. If he could have heard a man talking in a low tone of voice through an old tin dipper handle, at the south window on the ground floor, and occasionally swearing at a mosquito on the back of his neck, he would have hesitated.

An old-timer over there said that Woodworth would be a mighty good physician if he would let spiritualism alone. He claimed that no man could be a great physician and surgeon and still be a fanatic on spiritualism.

General Sheridan's Horse.

I HAVE always taken a great interest in war incidents, and more so, perhaps, because I wasn't old enough to put down the rebellion myself. I have been very eager to get hold of and hoard up in my memory all its gallant deeds of both sides, and to know the history of those who figured prominently in that great conflict has been one of my ambitions.

I have also watched with interest the steady advancement of Phil Sheridan, the black-eyed warrior with the florid face and the Winchester record. I have also taken some pains to investigate the later history of the old Winchester war horse.

"Old Rienzi died in our stable a few years after the war," said a Chicago livery man to me, a short time ago. "General Sheridan left him with us and instructed us to take good care of him, which we did, but he got old at last, and his teeth failed upon him, and that busted his digestion, and he kind of died of old age, I reckon."

"How did General Sheridan take it?"

"Oh, well, Phil Sheridan is no school girl. He didn't turn away when old Rienzi died and weep the manger full of scalding regret. If you know Sheridan, you know that he don't rip the blue dome of heaven wide open with unavailing wails. He just told us to take care of its remains, patted the old cuss on the head a little and walked off. Phil Sheridan don't go around weeping softly into a pink bordered wipe when a horse dies. He likes a good horse, but Rienzi was no Jay-Eye-See for swiftness, and he wasn't the purtiest horse you ever see, by no means."

"Did you read lately how General Sheridan don't ride on horseback since his old war horse died, and seems to have lost all interest in horses?"

"No, I never did. He no doubt would rather ride in a cable car or a carriage than to jar himself up on a horse. That's all likely enough, but, as I say, he's a matter of fact little fighter from Fighttown. He never stopped to snoot and paw up the ground and sob himself into bronchitis over old Rienzi.

He went right on about his business, and, like old King What's-his-name he hollered for another hoss, and the War Department never slipped a cog."

Later on I read that the old war horse was called Winchester and that he was still alive in a blue grass pasture in Kentucky. The report said that old Winchester wasn't very coltish, and that he was evidently failing. I gathered the idea that he was wearing store teeth, and that his memory was a little deficient, but that he might live yet for years. After that I met a New York livery stable prince, at whose palace General Sheridan's well-known Winchester war horse died of botts in '71. He told me all about, it and how General Sheridan came on from Chicago at the time, and held the horse's head in his lap while the fleet limbs that flew from Winchester down and saved the day, stiffened in the great, mysterious repose of death. He said Sheridan wept like a child, and as he told the touching tale to me I wept also. I say I wept. I wept about a quart, I would say. He said also that the horse's name wasn't Winchester nor Rienzi; it was Jim.

I was sorry to know it. Jim is no name for a war horse who won a victory and a marble bust and a poem. You can't respect a horse much if his name was Jim.

After that I found out that General Sheridan's celebrated Winchester horse was raised in Kentucky, also in Pennsylvania and Michigan; that he went out as a volunteer private; that he was in the regular service prior to the war, and that he was drafted, and that he died on the field of battle, in a sorrel pasture, in '73, in great pain on Governor's Island; that he was buried with Masonic honors by the Good Templars and the Grand Army of the Republic; that he was resurrected by a medical college and dissected; that he was cremated in New Orleans and taxidermed for the Military Museum at New York. Every little while I run up against a new fact relative to this noted beast. He has died in nine different States, and been buried in thirteen different styles, while his soul goes marching on. Evidently we live in an age of information. You can get more information nowadays, such as it is, than you know what to do with.

A Circular.

TO MY FRIENDS, REGARDLESS OF PARTY.—**Many friends having** solicited me to apply for a foreign mission under the present administration, I have finally consented to do so, and last week filed my application for such missions as might still remain vacant.

To insure my appointment, much will remain for you to do. I now call upon my friends to aid me by their united effort. I especially solicit the aid of my friends who have repeatedly heretofore promised it to me while drunk.

You will see at a glance that I can only make the application. You must support it by your petitions and letters. It would be of little use for one man to write five thousand letters to the president, but if five thousand people each write him a letter in which casual reference is made to my social worth and $7\frac{1}{3}$ octave brain, it will make him pay attention.

PLENTY OF CORRESPONDENCE.

My idea would be for each of my friends to set aside one day in each week to write to the president, opening it in a chatty way by asking him if he does not think we are having rather a backward spring, and what he is doing for his cut worms now, and how his folks are, etc., etc. Then gradually lead up to the statement that you think I would be an ornament to the administration if I should go abroad and linger on a foreign strand at $2,000 per linger and stationery.

This will keep the president properly stirred up, and cause him to earn his salary. The effect will be to secure the appointment at last, as you will see if you persevere.

I need not add that I will do what is right by my friends upon receiving my commission.

Do not neglect this suggestion because it comes to you in the form of a circular, but remember it and act upon it. Remember that, although the president is stubborn as Sam Hill, he will at last yield to fatigue, and when tired nature can hold out no longer, the last letter will drop from his nerveless hand and he will surrender.

NURSING THE FIERY STEED.

Some of you will urge that I have been an offensive partisan, but when you come to think it over I have not been so all-fired partisan. There have been days and days when it did not show itself very much. However, that is not the point. I want your hearty indorsement and I want it to be entirely voluntary, and if you do not give it, and give it freely and voluntarily, you hadn't better ask me for any more favors.

All the newspapers most heartily indorse me. The *Rocky Mountain Whoop* very truthfully says

"Mr. Nye called at our office yesterday and subscribed for our paper. We are proud to add him to our list of paid-up subscribers, and should he renew his subscription next year, paying in advance, we will cheerfully refer to it among other startling news."

I have a scrap-book full of such indorsements as this, and now, if my friends will peel their coats and write as they should, I can make this administration open its eyes.

Several papers in Iowa have alluded to my being in town, and referred to the fact that I had paid my bills while there. But press indorsements alone are not sufficient. What is needed is the written testimony of friends and neighbors. No matter how poor or humble or worthless you may be, write to Mr. Cleveland and tell him how much confidence you have in me, and if you can call to mind any little acts of kindness, or any times when I have got up in the night to give you a dollar, or nurse a colicky horse for you, throw that in. Throw it in anyhow. It will do no harm, and may do much good.

I can solemnly promise all my friends that if they will secure my appointment to a foreign country for four years, I will not return during that time. What more can I offer? I will stay longer if I am reappointed. I would do anything for my friends.

Do not throw this circular carelessly aside. Read it carefully over and act upon it. Some of you are poor spellers, and will try to get out of it in that way. Others are in the penitentiary and cannot spare the time. But to one and all I say, write, and write regularly, to the president. Do not wait for a reply from him, because he is pretty busy now; but he will be tickled to death to hear from you, and anything you say about me will give him great pleasure.

N. B.—Please be careful not to inclose this circular in your letter to the president.

The Photograph Habit.

NO doubt the photograph habit, when once formed, is one of the most baneful, and productive of the most intense suffering in after years, of any with which we are familiar. Some times it seems to me that my whole life has been one long, abject apology for photographs that I have shed abroad throughout a distracted country

Man passes through seven distinct stages of being photographed, each one exceeding all previous efforts in that line.

First he is photographed as a prattling, bald-headed baby, absolutely destitute of eyes, but making up for this deficiency by a wealth of mouth that would make a negro minstrel olive green with envy. We often wonder what has given the average photographer that wild, hunted look about the eyes and that joyless sag about the knees. The chemicals and the indoor life alone have not done all this. It is the great nerve tension and mental strain used in trying to photograph a squirming and dark red child with white eyes, in such a manner as to please its parents.

An old-fashioned dollar store album with cerebro-spinal meningitis, and filled with pictures of half-suffocated children in heavily-starched white dresses, is the first thing we seek on entering a home, and the last thing from which we reluctantly part.

The second stage on the downward road is the photograph of the boy with fresh-cropped hair, and in which the stiff and protuberant thumb takes a leading part.

Then follows the portrait of the lad, with strongly marked freckles and a look of hopeless melancholy With the aid of a detective agency, I have succeeded in running down and destroying several of these pictures which were attributed to me.

Next comes the young man, 21 years of age, with his front hair plastered smoothly down over his tender, throbbing dome of thought. He does not care so much about the expression on the mobile features, so long as his left hand, with the new ring on it, shows distinctly, and the string of jingling, jangling charms on his watch chain, including the cute little basket cut out of a peach stone, stand out well in the foreground. If the young man would stop to think for a moment that some day he may become eminent and ashamed of himself, he would hesitate about doing this.

Soon after, he has a tintype taken in which a young lady sits in the alleged grass, while he stands behind her with his hand lightly touching her shoulder as though he might be feeling of the thrilling circumference of a buzz saw. He carries this picture in his pocket for months, and looks at it whenever he may be unobserved.

Then, all at once, he discovers that the young lady's hair is not done up that way any more, and that her hat doesn't seem to fit her. He then, in a fickle moment, has another tintype made, in which another young woman, with a more recent hat and later coiffure, is discovered holding his hat in her lap.

This thing continues, till one day he comes into the studio with his wife, and tries to see how many children can be photographed on one negative by holding one on each knee and using the older ones as a back-ground.

The last stage in his eventful career, the old gentleman allows himself to be photographed, because he is afraid he may not live through another long, hard winter, and the boys would like a picture of him while he is able to climb the dark, narrow stairs which lead to the artist's room.

Sadly the thought comes back to you in after years, when his grave is green in the quiet valley, and the worn and weary hands that have toiled for you are forever at rest, how patiently he submitted while his daughter pinned the clean, stiff, agonizing white collar about his neck, and brushed the velvet collar of his best coat; how he toiled up the long, dark, lonesome stairs, not with the egotism of a half century ago, but with the light of anticipated rest at last in his eyes—obediently, as he would have gone to the dingy law office to have his will drawn—and meekly left the outlines of his kind old face for those he loved and for whom he had so long labored.

It is a picture at which the thoughtless may smile, but it is full of pathos, and eloquent for those who knew him best. His attitude is stiff and his coat hunches up in the back, but his kind old heart asserts itself through the gentle eyes, and when he has gone away at last we do not criticise the picture any more, but beyond the old coat that hunches up in the back, and that lasted him so long, we read the history of a noble life.

Silently the old finger-marked album, lying so unostentatiously on the gouty centre table, points out the mile-stones from infancy to age, and back of the mistakes of a struggling photographer is portrayed the laughter and the tears, the joy and the grief, the dimples and the gray hairs of one man's lifetime.

Rosalinde.

IN answer to a former article relative to the dearth of woman here, we are now receiving two to five letters per day from all classes and styles of young, middle-aged and old women who desire to come to Wyoming. Some of them would like to come here to work and obtain an honest livelihood, and some of them desire to come here and marry cattle kings.

A recent letter from Michigan, written in lead pencil, and evidently during hours when the writer should have been learning her geography lesson, is very enthusiastic over the prospect of coming out here where one girl can have a lover for every day in the week. She signs herself Rosalinde, with a small r, and adds in a postscript that she "means business."

Yes, Rosalinde, that's what we are afraid of. We had a kind of a vague fear that you meant business, so we did not reply to your letter. Wyoming already has women enough who write with a lead pencil. We are also pretty well provided with poor spellers, and we do not desire to ransack Michigan for affectionate but sap-headed girls.

Stay in Michigan, Rosalinde, until we write to you, and one of these days when you have been a mother eight or nine times, and as you stand in the golden haze in the back yard, hanging out damp shirts on an uncertain line, while your ripe and dewy mouth is stretched around a bass-wood clothes pin, you will thank us for this advice.

Michigan is the place for you. It is the home of the Sweet Singer and the abiding place of the Detroit *Free Press.* We can't throw any such influences around you here as those you have at your own door.

Do not despair, Rosalinde. Some day a man, with a great, warm, manly heart and a pair of red steers, will see you and love you, and he will take you in his strong arms and protect you from the Michigan climate, just as devotedly as any of our people here can. We do not wish to be misunderstood in this matter. It is not as a lover that we have said so much on the girl question, but in the domestic aid department, and when we get a long letter from a young girl who eats slate pencils and reads Ouida behind her atlas, we feel like going over there to Michigan with a trunk strap and doing a little missionary work.

The Church Debt.

I HAVE been thinking the matter over seriously and I have decided that if I had my life to live over again, I would like to be an eccentric millionaire.

I have eccentricity enough, but I cannot successfully push it without more means.

I have a great many plans which I would like to carry out, in case I could unite the two necessary elements for the production of the successful eccentric millionaire.

Among other things, I would be willing to bind myself and give proper security to any one who would put in money to offset my eccentricity, that I would ultimately die. We all know how seldom the eccentric millionaire now dies. I would be willing to inaugurate a reform in that direction.

I think now that I would endow a home for men whose wives are no longer able to support them. In many cases the wife who was at first able to support her husband comfortably, finally shoulders a church debt, and in trying to lift that she overworks and impairs her health so that she becomes an invalid, while her husband is left to pine away in solitude or dependent on the cold charities of the world.

My heart goes out toward those men even now, and in case I should fill the grave of the eccentric millionaire, I am sure that I would do the square thing by them.

The method by which our wives in America are knocking the church debt silly, by working up their husbands' groceries into "angel food" and selling them below actual cost, is deserving of the attention of our national financiers.

The church debt itself is deserving of notice in this country It certainly thrives better under a republican form of government than any other feature of our boasted civilization. Western towns spring up everywhere, and the first anxiety is to name the place, the second to incur a church debt and establish a roller rink.

After that a general activity in trade is assured. Of course the general hostility of church and rink will prevent *ennui* and listlessness, and the church debt will encourage a business boom. Naturally the church debt cannot be paid without what is generally known through the West as the "festival and hooraw." This festival is an open market where the ladies trade the groceries of their husbands to other ladies' husbands, and everybody has a "perfectly lovely time." The church clears $2.30, and thirteen ladies are sick all the next day.

This makes a boom for the physicians and later on for the undertaker and general tombist. So it will be seen that the Western town is right in establishing a church debt as soon as the survey is made and the town properly named. After the first church debt has been properly started, others will rapidly follow, so that no anxiety need be felt if the church will come forward the first year and buy more than it can pay for.

PUGILISM IN RELIGION.

The church debt is a comparatively modern appliance, and yet it has been productive of many peculiar features. For instance, we call to mind the clergyman who makes a specialty of going from place to place as a successful debt demolisher. He is a part of the general system, just as much as the ice cream freezer or the button-hole boquet.

Then there is a row or social knock-down-and-drag-out which goes along with the church debt. All these things add to the general interest, and to acquire interest in one way or another is the mission of the c. d.

I once knew a most exemplary woman who became greatly interested in the wiping out of a church debt, and who did finally succeed in wiping out the debt, but in its last expiring death struggle it gave her a wipe from which she never recovered. She had succeeded in begging the milk and the cream, and the eggs and the sandwiches, and the use of the dishes and the sugar, and the loan of an oyster, and the use of a freezer and fifty button-hole boquets to be sold to men who were not in the habit of wearing boquets, but she could not borrow a circular artist to revolve the crank of the freezer, so she agitated it herself. Her husband had to go away prior to the festivities, but he ordered her not to crank the freezer. He had very little influence with her, however, and so to-day he is a widower. The church debt was revived in the following year, and now there isn't a more thriving church debt anywhere in the country. Only last week that church traded off $75 worth of groceries, in the form of asbestos cake and celluloid angel food, in such a way that if the original cost of the groceries and the work were not considered, the clear profit was $13, after the hall rent was paid. And why should the first cost of the groceries be reckoned, when we stop to think that they were involuntarily furnished by the depraved husband and father.

I must add, also, that in the above estimate doctors' bills and funeral expenses are not reckoned.

A Collection of Keys.

I'M getting to be quite a connoisseur of hotel keys as I get older. For ten years I have been collecting these mementoes of travel and cording them away in my key cabinet. Some have square brass tags attached to them, others have round ones. Still others affect the octagonal, the fluted, the hexagonal, the scalloped, the plain, the polished, the docorated, the chaste, the Etruscan, the metropolitan, the rural, the cosmopolitan, the shirred, the tucked, the biased, the high neck and long sleeve or the *decolette* style of brass check.

I have, so far, paid my bills, but I have not returned the keys to my room. Hotel proprietors will please take notice and govern themselves accordingly. When my visit to a pleasant city has become a beautiful memory only, I all at once sit down on something hard and find that it is the key to my former room at the hotel. Sitting down on a key tag of corrugated brass, as big as a buckwheat pancake, would remind most anyone of something or other.

I generally leave my tooth-brush in my room and carry off the key as a kind of involuntary swap, so far as the hotel proprietor is concerned, but I do not think it is a mutual benefit, particularly. I cannot use the key to a hotel 500 miles away, and so far as a tooth-brush is concerned, it generally has pleasant associations only for the owner. A man is fond of his own tooth-brush, but it takes years for him to love the tooth-brush of a stranger.

There are a good many associations attached to those keys, like the tags They point backward to the rooms to which the keys belong. Here is a fat one that led to room number 33½ in the Synagogue hotel. It was a cheerful room, where the bell boy said an old man had asphyxiated himsolf with gas the previous week. I had never met the old man before, but that night, about 1 o'clock A. M., I had the pleasure of his acquaintance. He came in a sad and reproachful way, and showed me how the post-mortem people had disfigured him. Of course it was a little tough to be mutilated by an inquest, but that's no reason why he should come back there and occupy a room that I was paying for so that I could be alone. He showed me how he blew out the gas, and told me how a man could successfully blow down the muzzle of a shot-gun or a gas jet, but both of these weapons had a way of blowing back.

I have a key that brings back to me the memory of a room that I lived in two days at one time. I do not mean that I lived the two days at once, but that at one period I occupied that room, partially, for two days and two nights. I say I partially occupied it, because I used to occupy it days and share it nights with others; that is, I tried to occupy it nights. I tried to get the clerk to throw off something because I didn't have the exclusive use of the room. He wouldn't throw off anything. He even wanted to fight me because I said that the room was occupied before I got it and after I left it. Finally, I told him that if he would throw a bed quilt over his diamond, so I could see him, I would fight him with buckwheat cakes at five-hundred miles. I took my position the next morning at the place appointed, but he did not appear.

Extracts from a Queen's Diary.

JANUARY 1.—I awoke late this forenoon with a pain through the head and a taste of ennui in the mouth, which I can hardly account for. Can it be a result of the party last evening? I ween it may be so. We had a lovely card party last evening. It was very enjoyable, indeed. Whist was the game.

JANUARY 3.—Yesterday all day I was unable to leave my room, owing to a headache and nervous prostration, caused by late hours and too much company, the doctor said. It is too bad, and yet I do so much enjoy our card parties and the excitement of the game. To-night I am to take part in a little quiet game of draw poker, I think they call it. I have not had any experience heretofore in the game, but trust I shall soon learn it. There has been some talk about £1 ante and £5 limit. I do not exactly understand the terms. I hope it does not mean anything wrong.

JANUARY 4.—Poker is an odd game, indeed. I think it quite exciting, though at first the odd terms rather confused me. I had not been accustomed to such phrases as "show down," "bob-tail flush," and "King full." I must ask Brown, as soon as his knees are able to be out, to explain the meaning of these terms a little more fully to me. If poor Brown's knees are not better soon, I shall be on kneesy about him. [Here the diary has the appearance of being blurred with tears.] A bob-tail flush, I learn, is something very disagreeable to have. One gentleman said last evening that another bob-tail flush would certainly paralyze him. I gather from that that it is something like a hectic flush. I can understand the game called "old sledge," and have become quite familiar with such terms as "beg," "gimmeone," "I've got the thin one," "how high is that?" "one horse on me," "saw-off," etc., etc., but poker is full of surprises. It seems so odd to see a gentleman "show out on a pair of deuces" and gather in upward of two pounds with great merriment, while the remainder of the party seem quite bored. One gentleman last evening showed out on a full hand with "treys at the head," putting £3 12s. in his purse with great glee, while another one of the party who had not shown up, but I am positive had a better hand, became so angered that he got up and kicked four front teeth out of the mouth of a favorite dog worth £20. I took part in a spade flush during the evening and was quite successful, so that I can easily pay my traveling expenses and have a few shillings to buy ointment for poor Brown. It was my first winning, and made me quiver all over with excitement. The game is already very fascinating to me, and I am becoming passionately fond of it.

JANUARY 6.—I have just learned fully what a bob-tail flush is. It cost me £50. I like information, but I do not like to buy it when it comes so high. I drew two to fill in a heart flush last evening, and advanced the money to back up my judgment; but one of the hearts I drew was a club, which was entirely useless to me. I have sent out a sheriff with a bulldog to ascertain if he can find the whereabouts of the party who started this poker game, I do not know when I have felt so bored. After that I was so timid that I allowed a friend to walk off with £2 on a pair of deuces. I said to him that I called that a deuced bore, and he laughed heartily.

I find that you should not be too ready to show by your countenance whether you are bored or pleased in poker. Your opponent will take advantage of it and play accordingly. It cost me £8 10s. to acquire a knowledge of this fact. If all the information I ever got had cost me as much as this poker wisdom, I would not now have two pennies to jingle together in my purse. Still, we have had a good time, take it all in all, and I shall not soon forget the evenings we have spent here together buying knowledge regardless of cost. I think I shall try to control my wild thirst for information awhile, however, till I can get some more funds.

[Here the diary breaks off abruptly, and on turning the book over we find the royal signature at the foot of the last page, "The Queen of Spades."]

Shorts.

COLORADO burro has been shipped across the Atlantic and presented to the Prince of Wales. It is a matter of profound national sorrow that this was not the first American jackass presented to his Tallness, the Prince.

At Omaha last week a barrel of sauer kraut rolled out of a wagon and struck O'Leary H. Oleson, who was trying to unload it, with such force as to kill him instantly and to flatten him out like a kiln-dried codfish. Still, after thousands of such instances on record, there are many scientists who maintain that sauer kraut is conducive to longevity.

As an evidence of the healthfulness of mountain climate, the people of Denver point to a man who came there in '77 without flesh enough to bait a trap, and now he puts sleeves in an ordinary feather-bed and pulls it on over his head for a shirt. People in poor health who wish to communicate with the writer in relation to the facts above stated, are requested to enclose two unlicked postage stamps to insure a reply.

At Ubet, M. T., during the cold snap in January, one of the most inhuman outrages known in the annals of crime was perpetrated upon a young man who went West in the fall, hoping to make his pile in time to return in May and marry the New York heiress selected before he went.

While stopping at the hotel, two frolicsome young women hired the porter to procure the young man's pantaloons at dead of night. They then sewed up the bottoms of the legs, threw the doctored garment back through the transom and squealed "Fire!"

When he got into the hall he was vainly trying to stab one foot through the limb of his pantaloons while he danced around on the other and joined in the general cry of "Fire!" The hall seemed filled with people, who were running this way and that, ostensibly seeking a mode of egress from the flames, but in reality trying to dodge the mad efforts of the young man, who was trying to insert himself in his obstinate pantaloons.

He did not tumble, as it were, until the night watchman got a Babcock fire extinguisher and played on him. I do not know what he played on him. Very likely it was, "Sister, what are the wild waves saying?"

Anyway, he staggered into his room, and although he could hear the audience outside in their wild, tumultuous encore, he refused to come before the curtain, but locked his door and sobbed himself to sleep.

How often do we forget the finer feelings of others and ignore their sorrow while we revel in some great joy.

"We."

THE world is full of literary people to-day, and they are divided into three classes, viz: Those who have written for the press, those who are writing for the press, and those who want to write for the press. Of the first, there are those who tried it and found that they could make more in half the time at something else, and so quit the field, and those who failed to touch the great heart and pocketbook of the public, and therefore subsided. Those who are writing for the press now, whether putting together copy by the mile within the sound of the rumbling engine and press, or scattered through the country writing more at their leisure, find that they have to lay aside every weight and throw off all the incumbrances of the mossy past.

One thing, however, still clings to the editor like a dab of paste on a white vest or golden fleck of scrambled egg on a tawny moustache. One relic of barbarism rears in gaunt form amid the clash and hurry and rush of civilization, and in the dazzling light of science and smartness.

It is "we."

The budding editor of the rural civilizer for the first time peels his coat and sharpens his pencil to begin the work of changing the great current of public opinion. He is strong in his desire to knock error and wrong galley west. He has buckled on his armor to paralyze monopoly and purify the ballot. He has hitched up his pantaloons with a noble resolve and covered his table with virgin paper.

He is young, and he is a little egotistical, also. He wants to say, "I believe" so and so, but he can't. Perspiration breaks out all over him. He bites his pencil, and looks up with his clenched hand in his hair. The slimy demon of the editor's life is there, sitting on the cloth bound volume containing the report of the United States superintendent of swine diseases.

Wherever you find a young man unloading a Washington hand press to fill a long-felt want, there you will find the ghastly and venomous "we," ready to look over the shoulder of the timid young mental athlete. Wherever you find a ring of printer's ink around the door knob, and the snowy towel on which the foreman wipes the pink tips of his alabaster fingers, you will find the slimy, scaly folds of "we" curled up in some neighboring corner.

From the huge metropolitan journal, whose subscribers could make or bust a president, or make a blooming king wish he had never been born, down to the obscure and unknown dodger whose first page is mostly electrotype head, whose second and third pages are patent, whose news is eloquent of the dear dead past, whose fourth page ushers in a new baby, or heralds the coming of the circus, or promulgates the fact that its giant editor has a felon on his thumb, the trail of the serpent "we" is over them all. It is all we have to remind us of royalty in America, with the exception, perhaps, of the case now and then where a king full busts a bob-tail flush.

A Mountain Snowstorm.

SEPTEMBER does not always indicate golden sunshine, and ripening corn, and old gold pumpkin pies on the half-shell. We look upon it as the month of glorious perfection in the handiwork of the seasons and the time when the ripened fruits are falling, when the red sun hides behind the bronze and misty evening, and says good night with reluctance to the beautiful harvests and the approching twilight of the year.

It was on a red letter day of this kind, years ago, that Wheeler and myself started out under the charge of Judge Blair and Sheriff Baswell to visit the mines at Last Chance, and more especially the Keystone, a gold mine that the Judge had recently become president of. The soft air of second summer in the Rocky Mountains blew gently past our ears as we rode up the valley of the Little Laramie, to camp the first night at the head of the valley behind Sheep Mountain. The whole party was full of joy. Even Judge Blair, with the frosts of over sixty winters in his hair, broke forth into song. That's the only thing I ever had against Judge Blair. He would forget himself sometimes and burst forth into song.

The following day we crossed the divide and rode down the gulch into the camp on Douglass Creek, where the musical thunder of the stamp mills seemed to jar the ground, and the rapid stream below bore away on its turbid bosom the yellowish tinge of the golden quartz. It was a perfect day, and Wheeler and I blessed our stars and, instead of breathing the air of sour paste and hot presses in the newspaper offices, away in the valley, we were sprawling in the glorious sunshine of the hills, playing draw poker with the miners in the evening, and forgetful of the daily newspaper where one man does the work and the other draws the salary. It was heaven. It was such luxury that we wanted to swing our hats and yell like Arapahoes.

The next morning we were surprised to find that it had snowed all night and was snowing still. I never saw such flakes of snow in my life. They came sauntering through the air like pure, white Turkish towels falling from celestial clothes-lines. We did not return that day We played a few games of chance, but they were brief. We finally made it five cent ante, and, as I was working then for an alleged newspaper man who paid me $50 per month to edit his paper nights and take care of his children daytimes, I couldn't keep abreast of the Judge, the Sheriff and the Superintendent of the Keystone.

The next day we had to go home. The snow lay ankle-deep everywhere and the air was chilly and raw. Wheeler and I tried to ride, but the mountain road was so rough that the horses could barely move through the snow, dragging the buggy after them. So we got out and walked on ahead to keep warm. We gained very fast on the team, for we were both long-legged and measured off the miles like a hired man going to dinner. I wore a pair of glove-fitting low shoes and lisle-thread socks. I can remember that yet. I would advise anyone going into the mines not to wear lisle-thread socks and low shoes. You are liable to stick your foot into a snow-bank or a mud hole and dip up too much water. I remember that after we had walked through the pine woods down the mountain road a few miles, I noticed that the bottoms of my pantaloons looked like those of a drowned tramp I saw many years ago in the morgue. We gave out after a while, waited for the team, but decided that it had gone the other road. All at once it flashed over us that we were alone in the woods and the storm, wet, nearly starved, ignorant of the road and utterly worn out!

IT WAS TOUGH.

It was tough!

I never felt so blue, so wet, so hungry, or so hopeless in my life. We moved on a little farther. All at once we came out of the timber. There was no snow whatever! At that moment the sun burst forth, we struck a deserted supply wagon, found a two-pound can of Boston baked beans, got an axe from the load, chopped open the can, and had just finished the tropical fruit of Massachusetts when our own team drove up, and joy and hope made their homes once more in our hearts.

We may learn from this a valuable lesson, but at this moment I do not know exactly what it is.

Lost Money.

MOST anyone could collect and tell a good many incidents about lost money that has been found, if he would try, but these cases came under my own observation and I can vouch for their truth.

A farmer in the Kinnekinnick Valley was paid $1,000 while he was loading hay He put it in his vest pocket, and after he had unloaded the hay he discovered that he had lost it, and no doubt had pitched the whole load into the mow on top of it. He went to work and pitched it all out, a handful at a time, upon the barn floor, and when the hired man's fork tine came up with a $100 bill on it he knew they had struck a lead. He got it all.

A man gave me two $5 bills once to pay a balance on some store teeth and asked me to bring the teeth back with me. The dentist was fifteen miles away and when I got there I found I had lost the money That was before I had amassed much of a fortune, so I went to the tooth foundry and told the foreman that I had started with $10 to get a set of teeth for an intimate friend, but had lost the funds. He said that my intimate friend would, no doubt, have to gum it awhile. Owing to the recent shrinkage in values he was obliged to sell teeth for cash, as the goods were comparatively useless after they had been used one season. I went back over the same road the next day and found the money by the side of the road, although a hundred teams had passed by it.

A young man, one spring, plowed a pocket-book and $30 in greenbacks under, and by a singular coincidence the next spring it was plowed out, and, though rotten clear through, was sent to the Treasury, where it was discovered that the bills were on a Michigan National Bank, whither they were sent and redeemed.

I lost a roll of a hundred dollars the spring of '82, and hunted my house and the office through, in search for it, in vain. I went over the road between the office and the house twenty times, but it was useless. I then advertised the loss of the money, giving the different denominations of the bills and stating, as was the case, that there was an elastic band around the roll when lost. The paper had not been issued more than an hour before I got my money, every dollar of it. It was in the pocket of my other vest.

This should teach us, first, the value of advertising, and, secondly, the utter folly of two vests at the same time.

Apropos of recent bank failures, I want to tell this one on James S. Kelley, commonly called "Black Jim." He failed himself along in the fifties, and by a big struggle had made out to pay everybody but Lo Bartlett, to whom he was indebted in the sum of $18. He got this money, finally, and as Lo wasn't in town, Black Jim put it in a bank, the name of which has long ago sunk into oblivion. In fact, it began the oblivion business about forty-eight hours after Jim had put his funds in there.

Meeting Lo on the street, Jim said:

"Your money is up in the Wild Cat Bank, Lo. I'll give you a check for it."

"No use, old man, she's gone up."

"No! !"

"Yes, she's a total wreck."

Jim went over to the president's room. He knocked as easy as he could, considering that his breath was coming so hard.

"Who's there?"

"It's Jim Kelley, Black Jim, and I'm in something of a hurry."

"Well, I'm very busy, Mr. Kelley. Come again this afternoon."

"That will be too remote. I am very busy myself. Now is the accepted time. Will you open the door or shall I open it."

The president opened it because it was a good door and he wanted to preserve it.

Black Jim turned the key in the door and sat down.

"What did you want of me?" says the president.

"I wanted to see you about a certificate of deposit I've got here on your bank for eighteen dollars."

"We can't pay it. Everything is gone."

"Well, I am here to get $18 or to leave you looking like a giblet pie. Eighteen dollars will relieve you of this mental strain, but if you do not put up I will paper this wall with your classic features and ruin the carpet with what remains."

The president hesitated a moment. Then he took a roll out of his boot and paid Jim eighteen dollars.

"You will not mention this on the street, of course," said the president.

"No," says Jim, "not till I get there."

When the crowd got back, however, the president had fled and he has remained fled ever since. The longer he remained away and thought it over, the more he became attached to Canada, and the more of a confirmed and incurable fugitive he became.

I saw Black Jim last evening and he said he had passed through two bank failures, but had always realized on his certificates of deposit. One cashier told Jim that he was the homeliest man that ever looked through the window of a busted bank. He said Kelley looked like a man who ate bank cashiers on toast and directors raw with a slice of lemon on top.

Dr. Dizart's Dog.

A MAN whose mother-in-law had been successfully treated by the doctor, one day presented him with a beautiful Italian hound named Nemesis. When I say that the able physician had treated the mother-in-law successfully, I mean successfully from her son-in-law's standpoint, and not from her own, for the doctor insisted on treating her for small-pox when she had nothing but an attack of agnostics. She is now sitting on the front stoop of the golden whence.

So, after the last sad rites, the broken-hearted son-in-law presented the physician with a handsome hound with long, slender legs and a wire tail, as a token of esteem and regard.

The dog was young and playful, as all young dogs are, so he did many little tricks which amused almost everyone.

One day, while the doctor was away administering a subcutaneous injection of morphine to a hay-fever patient, he left Nemesis in the office alone with a piece of rag-carpet and his surging thoughts.

At first Nemesis closed his eyes and breathed hard, then he arose and ate part of an ottoman, then he got up and scratched the paper off the office wall and whined in a sad tone of voice.

A young Italian hound has a peculiarly sad and depressing song.

Then Nemesis got up on the desk and poured the ink and mucilage into one of the drawers on some bandages and condition-powders that the doctor used in his horse-practice.

Nemesis then looked out of the window and wailed. He filled the room with robust wail and unavailing regret.

After that he tried to dispel his *ennui* with one of the doctor's old felt hats that hung on a chair; but the hair oil with which it was saturated changed his mind.

The doctor had magenta hair, and to tone it down so that it would not raise the rate of fire insurance on his office, he used to execute some studies on it in oil—bear's oil

This gave his hair a rich mahogany shade, and his hat smelled and looked like an oil refinery.

That is the reason Nemesis spared the hat, and ate a couple of porous-plasters that his master was going to use on a case of croup.

At that time the doctor came in, and the dog ran to him with a glad cry of pleasure, rubbing his cold nose against his master's hand. The able veter-

BUSTLE AND CONFUSION.

inarian spoke roughly to Nemesis, and throwing a cigar-stub at him, broke two of the animal's delicate legs.

After that there was a low discordant murmur and the angry hum of medical works, lung-testers, glass jars containing tumors and other bric-a-brac, paper-weights and Italian grayhound bisecting the orbit of a red-headed horse-physician with dude shoes.

When the police came in, it was found that Nemsis had jumped through a glass door and escaped on two legs and his ear.

Out through the autumnal haze, across the intervening plateau, over the low foot-hills, and up the Medicine Bow Range, on and ever onward sped the timid, grieved and broken-hearted pup, accumulating with wonderful eagerness the intervening distance between himself and the cruel promoter of the fly-blister and lingering death.

How often do we thoughtlessly grieve the hearts of those who love us, and drive forth into the pitiless world those who would gladly lick our hands with their warm, loving tongues, or warm their cold noses in the meshes of our necks.

How prone we are to forget the devotion of a dumb brute that thoughtlessly eats our lace lambrequins, and ere we have stopped to consider our mad course, we have driven the loving heart and the warm wet tongue and the cold little black nose out of our home-life, perhaps into the cold, cold grave or the bleak and relentless pound.

Chinese Justice.

THEY do things differently in China. Here in America, when a man burgles your residence, you go and confide in a detective, who keeps your secret and gets another detective to help him. Generally that is the last of it. In China, not long ago, the house of a missionary was entered and valuables taken by the thieves. The missionary went to the authorities with his tale and told them whom he suspected. That's the last he heard of that for three weeks. Then he received a covered champagne basket from the Department of Justice. On opening it he found the heads of the suspected burglars packed in tinfoil and in a good state of preservation. These heads were not sent necessarily for publication, but as an evidence of good faith on the part of the Department of Unimpeded Justice. Mind you, there was no postponement of the preliminary examination, no dilatory motions and changes of venue, no pleas to the jurisdiction of the court, no legal delays and final challenges of jurors until an idiotic jury had been procured who hadn't read the papers, no ruling out of damaging testimony, and finally filing of bill of exceptions, no appeal and delay, or appeal afterward to another court which returned the defendant to the court of original jurisdiction for review, and years of waiting for the prosecuting witnesses to die of old age and thus release the defendant. There is nothing of that kind in China. You just hand in your orders to the judicial end of the administration, and then you retire. Later on, the delivery man brings in your package of heads, makes a salaam, and goes away.

Now, this is swift and speedy justice for you. I don't know how the guilt of the defendants is arrived at, but there's nothing tedious about it. At least, there's nothing tedious to the complainant. I presume they make it red-hot for the criminal.

Still this style of justice has its drawbacks. For instance, you are at dinner. You have a large and select company dining with you. You are about to carve the roast. There is a ring at the door. The servant announces that a judicial officer is at the drawbridge and desires to speak with you. You pull your napkin out of your bosom, lay the carving knife down on the virgin table cloth, and go to the door. There the minister of justice presents you with a champagne basket and retires. You return to the dining hall, leaving your basket on the sideboard. After a while you announce to your guests that you have just received a basket of Mumm's extra dry with the compliments of the government, and that you will, with the permission of those present, open a bottle. You arm yourself with a corkscrew, open the basket, and thoughtlessly tip it over, when two or three human heads, with a pained and grieved expression on the face, roll out on the table.

When you are looking for a quart bottle of sparkling wine and find instead the cold, sad features and reproachful stare of the extremely deceased and *hic jacet* Chinaman, you naturally betray your chagrin. I like to see justice moderately swift, and, in fact I've seen it pretty forthwith in its movements two or three times; but I cannot say that I would be prepared for this style.

Perhaps I'm getting a little nervous in my old age, and a small matter jars my equilibrium; but I'm sure a basket of heads handed in as I was seated at the table would startle me a little at first, and I might forget myself.

A friend of mine, under such circumstances, made what the English would call "a doosed clevah" remark once in Shanghai. When he opened the basket he was horrified, but he was cool. He was old sang froid from Sangfroidville. He first took the basket and started for the back room, with the remark: "My friends. I guess you will have to ex-queuese me." Then he pulled down his eyelids and laughed a hoarse English laugh.

Answers to Correspondents.

CALLER.—Your calling cards should be modest as to size and neatly engraved, with an extra flourish.

In calling, there are two important things to be considered. First, when to call, and, second, when to rise and hang on the door handle. Some make one-third of the call before rising, and then complete the call while airing the house and holding the door open, while others consider this low and vulgar, making at least one-fourth of the call in the hall, and one-half between the front door and the gate. Different authorities differ as to the proper time for calling. Some think you should not call before 3 or after 5 P M., but if you have had any experience and had ordinary sense to start with, you will know when to call as soon as you look at your hand.

AMATEUR PRIZE FIGHTER.—The boxing glove is a large upholstered buckskin mitten, with an abnormal thumb and a string by which it is attached to the wrist, so that when you feed it to an adversary he cannot swallow it and choke himself. There are two kinds of gloves, viz., hard gloves and soft gloves.

I once fought with soft gloves to a finish with a young man who was far my inferior intellectually, but he exceeded me in brute force and knowledge of the use of the gloves. He was not so tall, but he was wider than myself. Longitudinally he was my inferior, but latitudinally he outstripped me. We did not fight a regular prize-fight. It was just done for pleasure. But I do not think we should abandon ourselves entirely to pleasure. It is enervating, and makes one eye swell up and turn blue.

I still think that a young man ought to have a knowledge of the manly art of self-defense, and if I could acquire such a knowledge without getting into a fight about it I would surely learn how to defend myself.

The boxing glove is worn on the hand of one party, and on the gory nose of the other party as the game progresses. Soft gloves very rarely kill anyone, unless they work down into the bronchial tubes and shut off the respiration.

LECTURER, New York City.—You need not worry so much about your costume until you have written your lecture, and it would be a good idea to test the public a little, if possible, before you do much expensive printing. Your idea seems to be that a man should get a fine lithograph of himself and a $100 suit of clothes, and then write his lecture to fit the lithograph and the clothes. That is erroneous.

"HE EXCEEDED ME IN BRUTE FORCE."

You say that you have written a part of your lecture, but do not feel satisfied with it. In this you will no doubt find many people who will agree with you.

MAKING REPAIRS.

You could wear a full dress suit of black with propriety, or a Prince Albert coat, with your hand thrust into the bosom of it. I once lectured on the subject of phrenology in the southern portion of Utah, being at that time temporarily busted, but still hoping to tide over the dull times by delivering a lecture on the subject of "Brains, and how to detect their presence." I was not supplied with a phrenological bust at that time, and as such a thing is almost indispensable, I borrowed a young man from Provost and induced him to act as bust for the evening. He did so with thrilling effect, taking the entire gross receipts of the lecture course from my coat pocket while I was illustrating the effect of alcoholic stimulants on the raw brain of an adult in a state of health.

You can remove spots of egg from your full dress suit with ammonia and water, applied by means of a common nail brush. You do not ask for this recipe, but, judging from your style, I hope that it may be of use to you.

MARTIN F. TUPPER, Texas.—The poem to which you allude was written by Julia A. Moore, better known as the Sweet Singer of Michigan. The last stanza was something like this:

"My childhood days are past and gone,
 And it fills my heart with pain,
To think that youth will nevermore
 Return to me again.
And now, kind friends, what I have wrote,
 I hope you will pass o'er
And not criticise as some has hitherto here-
 before done."

Miss Moore also wrote a volume of poems which the farmers of Michigan are still using on their potato bugs. She wrote a large number of poems, all more or less saturated with grief and damaged syntax. She is now said to be a fugitive from justice. We should learn from this that we cannot evade the responsibility of our acts, and those who write obituary poetry will one day be overtaken by a bob-tail sleuth hound or a Siberian nemesis with two rows of teeth.

ALONZO G., Smithville.—Yes, you can learn three card monte without a master. It is very easy. The book will cost you twenty-five cents and then you can practice on various people. The book is a very small item, you will find, after you have been practicing awhile. Three card monte and justifiable homicide go hand in hand. 2. You can turn a jack from the bottom of the pack in the old sledge, if you live in some States, but west of the Missouri the air is so light that men who have tried it have frequently waked up on the shore of eternity with a half turned jack in their hand, and a hole in the cerebellum the size of an English walnut.

You can get "Poker and Three Card Monte without a Master" for sixty cents, with a coroner's verdict thrown in. If you contemplate a career as a monte man, you should wear a pair of low, loose shoes that you can kick off easily, unless you want to die with your boots on.

HENRY UBET, Montana.—No, you are mistaken in your assumption that Socrates was the author of the maxim to which you allude. It is of more modern origin, and, in fact, the sentence of which you speak, viz: "What a combination of conflicting and paradoxical assertions is life? Of what use are logic and argument when we find the true inwardness of the bologna sausage on the outside?" were written by a philosopher who is still living. I am willing to give Socrates credit for what he has said and done, but when I think of a sentiment that is worthy to be graven on a monolith and passed on down to prosperity, I do not want to have it attributed to such men as Socrates.

LEONORA VIVIAN GOBB, Oleson's Forks, Ariz.—Yes. You can turn the front breadths, let out the tucks in the side plaiting and baste on a new dagoon where you caught the oyster stew in your lap at the party You could also get trusted for a new dress, perhaps. But that is a matter of taste. Some dealers are wearing their open accounts long this winter and some are not. Do as you think best about cleaning the dress. Benzine will sometimes eradicate an oyster stew from dress goods. It will also eradicate everyone in the room at the same time. I have known a pair of rejuvenated kid gloves to break up a funeral that started out with every prospect of success. Benzine is an economical thing to use, but socially it is not up to the standard. Another idea has occurred to me, however. Why not riprap the skirt, calk the selvages, readjust the box plaits, cat stitch the crown sheet, file down the gores, sandpaper the gaiters and discharge the dolman. You could then wear the garment anywhere in the evening, and half the people wouldn't know anything had happened to it.

JAMES, Owatonna, Minn.—You can easily teach yourself to play on the tuba. You know what Shakspeare says: "Tuba or not tuba? That's the question."

How true this is? It touches every heart. It is as good a soliliquy as I ever read. P S.—Please do not swallow the tuba while practicing and choke yourself to death. It would be a shame for you to swallow a nice new tuba and cast a gloom over it so that no one else would ever want to play on it again.

FLORENCE.—You can stimulate your hair by using castor oil three ounces, brandy one ounce. Put the oil on the sewing machine, and absorb the brandy between meals. The brandy will no doubt fly right to your head and either greatly assist your hair or it will reconcile you to your lot. The great attraction about brandy as a hair tonic is, that it should not build up the thing. If you wish, you may drink the brandy and then breathe hard on the scalp. This will be difficult at first but after awhile it will not seem irksome.

Great Sacrifice of Bric-a-brac.

PARTIES desiring to buy a job-lot of garden tools, will do well to call and examine my stock. These implements have been but slightly used, and are comparatively as good as new. The lot consists in part of the following:

One three-cornered hoe, Gothic in its architecture and in good running order. It is the same one I erroneously hoed up the carnation with, and may be found, I think, behind the barn, where I threw it when I discovered my error. Original cost of hoe, six bits. Will be closed out now at two bits to make room for new goods.

Also one garden rake, almost as good as new. One front tooth needs filling, and then it will be as good as ever. I sell this weapon, not so much to get rid of it, but because I do not want it any more. I shall not garden any next spring. I do not need to. I began it to benefit my health, and my health is now so healthy that I shall not require the open-air exercise incident to gardening any more. In fact, I am too robust, if anything. I will, therefore, acting upon the advice of my royal physician, close this rake out, since the failure of the Northwestern Car Company, at 50 cents on the dollar.

Also one lawn-mower, only used once. At that time I cut down what grass I had on my lawn, and three varieties of high-priced rose bushes. It is one of the most hardy open-air lawn-mowers now made. It will outlive any other lawn-mower, and be firm and unmoved when all the shrubbery has gone to decay. You can also mow your peony bed with it, if you desire. I tried it. This is also an easy running lawn-mower. I would recommend it to any man who would like to soak his lawn with perspiration. I mowed my lawn, and then pushed a street-car around in the afternoon to relax my over-strained muscles. I will sacrifice this lawn-mower at three-quarters of its original cost, owing to depression in the stock of the New Jerusalem gold mine, of which I am a large owner and cashier-at-large.

Will also sell a bright new spade, only used two hours spading for angle-worms. This is a good, early-blooming and very hardy angle-worm spade, built in the Doric style of architecture. Persons desiring a spade flush, and lacking one spade to "fill," will do well to give me a call. No trouble to show the goods.

I will also part with a small chest of carpenter's tools, only slightly used. I had intended to do a good deal of amateur carpenter work this summer, but, as the presidential convention occurs in June, and I shall have to attend to that, and as I have already sawed up a Queen Anne chair, and thoughtlessly sawed into my leg, I shall probably sacrifice the tools. These tools are all well made, and I do not sell them to make money on them, but because I have no use for them. I feel as though these tools would be safer in the hands of a carpenter. I'm no carpenter. My wife admitted that when I sawed a board across the piano-stool and sawed the what-do-you-call-it all out of the cushion.

OPEN-AIR EXERCISE.

Anyone desiring to monkey with the carpenter's trade, will do well to consult my catalogue and price-list. I will throw in a white holly corner-bracket, put together with fence nails, and a rustic settee that looks like the Cincinnati riot. Young men who do not know much, and invalids whose minds have become affected, are cordially invited to call and examine goods. For a cash trade I will also throw in arnica, court-plaster and salve enough to run the tools two weeks, if ordinary care be taken.

If properly approached, I might also be wheedled into sacrificing an easy-running domestic wheelbarrow. I have domesticated it myself and taught it a great many tricks.

A Convention.

THE officers and members of the Home for Disabled Butter and Hoary-headed Hotel Hash met at their mosque last Saturday evening, and, after the roll call, reading of the moments of the preceding meeting by the Secretary, singing of the ode and examination of all present to ascertain if they were in possession of the quarterly password, explanation and signs of distress, the Most Esteemed Toolymuckahi, having reached the order of communications and new business and good of the order, stated that the society was now ready to take action, or, at least, to discuss the feasibility of holding a series of entertainments at the rink. These entertainments had been proposed as a means of propping up the tottering finances of the society, and procuring much-needed funds for the purpose of purchasing new regalia for the Most Esteemed Duke of the Dishrag and the Most Esteemed Hired Man, each of whom had been wearing the same red calico collar and cheese-cloth sash since the organization of the society Funds were also necessary to pay for a brother who had walked through a railroad trestle into the shoreless sea of eternity, and whose widow had a policy of $135.25 against this society on the life of her husband.

Various suggestions were made; among them was the idea advanced by the Most Highly Esteemed Inside Door-Slammer that, as the society's object was, of course, to obtain funds, would it not be well to consider, in the first place, whether it would not be as well for the Most Esteemed Toolymuckahi to appoint six brethren in good standing to arm themselves with great care, gird up their loins and muzzle the pay-car as it started out on its mission. He simply offered this as a suggestion, and, as it was a direct method of securing the coin necessary, he would move that such a committee be appointed by the Chair to wait on the pay-car and draw on it at sight.

The Most Esteemed Keeper of the Cork-screw seconded the motion, in order, as he said, to get it before the house. This brought forward very hot discussion, pending which the presiding officer could see very plainly that the motion was unpopular.

A visiting brother from Yellowstone Park Creamery No. 17, stated that in their society "an entertainment of this kind had been given for the purpose of pouring a flood of wealth into the coffers of the society, and it had been fairly successful. Among the attractions there had been nothing of an immoral or lawless nature whatever. In the first place, a kind of farewell oyster gorge had been given, with cove oysters as a basis, and $2 a couple as an after-thought A can of cove oysters entertained thirty people and made $30 for the society. Besides, it was found after the party had broken up that, owing to the adhesive properties of the oysters, they were not eaten; but the juice, as it were, had been scooped up and the puckered and corrugated gizzards of the sea had been preserved. Acting upon this suggestion, the society had an oyster patty debauch the following evening at $2 a couple. Forty suckers came and put their means into the common fund. We didn't have enough oysters to quite go around, so some of us cut a dozen out of an old boot leg, and the entertainment was a great success. We also had other little devices for making money, which worked admirably and yielded much profit to the society. Those present also said that they had never enjoyed themselves so much before. Many little games were played, which produced great merriment and considerable coin. I could name a dozen devices for your society, if desired, by which money could be made for your treasury, without the risk or odium necessarily resulting from robbing the pay-car or a bank, and yet the profit will be nearly as great in proportion to the work done."

Here the gavel of the Most Esteemed Toolymuckahi fell with a sickening thud, and the visiting brother was told that the time assigned to communications, new business and good of the order had expired, but that the discussion would be taken up at the next session, in one week, at which time it was the purpose of the chair to hear and note all suggestions relative to an entertainment to be given at a future date by the society for the purpose of obtaining the evanescent scad and for the successful flash of the reluctant boodle.

Come Back.

PERSONAL.—Will the young woman who used to cook in our family, and who went away ten pounds of sugar and five and a half pounds of tea ahead of the game, please come back, and all will be forgiven.

If she cannot return, will she please write, stating her present address, and also give her reasons for shutting up the cat in the refrigerator when she went away?

If she will only return, we will try to forget the past, and think only of the glorious present and the bright, bright future.

Come back, Sarah, and jerk the waffle-iron for us once more.

Your manners are peculiar, but we yearn for your doughnuts, and your style of streaked cake suits us exactly.

You may keep the handkerchiefs and the collars, and we will not refer to the dead past.

We have arranged it so that when you snore it will not disturb the night police, and if you do not like our children we will send them away.

We realize that you do not like children very well, and our children especially gave you much pain, because they were not so refined as you were.

We have often wished, for your sake, that we had never had any children; but so long as they are in our family, the neighbors will rather expect us to take care of them.

Still, if you insist upon it, we will send them away. We don't want to seem overbearing with our servants.

We would be willing, also, to give you more time for mental relaxation than you had before. The intellectual strain incident to the life of one who makes gravy for a lost and undone world must be very great, and tired nature must at last succumb. We do not want you to succumb. If anyone has got to succumb, let us do it.

All we ask is that you will let us know when you are going away, and leave the crackers and cheese where we can find them.

It was rather rough on us to have you go away when we had guests in the house, but if you had not taken the key to the cooking department we could have worried along.

You ought to let us have company at the house sometimes if we will let you have company when you want to. Still, you know best, perhaps. You are older than we are, and you have seen more of the world.

We miss your gentle admonitions and your stern reproofs sadly. Come back and reprove us again. Come back and admonish us once more, at so much per admonish and groceries.

"WE HOPE YOU WILL DO THE SAME BY US."

We will agree to let you select the tender part of the steak, and such fruit as seems to strike you favorably, just as we did before. We did not like it when you were here, but that is because we were young and did not know what the custom was.

If a life-time devoted to your welfare can obliterate the injustice we have done you, we will be glad to yield it to you.

If you could suggest a good place for us to send the children, where they would be well taken care of, and where they would not interfere with some other-cook who is a friend of yours, we would be glad to have you write us.

My wife says she hopes you will feel perfectly free to use the piano whenever you are lonely or sad, and when you or the bread feel depressed you will be welcome to come into the parlor and lean up against either one of us and sob.

We all know that when you were with us before we were a little reserved in our manner toward you, but if you come back it will be different.

We will introduce you to more of our friends this time, and we hope you will do the same by us. Young people are apt to get above their business, and we admit that we were wrong.

Come back and oversee our fritter bureau once more.

Take the portfolio of our interior department.

Try to forget our former coldness.

Return, oh, wanderer, return!

A New Play.

THE following letter was written, recently, in reply to a dramatist who proposed the matter of writing a play jointly.

HUDSON, WIS., NOV. 13, 1886.

SCOTT MARBLE, ESQ.—*Dear Sir:* I have just received your favor of yesterday, in which you ask me to unite with you in the construction of a new play

This idea has been suggested to me before, but not in such a way as to inaugurate the serious thought which your letter has stirred up in my seething mass of mind.

I would like very much to unite with you in the erection of such a dramatic structure that people would cheerfully come to this country from Europe, and board with us for months in order to see this play every night.

You will surely agree with me that someone ought to write a play. Why it has not been done long ago, I cannot understand. A well known comedian told me a year ago that he hadn't been able to look into a paper for sixteen months. He could not even read over the proof of his own press notices and criticisms, to ascertain whether the printer had set them up as he wrote them or not, simply because it took all his spare time off the stage to examine the manuscripts of plays that had been submitted to him.

But I think we could arrange it so that we might together construct something in that line which would at least attract the attention of our families.

Would you mind telling me, for instance, how you write a play? You have been in the business before, and you could tell me, of course, some of the salient points about it. Do you write it with a typewriter, or do you dictate your thoughts to someone who does not resent being dictated to?

Do you write a play and then dramatize it, or do you write the drama and then play on it? Would it not be a very good idea to secure a plot that would cost very little, and then put the kibosh on it, or would you put up the lines first, and then hang the plot or drama, or whatever it is, on the lines? Is it absolutely necessary to have a prologue? If so, what is a prologue? Is it like a catalogue?

I have a great many crude ideas, but you see I am not practical. One of my crude ideas is to introduce into the play an artist's studio. This would not cost much, for we could borrow the studio evenings and allow the artist to use it daytimes. Then we would introduce into the studio scene the artist's living model. Everybody would be horrified, but they would go. They would walk over each other to attend the drama, and we would do well. Our living model in the studio act would be made of common wax, and if it worked well, we would discharge other members of the company and substitute wax. Gradually we could get it down to where the company would be wax, with the exception of a janitor with a feather duster. Think that over.

But seriously, a play, it seems to me, should embody an idea. Am I correct in that theory or not? It ought to convey some great thought, some maxim or aphorism, or some such a thing as that. How would it do to arrange a play with the idea of impressing upon the audience that "the fool and his money are soon parted?" Are you using a hero and a heroine in your plays now? If so, would you mind writing their lines for them, while I arrange the details and remarks for the young man who is discovered asleep on a divan when the curtain rises, and who sleeps on through the play with his mouth slightly ajar till the close—the close of the play, not the close of his mouth—when it is discovered that he is dead. He then plays the cold remains in the closing tableau, and fills a new-made grave at $9 per week.

I could also write the lines, I think, for the young man who comes in wearing a light summer cane and a seersucker coat so tight that you can count his vertebræ. I could write what he would say without great mental strain, I think. I must avoid mental strain or my intellect might split down the back and I would be a mental wreck, good for nothing but to strew the shores of time with myself.

Various other crude ideas present themselves to my mind, but they need to be clothed. You will say that this is unnecessary. I know you will at once reply that, for the stage, the less you clothe an idea the more popular it will be, but I could not consent to have even a bare thought of mine make an appearance night after night before a cultivated audience.

What do you think of introducing a genuine case of small-pox on the stage?

You say in your letter that what the American people clamor for is something "catchy." That would be catchy, and it would also introduce itself.

I wish you would also tell me what kind of diet you confine yourself to while writing a play, and how you go to work to procure it. Do you live on a mixed diet, or on your relatives? Would you soak your head while writing a play, or would you soak your overcoat? I desire to know all these things, because, Mr. Marble, to tell you the truth, I am as ignorant about this matter as the babe unborn. In fact, posterity would have to get up early in the morning to know less about play-writing than I have succeeded in knowing.

If we are to make a kind of comedy, my idea would be to introduce something facetious in the middle of the comedy No one will expect it, you see, and it will tickle the audience almost to death.

A friend of mine suggests that it would be a great hit to introduce, or rather to reproduce, the Hell Gate explosion. Many were not able to be there at the time, and would willingly go a long distance to witness the reproduction.

I wish that you would reply to this letter at an early date, telling me what you think of the schemes suggested. Feel perfectly free to express yourself fully. I am not too proud to receive your suggestions.

The Silver Dollar.

IT would seem at this time, while so little is being said on the currency question, and especially by the men who really control the currency, that a word from me would not be out of place. Too much talking has been done by those only who have a theoretical knowledge of money and its eccentric habits. People with a mere smattering of knowledge regarding national currency have been loquacious, while those who have made the matter a study, have been kept in the background.

At this period in the history of our country, there seems to be a general stringency, and many are in the stringency business who were never that way before. Everything seems to be demonetized. The demonetization of groceries is doing as much toward the general wiggly palsy of trade as anything I know of.

But I may say, in alluding briefly to the silver dollar, that there are worse calamities than the silver dollar. Other things may occur in our lives, which, in the way of sadness and three-cornered gloom, make the large, robust dollar look like an old-fashioned half-dime.

I met a man the other day, who, two years ago, was running a small paper at Larrabie's Slough. He was then in his meridian as a journalist, and his paper was frequently quoted by such widely-read publications as the *Knight of Labor at Work*, a humorous semi-monthly journal. He boldly assailed the silver dollar, and with his trenchant pen he wrote such burning words of denunciation that the printer had to set them on ice before he could use the copy.

Last week I met him on a Milwaukee & St. Paul train. He was very thin in flesh, and the fire of defiance was no longer in his eye. I asked him how he came on with the paper at Larrabie's Slough. He said it was no more.

"It started out," said he, "in a fearless way, but it was not sustained."

He then paused in a low tone of voice, gulped, and proceeded:

"Folks told me when I began that I ought to attack almost everything. Make the paper non-partisan, but aggressive, that was their idea. Sail into everything, and the paper would soon be a power in the land. So I aggressed.

"Friends came in very kindly and told me what to attack. They would neglect their own business in order to tell me of corruption in somebody else. I went on that way for some time in a defiant mood, attacking anything that happened to suggest itself.

"Finally I thought I would attack the silver dollar. I did so. I thought that friends would come to me and praise me for my manly words, and that I could afford to lose the friendship of the dollar provided I could win friends.

"In six months I took an unexpired annual pass over our Larrabie Slough Narrow-Gauge, or Orphan Road, and with nothing else but the clothes I wore, I told the plaintiff how to jerk the old Washington press and went away The dear old Washington press that had more than once squatted my burning words into the pure white page. The dear old towel on which I had wiped my soiled hands for years, until it had almost become a part of myself, the dark blue Gordon press with its large fly wheel and intermittent chattel mortgage, a press, to which I had contributed the first joint of my front finger; the editor's chair; the samples of large business cards printed in green with an inflamed red border, which showed that we could do colored work at Larrabie's Slough just as well as they could in the large cities; the files of our paper; the large wilted potato that Mr. Alonzo G. Pinkham of Erin Corners kindly laid on our table—all, all had to go.

"I fled out into the great, hollow, mocking world of people who had requested me to aggress. They were people who had called my attention to various things which I ought to attack. I had attacked those things. I had also attacked the Larrabie Slough Narrow-Gauge Railroad, but the manager did not see the attack, and so my pass was good.

"What could I do?

"I had attacked everything, and more especially the silver dollar, and now I was homeless. For fourteen weeks I rode up the narrow-gauge road one day and back the next, subsisting solely on the sample of nice pecan meat that the newsboy puts in each passenger's lap.

"You look incredulous, I see, but it is true.

"I feel differently toward the currency now, and I wish I could undo what I have done. Were I called up again to jerk the Archimedean lever, I would not be so aggressive, especially as regards the currency. Whether it is inflated or not, silver dollars, paper certificates of deposit or silver bullion, it does not matter to me.

"I yearn for two or three adult doughnuts and one of those thick, dappled slabs of gingerbread, or slat of pie with gooseberries in it. I presume that I could write a scathing editorial on the abuses of our currency yet, but I am not so much in the scathe business as I used to be.

"I wish you would state, if you will, through some great metropolitan journal, that my views in relation to the silver coinage and the currency question have undergone a radical change, and that any plan whatever, by which to make the American dollar less skittish, will meet with my hearty approval.

"If I have done anything at all through my paper to injure or repress the flow of our currency, and I fear I have, I now take this occasion to cheerfully regret it."

He then wrung my hand and passed from my sight.

Polygamy as a Religious Duty.

DURING the past few years in the history of our republic, we have had leprosy, yellow fever and the dude, and it seemed as though each one would wreck the whole national fabric at one time. National and international troubles of one kind and another have gradually risen, been met and mastered, but the great national abscess known as the Church of Jesus Christ of Latter Day Saints still obstinately refuses to come to a head.

I may be a radical monogamist and a rash enthusiast upon this matter, but I still adhere to my original motto, one country, one flag and one wife at a time. Matrimony is a good thing, but it can be overdone. We can excuse the man who becomes a collection of rare coins, stamps, or autographs, but he who wears out his young life making a collection of wives, should be looked upon with suspicion.

After all, however, this matter has always been, and still is, treated with too much levity. It seems funny to us, at a distance of 1,600 miles, that a thick-necked patriarch in the valley of the Jordan should be sealed to thirteen or fourteen low-browed, half human females, and that the whole mass of humanity should live and multiply under one roof.

Those who see the wealthy polygamists of Salt Lake City, do not know much of the horrors of trying to make polygamy and poverty harmonize in the rural districts. In the former case, each wife has a separate residence or suite of rooms, perhaps; but in the latter is the aggregation of vice and depravity, doubly horrible because, instead of the secluded character which wickedness generally assumes, here it is the common heritage of the young and at once fails to shock or horrify.

Under the All-seeing eye, and the Bee Hive, and the motto, "Holiness to the Lord," with a bogus Bible and a red-nosed prophet, who couldn't earn $13. per month pounding sand, this so called church, hanging on to the horns of the altar, as it were, defies the statutes, and while in open rebellion against the laws of God and man, refers to the constitution of the United States as protecting it in its "religious belief."

In a poem, the patient Mormon in the picturesque valley of the Great Salt Lake, where he has "made the desert blossom as the rose," looks well. With the wonderful music of the great organ at the tabernaclo sounding in your ears, and the lofty temple near by towering to the sky, you say to yourself, there is, after all, something solemn and impressive in all this; but when a greasy apostle in an alapaca duster, takes his place behind the elevated desk, and with bad grammar and slangy sentences, asks God in a businesslike way to bless this buzzing mass of unclean, low-browed, barbarous scum of all foreign countries, and the white trash and criminals of our own, you find no reverence, and no religious awe.

The same mercenary, heartless lunacy that runs through the sickly plagiarism of the Book of Mormon, pervades all this, and instead of the odor of sanctity you notice the flavor of bilge water, and the emigrant's own hailing sign, the all-pervading fragrance of the steerage.

THE FAMILY WASH.

Education is the foe of polygamy, and many of the young who have had the means by which to complete their education in the East, are apostate, at least so far as polygamy is concerned. Still, to the great mass of the poor and illiterate of Mormondom this is no benefit. The rich of the Mormon Church are rich because their influence with this great fraud has made them so; and it would, as a matter of business, injure their prospects to come out and bolt the nomination.

Utah, even with the Edmunds bill, is hopelessly Mormon; all adjoining States and Territories are already invaded by them, and the delegate in Congress from Wyoming is elected by the Mormon vote.

I believe that I am moderately liberal and free upon all religious matters, but when a man's confession of faith involves from three to twenty-seven old corsets in the back yard every spring, and a clothes line every Monday morning that looks like a bridal trosseau emporium struck by a cyclone, I must admit that I am a little bit inclined to be sectarian in my views.

It's bad enough to be slapped across the features by one pair of long wet hose on your way to the barn, but to have a whole bankrupt stock of cold, wet garments every week fold their damp arms around your neck, as you dodge under the clothes line to drive the cow out of the yard, is wrong.

It is not good for man to be alone, of course, but why should he yearn to fold a young ladies' seminary to his bosom? Why should this morbid sentiment prompt him to marry a Female Suffrage Mass Meeting? I do not wish to be considered an extremist in religious matters, but the doctrine that requires me to be sealed to a whole emigrant train, seems unnatural and inconsistent.

The Newspaper.

AN ADDRESS DELIVERED BEFORE THE WISCONSIN STATE PRESS ASSOCIATION, AT WHITE-WATER, WIS., AUGUST 11, 1885.

MR. PRESIDENT AND GENTLEMEN OF THE PRESS OF WISCONSIN:

I am sure that when you so kindly invited me to address you to-day, you did not anticipate a lavish display of genius and gestures. I accepted the invitation because it afforded me an opportunity to meet you and to get acquainted with you, and tell you personally that for years I have been a constant reader of your valuable paper and I like it. You are running it just as I like to see a newspaper run.

I need not elaborate upon the wonderful growth of the press in our country, or refer to the great power which journalism wields in the development of the new world. I need not ladle out statistics to show you how the newspaper has encroached upon the field of oratory and how the pale and silent man, while others sleep, compiles the universal history of a day and tells his mighty audience what he thinks about it before he goes to bed.

Of course, this is but the opinion of one man, but who has a better opportunity to judge than he who sits with his finger on the electric pulse of the world, judging the actions of humanity at so much per judge, invariably in advance?

I need not tell you all this, for you certainly know it if you read your paper, and I hope you do. A man ought to read his own paper, even if he cannot endorse all its sentiments.

So necessary has the profession of journalism become to the progress and education of our country, that the matter of establishing schools where young men may be fitted for an active newspaper life, has attracted much attention and discussion. It has been demonstrated that our colleges do not fit a young man to walk at once into the active management of a paper. He should at least know the difference between a vile contemporary and a Gothic scoop.

It is difficult to map out a proper course for the student in a school of journalism, there are so many things connected with the profession which the editor and his staff should know and know hard. The newspaper of to-day is a library. It is an encyclopædia, a poem, a biography, a history, a prophecy, a directory, a time-table, a romance, a cook book, a guide, a horoscope, an art critic, a political resume, a *multum in parvo.* It is a sermon, a song, a circus, an obituary, a picnic, a shipwreck, a symphony in solid brevier, a medley of life and death, a grand aggregation of man's glory and his shame. It is, in short, a bird's-eye-view of all the magnanimity and meanness, the joys and griefs, the births and deaths, the pride and poverty of the world, and all for two cents—sometimes.

I could tell you some more things that the newspaper of to-day is, if you had time to stay here and your business would not suffer in your absence. Among others it is a long felt want, a nine-column paper in a five-column town, a lying sheet, a feeble effort, a financial problem, a tottering wreck, a political tool and a sheriff's sale.

If I were to suggest a curriculum for the young man who wished to take a regular course in a school of journalism, preferring that to the actual experience, I would say to him, devote the first two years to meditation and prayer. This will prepare the young editor for the surprise and consequent temptation to profanity which in a few years he may experience when he finds that the name of the Deity in his double-leaded editorial is spelled with a little "g," and the peroration of the article is locked up between a death notice and the advertisement of a patent moustache coaxer, which is to follow pure reading matter every day in the week and occupy the top of column on Sunday tf.

The ensuing five years should be devoted to the peculiar orthography of the English language.

Then put in three years with the dumb bells, sand bags, slung shots and tomahawk. In my own journalistic experience I have found more cause for regret over my neglect of this branch than anything else. I usually keep on my desk during a heated campaign, a large paper weight, weighing three or four pounds, and in several instances I have found that I could feed that to a constant reader of my valuable paper instead of a retraction.

Fewer people lick the editor though, now, than did so in years gone by. Many people—in the last two years—have gone across the street to lick the editor and never returned. They intended to come right back in a few moments, but they are now in a land where a change of heart and a palm leaf fan is all they need.

Fewer people are robbing the editor now-a-days, too, I notice with much pleasure. Only a short time ago I noticed that a burglar succeeded in breaking into the residence of a Dakota journalist, and after a long, hard struggle the editor succeeded in robbing him.

After the primary course, mapped out already, an intermediate course of ten years should be given to learning the typographical art, so that when visitors come in and ask the editor all about the office, he can tell them of the mysteries of making a paper, and how delinquent subscribers have frequently been killed by a well-directed blow with a printer's towel.

Five years should be devoted to a study of the art of proof-reading. In that length of time the young journalist can perfect himself to such a degree that it will take another five years for the printer to understand his corrections and marginal notes.

Fifteen years should then be devoted to the study of American politics, especially civil service reform, looking at it from a non-partisan standpoint. If possible, the last five years should be spent abroad. London is the place to go if you wish to get a clear, concise view of American politics, and Chicago or Milwaukee would be a good place for the young English journalist to go and study the political outlook of England.

The student should then take a medical and surgical course, so that he may be able to attend to contusions, fractures and so forth, which may occur to himself or to the party who may come to his office for a retraction and by mistake get his spinal column double-leaded.

Ten years should then be given to the study of law. No thorough, metropolitan editor wants to enter upon the duties of his profession without knowing the difference between a writ of *mandamus* and other styles of profanity. He should thoroughly understand the entire system of American jurisprudence, so that in case a *certiorari* should break out in his neighborhood he would know just what to do for it.

The student will, by this time, begin to see what is required of him and enter with great zeal upon the further study of his profession.

He will now enter upon a theological course of ten years and fit himself thoroughly to speak intelligently of the various creeds and religions of the world. Ignorance on the part of an editor is almost a crime, and when he closes a powerful editorial with the familiar quotation, "It is the early bird that catches the worm," and attributes it to St. Paul instead of Deuteronomy, it makes me blush for the profession.

The last ten years may be profitably devoted to the acquisition of a practical knowledge of cutting cordwood, baking beans, making shirts, lecturing, turning double handsprings, being shot out of a catapult at a circus, learning how to make a good adhesive paste that will not sour in hot weather, grinding scissors, punctuating, capitalization, condemnation, syntax, plain sewing, music and dancing, sculping, etiquette, prosody, how to win the affections of the opposite sex and evade a malignant case of breach of promise, the ten commandments, every man his own tooter on the flute, croquet, rules of the prize ring, rhetoric, parlor magic, calisthenics, penmanship, how to run a jack from the bottom of the pack without getting shot, civil engineering, decorative art, kalsomining, bicycling, base ball, hydraulics, botany, poker, international law, high-low-jack, drawing and painting, faro, vocal music, driving, breaking team, fifteen ball pool, how to remove grease spots from last year's pantaloons, horsemanship, coupling freight cars, riding on a rail, riding on a pass, feeding threshing machines, how to wean a calf from the parent stem. teaching school, bull-whacking, plastering, waltzing, vaccination. autopsy, how to win the affections of your wife's mother, every man his own washerwoman, or how to wash underclothes so they will not shrink, etc., etc.

But time forbids anything like a thorough list of what a young man should study in order to fully understand all that he may be called upon to express an opinion about in his actual experience as a journalist. There are a thousand little matters which every editor should know; such, for instance, as the construction of roller composition. Many newspaper men can write a good editorial on Asiatic cholera, but their roller composition is not fit to eat.

With the course of study that I have mapped out, the young student would emerge from the college of journalism at the age of 95 or 96, ready to take off his coat and write an article on almost any subject. He would be a little giddy at first, and the office boy would have to see that he went to bed at a proper time each night, but aside from that, he would be a good man to feed a waste paper basket.

Actual experience is the best teacher in this peculiarly trying profession. I hope some day to attend a press convention where the order of exercise will consist of five-minute experiences from each one present. It would be worth listening to.

My own experience was a little peculiar. It was my intention at first to practice law, when I went to the Rocky Mountains, although I had been warned by the authorities not to do so. Still, I did practice in a surreptitious kind of a way, and might have been practicing yet if my client hadn't died. When you have become attached to a client and respect and like him, and then when, without warning, like a bolt of electricity from a clear sky, he suddenly dies and takes the bread right out of your mouth, it is rough.

Then I tried the practice of criminal law, but my client got into the penitentiary, where he was no use to me financially or politically. Finally, when the judge was in a hurry, he would appoint me to defend the pauper criminals. They all went to the penitentiary, until people got to criticising the judge, and finally they told him that it was a shame to appoint me to defend an innocent man.

My first experience in journalism was in a Western town, in which I was a total stranger. I went there with thirty-five cents, but I had it concealed in the lining of my clothes so that no one would have suspected it if they had met me. I had no friends, and I noticed that when I got off the train the band was not there to meet me. I entered the town just as any other American citizen would. I had not fully decided whether to become a stage robber or a lecturer on phrenology At that time I got a chance to work on a morning paper. It used to go to press before dark, so I always had my evenings to myself and I liked that part of it first-rate. I worked on that paper a year and might have continued if the proprietors had not changed it to an evening paper.

Then a company incorporated itself and started a paper, of which I took charge. The paper was published in the loft of a livery stable. That is the reason they called it a stock company You could come up the stairs into the office or you could twist the tail of the iron-gray mule and take the elevator.

It wasn't much of a paper, but it cost $16,000 a year to run it, and it came out six days in the week, no matter what the weather was. We took the Associated Press news by telegraph part of the time, and part of the time we relied on the Cheyenne morning papers, which we got of the conductor on the early morning freight. We got a great many special telegrams from Washington in that way, and when the freight train got in late, I had to guess at what congress was doing and fix up a column of telegraph the best I could. There was a rival evening paper there, and sometimes it would send a smart boy down to the train and get hold of our special telegrams, and sometimes the conductor would go away on a picnic and take our Cheyenne paper with him.

All these things are annoying to a man who is trying to supply a long felt want. There was one conductor, in particular, who used to go away into the foot-hills shooting sage hens and take our cablegrams with him. This threw too much strain on me. I could guess at what congress was doing and make up a pretty readable report, but foreign powers and reichstags and crowned heads and dynasties always mixed me up. You can look over what congress did last year and give a pretty good guess at what it will do this year, but you can't rely on a dynasty or an effete monarchy in a bad state of preservation. It may go into executive session or it may go into bankruptcy.

Still, at one time we used to have considerable local news to fill up with. The north and middle parks for a while used to help us out when the mining camps were new. Those were the days when it was considered perfectly proper to kill off the board of supervisors if their action was distasteful. At that time a new camp generally located a cemetery and wrote an obituary; then the boys would start out to find a man whose name would rhyme with the rest of the verse. Those were the days when the cemeteries of Colorado were still in their infancy and the song of the six-shooter was heard in the land.

Sometimes the Indians would send us in an item. It was generally in the obituary line. With the Sioux on the north and the peaceful Utes on the south, we were pretty sure of some kind of news during the summer. The parks used to be occupied by white men winters and Indians summers. Summer was really the pleasantest time to go into the parks, but the Indians had been in the habit of going there at that season, and they were so clannish that the white men couldn't have much fun with them, so they decided they would not go there in the summer. Several of our best subscribers were killed by the peaceful Utes.

There were two daily and three weekly papers published in Laramie City at that time. There were between two and three thousand people and our local circulation ran from 150 to 250, counting dead-heads. In our prospectus we stated that we would spare no expense whatever in ransacking the universe for fresh news, but there were times when it was all we could do to get our paper out on time. Out of the express office, I mean.

One of the rival editors used to write his editorials for the paper in the evening, jerk the Washington hand-press to work them off, go home and wrestle with juvenile colic in his family until daylight and then deliver his papers on the street. It is not surprising that the great mental strain incident to this life made an old man of him, and gave a tinge of extreme sadness to the funny column of his paper.

In an unguarded moment, this man wrote an editorial once that got all his subscribers mad at him, and the same afternoon he came around and wanted to sell his paper to us for $10,000. I told him that the whole outfit wasn't worth ten thousand cents.

"I know that," said he, "but it is not the material that I am talking about. It is the good will of the paper."

We had a rising young horsethief in Wyoming in those days, who got into jail by some freak of justice, and it was so odd for a horsethief to get into jail that I alluded to it editorially. This horsethief had distinguished himself from the common, vulgar horsethieves of his time, by wearing a large mouth—a kind of full-dress, eight-day mouth. He rarely smiled, but when he did, he had to hold the top of his head on with both hands. I remember that I spoke of this in the paper, forgetting that he might criticise me when he got ont of jail. When he did get out again, he stated that he would shoot me on sight, but friends advised me not to have his blood on my hands, and I took their advice, so I haven't got a particle of his blood on either of my hands.

For two or three months I didn't know but he would drop into the office any minute and criticise me, but one day a friend told me that he had been hung in Montana. Then I began to mingle in society again, and didn't have to get in my coal with a double barrel shot gun any more.

After that I was always conservative in relation to horsethieves until we got the report of the vigilance committee.

Wrestling with the Mazy.

VERY soon now I shall be strong enough on my cyclone leg to resume my lessons in waltzing. It is needless to say that I look forward with great pleasure to that moment. Nature intended that I should glide in the mazy. Tall, lithe, bald-headed, genial, limber in the extreme, suave, soulful, frolicsome at times, yet dignified and reserved toward strangers, light on the foot—on my own foot, I mean—gentle as a woman at times, yet irresistible as a tornado when insulted by a smaller, I am peculiarly fitted to shine in society Those who have observed my polished brow, when under a strong electric light, say they never saw a man shine so in society as I do.

My wife taught me how to waltz. She would teach me on Saturdays and repair her skirts during the following week. I told her once that I thought I was too brainy to dance. She said she hadn't noticed that, but she thought I seemed to run too much to legs. My wife is not timid about telling me anything that she thinks will be for my good. When I make a mistake she is perfectly frank with me, and comes right to me and tells me about it, so that I won't do so again.

I had just learned how to reel around a ballroom to a little waltz music, when I was blown across the State of Mississippi in September last by a high wind, and broke one of my legs which I use in waltzing. When this accident occurred I had just got where I felt at liberty to choose a glorious being with starry eyes and fluffy hair, and magnificently modeled form, to steer me around the rink to the dreamy music of Strauss. One young lady, with whom I had waltzed a good deal, when she heard that my leg was broken, began to attend every dancing party she could hear of, although she had declined a great many previous to that. I asked her how she could be so giddy and so gay when I was suffering. She said she was doing it to drown her sorrow, but her little brother told me on the quiet that she was dancing while I was sick because she felt perfectly safe. A friend of mine says I have a pronounced and distinctly original manner of waltzing, and that he never saw anybody, with one exception, who waltzed as I did, and that was Jumbo. He claimed that either one of us would be a good dancer if he could have the whole ring to himself. He said that he would like to see Jumbo and me waltz together if he were not afraid that I would step on Jumbo and hurt him. You can see what a feeling of jealous hatred it arouses in some small minds when a man gets so that he can mingle in good society and enjoy himself.

WALTZING WITH JUMBO.

I could waltz more easily if the rules did not require such a constant change of position. I am sedentary in my nature, slow to move about, so that it takes a lady of great strength of purpose to pull me around on time.

Anecdotes of the Stage.

YEARS ago, before Laramie City got a handsome opera house, everything in the theatrical and musical line of a high order was put on the stage of Blackburn's Hall. Other light dramas on the stage, and thrilling murders in the audience, used to occur at Alexander's Theater, on Front street. Here you could get a glass of Laramie beer, made of glucose, alkali water, plug tobacco, and Paris green, by paying two bits at the bar, and, as a prize, you drew a ticket to the olio, specialties, and low gags of the stage. The idea of inebriating a man at the box office, so that he will endure such a sham, is certainly worthy of serious consideration. I have seen shows at Alexander's, and also at McDaniel's, in Cheyenne, however, where the bar should have provided an ounce of chloroform with each ticket in order to allay the suffering.

Here you could sit down in the orchestra and take the chances of getting hit when the audience began to shoot at the pianist, or you could go up into the boxes and have a quiet little conversation with the timid beer-jerkers. The beer-jerker was never too proud to speak to the most humble, and if she could sell a grub-staker for $5 a bottle of real per Heidsick, made in Cheyenne and warranted to remove the gastric coat, pants and vest from a man's stomach in two minutes, she felt pleased and proud.

A room-mate of mine, whose name I will not give, simply because he was and still is the best fellow in the United States, came home from the "theater" one night with his hair parted in the middle. He didn't wear it that way generally, so it occasioned talk in social circles. He still has a natural parting of the hair about five inches long, that he acquired that night. He said it was accidental so far as he was concerned, but unless the management could keep people from shooting the holders of reserved seats between the acts or any other vital spot, he would withdraw his patronage. And he was right about it. I think that any court in the land would protect a man who had purchased a seat in good faith, and with his hat on and both feet on the back of the seat in front of him, sits quietly in said seat, smoking a Colorado Maduro cigar and watching the play.

Several such accidents occurred at the said theater. Among them was a little tableau in which Joe Walker and Centennial Bob took the leading parts. Bob went to the penitentiary, and Joe went to his reward with one of his lungs in his coat pocket. There was a little difference between them as to the regularity of a "draw" and "show down," so Bob went home from the theater and loaded a double-barrel shot-gun with a lot of scrap-iron, and, after he had introduced the collection into Joe's front breadth, the latter's system was so lacerated that it wouldn't retain ground feed.

There were other little incidents like that which occurred in and around the old theater, some growing out of the lost love of a beer-jerker, some from an injudicious investment in a bob-tail flush that never got ripe enough to pick, and some from the rarified mountain air, united with an epidemic known as *mania rotguti.*

A funny incident of the stage occurred not long ago to a friend of mine, who is traveling with a play in which a stage cow appears. He is using what is called a profile cow now, which works by machinery. Last winter this cow ran down while in the middle of the stage, and forgot her lines. The prompter gave the string a jerk in order to assist her. This broke the cow in two, and the fore-quarters walked off to the left into one dressing-room, while the behind-quarters and porter-house steak retired to the outer dressing-room. The audience called for an *encore;* but the cow felt as though she had made a kind of a bull of the part, and would not appear. Those who may be tempted to harshly criticise this last remark, are gently reminded that the intense heat of the past month is liable to effect anyone's mind. Remember, gentle reader, that your own brain may some day soften also, and then you will remember how harsh you were toward me.

Prior to the profile cow, the company ran a wicker-work cow, that was hollow and admitted of two hired-men, who operated the beast at a moderate salary These men drilled a long time on what they called a heifer dance—a beautiful spectacular, and highly moral and instructive quadruped clog, sirloin shuffle, and cow gallop, to the music of a piano-forte. The rehearsals had been crowned with success, and when the cow came on the stage she got a bouquet, and made a bran mash on one of the ushers.

She danced up and down the stage, perfectly self-possessed, and with that perfect grace and abandon which is so noticeable in the self-made cow. Finally she got through, the piano sounded a wild Wagnerian bang, and the cow danseuse ambled off. She was improperly steered, however, and ran her head against a wing, where she stopped in full view of the audience. The talent inside of the cow thought they had reached the dressing-room and ran against the wall, so they felt perfectly free to converse with each other. The cow stood with her nose jammed up against the wing, wrapped in thought. Finally, from her thorax the audience heard a voice say:

"Jim, you blamed galoot, that ain't the step we took at rehearsal no more'n nuthin' If you're going to improvise a new cow duet, I wish you wouldn't take the fore-quarters by surprise next time."

It is not now known what the reply was, for just then the prompter came on the stage, rudely twisted the tail of the cow, rousing her from her lethargy, and harshly kicking her in the pit of the stomach, he drove her off the stage. The audience loudly called for a repetition, but the cow refused to come in.

George the Third.

GEORGE III. was born in England June 4, 1738, and ran for king in 1760. He was a son of Frederick, Prince of Wales, and held the office of king for sixty years. He was a natural born king and succeeded his grandfather, George II. Look as you will a-down the long page of English history, and you will not fail to notice the scarcity of self-made kings. How few of them were poor boys and had to skin along for years with no money, no influential friends and no fun.

Ah, little does the English king know of hard times and carrying two or three barrels of water to a tired elephant in order that he may get into the afternoon performance without money. When he gets tired of being prince, all he has to do is just to be king all day at good wages, and then at night take off his high-priced crown, hang it up on the hat-rack, put on a soft hat and take in the town.

George III. quit being prince at the age of 22 years, and began to hold down the English throne. He would reign along for a few years, taking it kind of quiet, and then all at once he would declare war and pick out some people to go abroad and leave their skeletons on some foreign shore. That was George's favorite amusement. He got up the Spanish war in two years after he clome the throne; then he had an American revolution, a French revolution, an Irish rebellion and a Napoleonic war. He dearly loved carnage, if it could be prepared on a foreign strand. George always wanted imported carnage, even if it came higher. It was in 1765, and early in George's reign, that the American stamp act passed the Legislature and the Goddess of Liberty began to kick over the dashboard.

George was different from most English kings, morally. When he spit on his hand and grasped the sceptre, he took his scruples with him right onto the throne. He was not talked about half so much as other kings before or since his time. Nine o'clock most always found George in bed, with his sceptre under the window-sash, so that he could get plenty of fresh air. As it got along toward 9 o'clock, he would call the hired girl, tell her to spread a linen lap-robe on the throne till morning, issue a royal ukase directing her to turn out the cat, and instructing the cook to set the pancake batter behind the royal stove in the council chamber, then he would wind the clock and retire. Early in the morning George would be up and dressed, have all his chores done and the throne dusted off ready for another hard day's reign.

George III. is the party referred to in the Declaration of Independence as the present king of Great Britain, and of whom many bitter personal remarks were made by American patriots. On this side of the water George was not

WRAPPED IN SLUMBER.

highly esteemed. If he had come over here to spend the summer with friends in Boston, during the days of the stamp act excitement, he could have gone home packed in ice, no doubt, and with a Swiss sunset under each eye.

George's mind was always a little on the bias, and in 1810 he went crazy for the fifth time. Always before that he had gone right ahead with his reign, whether he was crazy or not, but with the fifth attack of insanity, coupled with suggestion of the brain and blind staggers, it was decided to tie him up in the barn and let someone else reign awhile. The historian says that blindness succeeded this attack, and in 1811 the Prince of Wales became regent.

George III. died at Windsor in 1820, with the consent of a joint committee of both houses of congress, at the age of 82 years. He made the longest run as king, without stopping for feed or water, of any monarch in English history. Sixty years is a long time to be a monarch and look under the bed every night for a Nihilist loaded with a cut-glass bomb and Paris green. Sixty years is a long while to jerk a sceptre over a nation and keep on the right side, politically, all the time.

George was of an inventive turn of mind, and used to be monkeying with some kind of a patent, evenings, after he had peeled his royal robes. Most of his patents related to land, however, and some of the most successful soil in Massachusetts was patented by George.

He was always trying some scheme to make a pile of money easy, so that he wouldn't have to work; but he died poor and crazy at last, in England. He was not very smart, but he attended to business all the time, and did not get up much of a reputation as a moral leper. He said that as king of Great Britain and general superintendent of Cork he did not aim to make much noise, but he desired to attract universal attention by being so moral that he would be regarded as eccentric by other crowned heads.

The Cell Nest.

TO THE MEMBERS OF THE ACADEMY OF SCIENCE, AT ERIN PRAIRIE, WISCONSIN:

Gentlemen:—I beg leave to submit herewith my microscopic report on the several sealed specimens of proud flesh and other mementoes taken from the roof of Mr. Flannery's mouth. As Mr. Flannery is the mayor of Erin Prairie, and therefore has a world-wide reputation, I deemed it sufficiently important to the world at large, and pleasing to Mr. Flannery's family, to publish this report in the medical journals of the country, and have it telegraphed to the leading newspapers at their expense. Knowing that the world at large is hungry to learn how the laudable pus of an eminent man appears under the microscope, and what a pleasure it must be to his family to read the description after his death, I have just opened a new box of difficult words and herewith transmit a report which will be an ornament not only to the scrap-book of Mr. Flannery's immediate family after his death, but a priceless boon to the reading public at large.

Removing the seals from the jars as soon as I had returned from the express office, I poured off the alcohol and recklessly threw it away. A true scientist does not care for expense.

The first specimen was in a good state of preservation on its arrival. I never saw a more beautiful or robust proliferation epitherial cell nest in my life. It must have been secured immediately after the old epitherial had left the nest, and it was in good order on its arrival. The whole lobule was looking first-rate. You might ride for a week and not run across a prettier lobule or a more artistic aggregation of cell nests outside a penitentiary.

Only one cell nest had been allowed to dry up on the way, and this looked a good deal fatigued. In one specimen I noticed a carneous degeneration, but this is really no reflection on Mr. Flannery personally. While he has been ill it is not surprising that he should allow his cell nests to carneously degenerate. Such a thing might happen to almost any of us.

One of the scrapings from the sore on the right posterior fauces, I found on its arrival, had been seriously injured, and therefore not available. I return it herewith.

From an examination, which has been conducted with great care, I a led to believe that the right posterior rafter of Mr. Flannery's mouth is slightly indurated, and it is barely possible that the northeast duplex and parotid gable end of the roof of his mouth may become involved.

I wish you would ask Mr. Flannery's immediate relatives, if you can do so without arousing alarm in the breast of the patient, if there has ever been a marked predisposition on the part of his ancestors to tubercular gumboil. I do not wish to be understood as giving this diagnosis as final at all, but from what I have already stated, taken together with other clinical and pathological data within my reach, and the fact that minute, lobulated gumboil bactinæ were found floating through some of the cell nests, I have every reason to fear the worst. I would be glad to receive from you for microscopic examination a fragment of Mr. Flannery's malpighian layer, showing evidences of cell proliferation. I only suggest this, of course, as practicable in case there should be a malpighian layer which Mr. Flannery is not using. Do not ask him to take a malpighian layer off her cell nest just to please me.

From one microscopic examination I hardly feel justified in giving a diagnosis, nor care to venture any suggestion as to treatment, but it might be well to kalsomine the roof of Mr. Flannery's mouth with gum-arabic, white lime and glue in equal parts.

There has already been some extravatations and a marked multiformity I also noticed an inflamed and angry color to the stroma with trimmings of the same. This might only indicate that Mr. Flannery had kept his mouth open too much during the summer, and sunburned the roof of his mouth, were it not that I also discovered traces of gumboil microbes of the squamous variety. This leads me to fear the worst for Mr. Flannery However, if the gentlemanly, courteous and urbane members of the Academy of Science, of Erin Prairie, to whom I am already largely indebted for past favors, will kindly forward to me, prepaid, another scraping from the mansard roof of Mr. Flannery's mouth next week, I will open another keg of hard words and trace this gumboil theory to a successful termination, if I have to use up the whole ceiling of the patient's mouth.

Yours, with great sincerity, profundity and verbosity,

BILL NYE,

Microscopist, Lobulist and Microbist.

HUDSON, WIS., May 6.

Parental Advice.

THE past fifty years have done much for the newspaper and periodical readers of the United States. That period has been fruitful of great advancement and a great reduction in price, but these are not all. Fifty years and less have classified information so that science and sense are conveniently found, and humor and nonsense have their proper sphere. All branches are pretty full of lively and thoroughly competent writers, who take hold of their own special work even as the thorough, quick-eyed mechanic takes hold of his line of labor and acquits himself in a creditable manner. The various lines of journalism may appear to be crowded, but they are not. There may be too much vagabond journalism, but the road that is traveled by the legitimate laborer is not crowded. The clean, Caucasian journalist, as he climbs the hill, is not crowded very much. He can make out to elbow his way toward the front, if he tries very hard. There may be too much James Crow science, and too much editorial vandalism and gush, and too much of the journalism for revenue only. There may be too much ringworm humor also, but there is still a demand for the scientific work of the true student. There is still a good market for honest editorial opinion, reliable news and fearless and funny paragraph work and character sketches, as the song and dance men would say

All this, however, points in one direction. It all has one hoarse voice, and in the tones of the culverin, whatever that is, it says that to the young man who is starting out with the intention of filling the tomb of a millionaire, "Learn to do something well."

Lots of people rather disliked the famous British hangman, and thought he hadn't made a great record for himself, but he performed a duty that had to be done by someone, and no one ever complained much about Marwood's work. He warranted every job and told everyone that if they were dissatisfied he would refund their money at the door. No man ever came back to Marwood and said, "Sir, you broke my neck in an unworkmanlike manner."

It is better to be a successful hangman than to be the banished, abused and heart-broken, cast-off husband of a great actress. Learn to take hold of some business and jerk it bald-headed. Learn to dress yourself first. This will give you self-assurance, so that you can go away from home and not be dependent on your mother. Teach yourself to be accurate and careful in all things. It is better to turn the handle of a sausage grinder and make a style of sausage that is free from hydrophobia, than to be the extremely hence cashier of a stranded bank, fighting horseflies in the solemn hush of a Canadian forest.

People have wrong ideas of the respective merits of different avocations. It is better to be the successful driver of a dray than to be the unsuccessful inventor of a still-born motor. I would rather discover how to successfully wean a calf from the parent stem without being boosted over a nine rail fence, than to discover a new star that had never been used, and the next evening find that it had made an assignment.

Boys, oh, boys! How I wish I could take each of you by the ear and lead you away by yourselves, and show you how many ruins strew the road to success, and how life is like a mining boom. We only hear of those who strike it rich. The hopeful, industrious prospector who failed to find the contact and finally filled a nameless grave, is soon forgotten when he is gone, but a million tongues tell to forty million listening ears of the man who struck it rich and went to Europe.

Therefore make haste to advance slowly and surely I am aware that your ears ache with the abundance wherewith ye are advised, but if ye seek not to brace up while yet it is called to-day, and file away information for future reference and cease to look upon the fifteen-ball pool game when it moveth itself aright, at such time as ye think not ye shall be in pecuniary circumstances and there shall be none to indorse for you—nay, not one.

Early Day Justice.*

THOSE were troublesome times, indeed. All wool justice in the courts was impossible. The vigilance committee, or Salvation Army as it calledi tself, didn't make much fuss about it, but we all knew that the best citizens belonged to it and were in good standing.

It was in those days when young Stewart was short-handed for a sheep herder, and had to take up with a sullen, hairy vagrant, called by the other boys "Esau." Esau hadn't been on the ranch a week before he made trouble with the proprietor and got the red-hot blessing from Stewart he deserved.

Then Esau got madder and sulked away down the valley among the little sage brush hummocks and white alkali waste land to nurse his wrath. When Stewart drove into the corral at night, from town, Esau raised up from behind an old sheep dip tank, and without a word except what may have growled around in his black heart, he raised a leveled Spencer and shot his young employer dead.

That was the tragedy of the week only. Others had occurred before and others would probably occur again. It was getting too prevalent for comfort. So, as soon as a quick cayuse and a boy could get down into town, the news spread and the authorities began in the routine manner to set the old legal mill to running. Someone had to go down to "The Tivoli" and find the prosecuting attorney, then a messenger had to go to "The Alhambra" for the justice of the peace. The prosecuting attorney was "full" and the judge had just drawn one card to complete a straight flush, and had succeeded.

In the meantime the Salvation Army was fully half way to Clugston's ranch. They had started out, as they said, "to see that Esau didn't get away." They were going out there to see that Esau was brought into town.

*From the Chicago Rambler.

What happened after they got there I only know from hearsay, for I was not a member of the Salvation Army at that time. But I got it from one of those present, that they found Esau down in the sage brush on the bottoms that lie between the abrupt corner of Sheep Mountain and the Little Laramie River. They captured him, but he died soon after, as it was told me, from the effects of opium taken with suicidal intent. I remember seeing Esau the next morning and I thought there were signs of ropium, as there was a purple streak around the neck of deceased, together with other external phenomena not peculiar to opium.

THE SALVATION ARMY.

But the great difficulty with the Salvation Army was that it didn't want to bring Esau into town. A long, cold night ride with a person in Esau's condition was disagreeable. Twenty miles of lonely road with a deceased murderer in the bottom of the wagon is depressing. Those of my readers who have tried it will agree with me that it is not calculated to promote hilarity So the Salvation Army stopped at Whatley's ranch to get warm, hoping that someone would steal the remains and elope with them. They stayed some time and managed to "give away" the fact that there was a reward of $5,000 out for Esau, dead or alive. The Salvation Army even went so far as to betray a great deal of hilarity over the easy way it had nailed the reward, or would as soon as said remains were delivered up and identified.

Mr. Whatley thought that the Salvation Army was having a kind of walk-away, so he slipped out at the back door of the ranch, put Esau into his own wagon and drove away to town. Remember, this is the way it was told to me.

Mr. Whatley hadn't gone more than half a mile when he heard the wild and disappointed yells of the Salvation Army He put the buckskin on the backs of his horses without mercy, driven on by the enraged shouts and yells of his infuriated pursuers. He reached town about midnight, and his pursuers disappeared. But what was he to do with Esau?

He drove around all over town, trying to find the official who sighed for the deceased. Mr. Whatley went from house to house like a vegetable man, seeking sadly for the party who would give him a $5,000 check for Esau. Nothing could be more depressing than to wake up one man after another out of a sound sleep and invite him to come out to the buggy and identify the remains. One man went out and looked at him. He said he didn't know how others felt about it, but he allowed that anybody who would pay $5,000 for such a remains as Esau's could not have very good taste.

Gradually it crept through Mr. Whatley's wool that the Salvation Army had been working him, so he left Esau at the engine house and went home. On his ranch he nailed up a large board on which had been painted in antique characters with a paddle and tar the following stanzas:

☞ Vigilance Committees, Salvation Armies, Morgues, or young physicians who may have deceased people on their hands, are requested to refrain from conferring them on to the undersigned.

☞ People who contemplate shuffling off their own or other people's mortal coils, will please not do so on these grounds.

☞ The Salvation Army of the Rocky Mountains is especially hereby warned to keep off the grass! JAMES WHATLEY.

The Indian Orator.

I LIKE to read of the Indian orator in the old school books. Most every-one does. It is generally remarkable that the American Demosthenes, so far, has dwelt in the tepee, and lived on the debris of the deer and the buffalo. I mean to say that the school readers have impressed us with the great magnetism of the crude warrior who dwelt in the wilderness and ate his game, feathers and all, while he studied the art of swaying the audience by his oratorical powers.

I am inclined to think that Black Hawk and Logan must have been fortunate in securing mighty able private secretaries, or that they stood in with the stenographers of their day. At least, the Blue Juniata warriors of our time, from Little Crow, Red Iron, Standing Buffalo, Hole-in-the-Day and Sitting Bull, to Victoria, Colorow, Douglas, Persume, Captain Jack and Shavano, seem to do better as lobbyists than they do as orators. They may be keen, logical and shrewd, but they are not eloquent. In some minds, Black Hawk will ever appear as the Patrick Henry of his people; but I prefer to honor his unknown, unhonored and unsung amanuensis. Think what a godsend such a man would have been to Senator Tabor.

The Indian orator of to-day is not scholarly and grand. He is soiled, ignorant and sedentary in his habits. An orator ought to take care of his health. He cannot overload his stomach and make a bronze Daniel Webster of himself. He cannot eat a raw buffalo for breakfast and at once attack the question of tariff for revenue only. His brain is not clear enough. He cannot digest the mammalia of North America and seek out the delicate intricacies of the financial problem at the same time. All scientists and physiologists will readily see why this is true.

It is quite popular to say that the modern Indian has seen too much of civilization. This may be true. Anyhow, civilization has seen too much of him. I hope the day will never come when the pale face and the White Father will have to stay on their reservation, whether the red man does or not.

Indian eloquence, toned down by the mellow haze of a hundred years, sounds very well, but the clarion voice of the red orator has died away The stony figure, the eagle eye, the matchless presence, have all ceased to palpitate.

He does not say: "I am an aged hemlock. I am dead at the top. The forest is filled with the ghosts of my people. I hear their moans on the night winds and in the sighing pines." He does not talk in the blank verse of a century ago. He uses a good many blanks, but it is not blank verse. Even the Indian's friend would admit that it was not blank verse. Perhaps it might be called blankety verse.

Once he pleaded for the land of his fathers. Now he howls for grub, guns and fixed ammunition.

I tried to interview a big Crow chief once. I had heard some Sioux, and learned a few irrelevant and disconnected Ute phrases. I connected these with some Spanish terms and hoped to get a reply, and keep up a kind of running conversation that might mislead a friend who was with me, into the belief that I was as familiar with the Indian tongue as with my own. I began conversing with him in my polyglot manner. I did not get a reply. I conversed with him some more in a desultory way, for I had heard that he was a great orator in his tribe, and I wanted to get his views on national affairs. Still he was silent. He would not even answer me. I got hostile and used some badly damaged Spanish on him. Then I used some sprained and dislocated German on him, but he didn't seem to wot whereof I spoke.

Then my friend, with all the assurance of a fresh young manhood, began to talk with the great warrior in the English language, and incidentally asked him aboat a new Indian agent, who had the name of being a bogus Christian with an eye to the main chance.

My friend talked very loud, with the idea that the chieftain could understand any language if spoken so that you could hear it in the next Territory. At the mention of the Indian agent's name, the Crow statesman brightened up and made a remark He simply said: "Ugh! too much God and no flour."

You Heah Me, Sah!

COL. VISSCHER, of Denver, who is delivering his lecture, "Sixty Minutes in the War," tells a good story on himself of an episode, or something of that nature, that occurred to him in the days when he was the amanuensis of George D. Prentice.

Visscher, in those days, was a fair-haired young man, with pale blue eyes, and destitute of that wealth of brow and superficial area of polished dome which he now exhibits on the rostrum. He was learning the lesson of life then, and every now and then he would bump up against an octagonal mass of cold-pressed truth of the never-dying variety that seemed to kind of stun and concuss him.

One day Mr. Visscher wandered into a prominent hotel in Louisville, and, observing with surprise and pleasure that "boiled lobster" was one of the delicacies on the bill of fare, he ordered one.

He never had seen lobster, and a rare treat seemed to be in store for him. He breathed in what atmosphere there was in the dining-room, and waited for his bird. At last it was brought in. Mr. Visscher took one hasty look at the great scarlet mass of voluptuous limbs and oceanic nippers, and sighed. The lobster was as large as a door mat, and had a very angry and inflamed appearance. Visscher ordered in a powerful cocktail to give him courage, and then he tried to carve off some of the breast.

The lobster is honery even in death. He is eccentric and trifling. Those who know him best are the first to evade him and shun him. Visscher had failed to straddle the wish bone with his fork properly, and the talented bird of the deep rolling sea slipped out of the platter, waved itself across the horizon twice, and buried itself in the bosom of the eminent and talented young man. The eminent and talented young man took it in his napkin, put it carefully on the table, and went away.

As he passed out, the head waiter said:

"Mr. Visscher, was there anything the matter with your lobster?"

Visscher is a full-blooded Kentuckian, and answered in the courteous dialect of the blue-grass country.

"Anything the matter with my lobster, sah? No, sah. The lobster is very vigorous, sah. If you had asked me how I was, sah, I should have answered you very differently, sah. I am not well at all, sah. If I were as well, and as ruddy, and as active as that lobster, sah, I would live forever, sah. You heah me, sah?

"Why, of course, I am not familiar with the habits of the lobster, sah, and do not know how to kearve the bosom of the bloomin' peri of the summer sea, but that's no reason why the inflamed reptile should get up on his hind feet and nestle up to me, sah, in that earnest and forthwith manner, sah.

"I love dumb beasts, sah, and they love me, sah; but when they are dead, sah, and I undertake to kearve them, sah, I desiah, sah, that they should remain as the undertakah left them, sah. You doubtless heah me, sah!"

Plato.

PLATO was a Greek philosopher who flourished about 426 B. C., and kept on flourishing for eigty-one years after that, when he suddenly ceased to do so. He early took to poetry, but when he found that his poems were rejected by the Greek papers, he ceased writing poetry and went into the philosophy business. At that time Greece had no regular philosopher, and so Plato soon got all he could do.

Plato was a pupil of Socrates, who was himself no slouch of a philosopher. Many and many a day did Socrates take his little class of kindergarten philosophers up the shady banks of the Ilissus, and sit all day discoursing to his pupils on deep and difficult doctrines, while his unsandaled feet were bathed in the genial tide. Many happy hours were thus spent. Socrates would take his dinner or tell some wonderful tale to his class, whereby he would win their dinner himself. Then in the deep Athenian shade, with his bare, Gothic feet in the clear, calm waters of the Ilissus, he would eat the Grecian doughnut of his pupils, and while he spoke in poetic terms of his belief, he would dig his heel in the mud and heave a heart-broken sigh.

Such was Socrates, the great teacher. He got a small salary, and went barefoot till after Thanksgiving. He was a great tutor, and boarded around, teaching in the open air while the mosquitos bit his bare feet. No tutor ever tuted with a more unselfish purpose or a smaller salary.

Plato maintained, among other things, that evil is connected with matter, and aside from matter we do not find evil existing. That is true. At least, such evil as we might find apart from matter would be outside the jurisdiction of a police court. I think Plato was correct. Evil and matter are inseparable. That's what's the matter.

It is quite common for us to say that virtue is its own reward. Plato held that, while it was better to be virtuous as a matter of economy and ultimate peace than not to be virtuous at all, he believed in being virtuous for a higher reason. Probably it was notoriety. He would rather be right than be presi dent. He believed in being good just for the excitement of it, and the notice it would attract, and not because it paid. Plato was a great virtuoso.

Socrates would have been called a crank if he had lived in our day and age, and if Plato were to go into London or New York and talk of organizing a society for the encouragement of virtue among adult male taxpayers he would have a lonesome time of it. Be virtuous and you will be happy was a favorite motto with Plato. The legend is still quoted by those who love to ransack the dead past.

Pluto was quite another party, and some get him mixed up with Plato. They were not related in any way, Pluto being a son of Saturn and Rhea, who

NEPTUNE TAKING A RIDE.

flourished at about the same time as Plato. Pluto was a brother of Jupiter and Neptune, and when the estate of Saturn was wound up, Jupiter wanted the earth, and he got it. Neptune wanted the codfish conservatory and the mermaid's home, so he took the deep, deep sea, and even yet he rides around in a gold spangled stone boat on the pale green billows of the summer sea, jabbing a pickerel ever and anon with a three pronged fork. He leads a gay life, going to picnics with the mermaids in their coral caves, or attending their full evening dress parties, clad in a trident and a full beard. He loves the sea, the lone, blue sea, and those who have seen him turning handsprings on a sponge lawn, or riding in his water-tight chariot with his feet over the dashboard, beside a slim young mermaid with Paris green hair, and dressed in a tight-fitting, low-neck dorsal fin, say he is a lively old party.

But Pluto was different. He stood around till the estate was all closed up, and it looked as though he had got left. Just then the administrator says: "Why, here's Plute. He is going to come out of the little end of the horn. He will have to hustle for himself." Pluto resented this and clinched with the administrator. They fought till each had a watch pocket on the brow and an Irish sunset symphony in green under the eye, while Jupiter and Neptune stood by and encouraged the fight. Jupiter rather took sides with his brother, and Neptune stood in with the administrator. In the midst of the confusion Jupiter speaks up and says: "Swat him under the ear, Plute." Whereupon Neptune says to the administrator. "Give him—hail." The administrator paused and said that was a good suggestion. He would do so. And so he forgave Pluto and gave him—sheol.

The Expensive Word.

MUCH that is annoying in this life is occasioned by the use of a high priced word where a cheaper one would do. In these days of failure, shortage at both ends and financial stringency generally, I often wonder that some people should go on, day after day, using just as extravagant language as they did during the flush times. When I get hard up the first thing I do is to economize in my expressions in every day conversation. If there is a marked stringency in business, I lay aside first, my French, then my Latin, and finally my German. Should the times become greatly depressed and failures and assignments become frequent, I begin to lop off the large words in my own language, beginning with "incomprehensibility," "unconstitutionality," etc., etc.

Julius Cæsar's motto used to be, "Avoid an unusual word as you would a rock at sea," and Jule was right about it, too. Large and unusual words, especially in the mouths of ignorant people, are worse than "Rough on Rats" in a boarding-house pie.

Years ago there used to be a pompous cuss in southern Wisconsin, who was a self-made man. Extremely so. Those who used to hear him assert again and again that he was a self-made man always felt renewed confidence in the Creator.

He rose one evening in a political meeting, and swelling out his bosom, as his eagle eye rested on the chairman, he said:

"Mr. Cheerman! I move you that the cheer do appoint a committee of three to attend to the matter under discussion, and that sayed committee be clothed by the cheer with ominiscient and omnipotent powers."

The motion was duly seconded and the cheerman said he guessed that it wouldn't be necessary to put it to a vote.

"I guess it will be all right, Mr. Pinkham. I guess there'll be no declivity to that."

And so the committee was appointed and clothed with omniscient and omnipotent powers, there being no declivity to it.

We had a self-made lawyer at one time in the northern part of the State who would rather find a seventy-five cent word and use it in a speech where it did not belong than to eat a good square meal. He was more fatal to the King's English than O'Dynamite Rossa. One day he was telling how methodical one of the county officials was.

HE PAINTED THE FENCE GREEN.

"Why," said he, "I never saw a man do so much and do it so easy. But the secret of it is plain enough. You see, he has a regular rotunda of business every day"

If he meant anything, I suppose he meant a routine of business, but a man would have to be a mind reader to follow him some days when he had about six fingers of cough medicine aboard and began to paw around in the dark and musty garret of his memory for moth-eaten words that didn't mean anything.

A neighbor of mine went to Washington during the Guiteau trial and has been telling us about it ever since. He is one of those people who don't want to be close and stingy about what they know. He likes to go through life shedding information right and left. He likes to get a crowd around him and then tell how he was in Washington at the time of the "post mortise examination." "Boys, you may talk all your a mind to, but the greatest thing I saw in Washington," said he, "was Dr. Mary Walker on the street every morning riding one of these philosophers."

He painted the top of his fence green, last year, so it would "kind of combinate with his blinds."

If he would make his big words "combinate" with what he means a little better, he would not attract so much attention. But he don't care. He hates to see a big, fat word loafing around with nothing to do, so he throws one in occasionally for exercise, I guess.

In the Minnesota legislature, in 1867, they had under discussion a bill to increase the per diem of members from three dollars to five dollars. A member of the lower house, who voted for the measure, was hauled over the coals by one of his constituents and charged with corruption in no unmeasured terms.

To all this the legislator calmly answered that when he got down to the capital and found out the awful price of board, he concluded that his "per diadem" ought to be increased, and so he supported the measure. Then the belligerent constituent said:

"I beg your pardon and acquit you of all charges of corruption, for a legislator who does not know the difference between a crown of glory and the price of a day's work is too big a blankety blanked fool to be convicted of an intentional wrong."

Petticoats at the Polls.

THERE have been many reasons given, first and last, why women should not vote, but I desire to say, in the full light of a ripe experience, that some of them are fallacious. I refer more particularly to the argument that it will degrade women to go to the polls and vote like a little man. While I am not and have never been a howler for female suffrage, I must admit that it is much more of a success than prohibition and speculative science.

My wife voted eight years with my full knowledge and consent, and to-day I cannot see but that she is as docile and as tractable as when she won my trusting heart.

Now those who know me best will admit that I am not a ladies' man, and, therefore, what I may say here is not said to secure favor and grateful smiles. I am not attractive and I am not in politics. I believe that I am homelier this winter than usual. There are reasons why I believe that what I may say on this subject will be sincere and not sensational or selfish.

It has been urged that good women do not generally exercise the right of suffrage, when they have the opportunity, and that only those whose social record has been tarnished a good deal go to the polls. This is not true.

It is the truth that a good full vote always shows a list of the best women and the wives of the best men. A bright day makes a better showing of lady voters than a bad one, and the weather makes a more perceptible difference in the female vote than the male, but when things are exciting and the battle is red-hot, and the tocsin of war sounds anon, the wife and mother puts on her armor and her sealskin sacque and knocks things cross-eyed.

It is generally supposed that the female voter is a pantaloonatic, a half horse, half alligator kind of woman, who looks like Dr. Mary Walker and has the appearance of one who has risen hastily in the night at the alarm of fire and dressed herself partially in her own garments and partially in her husband's. This is a popular error. In Wyoming, where female suffrage has raged for years, you meet quiet, courteous and gallant gentlemen, and fair, quiet, sensible women at the polls, where there isn't a loud or profane word, and where it is an infinitely more proper place to send a young lady unescorted than to the postoffice in any city in the Union. You can readily see why this is so. The men about the polls are always candidates and their friends. That is the reason that neither party can afford to show the slightest rudeness toward a voter. The man who on Wednesday would tell her to go and soak her head, perhaps, would stand bareheaded to let her pass on Tuesday. While she holds a smashed ballot shoved under the palm of her gray kid glove she may walk over the candidate's prostrate form with impunity and her overshoes if she chooses to.

Weeks and months before election in Wyoming, the party with the longest purse subsidizes the most livery stables and carriages. Then, on the eventful day, every conveyance available is decorated with a political placard and driven by a polite young man who is instructed to improve the time. Thus every woman in Wyoming has a chance to ride once a year, at least. Lately, however, many prefer to walk to the polls, and they go in pairs, trios and quartettes, voting their little sentiments and calmly returning to their cookies and crazy quilts as though politics didn't jar their mental poise a minute.

It is possible, and even probable, that a man and his wife may disagree on politics as they might on religion. The husband may believe in Andrew Jackson and a relentless hell, while his wife may be a stalwart and rather liberal on the question of eternal punishment. If the husband manages his wife as he would a clothes-wringer, and turns her through life by a crank, he will, no doubt, work her politically; but if she has her own ideas about things, she will naturally act upon them, while the man who is henpecked in other matters till he can't see out of his eyes, will be henpecked, no doubt, in the matter of national and local politics.

These are a few facts about the actual workings of female suffrage, and I do not tackle the great question of the ultimate results upon the political machinery if woman suffrage were to become general. I do not pretend to say as to that. I know a great deal, but I do not know that. There are millions of women, no doubt, who are better qualified to vote, and yet cannot, than millions of alleged men who do vote; but no one can tell now what the ultimate effect of a change might be.

So far as Wyoming is concerned, the Territory is prosperous and happy. I see, also, that a murderer was hung by process of law there the other day. That looks like the onward march of reform, whether female suffrage had anything to do with it or not. And they're going to hang another in March if the weather is favorable and executive clemency remains dormant, as I think it will.

All these things look hopeful. We can't tell what the Territory would have been without female suffrage, but when they begin to hang men by law instead of by moonlight, the future begins to brighten up. When you have to get up in the night to hang a man every little while and don't get any per diem for it, you feel as though you were a good way from home.

The Sedentary Hen.

THOUGH generally cheerful and content with her lot, the hen at times becomes moody, sullen and taciturn. We are often called upon to notice and profit by the genial and sunny disposition of the hen, and yet there are times in her life when she is morose, cynical, and the prey of consuming melancholy. At such times not only her own companions, but man himself shuns the hen.

At first she seems to be preoccupied only. She starts and turns pale when suddenly spoken to. Then she leaves her companions and seems to be the victim of hypochondria. Then her mind wanders. At last you come upon her suddenly some day, seated under the currant bushes. You sympathize with her and you seek to fondle her. She then picks a small memento out of the back of your hand. You then gently but firmly coax her out of there with a hoe, and you find that she has been seated for some time on an old croquet ball, trying to hatch out a whole set of croquet balls. This shows that her mind is affected. You pick up the croquet ball, and find it hot and feverish, so you throw it into the shade of the woodshed. Anon, you find your demented hen in the loft of the barn hovering over a door knob and trying by patience and industry to hatch out a hotel.

When a hen imagines that she is inspired to incubate, she at once ceases to be an ornament to society and becomes a crank. She violates all the laws and customs of nature and society in trying to hatch a conservatory by setting through the long days and nights of summer on a small flower pot.

Man may win the affections of the tiger, the lion, or the huge elephant, and make them subservient to his wishes, but the setting hen is not susceptible to affection. You might as well love the Manitoba blizzard or try to quell the cyclone by looking calmly in its eye. The setting hen is filled with hatred for every living thing. She loves to brood over her wrongs or anything else she can find to squat on.

I once owned a hen that made a specialty of setting. She never ceased to be the proud anonymous author of a new, warm egg, but she yearned to be a parent. She therefore seated herself on a nest where other hens were in the habit of leaving their handiwork for inspection. She remained there during the summer hatching steadily on while the others laid, until she filled my barnyard with little orphaned henlets of different ages. She remained there night and day, patiently turning out poultry for me to be a father to. I brought up on the bottle about one hundred that summer that had been turned out by this morbidly maternal hen. All she seemed to ask in return was my kind regards and esteem. I fed her upon the nest and humored her in every way. Every day she became a parent, and every day added to my responsibility.

SUCCESS WITH CHICKENS.

One day I noticed that she seemed weak and there was a far away look in her eye. For the first time the horrible truth burst upon my mind. I buried my face in the haymow and I am not ashamed to say that I wept. Strong man as I am, I am not too proud to say that I soaked that haymow through with unavailing tears.

My hen was dying even then. Her breath came hot and quick like the swift rush of a hot ball that caves in the short-stop and speeds away to center-field.

The next morning one hundred chickens of various sizes were motherless, and if anything had happened to me they would have been fatherless.

For many years I have made a close study of the setting hen, but I am still unsettled as to what is best to do with her. She is a freak of nature, a disagreeable anomaly, a fussy phenomenon. Logic, rhetoric and metaphor are all alike to the setting hen. You might as well go down into the bosom of Vesuvius and ask it to postpone the next eruption.

A Bright Future for Pugilism.

THE recent prominence of Mr. John E. Dempsey, better known as Jack Dempsey, of New York, brings to mind a four days' trip taken in his company from Portland, Oregon, to St. Paul, over the Northern Pacific.

There were three pugilists in the party besides myself, viz, Dempsey, Dave Campbell and Tom Cleary. We made a grand, triumphant tour across the country together, and I may truthfully state that I never felt so free to say anything I wanted to—to other passengers—as I did at that time. I wish I could afford to take at least one pugilist with me all the time. In traveling about the country lecturing, a good pugilist would be of great assistance. I would like to set him on the man who always asks: "Where do you go to from here, Mr. Nye?" He does not ask because he wants to know, for the next moment he asks right over again. I do not know why he asks, but surely it is not for the purpose of finding out.

Well, throughout our long journey across the State of Oregon and the Territories of Idaho, Montana and Dakota, and the State of Minnesota, it was one continual ovation. Dempsey had a world-wide reputation, I found, co-extensive with the horizon, as I may say, and bounded only by the zodiac.

In my great forthcoming work, entitled "Half-Hours with Great Men, or Eminent People Which I Have Saw," I shall give a fuller description of this journey The book will be a great boon.

Mr. Dempsey is not a man who would be picked out as a great man. You might pass by him two or three times without recognizing his eminence, and yet, at a scrapping matinee or swatting recital, he seems to hold his audiences at his own sweet will—also his antagonist.

Mr. Dempsey does not crave notoriety. He seems rather to court seclusion. This is characteristic of the man. See how he walked around all over the State of New York last week—in the night, too—in order to evade the crowd.

His logic, however, is wonderful. Though quiet and unassuming in his manner, his arguments are powerful and generally make a large protuberance wherever they alight.

Nothing is more pleasing than the sight of a man who has risen by his own unaided effort, fought his way up, as it were, and yet who is not vain. Mr. Dempsey conversed with me frequently during our journey, and did not seem to feel above me.

I opened the conversation by telling him that I had seen a number of his works. Nothing pleases a young author so much as a little friendly remark in relation to his work. I had seen a study of his one day in New York last spring. It was an italic nose with quotation marks on each side.

It was a very happy little bon mot on Mr. Dempsey's part, and attracted a good deal of notice at the time.

Mr. Dempsey is not a college graduate, as many suppose. He is a self-made man. This should be a great encouragement to our boys who are now unknown, and whose portraits have not as yet appeared in the sporting papers.

But Mr. Dempsey's great force as a debater is less, perhaps, in the matter than in the manner. His delivery is good and his gestures cannot fail to convince the most skeptical. Striking in appearance, aggressive in his nature, and happy in his gestures, he is certain to attract the attention of the police, and he cannot fail to rivet the eye of his adversary. I saw one of his adversaries, not long ago, whose eye had been successfully riveted in that way.

And yet, John E. Dempsey was once a poor boy. He had none of the advantages which wealth and position bring. But, confident of his latent ability as a middle-weight convincer, he toiled on, ever on, sitting up until long after other people had gone to bed, patiently knocking out those who might be brought to him for that purpose. He never hung back because the way looked long and lonely. And what is the result? To-day, in the full vigor of manhood, he is sought out and petted by everyone who takes an interest in the onward march of pugilism.

It is a wonderful record, though .brief. It shows what patient industry will accomplish unaided. Had John E. Dempsey hesitated to enter the ring and said that he would rather go to school, where he would be safe, he might to-day be an educated man; but what does that amount to here in America, where everybody can have an education? He would have lost his talent as a slugger, and drifted steadily downward, perhaps, till he became a schoolteacher or a narrow-chested editor, writing things day after day just to gratify the morbid curiosity of a sin-cursed world.

In closing, I would like to say that I hope I have not expressed an opinion in the above that may hereafter be used against me. Do not understand me to be the foe of education. Education and refinement are good enough in their places, but how shall we attract attention by trying to become refined and educated in a land where, as I say, education and refinement seem almost to run rampant.

Heretofore, in America, pugilism has been made subservient to the common schools. Pugilism and polygamy have both been crowded to the wall. Now pugilism is about to assert itself. The tin ear and the gory nose will soon come to the front, and the day is not far distant when progressive pugilism and the prize-ring will take the place of the poorly ventilated common school and the enervating prayer meeting.

The Snake Indian.

THERE are about 5,000 Snake or Shoshone Indians now extant. the greater part being in Utah and Nevada, though there is a reservation in Idaho and another in Wyoming.

The Shoshone Indian is reluctant to accept of civilization on the European plan. He prefers the ruder customs which have been handed down from father to son along with other hairlooms. I use the word hairlooms in its broadest sense.

There are the Shoshones proper and the Utes or Utahs, to which have been added by some authorities the Comanches, and Moquis of New Mexico and Arizona, the Netelas and other tribes of California. The Shoshone, wherever found, is clothed in buckskin and blanket in winter, but dressed more lightly in summer, wearing nothing but an air of intense gloom in August. To this he adds on holidays a necklace made from the store teeth of the hardy pioneer.

HOLIDAY COSTUME.

The Snake or Shoshone Indian is passionately fond of the game known as poker among us, and which, I learn, is played with cards. It is a game of chance, though skill and a thorough knowledge of firearms are of great use. The Indians enter into this game with great zeal, and lend to it the wonderful energy which they have preserved from year to year by abstaining from the debilitating effects of manual labor. All day long the red warrior sits in his skin boudoir, nursing the sickly and reluctant "flush," patient, silent and hopeful. Through the cold of winter, in the desolate mountains, he continues to

'Hope on, hope ever,"

That he will "draw to fill." Far away up the canyon he hears the sturdy blows of his wife's tomahawk as she slaughters the grease wood and the sage brush for the fire in his gilded hell where he sits and woos the lazy Goddess of Fortune.

With the Shoshone, poker is not alone a relaxation, the game wherewith to wear out a long and listless evening, but it is a passion, a duty and a devotion. He has a face designed especially for poker. It never shows a sign of good or evil fortune. You might as well try to win a smile from a railroad right of way. The full hand, the fours, threes, pairs and bob-tail flushes are all the same to him, if you judge by his face.

GOING AWAY BROKE.

When he gets hungry he cinches himself a little tighter and continues to "rastle" with fate. You look at his smoky, old copper cent of a face, and you see no change. You watch him as he coins the last buckshot of his tribe and later on when he goes forth a pauper, and the corners of his famine-breeding mouth have never moved, His little black, smoke-inflamed eyes have never lighted with triumph or joy. He is the great aboriginal stoic and sylvan dude. He does not smile. He does not weep. It certainly must be intensely pleasant to be a wild, free, lawless, irresponsible, natural born fool.

The Shoshones proper include the Bannocks, which are again subdivided into the Koolsitakara or Buffalo Eaters, on Wind River, the Tookarika or Mountain Sheep Eaters, on Salmon or Suabe Rivers, the Shoshocas or White Knives, sometimes called Diggers, of the Humbolt River and the Great Salt Lake basin. Probably the Hokandikahs, Yahooskins and the Wahlpapes are subdivisions of the Digger tribe. I am not sure of this, but I shall not suspend my business till I can find out about it. If I cannot get at a great truth right off I wait patiently and go right on drawing my salary

The Shoshones live on the government and other small game. They will eat anything when hungry, from a buffalo down to a woodtick. The Shoshone does not despise small things. He loves insects in any form. He loves to make pets of them and to study their habits in his home life.

Formerly, when a great Shoshone warrior died, they killed his favorite wife over his grave, so that she could go to the happy hunting grounds with him, but it is not so customary now. I tried to impress on an old Shoshone brave once that they ought not to do that. I tried to show him that it would encourage celibacy and destroy domestic ties in his tribe. Since then there

THE HOME CIRCLE.

has been quite a stride toward reform among them. Instead of killing the widow on the death of the husband, the husband takes such good care of his health and avoids all kinds of intellectual strain or physical fatigue, that late years there are no widows, but widowers just seem to swarm in the Shoshone tribe. The woods are full of them.

Now, if they would only kill the widower over the grave of the wife, the Indian's future would assume a more definite shape.

Roller Skating.

I HAVE once more tried to ride a pair of roller skates. That is the reason I got down on the rink and down on roller skates. That is the reason several people got down on me. That is also the reason why I now state in a public manner, to a lost and undone race; that unless the roller-rink is at once abolished, the whole civilized race will at once be plunged into arnica.

I had tried it once before, but had not carried my experiments to a successful termination. I made a trip around the rink last August, but was ruled out by the judges for incompetency, and advised to skate among the people who were hostile to the government of the United States, while the proprietors repaired the rink.

On the 9th of June I nestled in the bosom of a cyclone to excess, and it has required the bulk of the succeeding months for nature to glue the bone of my leg together in proper shape. That is the reason I have not given the attention to roller-skating that I should.

A few weeks ago I read what Mr. Talmage said about the great national vice. It was his opinion that, if we skated in a proper spirit, we could leave the rink each evening with our immortal souls in good shape.

Somehow it got out that on Thursday evening I would undertake the feat of skating three rounds in three hours with no protection to my scruples, for one-half the gate money, Talmage rules. So there was quite a large audience present with opera glasses. Some had umbrellas, especially on the front rows. These were worn spread, in order to ward off fragments of the rink which might become disengaged and set in motion by atmospheric disturbances.

In obedience to a wild, Wagnerian snort from the orchestra, I came into the arena with my skates in hand. I feel perfectly at home before an audience when I have my skates in hand. It is a morbid desire to wear the skates on my feet that has always been my *bete noire*. Will the office boy please give me a brass check for that word so that I can get it when I go away?

My first thought, after getting myself secured to the skates, was this: "Am I in the proper frame of mind? Am I doing this in the right spirit?

Am I about to skate in such a way as to lift the fog of unbelief which now envelopes a sinful world, or shall I deepen the opaque night in which my race is wrapped?"

Just then that end of the rink erupted in a manner so forthwith and so *tout ensemble* that I had to push it back in place with my person. I never saw anything done with less delay or less languor.

The audience went wild with enthusiasm, and I responded to the encore by writing my name in the air with my skates.

This closed the first seance, and my trainer took me in the dressing-room to attend a consultation of physicians. After the rink carpenter had jacked up the floor a little I went out again. I had no fears about my ability to perform the mechanical part assigned me, but I was still worried over the question of whether it would or would not be of lasting benefit to mankind.

Those who have closely scrutinized my frame in repose have admitted that I am fearfully and wonderfully made. Students of the human frame say that they never saw such a wealth of looseness and limberness lavished upon one person. They claim that nature bestowed upon me the hinges and joints intended for a whole family, and therefore when I skate the air seems to be perfectly lurid with limbs. I presume that this is true; though I have so little leisure while skating in which to observe the method itself, the plot or animus of the thing, as it were, that my opinion would be of little value to the scientist.

I am led to believe that the roller skate is certainly a great civilizer and a wonderful leveler of mankind. If we so skate that when the summons comes to seek our ward in the general hospital, where each shall heal his busted cuticle within the walls where rinkists squirm, we go not like the moral wreck, morally paralyzed, but like a hired man taking his medicine, and so forth—we may skate with perfect impunity, or anyone else to whom we may be properly introduced by our cook.

No More Frontier.

THE system of building railroads into the wilderness, and then allowing the wilderness to develop afterward, has knocked the essential joy out of the life of the pioneer. At one time the hardy hewer of wood and drawer of water gave his lifetime willingly that his son might ride in the "varnished cars." Now the Pullman palace car takes the New Yorker to the threshold of the sea, or to the boundary line between the United States and the British possessions.

It has driven out the long handled frying pan and the flapjack of twenty years ago, and introduced the condensed milk and canned fruit of commerce. Along the highways, where once the hopeful hundreds marched with long handled shovel and pick and pan, cooking by the way thin salt pork and flapjacks and slumgullion, now the road is lined with empty beer bottles and peach cans that have outlived their usefulness. No landscape can be picturesque with an empty peach can in the foreground any more than a lion would look grand in a red monogram horse blanket and false teeth.

The modern camp is not the camp of the wilderness. It wears the half-civilized and shabby genteel garments of a sawed-off town. You know that if you ride a day you will be where you can get the daily papers and read them under the electric light. That robs the old canyons of their solemn isolation and peoples each gulch with the odor of codfish balls and civilization. Civilization is not to blame for all this, and yet it seems sad.

Civilization could not have done all this alone. It had to call to its aid the infernal fruit can that now desolates the most obscure trail in the heart of the mountains. You walk over chaos where the "hydraulic" has plowed up the valley like a convulsion, or you tread the yielding path across the deserted dump, and on all sides the rusty, neglected and humiliated empty tin can stares at you with its monotonous, dude-like stare.

An old timer said to me once "I've about decided, Bill, that the West is a matter of history When we cooked our grub over a sage brush fire we could get fat and fight Indians, but now we fill our digesters with the cold pizen and pewter of the canned peach; we go to a big tavern and stick a towel under our chins and eat pie with a fork and heat up our carkisses with antichrist coal, and what do we amount to? Nuthin! I used to chase Injuns all day and eat raw salt pork at night, bekuz I dassent build a fire, and still I felt better than I do now with a wad of tin-can solder in my stummick and a homesick feeling in my weather-beaten breast.

"No, we don't have the fun we used to. We have more swarrees and sciatica and one bloomin' thing and another of that kind, but we don't get one snort of pure air and appetite in a year. They're bringin' in their blamed telephones now and malaria and aigue and old sledge, and fun might as well skip out. There ain't no frontier any more. All we've got left is the old-fashioned trantler joos and rhumatiz of '49."

Behind the red squaw's cayuse plug,
  The hand-car roars and raves,
And pie-plant pies are now produced
  Above the Indian graves.
I hear the oaths of pioneers,
  The caucus yet to be,
The first low hum where soon will come
  The fuzzy bumble bee.

A Letter of Regrets.

MY DEAR PRINCESS BEATRICE.—I received your kind invitation to come up to Whippingham on the 23d inst. and see you married, but I have not been able to get there. The weather has been so hot this month, that, to tell you the truth, Beatrice, I haven't been going anywhere to speak of. At first I thought I would go anyhow, and even went so far as to pick out a nice corner bracket to take along for a wedding present. Not so much for its intrinsic value, of course, but so you would have something with my name to it on a card that you could show to those English dudes, and let them know that you had influential friends, even in America. But when I thought what a long, hard trip it would be, and how I would probably mash that bracket on the cars before I got half way there, I gave it up.

I am not personally acquainted with your inamorato, if that's all right, never having met him in our set; but I understand you have done well, and that your husband is a rising young man of good family, and that he will never allow you to put your hands into dishwater. I hope this is true and that he does not drink. Rum has certainly paralyzed more dukes and such things than war has. I attribute this to the fact that princes and dukes are generally more reckless about exposing themselves to the demon rum than to the rude alarums and one thing another of war.

If you keep a girl I hope you will get a good one who knows her business. A green girl in the house of a newly-married princess is a great source of annoyance. A friend of mine who got married last winter got a girl whose mind had been eaten by cut-worms and she had not discovered it. All the faculty that had been spared her was that power of the mind which enabled her to charge $3 a week. She lubricated the buckwheat pancake griddle for a week with soap grease and a dash of castor oil, and when she was discharged she wept bitterly because capital with the iron heel ground the poor servant girl into the dust.

Probably you will take a little tour after the wedding is over. They are doing that way a good deal in Boston this season. I thought you would like a pointer in the very lum-tumest thing to do, and so I write this. So long as you have the means to do this thing right, I think you ought to do so. You may never be married again, princess, and now is the time to paint the British Isles red.

You can also get more concessions from your husband now, while he is a little rattled, and temporarily knocked silly by the pomp and pageant of marrying into your family, and if you work it right you can maintain this supremacy for years. Treat him with a gentle firmness, and do not weep on his bosom if you detect the aroma of beer and bologna sausage on his young breath. Bologna and royalty do not seem to harmonize first-rate, but remember you can harass your husband if you choose, so that he will fall to even lower depths than bologna and Milwaukee beer. Do not aggravate him when he comes home tired, but help him do the chores and greet him with a smile.

I'd just as soon tell you, Beatrice, that this smile racket is not original with me. I read it in a paper. This paper went on to say that a young wife should always greet her husband with a smile on his return. I showed the article to my wife and suggested that it was a good scheme, and hoped she would try it on me sometime. She said if I would like to change off awhile, and take my smile when I got home instead of taking it down town, we would make the experiment. The trouble with the average woman of the age in which we live, Beatrice, is that she is above her business. She tries to be superior to her husband, and in many instances she succeeds. That is the bane of wedded life. Do not strive to be superior to your husband, Beatrice. If you do, it is good-bye, John.

Treat him well at all times, whether he treats you well or not; then when your mother gets tired of reigning and wants to come down and spend the hot weather with you, she will be kindly greeted by her son-in-law.

Do not allow the fact that you belong to the royal family to interfere with your fun, Beatrice. If you want to wear a Mother Hubbard dress on the throne during hot weather, or mash a mosquito with your mother's sceptre, do so. Conventionality is a humbug and a nuisance, and I'd just as soon tell you right here that if I could have gone to your wedding and worn a linen coat and a perspiration, I would have gone; but to stand around there all day in a tight black suit of clothes, in a mixed crowd of dukes, and counts, and princes of high degree, most of whom are total strangers to me, is more than I can stand.

I wish you would give my love to your mother and tell her just how it was. Make it as smooth as you can and break it to her gently. Tell her that the royal family is spreading out so that I can't leave my work every time one of its members gets married. Remember me to the Waleses, the Darmstadts, Princess Irene and Victoria, Mr. and Mrs. Prince Alexander of Bulgaria, also Prince Francis of Battenberg and the Countess Erbach Schomberg. They will all be there probably, and so will Lord Latham and Lord Edgcumbe. I know just how Edgcumbe will snort around there when he finds that I can't be there. Give my kind regards to any other lords, dukes, duchesses, dowagers or marchionesses who may inquire for me, and tell them all that I will be in London next year if the Prince of Wales will drop me a line stating that the moral tone of the city is such that it would be safe for me to come.

Venice.

WE arrived in Venice last evening, latitude 45 deg. 25 min. N., longitude 12 deg. 19 min. E.

Venice is the home of the Venetian, and also where the gondola has its nest and rears its young. It is also the headquarters for the paint known as Venetian red. They use it in painting the town on festive occasions. This is the town where the Merchant of Venice used to do business, and the home of Shylock, a broker, who sheared the Venetian lamb at the corner of the Rialto and the Grand Canal. He is now no more. I couldn't even find an old neighbor near the Rialto who remembered Shylock. From what I can learn of him, however, I am led to believe that he was pretty close in his deals, and liked to catch a man in a tight place and then make him squirm. Shylock, during the great panic in Venice, many years ago, it is said, had a chattel mortgage on more lives than you could shake a stick at. He would loan a small amount to a merchant at three per cent. a month, and secure it on a pound of the merchant's liver, or by a cut-throat mortgage on his respiratory apparatus. Then, when the paper matured, he would go up to the house with a pair of scales and a pie knife and demand a foreclosure.

Venice is one of the best watered towns in Europe. You can hardly walk a block without getting your feet wet, unless you ride in a gondola.

The gondola is a long, slim hack without wheels and is worked around through the damp streets by a brunette man whose breath should be a sad warning to us all. He is called the gondolier. Sometimes he sings in a low tone of voice and in a foreign tongue. I do not know where I have met so many foreigners as I have here in Europe, unless it was in New York, at the polls. Wherever I go, I hear a foreign tongue. I do not know whether these people talk in the Italian language just to show off or not. Perhaps they prefer it. London is the only place I have visited where the Boston dialect is used. London was originally settled by adventurers from Boston. The blood of some of the royal families of Massachusetts may be found in the veins of London people.

Wealthy young ladies in Venice do not run away with the coachman. There are no coaches, no coachmen and no horses in Venice. There are only four horses in Venice and they are made of copper and exhibited at St. Mark's as curiosities.

The Accademia delle Belle Arti of Venice is a large picture store where I went yesterday to buy a few pictures for Christmas presents. A painting by Titian, the Italian Prang, pleased me very much, but I couldn't beat down the price to where it would be any object for me to buy it. Besides, it would be a nuisance to carry such a picture around with me all over the Alps, up the Rhine and through St. Lawrence county. I finally decided to leave it and secure something less awkward to carry and pay for.

The Italians are quite proud of their smoky old paintings. I have often thought that if Venice would run less to art and more to soap, she would be more apt to win my respect. Art is all right to a certain extent, but it can be run in the ground. It breaks my heart to know how lavish nature has been with water here, and yet how the Venetians scorn to investigate its benefits. When a gondolier gets a drop of water on him, he swoons. Then he lies in a kind of coma till another gondolier comes along to breathe in his face and revive him.

She Kind of Coaxed Him.

I NEVER practiced law very much, but during the brief period that my sheet-iron sign was kissed by the Washoe zephyr, I had several odd experiences. I'm sure that lawyers who practice for forty years, especially on the frontier or in a new country, could write a large book that would make mighty interesting reading.

One day I was figuring up how much a man could save in ten years, paying forty dollars a month rent, and taking in two dollars and fifty cents per month, when a large man with a sad eye and an early purple tumor on the side of his head, came in and asked me if my name was Nye. I told him it was and asked him to take a chair and spit on the stove a few times, and make himself entirely at home.

He did so.

After answering in a loud, tremulous tone of voice that we were having rather a backward spring, he produced a red cotton handkerchief and took out of it a deed which he submitted to my ripe and logical legal mind.

I asked him if that was his name that appeared in the body of the deed as grantor. He said it was. I then asked him why his wife had not signed it, as it seemed to be the homestead, and her name appeared in the instrument with that of her husband, but her signature wasn't at the foot, though his name was duly signed, witnessed and acknowledged.

"Well," said he, "there's where the gazelle comes in." He then took a bite off the corner of a plug of tobacco about as big as a railroad land grant, and laid two twenty dollar gold pieces on the desk near my arm. I took them and tapped them together like the cashier of the Bank of England, and, disguising my annoyance over the little episode, told him to go on.

"Well," said the large man, fondling the wen which nestled lovingly in his faded Titian hair, "my wife has conscientious scruples against signing that deed. We have been married about a year now, but not actively for the past eleven months. I'm kind of *ex-officio* husband, as you might say. After we'd been married about a month a little incident occurred which made a riffle, as you might say, in our domestic tide. I was division master on the U. P., and one night I got an order to go down towards Sidney and look at a bridge. Of course I couldn't get back till the next evening. So I sighed and switched off to the superintendent's office, expecting to go over on No. 4 and look at the bridge. At the office they told me that I needn't go till Tuesday, so I strolled up town and got home about nine o'clock, went in with a latch key, just as a mutual friend went out through the bed-room window, taking a sash that I paid two dollars for. I didn't care for the sash, because he left a pair of pantaloons worth twelve dollars and some silver in the pockets, but I thought it was such odd taste for a man to wear a sash without his uniform.

"Well, as I had documentary evidence against my wife, I told her she could take a vacation. She cried a good deal, but it didn't count. I suffered a good deal, but tears did not avail. It takes a good deal of damp weather to float me out of my regular channel. She spent the night packing her trosseau, and in the morning she went away. Now, I could get a divorce and save all this trouble of getting her signature, but I'd rather not tell this whole business in court, for the little woman seems to be trying to do better, and if it wasn't for her blamed old hyena of a mother, would get along tip-top. She's living with her mother now and if a lawyer would go to the girl and tell her how it is, and that I want to sell the property and want her signature, in place of getting a divorce, I believe she'd sign. Would you mind trying it?"

"COAXING."

I said if I could get time I would go over and talk with her and see what she said. So I did. I got along pretty well, too. I found the young woman at home, and told her the legal aspects of the case. She wouldn't admit any of the charges, but after a long parley agreed to execute the deed and save trouble. She came to my office an hour later, and signed the instrument. I got two witnesses to the signature and had just put the notarial seal on it when the girl's mother came in. She asked her daughter if she had signed the deed and was told that she had. She said nothing, but smiled in a way that made my blood run cold. If a woman were to smile on me that way every day, I should certainly commit some great crime.

I was just congratulating myself on the success of the business, and was looking at the two $20 gold pieces and trying to get acquainted with them, as it were, after the two women had gone away, when they returned with the husband and son-in-law at the head of the procession. He looked pale and care-worn to me. He asked me in a low voice if I had a deed there, executed by his wife. I said yes. He then asked me if I would kindly destroy it. I said I would. I would make deeds and tear them up all day at $40 apiece. I said I liked the conveyancing business very much, and if a client felt like having a grand, warranty deed debauch, I was there to furnish the raw material.

I then tore up the deed and the two women went quietly away. After they had gone, my client, in an absent-minded way, took out a large quid that had outlived its usefulness, laid it tenderly on the open page of Estey's Pleadings, and said:

"You doubtless think I am a singular organization, and that my ways are past finding out. I wish to ask you if I did right a moment ago?" Here he took out another $20 and put it under the paper weight. "When I went down stairs I met my mother-in-law. She always looked to me like a firm woman, but I did not think she was so unswerving as she really was. She asked me in a low, musical voice to please destroy the deed, and then she took one of them Smith & Wesson automatic advance agents of death out from under her apron and kind of wheedled me into saying I would. Now, did I do right? I want a candid, legal opinion, and I'm ready to pay for it."

I said he did perfectly right.

Answering an Invitation.

HUDSON, WIS., January 19, 1886.

DEAR FRIEND.—I have just received your kind and cordial invitation to come to Washington and spend several weeks there among the eminent men of our proud land. I would be glad to go as you suggest, but I cannot do so at this time. I am passionately fond of mingling with the giddy whirl of good society. I hope you will not feel that my reason for declining your kind invitation is that I feel myself above good society. I assure you I do not.

Nothing pleases me better than to dress up and mingle among my fellow-men, with a sprinkling here and there of the other sex. It is true that the most profitable study for mankind is man, but we should not overlook woman. Woman is now seeking to be emancipated. Let us put our great, strong arms around her and emancipate her. Even if we cannot emancipate but one, we shall not have lived entirely for naught.

I am told by those upon whom I can rely that there are hundreds of attractive young women throughout our joyous land who have arrived at years of discretion and yet who have never been emancipated. I met a woman on the cars last week who is lecturing on this subject, and she told me all about it. Now, the question at once presents itself, how shall we emancipate woman unless we go where she is? We must go right into society and take her by the hand and never let go of her hand till she is properly emancipated. Not only must she be emancipated, but she must be emancipated from her present thralldom. Thralldom of this kind is liable to break out in any community, and those who are now in perfect health may pine away in a short time and flicker.

My course, while mingling in society's mad whirl, is to first open the conversation with a young lady by leading her away to the conservatory, where I ask her if she has ever been the victim of thralldom and whether or not she has ever been ground under the heel of the tyrant man. I then time her pulse for thirty minutes, so as to strike a good average. The emancipation of woman is destined at some day to become one of our leading industries.

You also ask me to kindly lead the German while there. I would cheerfully do so, but owing to the wobbly eccentricity of my cyclone leg, it would be sort of a broken German. But I could sit near by and watch the game with a furtive glance, and fan the young ladies between the acts, and converse with them in low, earnest, passionate tones. I like to converse with people in whom I take an interest. I was conversing with a young lady one evening at a recherche ball in my far away home in the free and unfettered West, a very brilliant affair, I remember, under the auspices of Hose Company No. 2. I was talking in a loud and earnest way to this liquid-eyed creature, a little louder than usual, because the music was rather forte just then, and the base viol virtuoso was bearing on rather hard at that moment. The music ceased with a sudden snort. And so did my wife, who was just waltzing past us. If I had ceased to converse at the same time that the music shut off, all might have been well, but I did not.

Your remark that the president and cabinet would be glad to see me this winter is ill-timed.

There have been times when it would have given me much pleasure to visit Washington, but I did not vote for Mr. Cleveland, to tell the truth, and I know that if I were to go to the White House and visit even for a few days, he would reproach me and throw it up to me. It is true I did not pledge myself to vote for him, but still I would hate to go to a man's house and eat his popcorn and use his smoking tobacco after I had voted against him and talked about him as I have about Cleveland.

No, I can't be a hypocrite. I am right out, open and above board. If I talk about a man behind his back, I won't go and gorge myself with his victuals. I was assured by parties in whom I felt perfect confidence that Mr. Cleveland was a "moral leper," and relying on such assurances from men in whom I felt that I could trust, and not being at that time where I could ask Mr. Cleveland in person whether he was or was not a moral leper as aforesaid, I assisted in spreading the report that he had been exposed to moral leprosy, and as near as I could learn, he was liable to come down with it at any time.

So that even if I go to Washington I shall put up at a hotel and pay my bills just as any other American citizen would. I know how it is with Mr. Cleveland at this time. When the legislature is in session there, people come in from around Buffalo with their butter and eggs to sell, and stay over night with the president. But they should not ride a free horse to death. I may not be well educated, but I am high strung till you can't rest. Groceries are just as high in Washington as they are in Philadelphia.

I hope that you will not glean from the foregoing that I have lost my interest in national affairs. God forbid. Though not in the political arena myself, my sympathies are with those who are. I am willing to assist the families of those who are in the political arena trying to obtain a precarious livelihood thereby I was once an official under the Federal government myself, as the curious student of national affairs may learn if he will go to the Treasury Department at Washington, D. C., and ask to see my voucher for $9.85, covering salary as United States commissioner for the Second Judicial District of Wyoming for the year 1882. It was at that time that a vile contemporary characterized me as "a corrupt and venal Federal official who had fattened upon the hard-wrung taxes of my fellow citizens and gorged myself for years at the public crib." This was unjust. I was not corrupt. I was not venal. I was only hungry!

Street Cars and Curiosities.

THERE is an institution in Boston which the Pilgrim Fathers did not originate. That is the street car. There is a street car parade all day on Washington street, and a red-light procession most of the night.

People told me that I could get into a car and go anywhere I wanted to. I tried it. There was a point in Boston, I learned, where there were some more relics that I hadn't seen. Parties told me where I could find some more fragments of the Mayflower, and an old chair in which Josiah Quincy had sat down to think. There were also a few more low price flint-lock guns and tomahawks that no man who visited Boston could afford to miss. Besides, there was said to be the lock that used to be on the door of a room in which General Washington had a good notion to write his farewell address. All these things were in the collection which I started out to find, and there were others, also.

For instance, there was a specimen of the lightning that Franklin caught in his demijohn out of the sky, and still in a good state of preservation; also some more clothes in which he was baptized, more swords of Bunker Hill, and a little shirt which John Hancock put on as soon as he was born. Hancock was a perfect gentleman from his birth, and it is said that the first thing he did was to excuse himself for a moment and then put on this shirt. His manners were certainly very agreeable, and he was very much polished.

I heard, too, that there was an acorn from the tree in which Benedict Arnold had his nest while he was hatching treason. I did not believe it, but I had an idea I could readily discover the fraud if I could only see the acorn, for I am a great historian and researcher from away back. I was told that in this collection there was a suspender button shed by Patrick Henry during his memorable speech in which he raised up to his full height on his hind feet and permitted the war to come in *italics*, also in SMALL CAPS and in **LARGE CAPS! ! !** with three astonishers on the end.

So I wanted to find this place, and as I had plenty of means I decided to ride in a street car. Therefore, I aimed my panic price cane at the driver of a cream-colored car with a blue stomach, and remarked, "Hi, there!" Before I go any further, and in order to avoid ambiguity, let me say that it was the car that had the blue stomach. He (the driver) twisted the brake and I went inside, clear to the further end, and sat down by the side of a young woman who filled the whole car with sunshine. I was so happy that I gave the conductor half a dollar and told him to keep the change. If by chance she sees this, I hope she still remembers me. Pretty soon a very fat woman came into the car and aimed for our quarter. She evidently intended to squat between this fair girl and myself. But ah, thought I to myself in a low tone of voice, I will fool thee. So I shoved my person along in the seat toward the sweet girl of the Bay State. The corpulent party, whose name I did not learn, had in the meantime backed up to where she had detected a slight vacancy, and where I had seen fit to place myself. At that moment she heaved a sigh of relief, and, assisted by the motion of the car, which just then turned a corner, she sat down in my lap and nestled in my bosom like a tired baby elephant.

PATRICK HENRY.

* * * * * * * *

Dear reader, if I were to tell you that the crystal of my watch was picked out from under my shoulder blades the next day, you would not believe it, would you? I will not strain your faith in me by making the statement, but that was the heaviest woman I ever held.

While all this was going on I lost track of my location. The car began to squirm around all over Boston, and finally the conductor came back and wanted more money. I said no, I would get off and try a dark red car with a green stomach for a while. So I did. I rode on that till I had seen a great deal of new scenery, and then I asked the conductor if he passed Number Clankety Clank, Blank street. He said he did not, but if I would go down two blocks further and take a maroon car with a plaid stomach it would take me to the corner of "What-do-you-call-it and What's-his-name streets," where, if k a seal brown car with squshed huckl berry trimmings it would take me to where I wanted to go. So I tried it. I do not know just where I missed my train, but when I found th seal brown car with scrunched huckleberry trimmings it was going the other way, and as it was late I went into a cafe and refi eshed myself. When I came out I discovered that it was too late to see the collection, ven if I could find it, for at 6 o'clock they take the relics in and put them into a refrigerator till morning.

TAKING A PRIZE.

I was now weary and somewhat disappointed, so I desired to get back to my headquarters, wherein I could rest and where I could lock myself up in my room, so no prize fat woman could enter. I hailed one of those sawed-off landaus, consisting of two wheels, one door behind, and a bill for two bits. I told the college graduate on the box where I wanted to go, gave him a quarter and got in. I sat down and heaved a chaste sigh. The sigh was only half hove when the herdic backed up to my destination, which was about 300 feet from where I got in, as the crow flies.

When I go to Boston again, I am going in charge of the police.

The street railway system of Boston is remarkably perfect. Fifty cars pass a given point on Washington street in an hour, and yet there are no blockades. You can take one of those cars, if you are a stranger, and you can get so mixed up that you will never get back, and all for five cents. I felt a good deal like the man who was full and who stepped on a man who was not full. The sober man was mad, and yelled out: "See here; condemn it, can't you look where you're walking?" "Betcher life," says the inebriate, "but the trouble is to walk where I'm lookin'."

The Poor Blind Pig.

I HAVE just been over to the Falls of Minnehaha. In fact I have been quite a tourist and summer resorter this season, having saturated my system with nineteen different styles of mineral water in Wisconsin alone, and tried to win the attention of nineteen different styles of head waiters at these summer hotels. I may add in passing that the summer hotels of Wisconsin and Minnesota have been crowded full the past season and more room will have to be added before another season comes around.

The motto of the summer hotel seems to be, "Unless ye shall have feed the waiter, behold ye shall in no wise be fed." Many waiters at these places, by a judicious system of blackmail and starvation, have reduced the guest to a sad state.

THE MAN WHO FEES THE WAITER.

The mineral water of Wisconsin ranks high as a beverage. Many persons are using it during the entire summer in place of rum.

The water of Waukesha does not appear to taste of any mineral, although an analysis shows the presence of several kinds of groceries in solution. The water at Palmyra Springs also tastes like any other pure water, but at Kankanna, on the Fox River, they have a style of mineral water which is different. Almost as soon as you taste it you discover that it is extremely different. Colonel Watrous, of the Milwaukee *Sunday Telegraph*, took some of it. I saw him afterward. He looked depressed, and told me that he had been deceived. Several Kankanna people had told him that this was living water. He had discovered otherwise. He hated to place his confidence in people and then find it misplaced.

A favorite style of Kankanna revenge is to drink a quart of this water, and then, on meeting an enemy, to breathe on him and wither him. One breath produces syncope and blind staggers. Two breaths induce coma and metallic casket for one.

Minnehaha is not mineral water. It is just plain water, giving itself away day after day like a fresh young man in society. If you want pure water you get it at the spring near the foot of the fall, and if you want it flavored with something that will leave a blazed road the whole length of your alimentary canal, you go to the "blind pig," a few rods away from the falls.

The blind pig draws many people toward the falls through sympathy. To be blind must indeed be a sad plight. Let us pause and reflect on this proposition.

By good fortune I have had a chance to watch the rum problem in all its phases this summer. Beginning in Maine, where the most ingenious methods of whipping the devil around the stump are adopted, then going through northern Iowa and tasting her exhilarating pop, and at last paying ten cents to see the blind pig at Minnehaha, I feel like one who has wrestled with the temperance problem in a practical way, and I have about decided that a high license is about the only way to make the sale of whisky odious. Prohibition is too abrupt in its methods, and one generation can hardly wipe out the appetite for liquor that has been planted and fostered by fifty preceding generations.

For fear that a few of my lady readers do not know what the Minnehaha blind pig looks like, and that they may be curious about it, I will just say that it is a method of evading the law, and consists of a dumb waiter, wherein, if you pay ten cents, you get a glass of stimulants without the annoyance of conversation. Many ladies who visit the falls, and who have heard incidentally about the blind pig, express a desire to see the poor little thing, but their husbands generally persuade them to refrain.

Minnehaha is a beautiful waterfall. It is not so frightfully large and grand as Niagara, but it is very fine, and if the State of Minnesota would catch the man who nails his signs on the trees around there, and choke him to death near the falls on a pleasant day, a large audience would attend with much pleasure. I believe that the fence-board advertiser is not only, as a rule, wicked, but he also lacks common sense. Who ever bought a liver pad or a corset because he read about it on a high board fence? No one. Who ever purchased a certain kind of pill or poultice because the name of that pill or poultice was nailed on a tree to disfigure a beautiful landscape? I do not believe that any sane human being ever did so. If everyone feels as I do about it, people would rather starve to death for pills and freeze to death in a perfect wilderness of liver pads than buy of the man who daubs the fair face of nature with names of his alleged goods.

I saw a squaw who seemed to belong in the picture of the poetic little waterfall. I did not learn her name. It was one of these long, corduroy Sioux names, that hang together with hyphens like a lot of sausage. The salaried humorist of the party said he never sausage a name before.

Translated into our tongue it meant The-swift-daughter-of-the-prairie-blizzard-that-gathers-the-huckleberry-on-the-run-and-don't-you-forget-it.

Daniel Webster.

I PRESUME that Daniel Webster was as good an off-hand speaker as this country has ever produced. Massachusetts has been well represented in Congress since that time, but she has had few who could successfully compete with D. Webster, Esq., attorney and counsellor-at-law, Boston, Mass.

I have never met Mr. Webster, but I have seen a cane that he used to wear, and since that time I have felt a great interest in him. It was a heavy winter cane, and was presented to him as a token of respect.

This reminds me of the inscription on a grave stone in the 280-year-old churchyard at LaPointe, on Lake Superior, where I was last week. It shows what punctuation has done for a lost and undone race. I copy the inscription exactly as it appears:

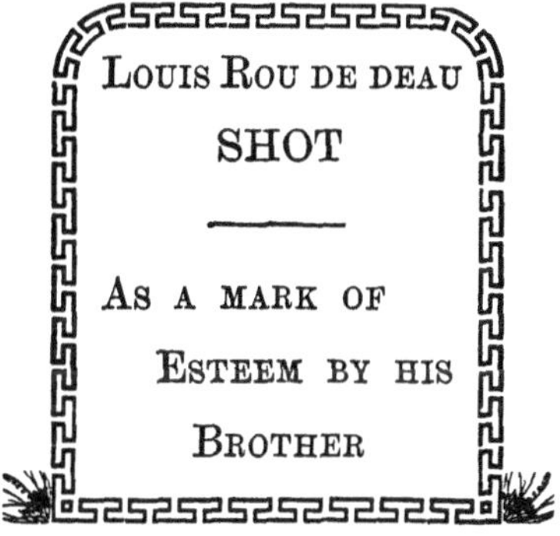

Daniel Webster had one of the largest and most robust brains that ever flourished in our fair land. It was what we frequently call a teeming brain, one of those four-horse teeming brains, as it were. Mr. Webster wore the largest hat of any man then in Congress, and other senators and representatives used to frequently borrow it to wear on the 2nd of January, the 5th of July, and after other special occasions, when they had been in executive session most all night and endured great mental strain. This hat matter reminds me of an incident in the life of Benjamin F. Butler, a man well known in Massachusetts even at the present time.

One evening, at a kind of reception or some such dissipation as that, while Jim Nye was in the Senate, the latter left his silk hat on the lounge with the opening turned up, and while he was talking with someone else, Mr. Butler sat down in the hat with so much expression that it was a wreck. Everyone expected to see James W Nye walk up and smite Benjamin F Butler, but he did not do so. He looked at the chaotic hat for a minute, more in sorrow than in anger, and then he said:

"Benjamin, I could have told you that hat wouldn't fit you before you tried it on."

Daniel Webster's brain was not only very large, but it was in good order all the time. Sometimes Nature bestows large brains on men who do not rise to great prominence. Large brains do not always indicate great intellectual power. These brains are large but of an inferior quality. A schoolmate of mine used to wear a hat that I could put my head and both feet into with perfect ease. I remember that he tied my shirt one day while I was laving my well-rounded limbs in the mill pond near my childhood's home.

I was mad at the time, but I could not lick him, for he was too large. All I could do was to patiently untie my shirt while my teeth chattered, then fling a large, three-cornered taunt in his teeth and run. He kept on poking fun at me, I remember, till I got dressed, and alluded incidentally, to my small brain and abnormal feet. This stung my sensitive nature, and I told him that if I had such a wealth of brain as he had, and it was of no use to think with, I would take it to a restaurant and have it breaded. Then I went away.

But we were speaking of Webster. Many lawyers of our day would do well to read and study the illustrious example of Daniel Webster. He did not sit in court all day with his feet on the table and howl, "We object," and then down his client for $50, just because he had made a noise. I employed a lawyer once to bring suit for me to recover quite a sum of money due me. After years of assessments and toilsome litigation, we got a judgment. He said to me that he was anxious to succeed with the case mainly because he knew I wanted to vindicate myself. I said yes, that was the idea exactly I wanted to be vindicated.

So he gave me the vindication and took the judgment as a slight testimonial of his own sterling worth. When I want to be vindicated again I will do it with one of those self-cocking vindicators that you can carry in a

Looking over this letter, I am amazed to see the amount of valuable information relative to the life of Mr. Webster that I have succeeded in using. There are, of course, some minor details of Mr. Webster's life which I have omitted, but nothing of real importance. The true history of Mr. Webster is epitomized here, and told in a pleasing and graceful manner, a style that is at once accurate and just and still elegant, chaste and thoroughly refined, while at the same time there are little gobs of sly humor in it that are real cute.

Two Ways of Telling It.

I REMEMBER one sunny day in summer, we were sitting in the Boomerang office, I and the city editor, and he was speaking enviously of my salary of $150 per month as compared with his of $80, and I had just given him the venerable minstrel witticism that of course my salary was much larger than his, but he ought not to forget that he got his.

Just then there was a revolver shot at the foot of our stairs, and then another. The printers rushed into the stairway from the composing room, and to save time I ran out on the balcony that hung over the sidewalk and which gave me a bird's-eye view of the murder. The next issue of the paper contained an account about like this:

COLD-BLOODED MURDER.—Yesterday, between 12 and 1 o'clock, in front of this office on Second street, James McKeon, in a manner almost wholly unprovoked, shot James Smith, commonly known as Windy Smith. Smith died at 2 o'clock this morning of his wounds. Windy Smith was not a bad man, but, as his nickname would imply, he was a kind of noisy, harmless fellow, and McKeon, who is a gambler and professional bad man, can give no good reason for the killing. There is a determined effort on foot to lynch the murderer.

This account was brief, but it seemed to set forth the facts pretty clearly, I thought, and I felt considerably chagrined when I saw an account of the matter latter on, as written up by the prosecuting attorney. I may be inaccurate as to dates and some other points of detail, but, as nearly as I can remember, his version of the matter was like this:

THE TERRITORY OF WYOMING, } ss.
COUNTY OF ALBANY. }

In Justice's Court, before E. W Nye, Esq., Justice of the Peace.

The Territory of Wyoming, plt'ff. }
vs. } Complaint.
James McKeon, def't. }

The above named defendant, James McKeon, is accused of the crime of murder, for that he, the said defendant, James McKeon, at the town of Laramie City, in the County of Albany and Territory of Wyoming, and on the 13th day of July, Anno Domini 1880, then and there being, he, the said defendant, James McKeon, did wilfully, maliciously, feloniously, wickedly, unlawfully, criminally, illegally, unjustly, premeditatedly, coolly and murderously, by means of a certain deadly weapon commonly called a Smith & Wesson revolver, or revolving pistol, so constructed as to revolve upon itself and to be discharged by means of a spring and hammer, and with six chambers thereto, and known commonly as a self-cocker, the same loaded with gun-powder and leaden bullets, and in the hands of him, the said defendant, James McKeon, level at, to, upon, by, contiguous to and against the body of one James Smith, commonly called Windy Smith, in the peace of the commonwealth then and there being, and that by means of said deadly weapon commonly called a Smith & Wesson revolver, or revolving pistol, so constructed as to revolve upon itself and to be discharged by means of a spring or hammer, and with six chambers thereto and known commonly as a self-cocker, the same loaded with gunpowder and leaden bullets and in the hands of him the said defendant, James McKeon, held at, to, upon, by, contiguous to and against the body of him, the said James Smith, commonly called Windy Smith, he, the said James McKeon, did wilfully, maliciously, feloniously, wickedly, fraudulently, virulently, unlawfully, criminally, illegally, brutally, unjustly, premeditatedly, coolly and murderously, of his malice aforethought with the deadly weapon aforesaid held in the right hand of him, the said defendant, James McKeon, to, at, against, etc., the body of him, the said James Smith, commonly called Windy Smith, he, the said defendant, James McKeon, at the said town of Laramie City, in the said County of Albany, and in the heretofore enumerated Territory of Wyoming, and on the hereinbefore mentioned 13th day of July, Anno Domini 1880, did inflict to, at, upon, by, contiguous to, adjacent to, adjoining, over and against the body of him, the said James Smith, commonly called Windy Smith, one certain deadly, mortal, dangerous and painful wound, to-wit: Over, against, to, at, by, upon, contiguous to, near, adjacent to and bisecting the intestines of him, the said James Smith, commonly called Windy Smith, by reason of which he, the said James Smith, commonly called Windy Smith, did in great agony linger, and lingering did die, on the 14th day of July, Anno Domini 1880, at 2 o'clock in the forenoon of said day, contrary to the statutes in such case made and provided, and against the peace and dignity of the Territory of Wyoming.

I am now convinced that although the published account was correct, it was not as full as it might have been. Perhaps the tendency of modern journalism is to epitomize too much. In the hurry of daily newspaper work and the press of matter upon our pages, very likely we are fatally brief, and sacrifice rhetorical beauty to naked and goose-pimply facts.

All About Menials.

THE subject of meals, lunch-counters, dining-cars and buffet-cars came up the other day, incidentally. I had ordered a little breakfast in the buffet-car, not so much because I expected to get anything, but because I liked to eat in a car and have all the other passengers glaring at me. I do not know which affords me the most pleasure—to sit for a photograph and be stabbed in the cerebellum with a cast-iron prong, to be fed in the presence of a mixed company of strangers, or to be called on without any preparation to make a farewell speech on the gallows.

However, I got my breakfast after awhile. The waiter was certainly the most worthless, trifling, half-asleep combination of Senegambian stupidity and poor white trash indolence and awkwardness that I ever saw. He brought in everything except what I wanted, and then wound up by upsetting the little cream pitcher in my lap. He did not charge for the cream. He threw that in.

SHOWING HIS INMOST THOUGHT

So all the rest of the journey I was trying to eradicate a cream dado from my pantaloons. It made me mad, because those pantaloons were made for me by request. Besides, I haven't got pantaloons to squander in that way To some a pair of pantaloons, more or less, is nothing, but it is much to me.

There was a porter on the same train who was much the same kind of furniture as the waiter. He slept days and made up berths all night. Truly, he began making up berths at Jersey City, and when he got through, about daylight, it was time to begin to unmake them again. All night long I could hear him opening and shutting the berths like a concertina. He sang softly to himself all night long:

> "You must camp a little in the wilderness
> And then we'll all go home."

He played his own accompaniment on the berths.

"Gentlemen, we talk about stringency and shrinkage of values, and all such funny business as that; but that's something I don't know a blamed thing about. What I can grapple with is this: If our county offices are worth $30,000, and there are other little after-claps and soft snaps, and walk-overs, worth, say $10,000, and the boys, say, are willing to do the fair thing, say, blow in fifteen per cent. to the central committee, and what they feel like on the outside, then politics, instead of a burden and a reproach, becomes a pleasing duty, a joyous occasion and a picnic to those whose lives might otherwise be a dreary monotone.

"Mr. Chairman, the past two years has wrecked four campaign saloons, and a tinner who socked his wife's fortune into campaign torches is now in a land where torchlights is no good. Overcome by a dull market, a financial depression and a reserved central committee, he ate a package of Rough on Rats, and passed up the flume. He is now at rest over yonder.

"Such instances would be common if we encouraged the eccentric economy of official cranks. It is an evil that is gnawing at the vitals of the republic. We must squench it or get left. There are millions of dollars in this country, Mr. Chairman, that, if we keep it out of the campaign, will get into the hands of the working classes, and then you and I, Mr. Chairman, and gentlemen of the convention, can starve to death. Keep the campaign money away from the soulless hired man, gentlemen, or good-bye John.

"Mr. Chairman, excuse my emotion! It is almighty seldom that I make a speech, but when I do, I strive to get there with both feet. We must either work the campaign funds into their legitimate channels, or every blamed patriot within the sound of my voice will have to fasten on a tin bill and rustle for angle-worms amongst the hens. You hear me?"

[Terrific applause, during which the delicate odor of enthusiasm was noticed on the breath of the entire delegation].

A Goat in a Frame.

LARAMIE has a seal brown goat, with iron gray chin whiskers and a breath like new mown hay.

He has not had as hard a winter as the majority of stock on the Rocky mountains, because he is of a domestic turn of mind and tries to make man his friend. Though social in his nature, he never intrudes himself on people after they have intimated with a shotgun that they are weary of him.

When the world seems cold and dark to him, and everybody turns coldly away from him, he does not steal away by himself and die of corroding grief; he just lies down on the sidewalk in the sun and fills the air with the seductive fragrance of which he is the sole proprietor.

One day, just as he had eaten his midday meal of boot heels and cold sliced atmosphere and kerosene barrel staves, he saw a man going along the street with a large looking glass under his arm.

The goat watched the man, and saw him set the mirror down by a gate and go inside the house after some more things that he was moving. Then the goat stammered with his tail a few times and went up to see if he could eat the mirror.

When he got pretty close to it, he saw a hungry-looking goat apparently coming toward him, so he backed off a few yards and went for him. There was a loud crash, and when the man came out he saw a full length portrait of a goat with a heavy, black walnut frame around it, going down the street with a great deal of apparent relish.

Then the man said something derogatory about the goat, and seemed offended about something.

Goats are not timid in their nature and are easily domesticated.

There are two kinds of goat—the cashmere goat and the plain goat. The former is worked up into cashmere shawls and cashmere boquet. The latter is not.

The cashmere boquet of commerce is not made of the common goat. It is a good thing that it is not.

A goat that has always been treated with uniform kindness and never betrayed, may be taught to eat out of the hand. Also out of the flour barrel or the ice-cream freezer.

To a Married Man.

ADELBERT G. GRIMES writes as follows. "I am a young man not yet twenty-two years of age. I am said to be rather attractive in appearance and a fluent conversationalist. Three years ago I very foolishly married and settled on a tree claim in Dakota, where we have three children, consisting of one pair of twins and an ordinary child, born by itself. We are a considerable distance from town, and to remain at home during the winter with no company besides my wife and children is very irksome, especially as my wife has never had the advantages that I have in the way of society. Her conversational powers are very inferior, and I cannot bear to remain at home very much. So I go to town, where I can meet my equals and enjoy myself.

"I fear that this will lead to an estrangement, for, when I return at night, my wife's nose is so red from sniveling all day that I can hardly bear to look at her. If there is anything in this world that I hate, it is a red-eyed, red-nosed woman who sheds tears on all occasions.

"Of course all this makes me irritable, and I say sharp things to her, as I have a wonderful command of language at such times. She surely cannot expect a young man twenty-two years old to stay at home day after day and listen to squalling children, when he is still in the heyday of life with joy beaming in his eye.

"Of course I do say things to my wife that I am afterward sorry for, but I made a great mistake in marrying the woman I did, and although some of my lady friends told me so at the time, I did not then believe it. Do you think I ought to bury myself on a tree claim with a woman far my inferior, while I have talents that would shine in the best of society? I am greatly distressed, and would willingly seek a legal separation if I knew how to go about it. Will you kindly advise me? What do you think of my penmanship?"

I hardly know how to advise you, Adelbert. You have got yourself into a place where you cannot do much but remain and take your medicine. Unfortunately, there are too many such young men as you are, Adelbert. You are young, and handsome, and smart. You casually admit this in your letter, I see. You have a social nature, and would shine in society. You also reluctantly confess this. That does not help you in my estimation, Adelbert. If you are a bright and shining light in society, you are probably a brunette fizzle as a husband. When you resolved to take a tree claim and make a home in Dakota, why didn't you put your swallow-tail coat under the bed and retire from the giddy whirl and mad rush of society, the way your wife had to?

I dislike very much to speak to you in a plain, blunt way, Adelbert, being a total stranger to you, but when you convey the idea in your letter that you

"I HAVE A WONDERFUL COMMAND OF LANGUAGE."

have made a great mistake in marrying at the age of nineteen, and marrying far beneath yourself, I am forced to agree with you. If, instead of marrying a young girl who didn't know any better than to believe that you were a man, instead of a fractional one, you had come to me, and borrowed my revolver and blown out the fungus growth which you refer to as your brains, you would have hit it. Even now it is not too late. You can still come to me, and I will oblige you. You cannot do your wife a greater favor at this time than to leave her a widow, and the sooner you do so the less orphans there will be.

Did it ever occur to you, Adelbert, that your wife made a mistake also? Did it ever bore itself through your adamantine skull that it is not an unbroken round of gayety for a young girl to shut herself up in a lonesome house for three years, gradually acquiring children, and meantime being "sassed" by her husband because she is not a fluent conversationalist?

Wherein you offend me, Adelbert, is that you persist in breathing the air which human beings and other domestic animals more worthy than yourself are entitled to. There are too many such imitation men at large. There should be a law that would prohibit your getting up and walking on your hind legs and thus imposing on other mammals. If I could run the government for a few weeks, Adelbert, I would compel your style of zoological wonder to climb a tree and stay there.

So you married a woman who was far your inferior, did you? How did you do it? Where did you go to find a woman who could be your inferior and still keep out of the menagerie? Adelbert, I fear you do your wife a great injustice. With just barely enough vitality to hand your name down to posterity and blast the fair future of Dakota by leaving your trade-mark on future generations, you snivel and whine over your blasted life! If your life had been blasted a little harder twenty years ago, the life of your miserable little wife would have been less blasted.

If you had acquired a little more croup twenty years ago, Dakota would have been ahead. Why did you go on year after year, permitting people to believe you were a man, when you could have undeceived them in two minutes by crawling into a hollow log and remaining there?

Your penmanship is very good. It is better than your chances for a bright immortality beyond the grave. Write to me again whenever you feel lonesome or want advice. I was a young married man myself once, and I know what they have to endure. Up to the time of my marriage, I had never known a harsher tone than a flute note; my early life ran quiet as the clear brook by which I sported, and so on. I was a great belle in society, also. I attended all the swell balls and parties in our county for years. Wherever you found fair women and brave men tripping the light bombastic toe, you would also find me. "Sometimes I played second violin, and sometimes I called off."

To an Embryo Poet.

THE following correspondence is now given to the press for the first time, with the consent of the parties:

WM. NYE, ESQ.—*Dear Sir*—I am a young man, 20 years of age, with fair education and a strong desire to succeed. I have done some writing for the press, having written up a very nice article on progressive euchre, which was a great success and published in our home paper, But it was not copied so much in other papers as I would like to have saw it, and I take my pen in hand at this time to write and ask you what there is in the article enclosed that prevents its being copied abroad all over our broad land. I write just as I hope you would feel perfectly free to write me at any time. I think that writers ought to aid each other. Yours with kind regards,

P. O. Box 202. ALGERNON L. TEWEY.

I have carefully read and pondered over the dissertation on progressive euchre which you send me, Algernon, and I cannot see why it should not be ravenously seized and copied by the press of the broad, wide land referred to in your letters. If you have time, perhaps it would be well enough to go to the leading journalists of our country and ask them what they mean by it. You might write till your vertebræ fell out of your clothes on the floor, and it would not do half so much good as a personal conference with the editors of America. First prepare your article, then go personally to the editors of the country and call them one by one out into the hall, in a current of cold air, and explain the article to them. In that way you will form pleasant acquaintances and get solid with our leading journalists. You have no idea, Algernon, how lonely and desolate the life of a practical journalist is. Your fresh young face and your fresh young ways, and your charming grammatical improvisations, would delight an editor who has nothing to do from year to year but attend to his business.

Do not try to win the editors of America by writing poems beginning:

Now the merry goatlet jumps,
And the trifling yaller dog,
With the tin can madly humps
Like an acrobatic frog.

At times you will be tempted to write such stuff as this, and mark it with a large blue pencil and send it to the papers of the country, but that is not a good way to do.

Seriously, Algernon, I would suggest that you make a bold dash for success by writing things that other people are not writing, thinking things that other people are not thinking, and saying things that other people are not saying. You will say that this advice is easier to give than to take, and I agree with you. But the tendency of the age is to wear the same style of collar and coat and hat that every other man wears, and to talk and write like other men; and to be frank with you, Algernon, I think it is an infernal shame. If you will look carefully about you, you will see that the preacher, who is talking mostly to dusty pew cushions, is also the preacher who is thinking the thoughts of other men. He is "up-ending" his barrel of sermons annually, and they were made in the first place from the sermons of a man who also "up-ended" his barrel annually. Go where the preacher is talking to full houses, and you will discover that his sermons are full of humanity and originality. They are not written in a library by a man with interchangeable ideas, an automatic cog-wheel thinker, but they are prepared by a man who earnestly and honestly studies the great, aching heart of humanity, and full of sincerity, originality and old-fashioned Christianity, appeals to your better impulses.

How is it with our poetry? As a fellow-traveler and sea-sick tourist across life's tempestuous tide, I ask you, Algernon, who is writing the poetry that will live? Is it the man who is sawing out and sandpapering stanzas of the same general dimensions as some other poet, in which he bewails the fact that he loved a tall, well-behaved, accomplished girl, sixteen hands high, who did not require his love?

Ah, no! He is not the poet whose terra cotta statue will stand in the cemetery, wearing a laurel wreath and a lumpy brow. Show me the poet who is intimate with nature and who studies the little joys and sorrows of the poor;

who smells the clover and writes about live, healthy people with ideas and appetites. He is my poet.

I apologize for speaking so earnestly, Algernon, but I saw by your letter that you felt kindly toward me, and rather invited an expression of opinion on my part. So I have written more freely, perhaps, than I otherwise would. We are both writers. Measurably so, at least. You write on progressive euchre, and I write on anything that I can get hold of. So let us agree here and promise each other that, whatever we do, we will not think through the thinker of another man.

The Great Ruler of the universe has made and placed upon the earth a good many millions of men, but He never made any two of them exactly alike. We may differ from every one of the countless millions who have preceded us, and still be safe. Even you and I, Algernon, may agree in many matters. and yet be very dissimilar. At least I hope so, and I presume you do also.

Eccentricities of Genius.

ALFONSO QUANTURNERNIT DOWDELL, Frumenti, Ohio, writes to know something of the effects of alcohol on the brain of an adult, being evidently apprehensive that some day he may become an adult himself. He says:

"I would be glad to know whether or not you think that liquor stimulates the brain to do better literary work. I have been studying the personal history of Edgar A. Poe, and learned through that medium that he was in the habit of drinking a good deal of liquor at times. I also read that Georgo D. Prentice, who wrote 'The Closing Year,' and other nice poems, was a hearty drinker. Will you tell me whether this is all true or not, and also what the effect of alcohol is on the brain of an adult?"

It is said on good authority that Edgar A. Poe ever and anon imbibed the popular beverages of his day and age, some of which contained alcohol. We are led to believe these statements because they remain as yet undenied. But Poe did a great deal of good in that way, for he set an example that has been followed ever since, more or less, by quite a number of poets' apprentices who emulated Poe's great gift as a drinker. These men, thinking that poesy and delirium tremens went hand in hand, became fluent drunkards early in their career, so that finally, instead of issuing a small blue volume of poems, they punctuated a drunkard's grave.

So we see that Poe did a great work aside from what he wrote. He opened up a way for these men which eradicated them, and made life more desirable for those who remained. He made it easy for those who thought genius and inebriation were synonymous terms to get to the hospital early in the day, while the overworked waste-basket might secure a few hours of much needed rest.

George D. Prentice has also done much toward weeding out a class of people who otherwise might have become disagreeable. It is better that these men who write under the influence of rum should fall into the hands of the police as early as possible. The police can handle them better than the editor can.

Do not try, Alfonso, to experiment in this way. Because Mr. Poe and Mr. Prentice could write beautiful and witty things between drinks, do not, oh do not imagine that you can begin that way and succeed at last.

The effect of alcohol on the brain of an adult is to congest it finally. Alcohol will sometimes congest the brain of an adult under the most trying and discouraging circumstances. I have frequently known it to scorch out and

THINKING ABOUT THE POEM.

paralyze the brain in cases where other experiments had not been successful in showing the presence of a brain at all.

That is the reason why some people love to fool with this great chemical. It revives their suspicions regarding the presence of a brain.

The habits of literary men vary a good deal, for no two of them seem to care to adopt the same plan.

I have taken the liberty of showing here my own laboratory and methods of thought. This is from a drawing made by myself, and represents the writer in his study and in the act of thinking about a poem.

Last summer I wrote a large poem entitled, *Moanings of the Moist, Malarious Sea*." I have it still. The back of it has a memoranda on it in blue pencil from the leading editors of our broad land, but otherwise it is just as I wrote it.

The engraving represents me in the act of thinking about the poem, and what I will do with the money when I get it.

I am now preparing a poem entitled, "*The Umbrella*." It is a dainty little bit of verse, and my hired man thinks it is a gem. I called it "The Umbrella" so that it would not be returned.

By looking at the drawing you will see the rapid change of expression on the face as the work goes on.

I give the drawing in order also, to show the rich furniture of the room. All poets do not revel in such gaudy trappings as I do, but I cannot write well in a bare and ill-furnished room. In these apartments there is also a window which does not show in the engraving. I have tried over and over again to write a poem in a room that had no window in it, but I cannot say that I ever wrote one under such circumstances that I thought would live.

You can do as you think best about furnishing your room as I have mine. You might, of course, succeed as well by writing in a plainer apartment, but I could not. All my poetical work that was done in the cramped and plainly furnished room that I formerly occupied over Knadler's livery stable, was ephemeral.

It got into a few of the leading autograph albums of the country, but it never got into the papers.

I would not use alcohol, however. Poe and Prentice could use it, but I never could. After a long debauch, I could always work well enough on the street, but I could not do literary work.

www.ingramcontent.com/pod-product-compliance
Lightning Source LLC
LaVergne TN
LVHW010525100826
845148LV00001B/97

* 9 7 8 1 4 2 5 5 7 3 6 1 4 *